CRITICAL PRAISE FOR R[...]
THE DEMON LOVER

"Frightening, but ultimately affirmative . . . Morgan builds a convincing case. . . . Of prime interest are her interviews with Palestinian women on the West Bank and Gaza Strip. . . . A book that women (and men) will overlook at their peril."

—*Kirkus Reviews*

"Brings a startling perspective to terrorism, which she sees as arising out of patriarchal societies' emphasis on power, control, domination, and violence."

—*Publishers Weekly*

"There is objective research and scholarship aplenty. . . . But the most moving parts of this provocative book are personal."

—*Detroit Free Press*

"A brilliant critique. . . . incisive analysis . . . compelling material."

—*Library Journal*

"Robin Morgan has continued to surpass herself as a passionate, cogent, and persuasive creator of feminist theory. THE DEMON LOVER represents yet another quantum leap in her work. This book is scholarly, impassioned, and packed with information."

—Mary Daly

"THE DEMON LOVER is strong stuff that demands consideration by women and men. . . . A major work in the developing study of terrorism."

—*West Coast Review of Books*

Books by Robin Morgan

Poetry

A Hot January: Poems 1996–1999

Upstairs in the Garden: Selected and New Poems

Depth Perception

Death Benefits

Lady of the Beasts

Monster

Fiction

Dry Your Smile

The Mer Child

Nonfiction

Saturday's Child: A Memoir

The Word of a Woman: Essays

A Woman's Creed

The Demon Lover

The Anatomy of Freedom

Going Too Far

Sisterhood Is Global (ed.)

Sisterhood Is Powerful (ed.)

The New Woman (co-ed.)

The Demon Lover

THE ROOTS OF TERRORISM

ROBIN MORGAN

PIATKUS

Copyright © 1989 by Robin Morgan
Introduction and afterword copyright © 2001 by Robin Morgan

First published in the UK in 2001 by
Judy Piatkus (Publishers) Ltd
5 Windmill Street, London W1T 2JA
e-mail: info@piatkus.co.uk

The moral right of the author has been asserted

A catalogue record for this book is available from the British Library

ISBN 0 7499 2312 1

This book has been printed on paper manufactured with
respect for the environment using wood from managed
sustainable resources

Printed and bound in Great Britain by
Mackays of Chatham Ltd, Chatham, Kent

For Isel Rivero

CONTENTS

𝕽𝕽𝕽𝕽𝕽𝕽𝕽𝕽𝕽

ACKNOWLEDGMENTS

𝍖𝍖𝍖𝍖𝍖𝍖𝍖𝍖𝍖

The completion of any book is, for its author, a triumph of tenacity over terror. In my case, the tenacity was strengthened by a number of people.

Bella Abzug, Alida Brill, Suzanna Dakin, Toni Fitzpatrick, Lesley Gore, Lois Sasson, and Karen Sunde encouraged me about the need for a feminist analysis of this grim subject; by their practice, they also reminded me of an alternative reality—the politics of affirmation in women's daily lives. Stimulating conversations with other women theorists generously taking time from their own work—Kathleen Barry, Mary Daly, Andrea Dworkin, Theresa Funiciello, Mim Kelber, Kate Millett, and Marilyn J. Waring—helped to focus me. Gloria Steinem and Koryne Horbal continued to offer cherished long-term friendship and added very concrete support for this project.

Chapter 8—on Palestinian women in the refugee camps of the Middle East—requires some special thanks. My deepest gratitude goes to the refugee women themselves, for honoring me with their time, their confidence, their stories. The sisterhood, advice, and networking provided in advance by Arab feminist activists Farida Allaghi, Fawzia Hassouna, and

Fatima Mernissi were acts of a political trust. Nawal El Saadawi's hospitality graced my stay in Egypt, as did Sherif Hetata's. The period in Jerusalem was lent a sense of sanity by the guidance of Lebanese-American feminist Karen Henry. Leila Diab, then of the Palestine Human Rights Campaign of the United States, was generous with suggested contacts, as was John Merriam with advice. My gratitude goes to Sallie Bingham for a grant-in-aid that permitted the transcribing and organizing of five densely jotted notebooks and over sixty hours of taped interviews with women in the camps. The trip itself was under the aegis of UNRWA (the United Nations Relief and Works Agency for Palestine Refugees in the Near East) ; the entire organization won my respect for extraordinary work performed against all odds. I wish to thank in particular the late John A. Miles, then Liaison Director in New York, R. S. Dillon, Deputy Commissioner-General at UNRWA headquarters in Vienna, Ron Wilkinson and William Lee of UNRWA's Public Information Office, and the various Field Directors and staffs in the region itself. The women of UNRWA who served as interpreters in the different fields were patient, sensitive, and educative. In the Gaza Field, especially, I am grateful to Peter Hawkins, then Field Director, and to Angela Williams, then Deputy Director and Field Administration Officer, the highest-ranking woman in UNRWA and a compassionate and inspiring person. Because of the commitment of Hawkins and Williams, the Gaza Field is by far the most advanced of all the UNRWA Fields in terms of women's services, facilities, activities, and consciousness. Christiane El Dabbagh, my sole interpreter for the entire Gaza stay, displayed indefatigable energy in adapting to what became virtually a twenty-hour-a-day schedule. I'm also indebted to Erskine B. Childers of the United Nations Development Programme for his aid in networking me with UNDP women's projects in the area. Keith Beavan, then Senior Political Adviser to UNTSO (the United Nations Truce Supervision Organization) was extremely helpful regarding

Lebanon, as were Hugh Brophy and Timor Göksel of UNIFIL (the United Nations Interim Force in Lebanon). The image of the United Nations as a round of diplomatic cocktail parties is markedly different from the reality of the UN in the field: I contracted a fierce loyalty to and affection for the non-nationalistic blue-and-white flag rippling above ramshackle, bullet-pocked, corrugated-iron "headquarter" huts in which international personnel risk their lives and lucidity in medical, educational, developmental, or peacekeeping assignments. Chapter 8 communicates only a tiny fragment of their dedication.

For the rest of this work, Edite Kroll, my literary representative, and Mary Cunnane, my Norton editor, earn my gratitude for their dual gifts of critical support and supportive criticism, and Esther Jacobsen deserves my thanks for her painstaking copy editing. My friend and son, Blake Morgan (Pitchford) has borne with me on this book as he has others, balancing a sense of justice with a sense of humor and always offering perspective. Marilyn J. Waring was a sustaining presence despite geographical distance, and the manuscript benefited from her challenging mind. My colleague at the Sisterhood Is Global Institute, Karen Berry, made time in between her responsibilities there to be of inestimable aid as a research associate, particularly regarding the international data throughout the book.

Last, I am grateful to Isel Rivero, who from the first had faith in the idea of *The Demon Lover,* and kept that faith in urging me to attempt and complete it. To her—because she has in her own life known terror, fled it, faced it, and transcended it—this book is lovingly dedicated.

Would that my skills were equal to my gratitude for the support of such colleagues and friends. As it is, the consciousness and vision in these pages is collective; the faults herein are singular, and mine alone.

R.M.

"Isolated Incidents":
Introduction to the 2001 Edition

What will it take to make them hear?

It's said that women are society's canaries in the mine—living alerts to danger—and it's true that a civilization can be gauged by the status of its female citizens. But miners pay *attention* to the canaries' health and reactions, since they know that this information is crucial to their own survival. So far—35 years into the current feminist wave, and despite remarkable gains won—warnings from female human beings still are not heeded sufficiently, and most male human beings still don't understand that their own lives depend on that heeding.

Since 1995, the international women's movement has been banging on doors about the extreme human-rights violations against women in Afghanistan. Gender apartheid, we've termed it. Actually, given the epidemic of female suicides there now, it is, in effect, "ethnic cleansing" in a new form: "gender cleansing." When a state murders minority populations, it's called genocide; when a state murders some of its general population (Stalin's USSR, Mao's Cultural Revolution), it's called democide. When a state murders its women citizens, it's not hyperbole to call it femicide. So we banged on doors. Some said it was those crazy feminists again, with their "victimology" whines (e.g., kill the messenger as well as the subject). Postmodernists waved us off with trendy "cultural relativism" arguments. The U.S. ignored us because oil-pipeline interests wanted to maintain dialogue with the Taliban. The UN sacrificed women to what was judged more important: striking a deal with the Taliban over ending opium-poppy farming. The world's fury was louder over Taliban destruction of two ancient statues, the great Bamian Buddhas, than over the abominations against women. *If they come for us at night and you do nothing, they will come for you in the morning.*

I sit at my desk in lower Manhattan, less than a mile and a half from where the Twin Towers once stood, writing this introduction to the new edition of *The Demon Lover* one month after the devastating attacks on the World Trade Center in New York and the Pentagon in Washington, D.C. My three public "Letters from Ground Zero," written in the anguished days immediately following the attacks, form an afterword to this new edition. But the task here is to try to update, however summarily, the subject of terrorism—and its real, deepest roots and connections—covering the twelve years since this work was originally finished.[1] In the interim, *The Demon Lover* has been published in various foreign editions, including British, Japanese, Italian, and Arabic.

I desperately wish this book was wrong and outdated. I feel Cassandran grief and horror to find that it's neither.

Much has changed since it was first published. Tragically, more has remained the same—and much has worsened.

[1] In the short time available for writing this introduction so as to meet the printer's deadline, friends and colleagues helped with research and ideas. My gratitude goes to Bill Lee of UNRWA; Jessica Neuwirth of Equality Now; Isel Rivero; Eleanor Smeal and Jennifer Jackman of The Feminist Majority Foundation; Gloria Steinem; Judith Curr and Rosemary Ahern of Washington Square Press; and especially Suzanne Braun Levine, whose determination that *The Demon Lover* be available in a new edition is in no small part responsible for the book in your hands.

Cyberterror is now a threat, as are the even more ominous biological, chemical, and nuclear terrorisms. Globalization has brought planetary jet-speed and light-speed electronic mobilities—of people, monies, materiel, images, information, ideas, and weapons. Secure borders are a delusion in an age when Chernobyl's fallout can ride the wind, and satellite-beamed TV images of one society's flaunted luxuries elicit envious outrage from viewers starving in a different society half a world away. Experts say this new battle will be fought with different tools: genomics, immunology, biotechnology. They address the means but miss the point.

Political and military figures vow to eradicate the leaders, to "decapitate" the problem. They address the image but miss the substance. Capturing or killing the leader(s) will no more end terrorism than would Bill Gates's dying of a heart attack end capitalism. *Item:* In 1992, Abimael Guzman, founder and leader of Peru's The Shining Path, was apprehended and sentenced to prison; his lover, Elena Iparraguirre, shares his cell. Since then, former Peruvian president Fujimori, who in 1992 cited terrorism as his excuse to establish martial law, fell from power due to rampant corruption and human-rights abuses, and fled into exile. Last year, The Shining Path was reported to be active and gaining momentum. *Item:* In 1994, after a worldwide manhunt and numerous escapes, the notorious "Carlos the Jackal" (Ilich Ramírez Sanchez) was caught and sentenced to prison for life, following several already incarcerated members of his "harem," his many female lovers (some of whom were aware of his exploits—and each other—and some of whom weren't). Carlos is believed responsible for as many as 90 murders in the name of insurgent causes; all the groups with which he was associated have engaged in violent action *since* his incarceration.[2]

---

[2] Meanwhile, this year, at age 52, Carlos announced plans to wed his attorney, Isabelle Coutant-Peyre, at the La Sante Prison in Paris; she confirmed the plans, saying "It's a meeting of hearts and of minds." Plus ça change . . .

That such groups reflect and feed off authentic grievances based on profound oppression suffered by their constituencies ought, by now, to be self-evident. There is a global, obscene imbalance of power, wealth, education, use/abuse of resources; a widening North/South divide wherein calls for peace, democratic procedures, and the rule of law are drowned out by screams for a bowl of rice; multigenerational suffering so chronic as to callous the soul until, joyless, it welcomes death. That addresses the justifications, but still misses the point. Violent acts committed by a man in a state of despair due to poverty, ignorance, and repression don't explain violent acts committed by men possessed of wealth, education, and power.

Something else is at work. We need to face it.

We need to look at the cross-cultural pattern that forms the central knot of terrorism: the intersection of violence, eroticism, and what is considered "masculinity." We need to change a definition of "manhood" toxic to men and lethal to women. And we—women *and* men—*can* change it. But it's not simple.

The evidence is so pervasive as to become virtually invisible against the background of the field, because it *is* the field. The terrorist (or, depending on one's view, the freedom fighter) is the ultimate sexual idol of a male-centered cultural tradition that stretches from pre-Biblical times to the present: he is the logical extension of the patriarchal hero/martyr. He is the Demon Lover, and society is (secretly or openly) fascinated by him. He walks with death and is thus inviolate; he is an idealist but a man of action, a fanatic of dedication and an archetype of self-sacrifice, a mixture of volatility, purity, severe discipline. He is desperate and therefore vulnerable, at risk and therefore brave, wholly given over to an idea. His intensity reeks of glamour. Women, we are told, lust to have him. Men, we are told, long to *be* him.[3] He is sexy because he is deadly;

---

[3] The devotees of ultra-masculinism recognize and applaud their brothers across considerable differences. "May the WAR be started," writes August Kreis, webmaster of the neo-Nazi Sheriff's Posse Comitatus group based in

he excites with the thrill of fear. He has been celebrated and evoked for centuries. Now he stalks among us.

As I write this, the U.S. population is living in fear. Airplanes. Tall buildings. Anthrax. Smallpox rumors. Other populations know fear, of course. Terror is the norm for entire peoples trying to survive in acute poverty; or under military, theocratic, or totalitarian rule; or in refugee or displacement circumstances. But this is new for the U.S. The populace is exhibiting post-traumatic stress syndrome. People are sleeping badly; they have nightmares, appetite loss, or irrational hungers; they experience sudden flashbacks, burst into tears for no immediate reason, sink into depression, can't seem to enjoy living, and—despite reassurances from authorities—keep obsessing about violence. Yet such symptoms aren't new to *everyone* in the U.S. These are exact descriptions of the rape survivor's condition, the battery survivor's reality; the abused child's experience. A terrified man isn't as much a cultural fixture as a terrified woman or cowering child for a reason: the latter are familiar images.[4] The spectrum of violence and terror ranges all the way from the fist in the face to the nuclear bomb. *It is the same spectrum, differing in degree but not in kind.* We can no longer afford to ignore it, dismiss it, or deal with it piecemeal.

Ulysses, Pennsylvania, "DEATH to God's enemies, may the World Trade Center BURN TO THE GROUND!" White supremacist National Alliance deputy Billy Roper cuts right to the manhood chase: "We may not want them marrying our daughter, just as they would not want us marrying theirs. But anyone willing to drive a plane into a building . . . is alright by me. *I wish our members had half as much testicular fortitude.*" White Aryan Resistance (WAR) leader Tom Metzger strikes the hero/martyr chord when he respectfully writes on his Web site: "These soldiers were aware that their lives would be sacrificed for their cause. If an Aryan wants an example of 'Victory or Valhalla,' look no further."

[4] On August 18, 1998, the *New York Times* reported that a new study of Vietnam veterans found that post-traumatic stress disorder was diagnosed in 20 to 30 percent, about half of whom have longterm psychiatric problems. The article also reported that the condition is found in less than 5 percent of the general population—but in *two-thirds* of prostituted women.

When I was writing *The Demon Lover,* I knew the centrality of this issue to women's worldwide struggle for freedom. Yet today it seems even clearer to me that understanding this politics is absolutely crucial to *men.* Well over 80 percent of terrorists are male; their average age is between 22 and 25. Female terrorists are rare, almost always "tokens" (see Chapter 6), and invariably involved because of their love for a particular man, a personal demon lover who draws them in. Furthermore, it's extraordinary how religious, aesthetic, political, and erotic paths meet at this crossroads: the sexual politics of terrorism.

Religious fundamentalisms pave one major route. Fundamentalism, anywhere you find it, is a political movement with a political agenda.[5] Yet fundamentalism didn't spring from nowhere. The truth is that *organized religion has always been about power, and thus has always been political.* But during the past 30 to 40 years, the religious far right in the U.S. has become more strategic in planning *and* mobilized toward voting. (As Ralph Reed, former executive director of The Christian Coalition, boasted in 1991: "I do guerrilla warfare. I paint my face and travel at night. You don't know it's over until you're in a body bag.") Internationally, fundamentalism is more complex. Modern tyrants understand, as the pharaohs did, that promises of a vivid afterlife are especially attractive when conditions in this life are wretched. So religion gets further entangled with

---

[5] Few examples better expose this than the recent coalition between the Vatican, evangelical Christian organizations, and Islamic fundamentalist groups (sometimes called Islamists). This trio formed to combat gains in reproductive rights, microcredit/economic empowerment campaigns, and progress in divorce, custody, and inheritance rights that women were making at UN conferences throughout the 1990s. For decades, Islamists had denounced feminism as a Western, un-Islamic phenomenon (conveniently ignoring centuries of women's rebellion in Islamic societies, back to 12th-century harem revolts in what is now Turkey). Suddenly, the mullahs could forget the Crusades and celebrate male bonding with the Holy See. In *Israel,*

nationalism, ethnic pride, rebellion against colonial or neo-colonial forces. It becomes an affirmation of cultural integrity, a personal identity.

But globally or nationally, fundamentalists' agendas are revealingly interchangeable. One refrain they share is their demand for high birth rates (the better to build their constituencies). Another is women's insatiable carnality and the consequential temptation we inflict on apparently helpless males. Indeed, the *consistent element* to religious extremism throughout history is that women are the first target. Why? Because women stand at the political, economic, and psychological intersection of the core societal issues: *sexuality, reproduction, and family structure*. To control the population, you *must* control women's bodies. From there, you move to control *everyone's* sexuality: homophobia, female genital mutilation, arranged marriage, child marriage, purdah, etc.[6]

Orthodox political parties are steadily gaining more power. Israeli feminists mourn their country betraying its founding vision as a secular socialist state. They trace one flaw to the vein of theocracy buried in that founding vision, though it "only" affects women—who are subject to rabbinical courts in most "personal status" matters, including marriage, divorce, and custody; men alone can serve as judges in those courts. Today, the impact of Orthodoxy is shuddering through the general populace, even affecting world Jewry, as the Orthodox claim sole right to define who is a Jew. Not surprisingly, the only celebrants are religious extremists on *both* sides of Israel's political divide: ultra-Orthodox Jews, and the Islamic fundamentalist group Hamas. They understand and respect each other.

[6] The following are some international examples of this murderous misogyny (we'll return to the U.S. later): *Iran, 1979:* Farrokhrou Parsa—a medical doctor, former member of parliament, feminist—is charged with "expansion of prostitution and warring against God," sentenced, wrapped in a dark sack, and machine-gunned to death; neighborhood-watch mullahs take to punishing any woman whose *chodor* is not pulled down far enough on her forehead by fixing it there—with a thumbtack. *Senegal, Malaysia, Jordan, Indonesia:* beginning in the early 1970s, there are reports of women being summarily executed by stoning and burning to death after accusations of adultery. (Adultery, depending on the mullahs, can be defined as being seen in the company of a man who is not a relative, or dating a man, or even as having

But life—chaotic, dynamic, electric, *messy*—is ultimately not controllable. Still, if life can't be controlled, perhaps death can be. "There are thousands of young men who look forward to death," an Al Qaeda spokesman bragged on October 10, 2001. A week later, Taliban leader Mullah Omar flatly stated, "The *goal* is martyrdom." People who have nothing to live for do find it easy to die—and to take others with them. But the process of indoctrination must *ensure* that those who have nothing to live for also have everything to die for. Sometimes this is done pragmatically, when such groups as the Lebanese Hezbollah and Palestinian Hamas guarantee lifetime stipends and medical care (plus access to heaven) for families of deceased *shaheed* (martyrs)—young men who, when alive, educated or not, felt "unmanned" by being unable to find jobs in devastated economies. Usually it is accompanied by the promise of forgiveness of sins and instant admission to paradise, where harems of virgin odalisques await. Always it is grounded by earthly respect, even celebrity, in the community. Young males who pledge themselves to such acts get to wear white clothing

survived a rape.) *Pakistan, Turkey:* throughout the 1980s, feminists resist Islamist attacks against women's rights; in the 1990s those attacks broaden to attempted takeovers of the entire government. *Egypt, 1983:* Nawal el Sadaawi, feminist author, is jailed and denounced in a *fatwa* (religious edict) of death; her books are banned. *Bangladesh, 1994:* novelist Taslima Nasreen flees her country under threat of a *fatwa* for "heretical" writing. *Algeria, 1994:* 28-year-old Dirouche Mimouna is accused of "un-Islamic attitudes of disobedience" and decapitated in front of her five children; *Algeria, 1997:* Islamic radicals hack to death 43 women and girls in an overnight raid on a village, for "refusing to cooperate." *Sudan, 1996:* Khartoum passes a "public order" law requiring the separation of the sexes by barriers at all public functions. Meanwhile, in *India and Pakistan,* Hindu fundamentalists boast of attacks on non-Hindus, riots, and assassinations. Indian feminists believe this trend began with the reprise of *sati* (widow burning)—but that "merely" affected women, so not much general attention was paid. In *Japan,* phenomena termed The New Religions—which blend forms of nationalistic Shintoism with militant Buddhist sects—are proliferating. Calling for a return to samurai masculinism, the leaders denounce the Japanese women's movement as "destructive to family values."

(symbolic of shrouds), strap practice toy grenades to their belts, grant autographs to kids who hero-worship them as "living martyrs," literal dead men walking. Their faces appear on posters; they swagger on videotape; small boys swap martyr-and-mullah trading cards. At their funerals, men laud their manliness. At their wakes, their mothers must weep in secret, pretending to celebrate their deaths when husbands and mullahs are near.

Such an environment fosters the attitude that life is best enjoyed when its intensity is heightened by proximity to death. Kiramat Ullah, a mujahadeen in Pehsawar, Pakistan, prefers war to playing with his children: "When we start fighting and bullets are flying and we are firing at the enemy and they are crying out and in trouble, and when some of my men are being injured and becoming martyrs—that is the peak!"[7] But lest we think such an attitude unique to men of a particular culture, we're reminded otherwise by Americans training as Rangers, Green Berets, and elite Delta Forces at Fort Bragg, North Carolina, singing their traditional combat-training hymn: "Glo-ry, Glo-ry, what a hell of a way to die!"[8]

Toughness must be learned and maintained at all costs. So it was with Mohammed Atta, the 33-year-old man believed to be the ringleader of the World Trade Center attacks and to have piloted the plane that slammed into the first tower. The youngest child and only boy in a middle-class Egyptian family, he grew up, like his older sisters, in terror of their father. Mohammed al-Amir Atta Sr., a lawyer, has given interviews in which he prides himself on having been such a strict disciplinarian that his children "almost never left the house except for school. . . . That is why my two daughters and my son are academically and morally excellent." But Junior was a disappointment. "He was so gentle. I used to tell him, 'Toughen up, boy!'" The father regarded others in their economically declining neighborhood

[7] Quoted in the *New York Times*, October 7, 2001.
[8] Quoted in the *New York Times*, October 9, 2001.

with contempt, certain that his family was superior. He fought with his wife over her milder methods of child-raising, especially with regard to their "sissy" son. "I used to tell her that she is raising him as a girl and that [therefore] I have three girls, but she never stopped pampering him. . . . I told him I needed to hear the word 'doctor' in front of his name . . . your sisters are doctors and their husbands are doctors and you are [supposed to be] the man of the family." The slender boy grew up timid and introverted, as abused children often are, and had no friends: "I never saw him playing. I think he wanted to," a former classmate recalled, "but his father wanted him to always perform in school in an excellent way." He did, as a perfectionist, meticulous student. His sole rebellion was to become more religiously devout than the rest of the family—the one thing his father could hardly criticize. Otherwise, he did his father's bidding and became an engineer. But his degree meant nothing in an Egypt where jobs were scarce. So, though unhappy at leaving his mother and sisters, he again obeyed his father's orders and sought an advanced degree in Germany. There, pursuing studies in urban planning, his religiosity so warped into fundamentalism that, on graduating with honors from Hamburg Technical University, he refused to shake hands with one of the judges because she was a woman. All his life he'd been painfully shy around girls, saying he doubted he would marry since most women were "insufficiently devout." His fixations on strict observance, on destiny, and on purity intensified. He disappeared for months at a time. In 1996, after becoming involved with the Al Qaeda network and finding his purpose in life (and employment) as a "jihadi," he wrote his will, requiring strict Muslim burial. He added, "the person who will wash my body near the genitals must wear gloves on his hand so he won't touch my genitals," and specified, "I don't want any women to go to my grave at all during my funeral or any occasion thereafter. I don't want a pregnant woman or other person who is not clean to come and say goodbye to me because I don't approve of it." Only once did his self-disciplined purity apparently desert him, two nights before the day he knew he would die. Then, in a display so ironic even a feminist could not have invented it, he and two confederates went to the Pink Pony Strip Club at Red Eyed Jack's Sports Bar in Daytona Beach, Florida, near where they had attended flight school. There they drank, vowed bloodshed against America, played video games, and spent up to $300 apiece on vodka—and on lap dances. When told of this back in Cairo, Atta Sr. flew into a rage, less about growing proof of his son's involvement with Al Qaeda than about the vodka and the women. Three refrains dominated the instructions to colleague operatives found in the son's effects after the attacks: "Do not disagree, but obey," "Fear is a great worship," and "Dedicate the slaughter to your fathers."[9]

Women's very existence is perceived as a threat to this kind of masculinity, whose partisans react in two basic ways. One is denial (erasure) or flight. When the Taliban seized power, officials announced the importance of sending small boys to the *madrassas* (religious schools) "to remove them from the influence of women." The other response—if female contamination is unavoidable—is by ownership and control (containment, purdah). Hafiz Sadiqulla Hassani, who escaped to Pakistan after having been a Taliban enforcer and Mullah Omar's former bodyguard, related how, before combat, soldiers were given blank marriage certificates signed by a mullah, and were encouraged to "take wives during battle": a license to rape. Either way, sexual obsession is central to this masculinism. If being a man is defined as *not* being a woman, then a man must either keep separate from women (purity) or enslave them (mastery).

After all, women get in the way of the major players, who are engaged in the passionate power struggle between father and son. Osama bin Laden triumphantly turned on all three of his fathers: his blood father, his country, and the United States (which financed and trained him to fight against the

[9] Culled from *New York Times* articles on September 29, October 4, October 7, and October 10, 2001, and the Associated Press, September 17, 2001.

USSR in Afghanistan).[10] Bin Laden is not the desperate, unemployable, middle- or lower-class operative, the zealous follower who carries out the attacks (those poor guys are called "disposables"). No, bin Laden perfectly mirrors the profile of the mythic hero: the once-profligate princeling who abjures luxury for a holy quest.[11] Bin Laden—he of the sorrowful gaze reminiscent of that fanciful image on the Shroud of Turin—doesn't need to shout. He can afford the quiet voice, mournful smile, and pious demeanor of one who understands he is both figurehead and sacrificial king. He can finance his endeavors by stock-market trading, and can wield the newest satellite phones, best encryption devices, and latest armaments, while calling for a return to the good old days of the Middle Ages. On the one hand, he has said that—though he was enraged at the corrupt despotism of the Saudi Wahabi royal family and the posting of U.S. troops in Saudi Arabia—the *real* turning point for him was seeing a photograph of two "immodest" women, U.S. soldiers, sitting in a jeep inside their base, wearing short-sleeved shirts in the 110-degree Fahrenheit desert heat. On the other hand, he uses the Internet to send coded

[10] The youngest of 52 children by a father who had multiple wives, bin Laden was his mother's only child. Al-Kalifa, a Syrian who never quite fit into the religious severity of Saudi Arabia and who used to doff the *burka* and wear Chanel suits when she traveled abroad, is reportedly living in Syria and France, where she has been treated for cancer at the American Hospital in Paris.

[11] If someone with such wealth and presence didn't exist, they would have had to invent him—and may well have. Anyone who has studied the region and spent time there, as I have, assumes that the real political and strategic brain behind Al Qaeda is Ayman al-Zawahiri, a former surgeon and head of the Egyptian Islamic Jihad (and, before that, active in the Muslim Brotherhood, the world's oldest, original Islamist group). His lieutenant, Muhammed Atef, a former Egyptian policeman, now heads Al Qaeda's military division. In 2001, bin Laden's 19-year-old son wed Atef's daughter, age 14. A bin Laden daughter that age has been married off to Mullah Omar, the Taliban chief. Patriarchal alliances are still being cemented by trading women and girls.

maps and signals to Web sites that provide their regular customers with sports news—and pornography. Despite his own four wives, bin Laden inhabits a male universe, wherein women are alien beings. In a 1998 interview, he pointedly said, "Our enemy is every American male, whether he is directly fighting us or paying taxes." This bizarre chivalry regards the thousands of women killed in the process—whether in the U.S., Afghanistan, or anywhere else—as incidental collateral damage. Our deaths are as invisible as lives.

But the manhood theme is most plainly stated in the case of Zacarias Moussaoui, a French-Moroccan alleged Al Qaeda operative who was arrested in Minnesota and is currently in custody on numerous charges stemming from alleged activities in the U.S., France, Afghanistan, Pakistan, Kosovo, and Chechnya. He is refusing to talk to authorities, but evidence suggests that had he not been apprehended, he might have been the twentieth hijacker on September 11. His mother was interviewed at her home in Narbonne, France, where she was distraught at the idea that her son might be a part of such violence. She hadn't heard from him in more than a year since, in his intensifying fundamentalism, he had told her he wanted nothing to do with a mother who didn't say daily prayers and who refused to wear the veil. She had thought he was living in England when, suddenly, his face appeared on her TV in connection with terrorist activity. "How could he be involved in such a thing?" she wept, "I cannot eat. I cannot sleep. . . . All my children, they each had their own rooms. They had pocket money. They went on vacations. I could understand it if he had grown up unhappy or poor. But they had everything." She had certainly tried. Married at age 14 in an arranged match to a man she says she never loved, she'd been brought to France from Morocco by her husband. Ten years and four children later, she managed to divorce him, worked as a seamstress and cleaning woman, took night classes, became a civil servant, raised her children. When Zacarias was a teenager, she moved the family to a suburb of Narbonne, because "I wanted them to be away from the city and the drugs and all the trouble there. I just asked that they get a profession." Her younger son, a slow worker in high school, was "a likeable boy, tenacious," and "full of good will"; in time, he would earn several technical degrees. All four children, boys as well as girls, were raised to share the housework—make their beds, do the dishes, vacuum. The trouble began, according to the mother, when a cousin came to visit—a girl who preached Islamic femininity to the daughters and told Zacarias and his brother they should never do housework. "She told them that they were not acting like men. She told them Muslim men should have four wives. She started criticizing me because I did not wear a veil. The boys liked what they heard."[12]

The mother rocks herself and weeps. The boys liked what they heard.

So now we rock ourselves and weep. Now we shudder in another war, a war one side calls "holy" and the other calls "just."

But we didn't arrive at this place spontaneously. Here is a timeline of events that have occurred since *The Demon Lover* was first published. These are samples; a full list would take another book. Some would term these "isolated incidents."

• In 1989, Kim Hyon-hui, called the "virgin terrorist," is sentenced to death in Korea for killing 115 people with a bomb planted aboard a South Korean jet in 1987. Described in the press as "beautiful" and "glamorous," she is a perfect "token terrorist"; news reports of her trial note that her "beauty, humility, alleged virginity, and unquestioning obedience appeal to Korean males."

• January 1989. Ted Bundy, confessed serial killer of as many as 36 women, is executed in Florida. Handsome, articulate, with all-American boy-next-door charm and a taste for

---

[12] "Mysterious Life of a Suspect from France," by Suzanne Daley, in the *New York Times*, September 21, 2001.

violent pornography, Bundy becomes a folk hero to many men; there are T-shirts lauding his exploits, songs written about his "romances." Statistics show serial murder increasing in the U.S.: 649 such murders—5.9 percent of all murders in 1966; 4,118 sex murders—19.6 percent of all murders in 1982.[13]

• December 6, 1989. "It's the women I've come for. You're all feminists. I'm against feminism. That's why I'm here." Those are the last words ever heard by 14 young women engineering students before they die, shot by a 22-year-old man who wounds 13 other people—nine of them women—during his semiautomatic-rifle rampage through the halls of the University of Montreal, in Canada. His final act is to kill himself. He has bought the rifle legally because he had no criminal or psychiatric record—despite numerous complaints of former girlfriends and women neighbors about his violent behavior. He has been addicted to such combat magazines as *Soldier of Fortune,* to pornography, war movies, gun shops, and combat fatigues. The note found on his body blames females for everything wrong in his life: his inability to graduate from college, loss of jobs, failure to get into graduate school, breakups of relationships with women. The note contains an enemies list of 15 prominent Quebec women, potential targets. (Many of them hadn't characterized themselves as feminists, but neither had most of the slaughtered students. That didn't matter. They were women: they endangered men: they must be destroyed.) Analyses of the massacre multiply. Because Marc Lépine, the gunman, was half Algerian, some use the occasion to Arab-bash. Because his uneven scholastic record meant he hadn't graduated college, others cite class resentment as his motive.

[13] Some historical perspective might be useful. From 1882 to 1927, more than 3,400 African American men were lynched in 17 southern and border states, lynching being a powerful means of maintaining white supremacy during post–Civil War Reconstruction. That era is a ghastly scar on U.S. history—yet more women and children are killed by various Ted Bundys *every* year than there were deaths in the entire 45-year span of hideous lynchings.

Because the rifle was U.S.-manufactured, the importation of such products—and of "American violence"—was deplored (as if Canada had no homegrown misogyny). Because the victims were women training for non-traditional jobs, some tsktsk that, saying "This is what happens when women refuse to stay home and have babies." Because he was raised by a woman, this must be her fault. Because his background included a broken home and battery, heads are shaken over "the demise of the family."[14] Every possible analysis is promulgated—except that based on the spoken and written words of Lépine, himself. The media consensus is that this is another isolated incident.

• 1989. The Palestinian Intifada ("uprising"), begun in 1987 in the Occupied Territories, reaches fever pitch. When I return to the refugee camps I'd first visited in 1986 (see Chapter 8), the bleak conditions have shifted from unspeakable to unthinkable.[15] The men and boys are now obsessed with martyrdom; the women and girls are still trying to sustain life amidst the death surrounding them. They call their struggle "the intifada within the intifada, the *women's* intifada," and meet secretly to conduct now-forbidden literacy classes, form feminist groups to fight "honor killings," persist in painful dialogue with courageous Israeli feminist peace activists. Palestinian feminist leaders tell me with pride how they've already begun drafting articles for the proposed Constitution, toward a someday state—including provisions

---

[14] The broken home *should* have been broken. The father, Rachid Gharbi, had battered his wife and children for years—until she divorced him and he returned to Algeria. That wife, Monique Lépine, reclaimed her own name, raised both children as a single mother, worked hard to support her family. In the divorce-hearing transcript, she testified that Gharbi insisted women were not the equals of men, but were born to serve men. The son—only seven when the father whom he feared had left—had already learned his lesson.

[15] This second trip back into the camps is described in the essay "Women in the Intifada," in my collection of essays, *The Word of a Woman: Feminist Dispatches* (W.W. Norton, second edition, 1994).

that women will be covered by secular law, not religious *(sharia)* law. This would be a first in any Islamic country (and in the region, including Israel). Palestinians have heretofore been the most secular people in the Arab world, yet now fundamentalism is rising. But there's a story behind that story: the Israeli Occupying Authority has outlawed any secular meetings of more than five Palestinians, yet prides itself on freedom of religious expression. So naturally hundreds suddenly begin meeting with impunity in the mosques (to the delight of Hamas and other fundamentalist groups). The women say that despair leaks in like sand through the rag-stuffed cracks in their hovels. In Rashideyeh Camp in Lebanon, the hunger becomes so great that, after the rats have been caught and eaten, the men petition the mullahs for dispensation to eat human flesh. No one asks who will cook it. Everyone knows that this is the job of women, who are already "unclean."

• 1989. The U.S. football star O. J. Simpson faces charges of domestic violence and battery against his wife, Nicole Brown Simpson. The arresting cops ask for his autograph. The situation is smoothed over with an anger-management class.

• Starting in the 1980s and persisting through the 1990s, a U.S. group calling itself the Christian Reconstructionism Movement builds its campaign calling for the death penalty in all cases of adultery, abortion (providers and clients both), homosexuality, and "incorrigible children." Acknowledging that such an increase in executions would be costly for the taxpayer, the CRM recommends reviving public stoning as the cheapest, most efficient, and Bible-approved method of capital punishment. Feminists calling attention to this group are chuckled at for being alarmist.

• In 1990, new surveys on violence against women in the U.S. report a rape being committed every six minutes, with domestic violence being the single largest cause of injury to women. Other indicators: 55 percent of all female victims of domestic sexual abuse are children under age 11; 51 percent of college men said they would rape if they could get away with it; 52 percent of men convicted for rape will be arrested again within three years; one woman in four will be assaulted in her lifetime. That year, government funding for battered women's shelters is cut by 35 percent.

• In 1990, Iraq invades Kuwait; the Gulf War ensues. One side calls for rivers of blood in "the Mother of Battles." The other uses football-game metaphor and modern phallocentric rhetoric ("penetrating their tight defenses"). The U.S. navy admits its pilots are shown violent porn videos before flying bombing missions, "to get that adrenaline going." In Riyadh, 47 Saudi women disobey the law forbidding them to drive cars; they are jailed; many lose jobs, travel papers, homes. Back in the U.S., a Harris poll reports that 48 percent of men favor attacking Iraqi forces occupying Kuwait, while an equal number of men oppose it; women oppose it by 73 to 22 percent. Interestingly, Harris finds women *and* men in agreement on Gulf strategies that don't involve killing or dying: a majority of both women and men want the U.S. to wait and let an embargo take its longer-term effect. They are not listened to. Meanwhile, a millionaire Saudi playboy leaves his country in protest at the presence of U.S. troops. His name is Osama bin Laden. Around the same time, a young U.S. soldier is shipped to the Gulf, where he will hone his skills and get "properly hardened." His name is Timothy McVeigh.

• In 1991, OMON[16] units on duty in Lithuania and Latvia have as their mission the prevention of those countries' secession from the USSR, but their zeal outstrips their orders, and atrocities are reported. Some of these units will be sent to Afghanistan as well. These anti-U.S. cold-war soldiers jovially nickname each other after "heroes" seen in Hollywood movies: Krueger. Snake. Ninja. Rambo.

---

[16] OMON (in Cyrillic: Special Assignment Militia Detachment) was created in 1987 as an elite paramilitary unit of the then-Soviet Interior Ministry. OMON members were labeled "angels of death in black berets."

• In 1991, Jack Ryan dies in Los Angeles. An obituary describes him as (1) a former husband of Zsa Zsa Gabor, (2) a designer of Hawk and Sparrow missiles for the Raytheon Company, and (3) the inventor of the Barbie doll. (I did not make this up.)

• 1991–1993. More than 50,000 women and girls in the former Yugoslavia are raped (more than 20,000 in Bosnia alone, according to the conservative European Community estimate), and at least another 100,000 killed. Although the overwhelming number of rapes and forced pregnancies are committed by Serbian men against Bosnian Muslim women, men of *all* the opposing sides—Serbian, Croatian, and Bosnian Muslim—are raping "each other's" women. That is the point: women are envelopes to carry the message of conquest from one group of men to another. Investigations will later find truth to the charges that UN Protection Forces in Croatia and Bosnia have frequented the brothel/death camps there. The previous year, when the UN Transition Authority in Cambodia received protests about troops' behavior there, UNTAC chief Yasushi Akashi replied that "18-year-old, hot-blooded soldiers" have a right to drink and chase "young, beautiful beings of the opposite sex." That year, men of warring clans in Somalia rape women of opposing clans, and there are reports of rapes by UN peacekeeping forces. Compounding the horror, Islamic fundamentalists blame Somali women rape survivors as adulterers: five women are stoned to death and a sixth lashed 100 times as punishments for this "adultery."[17]

• February 1993. The World Trade center is bombed.

• March 1993. Dr. David Gunn, an abortion provider, is shot and killed entering a Pensacola, Florida, clinic.

[17] In 1998, after decades of pressure from the global women's movement, rape as a war crime (and also as a form of forced-pregnancy ethnic-cleansing genocide) was successfully prosecuted at the UN International Criminal Tribunal for Rwanda. The Tribunal's sole woman member and its president, Judge Navinathem Pillay of South Africa, was presiding.

• April 1993. The FBI attacks the Branch Davidian compound in Waco, Texas, after a 51-day siege following a shootout that leaves four agents and six Davidians dead. The doomsday-prophet leader of the group, a spin-off sect of apocalyptic Seventh-Day Adventism, is 33-year-old Vernon Howell—self-renamed David Koresh—a barely literate, good-looking, failed wanna-be rock guitarist who can quote the Bible's apocalyptic Book of Revelations verbatim. By his own admission, he's fixated on Harley bikes, Marlboro cigarettes, and sex with little girls. He regards himself as a "sinful Messiah anointed by God to deflower virgins," sire dozens of children for a new House of David, and generate an army of followers to provoke Armageddon against Babylon. He uses his music and self-proclaimed "religious magnetism" as a way to get women. "I'll have women begging me to make love to 'em. Just imagine, virgins without number, man, this is how we're going to do it," he tells Davidian Marc Breault.[18] David Thibodeau, another follower, confirms stories of Koresh's multiple "marriages" to girls as young as age 12.[19] In later court testimony, Kiri Jewell will relate having been forcibly "wed" to Koresh and raped by him at age 10. All male followers (including married men) are required to renounce sex and turn their wives and daughters over to Koresh, so he can assume the "burden of sexuality" for other men, since "sex is a huge stumbling block, a major source of pain and lies between men and women." The women wear long skirts and no makeup, so as not to tempt the men. But Koresh—to Thibodeau a father figure—sometimes taunts the guys: "I got all the women, aren't you jealous?" During the final siege, Koresh sees the government assault as sexually driven. Thibodeau writes: "David said this was a man-to-man challenge. He said, 'You have to under-

[18] Quoted in Breault's book, *Inside the Cult* (Signet, 1993).
[19] David Thibodeau, *A Place Called Waco: A Survivor's Story* (Public Affairs, 1999).

stand the basic concept of them coming after me. Do you think they like the idea that this guy is in here with all these wives?'" Among the 75 people who die in the compound conflagration are 36 women and children, variously shot by Davidian men in cult-murder/suicides, or burned, suffocated, or buried alive by incendiary devices fired by government forces.

• August 1993. Randall Terry, founder of Operation Rescue, publicly instructs his followers, "I want you to let a wave of intolerance, of hatred, wash over you. . . . We have a Biblical duty to conquer this country." That month, Dr. Wayne Patterson, owner of the clinic where Dr. David Gunn was killed, is shot to death in Mobile, Alabama.

• 1994. Nicole Brown Simpson is found murdered, along with Ron Goldman, a young waiter who brought back a pair of eyeglasses she'd inadvertently left at a restaurant.

• 1994. The earliest reports coming out of a small African country called Rwanda focus on what appears to be an organized campaign of rape-murders of Tutsi women by young Hutu men calling themselves Interahamwe ("our heroic boys"). The Canadian commander of the small UN force in Rwanda, Lt. Gen. Romeo Dallaire, warns headquarters that the situation is serious. But HQ notes that so far only women seem to be targeted. So the world will wait for genocide to warrant its attention. Even then, too little action, too late.

• 1994. Islamist clerics in Bangladesh beat a man almost to death for having disobeyed their orders to stop teaching illiterate village women to read. That year, in Algeria, two women students, ages 18 and 19, are shot to death at an Algiers bus stop for being unveiled; in retaliation, and in response to fundamentalist threats to kill more unveiled women, a secular vigilante organization, Free Young Algerians, issues a tract vowing to kill 30 *veiled* women.

• 1994. Dr. John Bayard Britton and volunteer clinic escort Lt. Col. James Barrett are shot and killed in the clinic driveway in Pensacola, Florida. The same year, in Brookline, Massachusetts, staff members Shannon Lowney and Leanne Nichols are shot to death at the reception desks of their respective neighboring clinics.

• 1995. Women's groups note that Saudi Arabia's interpretation of Islamic justice has set a new record: 11 women have been publicly beheaded in less than three years.[20] Not a single embassy is reported to have protested the beheadings—nor the increasingly fierce public lashings for misdemeanors allegedly committed by the hundreds of foreign female workers in the Gulf states.

• 1995. A group is coming to power in Afghanistan (a country to which few in the West pay much attention, since the Russians have given up on it). Calling itself the Taliban, a movement of Islamic students, it gains followers for establishing order in the chaotic, post-war state of the country, particularly for defending women against prevalent rape by warlords. This "protection" soon requires women's seclusion, however. By November, Taliban enforcers are mobilizing mobs to assault women on their way to work at international aid agencies. The UN expresses concern over this "dilemma," but then discharges the female workers, diplomatically sacrificing women so as to maintain relations with religious militants on the verge of taking Kabul.

• 1995. The Aum Shinri-kyo (Supreme Truth Sect) releases sarin nerve gas in Tokyo's subway system, killing 12 and injuring almost 5,000. This Buddhist-fundamentalist sect (later to rename itself Aleph in trying to repair its image) acknowledges and apologizes for the attack, offering to pay $1.1 million a

[20] Three were sentenced for alleged drug-related offenses; eight for alleged murders (four for killing their husbands, one for killing her father, others for killing employers in claimed self-defense against rape). Most were under age 30, some as young as age 14; most were Filipino, Sri Lankan, Nigerian, Indonesian, and Pakistani women and girls working in the Gulf as domestic servants.

year as "compensation." The money will come out of cult assets from such successful enterprises as construction and publishing companies, computer firms that supply and service Japan's 100 top corporations, and a string of discount chain stores that bring in $66 million a year. Aum Shinri-kyo has a history of failed attempts at political power (leaders ran for parliament and lost), and of violence (kidnappings, beatings, disappearances) against members who rebel. Shoko Asahara, the sect leader, a blind "guru" in his forties, is sentenced to prison along with several of his associates. His teenage daughter is then fronted as his spiritual heir. Three years later, Fumihiro Joyu—the 38-year-old second-in-command thought to be the organizational genius of the group—is released from prison. He begins openly rebuilding the organization. Handsome and charismatic, Joyu inspires rock-star-level adulation among hordes of teenage fans, girls and boys alike; called "Joyu chasers," they wait for sightings and autographs. His nickname is "Killer Sexy Guru."

• 1995. The then-worst single terrorist act in U.S. history explodes in Oklahoma City, Oklahoma, when the Alfred P. Murrah Federal Building is bombed. Government officials assume the perpetrators are Muslim extremists until the arrest of Timothy McVeigh and his confederates. McVeigh, a Gulf War vet, is a sometime right-wing-militia member, follower of the Christian Identity Movement, gun-show addict, and illegal gun merchant who admittedly has "trouble with women." He is infuriated over what he considers the Branch Davidians' martyrdom; this is his act of revenge for Waco. Throughout his trial, 1997 conviction, and eventual execution in 2001, he remains "proud to act like a man," and "resolute," though he acknowledges that the deaths of women and children in the bombing were unfortunate—but were "collateral damage," a phrase he learned in the Gulf War.

• 1995. After a lengthy, costly, racially controversial, media-circus trial, O. J. Simpson is found not guilty of the murders of Nicole Brown Simpson and Ron Goldman.

• Throughout the 1990s, a "soldiers of fashion" vogue, begun in the late 1980s, increases: army-surplus trousers, military-style jackets, camouflage jumpsuits, and special radical chic items: "urban body armor"—bulletproof clothes—what rappers call "vesting up." Sales jump in Jeeps and Land Rovers, by consumers ostensibly not expecting to engage in combat while driving to the supermarket. The "gangsta look" grows in popularity.

• 1995. The Million Man March summons hundreds of thousands of African American men to Washington, D.C. The theme is reclaiming manhood.

• Throughout the 1990s and the first years of the new century, school slaughters, mostly by gun or automatic weapon, are on the rise. The boldest headlines focus on Columbine High School in Colorado: two killers—a 17-year-old and an 18-year-old; 14 students plus one teacher slain. The following school shooters warrant smaller headlines: a 17-year-old in Tennessee; a 16-year-old in Mississippi; another 16-year-old in Alaska; 15-year-olds in Oregon, Georgia, California; 14-year-olds in Kentucky, Washington, Arkansas, Pennsylvania, Virginia; 13-year-olds in Oklahoma and Florida; a 12-year-old in New Mexico; an 11-year-old and a 13-year-old in Arkansas; a *six-year-old* in Michigan. These shootings were described and deplored as "children killing children." *Notice the language.* But these killings were done by little boys, often deliberately aimed at little girls and female teachers. What does this tell us about the expendability of female people and the necessity to commit violent acts in order to be considered a real boy or a real man? As Michael Kimmel, professor of sociology at SUNY, Stonybrook, notes, "Experts continue to seek the 'deeper truth' of school violence . . . but they continue to miss what is right in front of them: these are not troubled 'teenagers,' 'youths,' or 'children,' but boys. Men and boys are responsible for 95 percent of all violent crimes in this country. . . . Moreover, nearly 90 percent of all homicides among boys aged 15 to 19 are firearm-related. . . . Unless we confront the lethal equation of masculinity and violence, the deeper truths about school violence will elude us."[21]

• 1996. The decade-long search for the Unabomber ends with the arrest of Ted Kaczynski, after a tip from his brother, following their father's suicide. Kaczynski, a Harvard graduate with a Ph.D. in mathematics, offers a manifesto denouncing modernity and technology. He pleads guilty to 13 bombing and murder charges, and in 1998 is sentenced to four consecutive life terms. The psychiatric report diagnoses him as a delusional paranoid schizophrenic with "an almost total absence of interpersonal relationships," and notes that his "lack of ability to get along with women haunted him from the age of 15, when he was told by an older woman that he was a 'beautiful boy.'" In his journals, Kaczynski attributes his acute depressions to two significant events: the first when he skipped two grades in school, couldn't fit in, and was bullied; the second at age 25, when he sought psychiatric help after "experiencing severe, intense, and persistent sexual excitement involving fantasies of being a female." He considered seeking a sex-change operation, he writes, but was stopped by feelings of "rage, shame, and humiliation" at the disgusting idea of being female.

• 1996. A booby-trapped truck full of explosives is detonated outside Khobar Towers, an apartment complex in Dhahran, Saudi Arabia, housing U.S. military personnel.

• 1997. In a civil suit, O. J. Simpson is found culpable for the wrongful deaths of Nicole Brown Simpson and Ron Goldman. He declares bankruptcy and pays no damages. Three years later, after several court battles with his former in-laws, he's granted sole custody rights to his and Nicole's two children. Nicole's diary is published. In it she writes that she knows her husband will someday kill her—and get away with it.

---

[21] May 4, 1999, Letter to the Editor, the *New York Times*.

• 1997. Agudath Israel of America is sponsoring a gathering expected to fill New York City's Madison Square Garden. Like the African American Million Man March and the Christian evangelical Promise Keepers, it too is for men only (in this case, male Torah-readers, though women are permitted to observe from sex-segregated sections); 70,000 tickets are sold to the Garden and satellite-linked sites around the country.

• 1998. Coordinated car-bomb attacks against U.S. embassies in Nairobi, Kenya, and Dar es Salaam, Tanzania, kill 224 and leave thousands wounded.

• 1998. In January, off-duty police officer Robert Sanderson is killed in a bomb explosion at New Woman, All Women Clinic in Birmingham, Alabama. The Army of God claims credit. In October, Dr. Barnett Slepian, an abortion provider, is killed in his Amherst, New York, home by a sniper with a high-powered rifle. That month, Matthew Shephard is tortured and crucified to death in Laramie, Wyoming, for, according to his attackers, being "a sissy gay guy."

• 1999. An Irish government task force reports that the rate of suicides of males age 15 to 24 is 19 per 100,000, higher than in most European countries and apparently growing. Since 1987, the number has doubled (to about 500 deaths per year); men are responsible for four out of five of those deaths. Psychologists believe the rising young male suicide rate is due to men being "unsure of their roles" now that: (1) women have more equality, (2) political violence in Northern Ireland is on the decline, and (3) there is a shrinking availability of firearms.[22]

• 1999. More than 12,000 men pack a basketball arena in Hartford, Connecticut, in another rally of The Promise Keepers

---

[22] The following is excerpted from the IANSA (International Action Network on Small Arms) Women's Caucus 2001 Statement to the Third Preparatory Committee toward the UN Conference on Illicit Trade of Small Arms and

(TPK). An all-male evangelical Christian movement with a military structure and an annual budget of $115 million (which subsequently claims bankruptcy and faces fraud investigations), TPK draws crowds of up to 40,000 men in its prayer rallies. Promise Keepers sometimes talk about male responsibility but link that to strengthening male authority in the family. They call for "taking back power" from women, for "family obedience," and for defeating the "abominations" of reproductive choice and lesbian/gay rights.

• 2000. UNFPA (UN Fund for Population Activities) and Unicef (UN Children's Fund) update their statistics on women's status. A sampling: given approximately 80 million unwanted pregnancies a year and 20 million unsafe abortions, one woman a minute dies of pregnancy-related causes. Sexually transmitted diseases afflict five times more women than men. Two-thirds of the 300 million children without access to education are girls, and two-thirds of the 880 million illiterate adults are women. Ninety-nine percent of the

Light Weapons in All Its Aspects: "Of the 49 regional conflicts waged since 1990, small arms and light weapons have been the weapons of choice in 46. Small arms kill almost as many people in countries not at war [where] interpersonal violence replaces violence between warring factions . . . small arms figure prominently in criminal violence, domestic violence, suicides, and accidents. An estimated 500,000 to 700,000 lives each year are claimed by the use of these weapons, an average of 1,700 deaths per day or one person dying every minute. *The easy availability of small arms during and after a conflict is responsible for the militarization and the masculinization of society where guns become a symbol of male power and normalize the violent resolution of a conflict. In times of "peace" high levels of violent crimes, domestic assault, sexual violence, suicides, and firearms accidents are recorded due to the ready availability of these weapons—legally or illegally possessed.* Studies in post-conflict societies have shown that women's perception of security differs considerably to men's: women experience the presence of small arms in the household as threatening while many men feel more secure in the presence of a weapon. Women are mostly the victims of the use of small arms while men are the major users of small arms and perpetrators of violence *Civilian women have a higher death rate than soldiers in war.*" (Italics mine.)

500,000 deaths from maternal mortality each year are in developing countries. Unicef reports a rise in violence against women. In Bangladesh, acid-throwing attacks on women and girls (usually by men and boys they have rejected) have risen from 47 disfiguring assaults in 1996 to more than 200 in 1998. In India, more than 6,000 "bride burnings" or dowry deaths are reported, along with 10,000 cases of female infanticide annually. Meanwhile, because of pressure from the U.S. Congress, the UN announces budget cuts; the deepest are in administrative services: statistical and policy analyses, and planning programs to fight poverty and enhance the status of women.

• 2000. Irked by the continuing peace process and facing a political campaign, Israeli arch-conservative Ariel Sharon makes a bid to position himself further right than his Likud rival Benjamin Netanyahu. He visits a volatile site sacred to Jews and Muslims: what Israel terms "The Temple Mount," called Haram Al-Sharif by the Palestinians. The ploy works. Sharon's presence near the Al Aksa Mosque—escorted by almost 1,000 Israeli army and police—is viewed as deliberate provocation. The peace talks halt. Sharon becomes prime minister. The second Intifada erupts. TV coverage again runs daily footage of street fights, bombings, dead and wounded children and adults, funerals, wailing women. The Israeli death toll mounts; the Palestinian death toll mounts higher. In October, while refueling in the Port of Aden, the USS *Cole*, a guided missile destroyer, is attacked by a suicide mission: 17 die, 39 are wounded.

• 2000. George W. Bush, campaigning for the presidency of the United States, is asked his opinion of the Taliban. "Is that a rock group or something?" he asks in return.

• 2000. The July 23 *New York Times* reports on the popularity of McFarlane Toys' new product: "Death Row Marv," a battery-operated toy electric chair, complete with strapped-in inmate, marketed at $20; the typical buyer is the 15- to 45-year-old male. The ad copy reads: "Watch Marv convulse as the switch is thrown, then hear him say 'That the best you can do?'" and exhorts the buyer to watch him "glow red as he fries." Marv, "half convict, half hero, is the guy who never gets the girl . . . the loser that guys desperately want to see win."

• 2000. In a historic decision, after decades of activist lobbying, the UN Security Council passes Resolution 1325, which recognizes the crucial role of women in the prevention, resolution, and management of conflicts, as well as in peace-building. The UN has no specific plans to implement the Resolution.

• The years 1991 to 2001 witness multiple terrorist attacks on U.S. clinics and medical personnel who provide contraception and abortion services, leaving eight dead and 33 seriously wounded. In addition, there have been 20 arsons and attempted arsons, 10 bombings and attempted bombings, and clinics in 23 states have received threats of anthrax and chemical offensives. In the wake of the September 11, 2001, attacks, an American Life League ad attacking Planned Parenthood runs in the *Washington Times*, declaring "Abortion is the ultimate terrorism."

• 2001. Ten days after the World Trade Center attacks, Clayton Lee Waagner joins Osama bin Laden on the FBI's Most Wanted List, but this receives little attention during the global hunt for Al Qaeda operatives. Waagner escaped federal custody in February 2001 while awaiting sentencing on federal weapons and stolen vehicle charges, facing a possible sentence of 15 years to life. At his trial, he admitted he'd stalked doctors and regretted he hadn't managed to kill one yet. "They're right," he crows in a statement newly posted on the Army of God web site, "I am a terrorist. God freed me [from jail] to make war on His enemy. . . . It doesn't matter to me if you're a nurse, receptionist, bookkeeper, or janitor, if you work for the abortionist I'm going to kill you."

Stunned, we stagger through a wilderness of griefs.

The long fuse of manhood that's been burning for centuries has, in this age of globalization, become a conflagration of heroes/martyrs/killers. It is the era of the Demon Lover. Yet we *can* free men from having to incarnate his model, we *can* free women from his thrall. We *can* save our children—but only if we raise them differently. And the same globalization that furthers the Demon Lover offers solutions to undo him. We too can communicate across borders on this small, endangered planet. We can feed one another—rice, ideas, strategies, laughter, love. We can dare to recognize the same mitochondrial DNA alive in each other's fragile, temporary flesh.

The genius of our species is its adaptability. *We can change this.*

Terrorism begins in the deepest recesses of the human heart, and it is there we must track it, to its ultimate end. Who stands a better chance of survival, after all: those enamored of death? Or those in love with life?

—Robin Morgan
October 2001
New York City

INTRODUCTION

༜༜༜༜༜༜༜

A friendly warning is in order: this book does not have the laudable if absurd function of providing "answers." It will "prove" nothing, "solve" nothing, and reassure no one. That is not its intention. Rather, it is meant to perform the humbler if irritating function of asking questions, sensing connections, and suggesting perspectives. These may validate a few readers, challenge others, and unsettle some.

The Demon Lover has been gestating since the mid-1960s. It could doubtless have gestated longer, but the crises of history impose their own deadlines on the writer who sees her work as politically engaged. Despite the two-decade renaissance of feminist letters, theory, and scholarship, there has been no feminist analysis of the phenomenon called "terrorism." That seems both a dangerous gap and an obvious need—which this work tries to address.

No single book is ever quite worthy of its subject. For the author blessed and burdened by feminist consciousness, no single subject can ever quite be separated from the rest: each work is in effect about everything—the world as we experience it and the world as we envision it. In this case, it is necessary to place terrorism in multiple contexts—national, international, cultural, historical, philosophical, religious, aesthetic, psychological, economic, etc.—and to locate it along an entire spectrum of patriarchal violence, which I call the politics of Thanatos.

In one sense, *The Demon Lover* expands the theory of metaphysical feminism on which I first began working in *Going Too Far* (1977) and which I continued to develop via the metaphor of quantum physics in *The Anatomy of Freedom* (1982). In another sense, this book is a radical departure. Because the world changes and because, in my own subjective becoming, I am again a different woman, I now have less need to overlook, escape, or minimize certain core elements of that evolving theory which I had previously managed to treat superficially or to avoid altogether. While affirming those previous attempts, I am nevertheless excited by and grateful for these new perceptions. I can't help noticing, however, an ironic consistency of anti-linear form, in which, by the end of each book, the words struggle increasingly to break free from the page that is their vehicle, as if the thoughts they convey yearn for more direct and urgent communication with the reader. Because, I confess, I am more drawn to preludes than to conclusions, this book's structure also reflects a process from the linear to the radiant—questions and possibilities spinning out from the hub of what is simultaneously an intellectual premise, a metacognitive intuition, and an experienced reality for the more than half of humanity that is female.

We begin, therefore, with a review of the scholarly literature and terminology* of terrorism. I trust this will reassure some

---

* A word about variant names of terrorist groups is in order. The reader will sometimes encounter differing appellations for the same group—for example, the Weathermen / Weatherpeople / Weather Underground, the Japanese Red Army / Japanese Red Armies, the Baader-Meinhof Group / Red Army Faction. These variants are intentional; they reflect development phases, schisms, and re-formations in the evolution of the particular groups.

that I've done my homework, and I hope it will amuse others: the paucity of thought in this field certainly shows a need for some healthily abrasive feminist energy. Since the continuum of violence is internal as well as external, we then trace the incarnation of terror in myth and legend, across the world and across time. The third chapter considers what is lightly termed "culture"—religion, philosophy, and aesthetics—as the means by which we are conditioned to view existence itself in a double negative: at worst a state of fear, at best the lack thereof.

Had this book been written in the 1970s, it might not have been necessary to examine State terrorism to the degree that the fourth chapter attempts. But the power of the State has grown alarmingly since then, and our vigilance about that seems to have shrunk. In the United States, with the rise of an ultra-conservative movement and two terms of a Right-wing administration, I cannot assume that an average reader any longer necessarily notices or cares that the State, too, can be a terrorist. Elsewhere, centralized theocratic governments—whether religious-fundamentalist ones or secular communist ones—also reinforce the power and terror of the State. It's not possible to examine insurgency unless one understands incumbency, and the reverse.

On the other hand, had this been written in the mid-1970s, neither would it have been possible to expose "revolutionary" terrorism to the extent hazarded by the fifth chapter. Even today, much written there may be misunderstood. Those too young to have been involved in or affected by the political ferment of the sixties tend to romanticize that period. Men *of* that time tend to glamourize it in a nostalgia almost as embarrassing as that of war veterans going misty-eyed while reminiscing about days at "the front." Sometimes I think that we women survivors of the time are "alone escaped to tell."

There are women who never escaped to tell, of course—which is the point of the sixth chapter, on "token terrorists." Because some women have been, still are, and will continue to be involved in terrorist acts, it's vital to comprehend how and why. And the next chapter brings it all back home in a personal testimony—because I was once such a woman.

The eighth chapter could easily have become an entire book in itself—stories of women in the refugee camps of the Middle East, where I spent almost two months in 1986. Those stories comprise the *de facto* answer to women who believe terrorism is a route to freedom for women—or for anyone.

The penultimate chapter of the book brings it all back home again—this time in a societal as well as a personal context: facing the normalization of terror that pervades the details of our everyday lives; women in particular live in this state as a matter of commonplace common space. And the final chapter is a meditation, a metaphoric leap beyond our species to freshen our thinking. It intuits a politics of Eros through options that might transform us *as* we transform society, and explores ways by which we might create in ourselves a committed ferocity too intelligent and pragmatic to settle for violent means.

I am not an "expert" on terrorism. I am a poet, a writer, a political creature, a feminist. My expertise is experiential. Because I once participated in what some called terrorist activities, and extricated myself barely in time to avoid the fate of a number of colleagues—fugitivity, prison, or death—I especially want to understand the phenomenon, understand why I became involved and why I severed that involvement when I did. More importantly, my expertise is rooted in my experience as a woman—which means that I share a democratization of fear with every other woman on earth. I want to understand more about that fear, and how to be free of it.

This much I know: unless the majority of the human species, which women constitute—the majority that has lived daily and nightly under a terrorism so ancient and omnipresent as to be called civilization—unless that enormous body of ordinary experiential experts addresses and engages this issue, it can never be understood, much less solved.

Such a task ranges from complex thinking to audaciously simple feeling, *from the personal to the political*—which feminists for decades have recognized and named as the same thing.

So this book contains no facile denunciations or defenses of terrorism, no strategies for combating it, no blueprints for stopping it. In a sense, this is a nonfiction work of fiction: it unearths realities buried under an abstract truth, and depicts truths immured under an imposed reality. Such fictions may be the only trustable repositories of fact left to us in a world where "megadeath" is a conceivable thought, where the beauty of language and the precision of mathematics are manipulated to make that concept feasible as fact.

I offer this book, then, for what use the reader may make of it, which is not up to me to prescribe or proscribe. The reader will use my work in ways more imaginative and constructive than I can conjure; she always has, so far. I trust her. Whatever my errors, in this I have never been wrong.

Robin Morgan
August 1988
New York City

THE DEMON LOVER

CHAPTER 1

𝔯𝔯𝔯𝔯𝔯𝔯𝔯𝔯𝔯

EVERYMAN'S POLITICS: THE DEMOCRATIZATION OF VIOLENCE

Terror, the human form divine . . . / WILLIAM BLAKE

Look closely at her.

She crosses a city street, juggling her briefcase and her sack of groceries. Or she walks down a dirt road, balancing a basket on her head. Or she hurries toward her locked car, pulling a small child along with her. Or she trudges home from the fields, the baby strapped to her back.

Suddenly there are footsteps behind her. Heavy, rapid. A man's footsteps. She knows this immediately, just as she knows that she must not look around. She quickens her pace in time to the quickening of her pulse. She is afraid. He could be a rapist. He could be a soldier, a harasser, a robber, a killer. He could be none of these. He could be a man in a hurry. He could be a man merely walking at his normal pace. But she fears him. She fears him because he is a man. She has reason to fear.

She does not feel the same way—on city street or dirt road,

2 3

in parking lot or field—if she hears a woman's footsteps behind her.

It is the footstep of a man she fears. This moment she shares with every human being who is female.

This is the democratization of fear.

———

The majority of terrorists—and those against whom they are rebelling—are men. The majority of women, caught in the middle, want no more of this newly intensified form of the old battle to the death between fathers and sons. Always the mothers, daughters, sisters, and wives are, in the words of an ancient Vietnamese proverb, "the grass that gets trampled when the elephants fight." Always we mourn, grieve, voluntarily staff emergency food lines and medical centers. Always we beg the insurgents to be careful, beg the officials to be merciful. Even when we collaborate—and we do, either in traditional roles of support or as tougher-than-thou token militants—we do so out of a disbelief, a suspended knowledge, a longing for acceptance, a tortured love we bear for the men we have birthed and sustain. But whether we collaborate or beg, support or oppose, always it is a case of *cherchez l'homme*.

The explosions going off today world wide have been smoldering on a long sexual and emotional fuse. The terrorist has been the subliminal idol of an androcentric cultural heritage from prebiblical times to the present. His mystique is the latest version of the Demon Lover. He evokes pity because he lives in death. He emanates sexual power because he represents obliteration. He excites with the thrill of fear. He is the essential challenge to tenderness. He is at once a hero of risk and an antihero of mortality.

He glares out from reviewing stands, where the passing troops salute him. He strides in skintight black leather across the stage, then sets his guitar on fire. He straps a hundred pounds of weaponry to his body, larger than life on the film screen. He peers down from huge glorious-leader posters, and confers with himself at summit meetings. He drives the fastest cars and wears the most opaque sunglasses. He lunges into the prize-fight ring to the sound of cheers. Whatever he dons becomes a uniform. He is a living weapon. Whatever he does at first appalls, then becomes faddish. We are told that women lust to have him. We are told that men lust to be him.

We have, all of us, invoked him for centuries. Now he has become Everyman. This is the *democratization of violence*.

———

"All politics is a struggle for power," writes C. Wright Mills in *The Power Elite,* "and the ultimate kind of power is violence."[1]

"Power and violence are opposites," writes Hannah Arendt in *On Violence,* as if in reply to him. "Violence appears where power is in jeopardy, but left to its own course it ends in power's disappearance. . . . The chief reason warfare is still with us is neither a secret death wish of the human species, nor an irrepressible instinct of aggression, nor . . . the serious economic and social dangers inherent in disarmament, but the simple fact that no substitute for this final arbiter in international affairs has yet appeared on the political scene."[2]

That substitute has now appeared. As with every major shift in human history, it manifests itself naively, from an unexpected and faintly ridiculous direction. Only after such a shift has demonstrated its energy as a transformative wave does it in retrospect seem obvious and inevitable.

That substitute—that transformative wave at this stage in the saga of the human species—is *women as a global political force.*

The vast majority of women, cross-culturally and through history, have suffered from and appeared to disagree with C. Wright Mills's definition of violence as "the ultimate kind of power." It's both fact and tragedy that the vast majority of men, cross-culturally and through history, also have suffered from it but appeared to agree with it.

This isn't the first, or even the second, wave of international feminism; it's more like the ten thousandth. Not much is required to realize that: a sense of curiosity, a historical perspective, a willingness to burrow behind the wall of androcentric history, and an openness to understanding the pluralism inherent in feminist politics. The evidence is there:

The twelfth-century harem revolts and the ancient Arab concept of *Nuśuz,* a word specifically meaning "women's rebellion." The Yellow Turban Uprising (200 C.E.) at the end of China's Han dynasty; the White Lotus Rebellion, calling for women's rights (1790s); the forty armies of 2,500 women each marching for women's freedom during the 1851 Taiping Rebellion; the nineteenth-century woman silkworkers' anti-marriage societies. The four-hundred-year-long witchcraft "craze" in Europe. The founding of the Argentinian Feminist Party in 1918. The reform movements—on health, on child labor, on prison conditions, on abolition of slavery, on suffrage. The thousands of peace movements—national, regional, international—founded, staffed, and embodied by women.[3] The stubborn women of Greenham Common. The seventeen thousand women assembled at the 1985 Third United Nations World Conference on Women in Nairobi, Kenya—who thundered that peace, development, and freedom were inseparable; seven thousand had attended the first conference ten years earlier in Mexico City, eleven thousand the second in 1980 in Copenhagen; a vertical curve.

The evidence is there. The evidence shows in women who at this moment, in the small towns of the midwestern United States, in the villages of Africa, on the islands of the Pacific, in the cities of Europe, the *favelas* of Latin America, the plantations of Asia, the refugee camps of the Middle East, are rejecting "the ultimate kind of power"—and rising in numbers and visibility as never before, to demand sanity, justice, joy, an end to violence.

The women who dare to say *No.*

This is not an oppressed minority organizing over limited grievances, however valid. *This is the majority of the human species, insisting that all issues are women's issues.* This is feminism.

Biological determinism has for years struck me as a failure of intellectual nerve. So I don't mean to counter sexist theories along those lines with a mirror-image feminist version. We have as yet no truly value-free science, uninfluenced by masculinist (among other biases) prejudice. Consequently—although on certain bleak days I am sorely tempted to agreement with what we feminists have termed the "acute terminal testosterone-poisoning" theory of patriarchal history—I do not make the argument that women are *inherently* more peaceable, nurturant, or altruistic than men. (For one thing, this permits men the laziest of justifications for their own behavior.) Yet it is undeniable that history is a record of most women *acting peaceably,* and of most men *acting belligerently*—to a point where the capacity for belligerence is regarded as an essential ingredient of manhood and the proclivity for conciliation is thought largely a quality of women.

Such a convenient use of women as repositories of pacific ideals (with women all the while kept powerless to incarnate those ideals in the body politic) has allowed men to dwell in a state of political savagery that is alternately denied or affirmed, regarded sheepishly or pridefully, and mostly kept un- or misnamed. Among ourselves, women know quite well that we're not incapable of belligerence, although for many of us, perhaps even most, that knowledge is so alarming that we have distanced it to a degree where we feel uneasy even in expressing anger. Still, the questions must eventually be addressed: If violence is the symptom of despair and powerlessness, then why have powerful men taken such joy in it? More curiously, why have women, suffering greater powerlessness and having greater cause for despair than the most powerless of men, avoided resorting to it on our own behalf? Why is our horror of it so intense? Why are women the ones now doing the *naming* of political savagery—and the renaming of power in totally different terms?

Perhaps it's because we exist outside that body politic, except as victims or tokens. Or perhaps it's the intolerable outrage felt by the many at watching the entire world destroyed by the few. Whatever the reason, it is this barbaric state of institutionalized violence—so pervasive now as to be virtually invisible—that women *and* men must confront, if sentient life on this planet is to survive.

We are human creatures, so we use language. Not the lovely mysterious language of the great whales and dolphins, a sophisticated singing that can resonate through ocean depths beyond the soundings of the most acute audio technology. Mere words. Words can create, communicate, clarify, and as effectively as silence, obfuscate.

A relatively new word has entered our usage with unsettling frequency: "terrorist." It's the latest in a litany of words meaning much the same thing: warrior, brave, caballero, samurai, knight, cadre, soldier, villain, hero. The definitions depend, like everything else, on perspective: the eye of the beholder—and the ideological polemics of the definer.

What is terrorism?

It's been called "the politics of last resort." Of course, this characterization has been made by the same men who brought us "the final solution," "the war to end all wars" (World War I), "the end of empire," "the definitive weapon," and "the ultimate deterrent." So we needn't be surprised that the politics of last resort has become commonplace world wide. In Europe, Asia, Africa, the Pacific, Latin America, and even in insulated North America, terrorist tactics (so we're told) are on the rise.

Political theorists lament that such extreme acts stem from a desperation over all traditional means of insurgency having failed. Political leaders adopt unyielding, nonnegotiating postures regarding terrorism in public—and then parley secret deals in private. Political analysts try to categorize terrorist individuals, groups, leaders, coalitions, funders, and suppliers—but encounter a company of shifting loyalties, of idealists, mercenaries, fanatics, adventurers, professionals, opportunists, fumblers. Books are written about terrorist cells, networks, hierarchies, arms and munitions transactions. Official hearings are held, think tanks are formed, conferences convened, resolutions and declarations passed. New counterterrorist measures are devised, research-and-development contracts are awarded, state-of-the-art security devices—surveillance equipment, screening and tracing apparatuses, weapons—are invented, tested, patented, manufactured, sold. New jobs are created: airport screening personnel, special task forces in police departments, animal trainers to teach dogs to sniff explosives. Scholarly journals on the subject are founded, psychological profiles are researched, fellowships granted, surveys done, papers published, academic careers furthered. Experts are proclaimed. What Noam Chomsky once termed "the façade of toughmindedness and pseudo-science" masking intellectual vacuity has now descended upon a fresh subject, inventing a bustling growth industry: the study of terrorism.

Meanwhile, other kinds of professionals—the generals and admirals, the CIA, KGB, Mossad, British Secret Service, and Interpol fellows—are involved in "intelligence," that appalling misuse of the word. Meanwhile, too, the infiltrators, agents, and "boys in the field" fix their scornful gaze on the flurry of academic and diplomatic activity. They don't need to study the issue: they're men of action; they know what must be done and are ready to do it.

When solutions are offered us by the people who originally brought us the problem, we do well to be suspicious.

Epidemic poverty spreads in the United States; bankruptcy looms in the industrialized world; famine is entrenched as a normal state of affairs in the Third World. The academic experts continue to examine the causes of terrorism, and to propose responses. Water, land, air, and even the stratosphere become polluted and depleted. Global war is seriously considered a "triage solution" by some in response to such crises. The military experts continue to scoff at terrorism, and to propose strategies.

So terrorism appears to escalate in frequency, sophistication, deadliness, and even spontaneity. The battlefront expands to the supermarket, the airport, the local movie theater and discotheque. "Disinformation" campaigns are mounted by government officials, exaggerating or minimizing statistics as convenient for policy purposes. Rumors are spread, believed, discounted, spread anew. No one is uninvolved or unimperiled. No one is a civilian anymore. Every day, we're told, more and more ordinary people die from terrorist attacks.

Every day, more and more ordinary people live in fear.

Consider the public reaction. In a 1986 national poll, U.S. citizens listed "terrorism" as their number-one issue of concern—ahead of the economy, unemployment, the agricultural crisis, poverty and homelessness, drugs, corruption in government, environmental pollution, and external national attack. This despite the fact that in no one year of the 1980s was the number of U.S. civilian fatalities due to terrorism higher than thirty—far below the number of homicides annually reported in any one of the twenty largest U.S. cities—and despite the additional fact that in 1985, when a total of twenty-three U.S. citizens died in terrorist incidents around the world, one hundred were killed by lightning.[4]

Consider our growing familiarity with the names of targets, places, groups, persons, and causes which until recently meant little to most people. *Achille Lauro*, Entebbe, Sabra and Shatila, *Rainbow Warrior*. The Baader-Meinhof Group. Action Directe. The Red Brigades. Jihad. Hizbollah. Black September. The Jewish Defense League. The Aryan Nation. The Shining Path. The Silent Brotherhood. The Bandera Roja. The Army of God. The Contras. The Basque struggle for ethnic autonomy—and that of the Kurds, the Eritreans, the Moluccans, the Kanaks, the Polisario, the Croats, the Armenians, the Walloons, the Tamils, the Miskitos. Abu Nidal. "Carlos." The Reverend Ian Paisley and Rabbi Meir Kahane. Euroterrorism, narcoterrorism, religious-fundamentalist terrorism, ecoterrorism.

Some of the embattled causes have calcified around ancient enmities, like the eight-hundred-year-long Irish agony: the Provisional IRA *and* the Ulster Defense Association. Others, more recent, already have become yesterday's headlines: the FALN (Fuerzas Armadas de la Liberación Nacional) of Puerto Rico, the Tupamaros of Uruguay, the Front de Libération du Québec. And the Weathermen, the Symbionese Liberation Army, the Black Liberation Army, the May 19 Organization—all born in the U.S.A.

The schisms within and the conflicts between various factions ought to make us wary of the oversimplistic "international conspiracy" theory—wary of those who claim this is all the doing of the Soviet Union, the handiwork of Fidel Castro, or the machinations of Colonel Muammar Qaddafi. Certainly some countries support and exploit such groups for their own economic, political, and foreign-policy purposes, but to a lesser degree than Rightists believe, if to a greater extent than Leftists admit. Nonetheless, if blame is going to be laid at the doors of terrorist training centers in Eastern Europe, Cuba, North Korea, or Libya, then the same attention should be paid to Frank Camper's Reconnaissance Commando School near Birmingham, Alabama. One of about a dozen in the United States, this institution offers Rambo-oriented curricula that include courses in how to make time bombs and efficiently execute silent killings, throat cutting, ear removal; how to ambush, patrol, rappel, camouflage, set booby traps; and—in a special predawn seminar—how to commit torture. Graduates are churned out as "men of fortune," ready to fight against Nicaragua's Sandinista government or as plain mercenaries in any other old war they can find. The school happened as well to train the group of Sikhs accused of attempting Rajiv Gandhi's assassination, also thought to have engineered the 1985 Tokyo airport explosion, and also suspected of having sabotaged the Air-India jet that in 1985, with 329 people aboard, plunged into the Atlantic Ocean.[5] The hypothesis of a single international conspiratorial source won't wash as an explanation for terrorism.

But then what is it, this phenomenon? Is it in fact a new historical development, or an old one, recently named? Why is it so much in the headlines *now*? Why is the average citizen not merely repelled by it, but also morbidly fascinated?

Political violence is as old as recorded patriarchal history. Machiavelli defined war as a necessary social force, and Clausewitz declared it "the continuation of politics by other means." As for militant rebellion against the State, Cicero, Aquinas, Locke, Milton, and Jefferson were only a few among many who advocated the violent overthrow of a tyrannical government. However, in terms of terrorism per se as one genre of violence, we can hazard a genealogy, at least since the nineteenth century.

Most political scientists see terrorism as a descendant of one branch of the anarchist tradition. Anarchism—itself a political philosophy that has been given different interpretations—can be traced back as far as Zeno of Citium, the father of Stoic philosophy. Both the sixteenth-century Anabaptists and the seventeenth-century Levelers in England could be said to have been religio-political anarchists. (So, for that matter, could the medieval mystics, including Saint Teresa of Avila and Saint Francis of Assisi.) "Modern" political anarchism was outlined in the late eighteenth century by William Godwin, at about the same time his wife, Mary Wollstonecraft, was writing *A Vindication of the Rights of Woman*. Quite a couple, they believed that all external and constricting forms of society—institutions of marriage and the family, structures of State and Church—should and eventually would be abolished. But it was Pierre Joseph Proudhon in the middle nineteenth century who extended the philosophy to include abolition of private property, and who is credited with coining the word "anarchism." The nihilists (the word was originated by Turgenev in his novel *Fathers and Sons*) developed an allied philosophy and had a constructive program, but emphasized the necessity to destroy the status quo first (what in the 1960s some of us meant by the slogan "Level everything—*then* we'll talk politics"). By 1868, Mikhail Bakunin was expounding—but militantly—"anarchism, collectivism, and atheism" in the First International. Kropotkin and Trotsky tried to affirm Bakunin's politics while rejecting his tone, and he was finally defeated by Marx, but his political philosophy—and his call for violence to achieve it—was adopted by small fragmented groups. After the Russian Revolution, anarchism was denounced as violence and was suppressed in all its forms by the Bolsheviks (rather violently). Yet the strategy of "propaganda by deed," complete with Bakunin's tone, persisted. It was, for example, adopted by the Syndicalists, particularly in Spain. Stereotyping of all anarchists as violent had by now become the order of the day. After the 1886 Chicago Haymarket riot and the 1901 assassination of President McKinley, the United States had passed legislation forbidding any anarchist to enter the country. As late as 1927, the execution of Sacco and Vanzetti was fueled by anti-anarchist bigotry. It is this perception of the anarchist as a deranged killer skulking about with a bomb hidden under his long black coat that even today colors our attitudes toward terrorism.

But the terrorist does exist, you say. The broken bodies, the shredded and bleeding flesh, the hollow-eyed hostages, the coffins, the assassinations and hijackings and abductions and raids, they exist. Surely the terrorist is not a figment of our imagination.

Yes, the murder exists. The fear exists. The grief exists. But yes, the terrorist *is* a figment of our imagination—and more, a figment of our lack of imagination.

The terrorist is the logical incarnation of patriarchal politics in a technological world.

The terrorist is the son practicing what the father has practiced, and claiming to have found his identity in doing so. As usual, with a paternal mixture of pride and alarm, the father affirms or disowns the son according to how closely the son follows in his footsteps or diverges from them. Listen to the fathers preaching and practicing:

To the Reagan administration in the United States, the Nicaraguan Contras were "freedom fighters" and the disappearance squads of General Pinochet in Chile "law enforcers," yet militant black South Africans and Palestinian paramilitary groups were "terrorists." To the Soviet Union, on the other hand, the People's Army in El Salvador was a "revolutionary force" while the People's Resistance in Afghanistan was a "terrorist phenomenon."

How do we rescue—or invent—any truths out of such a morass of hypocrisies? Where are any unsullied *terms?* Are we discussing national liberationists or transnational revolutionaries? Radicals or reactionaries? Do we examine the terrorist as a militant-idealist or as a desperado, as a Right-wing crusader or a dedicated Leftist, as a professional or a fanatic, an adventurer or a martyr, a mercenary or a sociopath?

For that matter, are we differentiating between acts of violence—for example, violence against property as opposed to violence against persons? Do we further differentiate between acts of violence against persons on the basis of their power: assassination of a head of state or diplomat or police chief or industrialist as opposed to the killing of tourists on holiday, homemakers shopping in a department store, patients lying in a refugee-camp hospital, or secretaries opening letter bombs?

No serious attempt to find a definition can be made in a vacuum, in the absence of social, political, national, and cultural context. Nor can it be made in the absence of historical context. Were the original Hebrew Zealots *merely* zealots in their terrorist acts against the Roman Empire? And what was the Inquisition? The Saint Bartholomew's Day massacre of 1572? The French Revolution spawned an era known literally as the Reign of Terror, but was it terror*ist*—and if not, then was Charlotte Corday a revolutionary committing tyrannicide or an assassin? How do we categorize the People's Will in their insurgency against the tsar? What was the Boston Tea Party? Were Anita and Giuseppe Garibaldi in their fight for Italian unification admirable only up to the point when, influenced by Giuseppe Mazzini, they began calling for violence? How do we characterize the Mafia, which was created after all as an eighteenth-century Sicilian nationalist movement in resistance to the Neapolitan monarchy? But then what about the Fascist Squadrons of the 1920s? Where do we fit in the French resistance to the Pétain regime or the response of the Dutch underground to the Nazi occupation? Do we include labor and trade-union-movement organizing—from the saboteurs of the nineteenth century through the "Wobblies" (Industrial Workers of the World) into twentieth-century attacks on scabs and strikebreakers? How can we leave out the Ku Klux Klan: threats, house burnings, kidnappings, beatings, lynchings? And where do we place Right-wing fundamentalist bombings of abortion clinics?

But wait. What do we do with terrorism practiced by the State? The scars of officially sanctioned terror deform all periods of history: denial of human rights and civil liberties, preventive detention, raids, torture, corporal and capital punishment, genocide, colonialism, slavery through serfdom through class exploitation, plus, in our own time, concentration camps, the Gulag, apartheid, "disappearances," the arms race, chemical and germ and atomic warfare, nuclear experimentation? If we exclude the activities of established nation-states from our definition of terrorism (as most experts do), then aren't we settling uncomfortably into automatic respect for those who already hold power, though claiming we do so in order to limit our focus of analysis to manageable proportions? Even could we justify this ethically repugnant and intellectually feeble limitation of our focus (as most experts do), wouldn't we still have to acknowledge that at least three sovereign twentieth-century nations were brought into existence in part by terrorist campaigns: the Federal Republic of Yugoslavia, the Republic of Ireland, and the State of Israel? (This doesn't begin to take into account scores of decolonized nations in the Third World, virtually all of which fought free—of England, France, Spain, Portugal, Belgium, the Netherlands, and other colonial powers—by at times employing "terrorist" measures.)

Where, then, *do* we place terrorism in this spectrum of violence?

Documents from the international community have concentrated on outlawing specific acts, based on frequency of occurrence and level of destructiveness: assassination, hostage taking, and hijacking. The League of Nations forged and adopted a convention for the prevention and punishment of terrorism as early as 1937, in the wake of the assassination of King Alexander of Yugoslavia. But the convention never formally came into effect, and was ratified by only one state (India) because most nations in the League were busy by then with the legitimized violence that was about to become World War II. Since then, repeated attempts by the United Nations to organize an international conference on the issue have come to nothing, the plans impeded by one member state or another for self-serving political reasons.[6]

Unlike the United Nations, the U.S. State Department doesn't restrict its definition to specific named acts: "Terrorism is premeditated, politically motivated violence, perpetrated against noncombatant targets by subnational groups or clandestine state agents."[7] Some of us might find this a fairly workable description of rape, battery, child abuse, homophobia, sexual harassment, economic exploitation, educational discrimination, and religious manipulation. We must be confused. But "subnational groups" does bring to mind the *Fortune* 500 corporate brotherhood. "Clandestine state agents" are instantly recognizable to the mother waiting on line in any welfare office, and to the convict on death row, and to the scientist informed that a vocation of pure research can be pursued only under funding requirements of the Defense Department. To Afro-Americans, Native Americans, Hispanic and Asian Americans, and other peoples of color not only in North America but globally, a "noncombatant target" must for a long time now feel a lot like oneself, and "subnational groups" must look disconcertingly similar, conspiratorial, and Caucasian. Unless one regards the president of the United States as a "combatant" (an interesting semantic exercise, given the history of that office), then the above definition could resurrect public paranoia about "clandestine state agents" and just who Lee Harvey Oswald *was* working for when he shot John F. Kennedy. I could go on, but the difficulty is obvious. We have here, as the saying goes, a failure in communication.

Jeane J. Kirkpatrick, former U.S. ambassador to the United Nations, is the sort of woman who helps keep feminists honest. With her on the scene we dare not fall into the rhetorical all-men-are-evil-all-women-are-wonderful trap. Ms. Kirkpatrick has given us a terrorism construct too tottery for its elegant façade to conceal: ". . . it cannot be that terror wreaked on a civilian population by a revolutionary movement is liberation, while violence committed by a government responding to a guerrilla threat is repression."[8] (Notice the lumping together of terror, revolutionary movement, and guerrilla threat.) Two can play at this game: *It cannot be that terror wreaked on a civilian population by a government is law, while violence committed by a revolutionary movement responding to oppression is terrorism.* To put it another way, you can't have one without the other; no double standards need apply. Most women, and some men, would prefer to do without both.

As for the experts, they differ drastically on how terrorism should be defined. They disagree even on the methodology for arriving at a definition. Some of them display thought processes that are embarrassing parodies of ratiocination.

For example, Dr. Richard Clutterbuck, a former army major general and the author of *Living with Terrorism*, defines terrorism as a Left-wing phenomenon, a "disease" caused by "Marxist indoctrination" in the universities; this "psychosis" especially infects "rejected, or rootless" people "suffering from personal or social inadequacies," as well as the "criminal fringe" of society. He is worried that such insurgents are potentially "so powerful that they can overthrow civilized society altogether."[9] Dr. Clutterbuck seems ignorant of the non-Marxist, nationalist emphasis of groups like the Basque or Croatian separatists, and innocent of occasions when "civilized society" has employed terrorist means (the French OAS in Algeria, for instance). He appears unaware of a number of "Marxist" denunciations of terrorism: Trotsky's article "The Bankruptcy of Terrorism," among others. Last, he seems uninformed about abundant research findings on the psychoses of rejected or rootless people—in the military.

But he's not alone in his analysis. Anthony Burton (another former officer), in his book *Urban Terrorism* tautologically proclaims that the terrorist "aims to kill the innocent" with one purpose: "to terrorize." He then proceeds to include political assassination in his definition, untroubled by such questions as the innocence of the tsar, and uncurious about possible motives for regicide or tyrannicide beyond terrorizing the citizenry. Burton, like Clutterbuck, diagnoses the terrorist as "emotionally stunted."[10]

Professor Ernst Halperin, who joins Kirkpatrick and Clutterbuck in seeing no difference between the guerrilla and the terrorist, apparently suffers a similar blur regarding sanity and madness. In *Terrorism in Latin America*, he tells us that the silly idea that Latin America is poor because the United States is rich "produces a state of mind that can only be described as a collective psychosis, a vampire complex" in those south of the border.[11] (The situation also conveniently produces metals, livestock, wheat, produce, and cheap labor for those north of the border.)

There's an interesting overlap between pronouncements by career militarists and reductive analyses by pseudoscientists. The "terrorist psychology" concept is a convenient way of evading complexities, including political ones. Some of its advocates have solemnly announced that terrorists are created by "inadequate or absent mothering" that has resulted in depression, hypochondria, dysphoria, and destructiveness.[12] When in doubt, blame mothers.

The political scientists and sociologists—"honorable men"— show more sophistication in addressing the problem.

Yehezkel Dror, a professor of political science and public administration at Hebrew University in Jerusalem, chooses to limit discussion of terrorism to "the use of selective intense violence by small groups to undermine *democratic government*, and to bring about changes (usually ill-defined) in regime and society, and to force governments to adopt dictated decisions of a political and / or economic nature"[13] (italics mine). We might question whether the last clause isn't in direct contradiction to the adjective "ill-defined," but let it go. This limitation, Dror feels, helps him avoid value-dependent concepts about "terrorist" versus "freedom fighter." It certainly does. A seemingly value-free approach, it presupposes that nation-states, and particularly democracies, never indulge in either subtle or blatant terrorism. It also ignores the difference between *functioning* democracies and those I would call pseudo-democracies, where electoral participation or representation is hampered by economic or educational disadvantage, by racial or sexual bigotry, by unequal access to funds for the escalating costs of campaigning, or by voter apathy caused by disillusion with the corrupted process (the result of which, for example, brought Ronald Reagan to the White House in 1980 with less than 35 percent of the eligible electorate voting). If, as Dror generalizes, "democracies" are especially prone to terrorist attacks, why are such attacks so rare in the Scandinavian countries?

Paul Wilkinson, professor of international relations at the University of Aberdeen, Scotland, and the author of numerous books on the subject, writes rationally much of the time. Yet even he, in *Political Terrorism*, genuflects to the State in viewing terrorism as distinct from warfare, because it's "undeclared" (like the U.S. "police action" in Korea, the U.S. "preemptive incursion" in Cambodia, the U.S. "intervention" in Grenada, the U.S. "defensive strike" against Libya?), and also because even wartime saturation bombing isn't "terroristic" if it can be proven that civilian deaths resulted only " 'incidentally' in the course of realizing purely military objectives. . . ."[14] Thus the citizens of London during World War II and the citizens of Hanoi and Haiphong during the (undeclared) Vietnam War had no reason to feel terrorized.

On the other hand, Irving Louis Horowitz, a professor of sociology and political science at Rutgers University, describes terrorism as a mix of three elements: "unconventional warfare" usually aimed at civilian targets, using threat or violence to change law and authority through "a culturally unacceptable form." I'm afraid Professor Horowitz doesn't intend the inherent irony: does he mean as opposed to conventional warfare aimed at civilian targets? And culturally unacceptable to whom—those who have the power to name their actions "defensive preemptive strikes" and get away with it? But Horowitz does concede that "terrorism has emerged partly in relation to the *decline in mass* [political] *participation*"[15] (italics mine).

Which is significant.

In numerous books and articles on the subject, Luigi Bonanate of the University of Turin has built his analysis around that significance, hypothesizing that societies afflicted with terrorism are "blocked"—incapable of disintegrating but unable to progress. He posits two forms of "internal terrorism": state terrorism and revolutionary terrorism; and two forms of "international terrorism": colonial and anti-colonial. Furthermore, he differentiates between "instrumental terrorism," a means to a specific objective, and "finalistic terrorism," a necessary but not sufficient component of the struggle.[16]

While not using the same terminology, the late Edward Hyams gave an example of "finalistic terrorism," noting that terrorists rarely benefit directly from their acts:

> It was the Irish nationalist moderates who were made heirs to the new order in Ireland which the extremists had wrung from the British Government. Not for themselves but for the Jewish Agency and Haganah, which had repudiated their methods with horror, did the Irgun Zvai Leumi and the so-called Stern Gang drive the British Government to relax its hold on Palestine.[17]

Or, as the nineteenth-century Irish nationalist William O'Brien put it, sometimes "violence is the only way of ensuring a hearing for moderation." Hyams's own conclusion about terrorism was that it is to the sick body politic what fever is to the sick body; he sensibly recognized cause and effect. Terrorism, he noted, "is a manifestation of social war."

Conor Cruise O'Brien, former editor of *The Observer* (London), also makes a few of the connections. He names State terrorism as usually the *initiating* agent, followed by reactive militance by the less powerful or outright powerless. As for terrorism in democratic states:

> If a minority is denied all participation in democratic process other than that of voting and being automatically outvoted, if it is denied the benefit of freedom of expression and the rule of law, and thus deprived of any peaceful means of improving its situation, then . . . it would be inappropriate to describe as terrorists those who use political violence on behalf of such a minority. They are in a position closely comparable to the subjects of arbitrary power. . . . [But] if a minority, in addition to being allocated its due proportion of seats in parliament, enjoys the benefits of freedom of expression and the rule of law, then I would not hesitate to describe as terrorists any persons who might resort to political violence on behalf of such a minority.[18]

For O'Brien *consent* and *participation* are crucial—not only the consent of the governed, but their full participation in the process of consenting *and* governance.

In an academic field where a female voice is seldom heard, Martha Crenshaw's insights are refreshing. She writes with lucidity that "terrorists may be revolutionaries . . . [or] nationalists fighting against foreign occupiers . . . [or] minority separatists . . . [or] reformists (the bombing of nuclear construction sites is meant to halt nuclear power, not to overthrow governments)* . . . [or] anarchists or millenarians† . . . [or] reaction-

---

* Considering how thoroughly the military-industrial complex pervades society, I would quibble with this particular interpretation.
† She characterizes as millenarian the original nineteenth-century anarchist movement and such contemporary groups as the Italian Red Brigades.

aries acting to prevent change from the top." She further notes the existence of "factional terrorism," which, for example, has plagued the Palestinian movement. She coolly dismisses the "terrorists are deranged" theorists: "What limited data we have on individual terrorists . . . suggests that *the outstanding common characteristic of terrorists is their normality*"[19] (italics mine). Crenshaw, a professor of government at Wesleyan University and the author of *Revolutionary Terrorism: The FLN in Algeria, 1954–1962*, has also edited the anthology *Terrorism, Legitimacy, and Power: The Consequences of Political Violence*. In both the Introduction to the volume and the Conclusions, she explores terrorism's meanings, uses, and effects— as an instrument of foreign policy, as a response to and / or an escalation of the erosion of human rights and civil liberties, and as revolving around the pivotal matter of *legitimacy*. She questions assumptions about the infallible legitimacy of the State, and notes that—even when specific demands cannot be met and attention seems all terrorists can hope to gain—legitimacy (requiring recognition of the justice of their cause by a significant segment of the public) is the real goal.[20]

Legitimacy—of those in power or of those who would be in power. A way, as we'll see, of finding out who one is.

Yet why, when acts terrorist in nature have been committed with every possible excuse for centuries, why this seeming upsurge of terrorism now? Can the writings which so affected the generation that came of age in the 1960s—Mao Tse-tung, Ho Chi Minh, General Giap, Frantz Fanon, Albert Memmi, Régis Debray, and Ernesto "Ché" Guevara, among others—be having an even greater effect today? Yet the printed word has less impact than it did a decade ago; the electronic media have far greater influence. In fact, technological advances contribute greatly to what Crenshaw calls the "preconditions" (as distinct from the more immediate "precipitants") for terrorist activity. She notes:

> Sophisticated networks of transportation and communication offer mobility and the means of publicity. . . . The terrorists of Narod-

naya Volya would have been unable to operate without Russia's newly established rail system, and the Popular Front for the Liberation of Palestine could not indulge in hijacking without the jet aircraft. In Algeria, the FLN only adopted a strategy of urban bombings when they were able to acquire plastic explosives. . . . Today, we fear that terrorists will exploit the potential of nuclear power, but it was in 1867 that Nobel's invention of dynamite made bombings a convenient terrorist tactic.[21]

Urbanization is another factor, providing "a multitude of targets, mobility, communications, anonymity, and audiences [as well as] a recruiting ground among the politicized and volatile inhabitants."[22]

Many analysts place a large share of the blame on the press. Numerous forums and conferences have been held on this issue alone. Back and forth go the expectable arguments. Yes, obviously, terrorists seek and need coverage of their acts; in many cases, such attention seems to be the point of their tactics. Yes, the press is not innocent: violence sells papers. (But then aren't we left with the question of who buys those papers, and why the public wants to buy violence?) And yes, at times this causes an almost symbiotic relationship, what some term "media terrorism." But yes, surely a free press cannot tolerate government censorship—or self-muzzling—in the foolish hope that news blackouts will act as a deterrent to news. (Nor has it. Witness the repeated clamp-downs on both the domestic and the foreign press by the South African government, an ostrich-head-in-the-sand strategy that assumes if nobody abroad knows how bad things are, the country will look good, and if nobody at home knows—except by looking around—then it will all magically go away.)

Brian Jenkins, a former U.S. Army Special Forces officer who served in Vietnam and the Dominican Republic, and who now heads the Rand Corporation program on political violence, takes a more jaded view: "The impact of terrorists . . . has declined in terms of the publicity they can achieve. Continuing media coverage acts like inflation; it reduces the value of the currency.

Repetition decreases the novelty and news value of terrorist incidents. The first hijacking is page-one news. After 87 hijackings, people tend to ignore them."[23] Yet some say this raises the stakes, inciting the terrorist to dream up more dramatic action which *will* get on page one. Even more importantly, Jenkins's statement opens up the question of the normalization of terror. He doesn't pursue it. We shall—and in depth.

For now, however, the preceding overview of social science literature on terrorism must suffice, although the experts leave us with the basic connection not made. It's not enough to examine social, political, and historical context. What about cultural context? And what about—unfashionable as it may be—moral context?

Once, assassination attempts were focused on those who held power; the nineteenth-century Russian Populists suspended their first attempt to kill Grand Duke Sergei by throwing a bomb into his carriage when they saw that his wife and two small children, his nephews, were riding with him. Once, attacks were carefully aimed for strategic reasons at particular sites (a barracks, a fortress, a police station). Once, hostages were taken for clearly defined ransom or negotiating purposes. Now, it's not uncommon that a bomb detonates at Harrods department store in London, a grenade is thrown into a tourist cafe on the Via Veneto, or a hostage is held by a sub-sub-splinter group in Lebanon with no bargaining terms specified. (In 1987 a total of seven U.S. citizens were killed by terrorism—three of them accidentally. More to the point, not one of them was a diplomat.)

What caused that shift?

For one thing, those who hold power have seen to it that they're better guarded.

But there are deeper reasons.

I come of a generation that has grown up under the mushroom cloud, in an age of technologically feasible violence more epidemic and sophisticated than any in the planet's previous history. I think it's not coincidental that random murder of average citizens, including those in no way connected to power, emerged as a strategy of insurgent struggle *after* the random murder of average citizens had become a "legitimate" military tactic in conventional warfare. The London blitz. The bombing of Cologne and Dresden. Hiroshima. Nagasaki. Of course citizen fatalities have always been an element of war, but a new level of desensitization to civilian death on a mass scale was set in motion in the twentieth century, and it isn't surprising that those already numbed by powerlessness should move with it.

Added to this sense of civilian vulnerability is a fatalism, a mainstreaming of despair that George Wald noticed when he wrote, "What we are up against is a generation that is by no means sure it has a future."[24] We live hourly under the threat of instant nuclear extermination, either by intent or by accident. Many of us feel unable to stop this juggernaut, unable even to delay its course. Furthermore, we live daily under systems growing more centralized, blanding out diversity and individuality into one shapeless more manipulable cipher. Television anchorpersons all over the world now look the same, dress the same, and employ the same calmative inflections in their delivery of the news, no matter what their language. Multinational corporate systems and advertising techniques come more and more to resemble one another in their race to create one homogeneous consumer market. The elite in every culture use an identical social science terminology of abstraction—e.g., "poverty" and "homelessness"—to disguise who the poor and homeless *are*, use the identical political maneuvers to perpetuate these systems and the identical technology to enforce them. This is what Simone Weil denounced as the bureaucratic machine "which excludes all judgment and all genius" in its drive to localize all powers in itself. One response to this trend has been the literally *re*-actionary shattering of societies along tribal fault lines—ethnic animosities, language wars, religious fanaticisms—as if a Them-versus-Us solution would any longer suffice to bring about an affirmable integrity, a resurrected sense of "I."

The greater the centralization and bureaucracy, the greater the sense of apathy, what Arendt termed "the severe frustration of the faculty of action in the modern world."[25] And the combination of a sense of apathy among the many with a situation urgent and threatening to all will inevitably induce among the few a tried-and-true reaction: *violence*.

The violence, of course, serves to perpetuate the cycle, not only of more violence, but also of more centralization, more bureaucracy, and greater technological investment in more lethal means of control. Violence, after all, is horrifyingly good business. "Violence is the accelerator of economic development," in Engels's words. Violence requires and supports more surveillance systems and more deadly "counterterrorist" weaponry—the development and trading of more pistols and rifles, more rocket launchers, more detonators and plastique, more submachine guns, than were originally sold via the international arms trade to the terrorists in the first place. J. Bowyer Bell was quite right when, in his work *Transnational Terror,* he observed that "to the threatened, all revolutionaries are terrorists."[26] I would add: to the businessman, they are also a *market*.

Multinational corporations have long since accommodated themselves to this periodically inconvenient but on the whole economically accelerative process. The private sector takes out kidnapping insurance as a matter of regular practice;* corporate public-relations departments have been known to buy space

---

* Lloyd's of London, the titan of the insurance world, has profited considerably. Between 1970 and 1976 its premium income in kidnapping insurance grew from $150,000 to $5 million, and it spun off a consulting firm, Control Risks Ltd., to advise clients on kidnapping risk and avoidance, contingency planning, crisis management, and even negotiation techniques if held hostage. In their book *The Weapons of Terror: International Terrorism at Work* (London: Macmillan, 1979), Christopher Dobson and Ronald Payne examine the growing bizarre economic interdependence between terrorism and industry: "The Libyan fanatic [Quadaffi] has become to terrorism what Lloyd's of London are to shipping. And, in fact, their worlds overlap because Lloyd's pays out on the aircraft hijacked by the men whose lives Qadaffi insures."

for terrorist "advertising"; business executives are smoothly ransomed by their companies behind the scenes while representatives out front on stage bluster about their no-ransom-no-negotiating policies.[27]

We have had few clearer examples of this amazing cabal than the tip of the iceberg exposed in the U.S. Iran-Contra scandal—which involved governments, private companies, corporations large and small, presidents, kings, sultans, the military, rabbis and mullahs, bankers, diplomats, attorneys, drug pushers, the global network of arms dealers, and machinations across thirteen different countries on five continents—all of them involved in selling arms to one set of terrorists in order to fund another set of terrorists, and all of them meanwhile denouncing terrorism. Another instance of business as usual is the French government's arrest of Abu Daoud (a Palestinian who allegedly participated in the Munich murders of Israeli athletes), and their subsequent release of him so as not to upset French business deals with Arab nations.

It isn't unusual for terrorism specialists to speak in unashamedly economic terms: ". . . terrorism belongs in part to the difficult category of very low probability and very high impact contingencies, along with nuclear war, earthquakes, or fatal diseases produced by genetic engineering. . . . [Consequently] *the opportunity costs of contingency preparations for unconventional terrorism are very different from cost-benefit assessment.*"[28] (Italics mine.) Or, to put it bluntly, it's less expensive to rush bleeding flesh to hospital emergency rooms and cemeteries than to invest in real preventive measures that address root causes. That wouldn't be cost-effective. It's better economics to make the world safe for murder.*

---

* For a thoroughly documented analysis of how the patriarchal world economic order—in the form of the United Nations System of National Accounts—institutionalizes placing its highest value on the means of death while erasing such positive contributions as women's labor or environmental replenishment, see Marilyn J. Waring, *If Women Counted: A New Feminist Economics* (New York and San Francisco: Harper and Row, 1989).

Nor is it only the official and unofficial arms dealers and the biggest businesses—computer, munitions, and chemical manufacturers—who profit. Just as violence has for so long vitalized the patriarchal world's economy in general, so terrorism in particular now does. This demands the glamorization of terrorism. Major department stores, boutiques, fashion advertisements, display the newest chic clothing: fatigues (complete with camouflage markings), ammo belts, and combat boots. Fetish as fashion. *Soldier of Fortune* magazine sits side by side on the racks with its brothers *Hustler* and *Penthouse* in their mutual message of pornographic violence and violent pornography. The film industry does its part. From *Exodus* through *Black Sunday* and *Day of the Jackal* to *The Little Drummer Girl*, Hollywood gives us the glowering, sexy, terrorist hero, in contrast to the emphatically *un*glamorous image offered by most film makers from abroad, from *Odd Man Out* and John Ford's classic *The Informer* through *The Battle of Algiers*, *The Sentimental Englishwoman*, Costa-Gavras's *Z*, *Missing*, and *Betrayed*, and Margarethe von Trotta's stunning *Marianne and Juliane*. (Exceptions prove the rule, of course, and one can always count on Lina Wertmuller to manage retrograde versions of the subject, promulgating tired old myths about women as sexually masochistic political reactionaries, about men as attractive when violent and more so when terrorists.)

Compare that image with the reality.

My morning newspaper reports the agony of 1,200 Tamil women, children, and old men—victims of ethnic civil war—standing in line at a Hindu temple, waiting for food rations. Their homes, in Valvedditturai, a rural area of Sri Lanka, have been bombed by the Sinhalese who hold power in the government. Officials claim that this "carpet bombing," which killed 500 to 600 peasants, was "not aimed at terrorizing civilians but at routing guerrillas from a three-mile system of tunnels. . . . The only way to destroy the tunnels was to bomb the whole area." The government also has arrested four thousand local young men as terrorist suspects, in partial response to a Tamil hijacking and shooting of a busload of Sinhalese women and children a few weeks earlier. There is panic and mourning among women on both sides. Tamil women surround a visiting government official, beseeching him for help regarding the four thousand detainees, stuffing papers with the names of sons, fathers, brothers, and husbands into his hands, begging that their loved ones not be tortured in prison. In a speech, he tries to "soothe their fears, promising that several women's organizations" have volunteered to try to arrange for mail service to those in prison—thus taking credit for voluntary civilian female action. To the women, the guerrillas *and* the army bring disaster. They complain that both sets of men steal, loot, and molest women and girls. They hate the government army for doing this, but they're terrified as well of the insurgent forces ostensibly fighting to free them. Of their own Tamil men, one says wearily, "If the boys come back, we will have the same experience all over again. We want to be left in peace."[29]

Yet the connections remain unnoticed by the experts. The connections are, if anything, assiduously avoided.

———

Look closely at her, observe her again. She walks down the dirt road, balancing a huge basket on her head, a baby on her hip. Or she exits from her office building after hours, having worked late. Or she moves through the early summer morning, to draw and haul water from the well, or just because it's a lovely day and she runs for exercise. There are footsteps behind her, a man's footsteps. She fears. She has reason to fear. *She does not feel the same way if she hears a woman's footsteps behind her.*

Now look closely at him. He hurries through the airport to catch his plane. Or he pedals his bicycle, basket laden with books, to the university. Or he mounts the steps to his embassy on official business. Or he snaps a fresh roll of film into his camera and starts out on assignment. Suddenly there are footsteps behind him. Heavy, rapid. A man's footsteps. In the split second before he turns around, he knows he's afraid. He tells himself he has no reason to fear. But he fears. *He does not feel the same way if he hears a woman's footsteps behind him.*

Is it possible that terrorism attracts so much attention today because men, as well as being its main perpetrators, are also among its victims? Not victims in the legitimate, accepted "civilized" circumstances of war, combat, the boxing ring, the corner bar, the locker room, the boardroom, the courtroom—but victims across class, age, race, occupation, nationality? Victims of a casual, anomic, spontaneous violence in a contest over their heads, a violence so ordinary as to be called politics?

If *men* are now afraid in daily circumstances, why then the situation must be taken seriously, attention must be paid. This also is patriarchal democracy.

Not until we understand the connections between society's crisis and our own individual lives, not until we expose this continuum of the sexuality of violence, not until we fathom who the Demon Lover really is, can we truly conceive other approaches, which will permit us to reclaim our rightful place on this sweet, imperiled landscape we call home.

That journey toward understanding is internal and external at the same time.

That journey itself is one of terror.

CHAPTER 2

🭯🭯🭯🭯🭯🭯🭯🭯🭯

THE DEADLY HERO: THE OLDEST PROFESSION

Pity is the feeling which arrests the mind in the presence of whatever is grave and constant in human sufferings and unites it with the human sufferer. Terror is the feeling which arrests the mind in the presence of whatsoever is grave and constant in human sufferings and unites it with the secret cause. / JAMES JOYCE

We don't need another hero. / TINA TURNER

If I had to name one quality as the genius of patriarchy, it would be compartmentalization, the capacity for institutionalizing disconnection. Intellect severed from emotion. Thought separated from action. Science split from art. The earth itself divided; national borders. Human beings categorized: by sex, age, race, ethnicity, sexual preference, height, weight, class, religion, physical ability, *ad nauseam*. The personal isolated from the political. Sex divorced from love. The material ruptured from the spiritual. The past parted from the present disjoined from the future. Law detached from justice. Vision dissociated from reality.

We are all affected by, wounded by, this capacity. It's reinforced by every institution around us each day. As a consequence, survival requires a coarsening of the sensibility—or so we've come to believe. We learn it as children: to pass quickly by the bum or the shopping-bag lady on the street. We read in the newspaper that certain U.S. states have now reinstated the death penalty, that yesterday another prisoner was murdered with gas or electricity or by injection; we wince, and turn the page. We justify our lies, in business, in friendship, in love. We're accustomed to atrocity on our nightly television news, sandwiched between heartwarming "human interest" stories and headache-remedy commercials. We think little—or nothing—of it. We fear that to dwell on it, to truly *notice* and *connect,* is to invite madness.

Hannah Arendt was not the first to perceive this state of being, but the name she gave to it is so precise as to be a candidate for describing the entire twentieth century—and, to me, a phrase synonymous with patriarchy: *the banality of evil.*

Twentieth-century so-called sophistication has gone one step further into horror. It has created what I would term *the banality of good.* This fosters a variety of violations. It degrades language into commercial slogans and political jargon. It cheapens emotion. It warps conceptual thinking into such contortions as "adaptation and survival-odds for nuclear catastrophe." It permits religious fundamentalists to fire-bomb birth-control clinics and houses of worship in the name of divine love and morality. It also requires the rapid ingestion of positive new ideas and the almost instantaneous vomiting out of them, no digestion having taken place in the interim.

For example, there are those who claim that feminism is now "passé." An amusing expression of wishful thinking, that pronouncement has been droned with tedious regularity every year for the past two decades, since the first rising of this feminist wave. (It was also droned against earlier waves. Self-proclaimed "post-feminist" women who protested that they were "pro-woman without being anti-man" formed a bohemian group in New York, and published a literary journal to keep alive these passé ideas—in 1919.[1]) Our demise, we chuckle, is repeatedly exaggerated. Yet it's true that the androcentric power structure managed to go directly from ridicule through defensiveness to boredom on this subject without passing through comprehension. Backlash, yes. Repression, certainly. Co-optation, where and when possible. Understanding, no. First the idea was too new, when actually it was ancient. Then the idea was old hat, when it had hardly begun to make its mark.

So long as women's reality remains invisible, suffering will be ignored. So long as the reality of suffering remains invisible, women will be ignored. But it's easier to face terror and feel united with secret abstract "causes" than to hazard pity (in its oldest sense of compassion and *caritas*) and risk encountering and uniting with the specific human sufferer. Androcentric politics seems to have taken as a motto the bitter old line "I love humanity; it's people I can't stand."

If I had to characterize one quality as the genius of feminist thought, culture, and action, it would be *connectivity*. In its rejection of the static, this capacity is witty and protean, like the dance of nature itself as reflected in the spectrum from microbiology to astrophysics. It is therefore a volatile capacity—and dangerous to every imaginable status quo, because of its insistence on *noticing*. Such a noticing involves both attentiveness and recognition, and is in fact a philosophical and activist technique for being in the world, as well as for changing the world. Noticing, in this sense, requires that survival become a consciously sensitizing process instead of a coarsening one. That requirement in turn is crucial, both for individuals and for humanity.

Using these techniques of noticing, then, we can explore—and make the connections as we explore—the mythic underpinnings of the terrorist mystique, and the often-denied but nevertheless real charisma that mystique holds for us. Those underpinnings constitute a foundation—*the* foundation of every androcentric society in the world. Myth is simply another form of history, the encoded history of human beliefs. It works on us still, possibly more than ever, since we no longer acknowl-

edge it, leaving its numinous archetypes free to affect us sub-
liminally.

Georges Sorel acknowledged the potential impact of myth
on politics; in his controversial 1908 essay *Réflexions sur la
violence,* he counseled contemporary revolutionaries that

the framing of a future . . . happens when the anticipations of the
future take the form of those myths which enclose . . . the strongest implications of a people, of a party, or of a class . . . [,] which
recur to the mind with the insistence of instincts . . . [,] and which
give an aspect of complete reality to the hopes of immediate action
by which, more easily than by any other method, man *[sic]* can
reform the desires, passions, and mental activity.[2]

When listing the "strongest implications" of a people, party,
or class (no doubt why Mussolini admired him), Sorel overlooked the most basic "insistence of instincts"—that of sex and
gender. But then, Sorel actually *was* talking about man.

So is the entire culture.

The terrorist mystique is twin brother to the manhood mystique—and the mythic father of both is the hero. The terrorist
has charisma *because* he is the technological-age manifestation
of the hero.

He is the Hero Triumphant when he wins his revolution and
moves into the presidential palace (George Washington, Mao
Tse-tung, Fidel Castro, Anwar Sadat, Menachem Begin), and
he is the Hero Martyred when he loses and is destroyed (Spar-
tacus, Crazy Horse, Zapata, Patrice Lumumba, Ché Guevara).
Because he carries within him the double potential of trium-
phal power and sacrificial power, he personifies in patriarchal
terms all that remains to us—after centuries of manipulation,
diminution, and corruption—of what once was passion. We
can follow his trail back in patriarchal time, with the blood
spots as a spoor.

The Greeks, emphasizing moderation in all things, regarded
intense erotic love as a frenzy, a "divine enthusiasm," and cod-

ified passion as a form of madness, respecting but isolating it in an attempt to contain it. The Judeo-Christian tradition bifurcated passion into the acceptable (passion for God) and the unacceptable (earthly or carnal passion)—and blamed women as instigators of the latter. By the Middle Ages, repressed images of passionate sexual freedom had resurfaced in myth, legend, popular culture, and even mass hallucination: the incubus or succubus lover who preyed on the beloved, the Black Knight, the bestial paramour, the concept of "possession" (by a satanic or seraphic lover) in multi-layered meanings. Both as victims and as provocateurs, women were targeted by the Renaissance as carnality personified, and institutionalized persecution of girls and women as agents of passion reached new heights with the mass witch burnings. In the Enlightenment, passion was again repressed, this time with ridicule and trivialization, beneath the weight of ostensible reason. Inevitably, in the modern period we're again witnessing the eruption of passion, too vital a force to be tamed, but by now, after centuries of distortion and denial, a force almost inextricable from violence. And this is only Western culture. When we follow the hero's spoor through the terrain of religion and aesthetics— which requires a chapter unto itself—we'll glimpse an enormous cross-cultural pattern that ineluctably forms the psychic field on which we suffer today. For the moment, though, an exploration of myth lies before us.

And here is Jillian Becker including in the list of "hungers" that can motivate a terrorist "very commonly, a straightforward and immature lust for the role of hero."[3] Here is Edward Hyams pointing out that the first act of nineteenth-century terrorist cells in Europe was to adopt a structure of secret signs and mythic rituals from the Freemasons.[4] Here is Martha Crenshaw acknowledging that "social myths, traditions, and habits permit the development of terrorism as an established political custom. An excellent example . . . is Ireland, where the tradition of physical force dates from the eighteenth century, and the legend of Michael Collins in 1919–21 still inspires

and partially excuses the much less discriminate and less effective terrorism of the contemporary Provisional IRA in Northern Ireland."[5] Crenshaw doesn't go back far enough, especially
with respect to Ireland. For example, the Fenians, a paramilitary group of the nineteenth and early twentieth century, named
themselves after the Fenians, or Fianna, colleagues of the mythic
hero-warrior Oisin, son of the demigod Finn MacColl. The
poems and plays of William Butler Yeats and Lady Gregory,
the fiction of James Joyce, are alive with linkages between the
legendary past of pre-Christian Eire—its gods, heroes, giants,
supernatural folk, and divine warrior-kings—and the contemporary Irish political struggle.

Nor is Ireland the sole example available. The Third Reich
made clever use of the Nibelung legends. Contemporary Italian
Right-wing terrorists deliberately re-identify themselves with a
more recent historical myth, Fascism, and the charisma that it
exerted over Italians in the 1930s and 1940s: one group goes
so far as to call itself the Mussolini Action Squad. The Maoist-
oriented Sendero Luminoso (Shining Path) of Peru combines
revolutionary violence with a quasi-mystical image, claiming
to fulfill the prophecy that one day the ancient Incan rulers
would return to avenge their people. Back in the United States,
the name of the Minutemen—an extremist ultraconservative
organization sometimes allied with the Ku Klux Klan—echoes
in identification with the Minutemen of the Colonies' revolution against England. On the other side of the ideological barricades, the Weathermen drew their name from the Bob Dylan
phrase "You don't need a weatherman to know which way the
wind blows" in his song "Subterranean Homesick Blues." (In
the process, they reversed his meaning.) The mythmaker may
be ancient, recent, or contemporary. The myth—and arraying
oneself in its power—is the message.

Without the propaganda of the hero myth, murder is a sor-
did business. With the hero myth, any act of violence is made
not only possible but inevitable: the rapist is transformed into
the seducer, the tyrant rules by divine right, the terrorist reconstitutes the hero.

There he stands: young, lean, garbed in black, his face in shadow or masked by a balaclava, his gestures swift and economical as a predatory cat's, his muscled body not only bearing the magic tools of death but a magic tool of death itself, his commitment total. He is a fanatic of dedication, a mixture of impetuosity and discipline; he is desperate and therefore vulnerable; he is totally at risk and therefore brave; he is an idealist yet a hardened realist. Most of all, he is someone wholly given over to a passion. But his passion is death.

He is what passes for manhood. He is why a seventeen-year-old male Palestinian refugee, huddled over a charcoal stove in a camp near Damascus, can brag that he became a guerrilla fighter at age fourteen, and add, "I want to do a suicide mission with an explosive belt."[6] In that he seeks (or risks) exalted annihilation, and threatens (or promises) the same, he magnetizes us as an avatar of power.

We recognize this as an unhealthy power. We recognize less what lies behind his ski mask or feature-contorting nylon stocking: the leading man of popular-entertainment culture, the hero of millions. Mae West's sexy Masked Man. The Lone Ranger. Zorro. The comic-book heroes Spider-Man and the Green Lantern. The depersonalized abandon of Mardi Gras, Carnival, and the masked ball. The swashbuckler, the highwayman, the pirate, the daredevil, the outlaw. The Frog Prince. The Beast menacing Beauty. The costumes, uniforms, disguises, worn by men of the church and the military (as Virginia Woolf noted in *Three Guineas*), *and* by men of the corporation, *and* by the hip-radical or the Yuppie, the biker or the chieftain. The hero's disguises and the emperor's clothes were cut by the same tailor, and for the same purpose.

"But this is nonsense," one might respond. "The terrorist is a man who wears a ski mask or a stocking mask because he doesn't want to betray his identity; he simply doesn't want anyone to know who he *is*, that's all."

My point exactly.

From historical T. E. Lawrence to fictional Rhett Butler (who was a gunrunner, remember?), from fictional Superman to historical *Obermensch,* from war toy to war game, he is El Hombre, "the Man." The manufacturer of the $150,000 Lamborghini sports car smiles cynically as he purrs in a televised interview, "The Lamborghini is the ultimate outlaw statement."

The mask, you see, is imperative.

It preserves and enhances his mystery. It impedes revelation. It keeps us from recognizing him with each deadly reappearance. It also serves to keep him from attaining what he so desperately claims to pursue: self-knowledge.

Joseph Campbell, in his major work *The Hero with a Thousand Faces,* writes, "The hero is the man of self-achieved submission. But submission to what? That precisely is the riddle that today we have to ask ourselves and that it is everywhere the primary virtue and historic deed of the hero to have solved."[7] The hero has not solved it. Had he done so, he would have made himself unnecessary.

Campbell tracks the archetype through 416 pages dense with examples from scores of cultures, past and present, all over the planet. He delineates two types of hero: the tribal / local / ethnic savior, whom he sees in the Hebraic Moses or the Aztec Tezcatlipoca; and the universal savior, whom he characterizes as a Muhammad, a Jesus, or a Gautama Buddha. Perceptively, Campbell warns that whereas the former "prevails over his personal oppressors, the latter brings back from his adventure the means for the regeneration of his society as a whole. Tribal or local heroes . . . commit their boons to a single folk; universal heroes . . . bring a message for the entire world." Later, Campbell observes further, "If the God is a tribal, racial, national, or sectarian archetype, we are the warriors of his cause; but if he is a lord of the universe itself, we then go forth as knowers to whom *all* men are brothers."[8] But Campbell's insight is clouded by three central misperceptions.

First, he overlooks the unfortunately universal ethnocentricism inherent in the compartmentalization process. To all peoples, their own unique "folk-ness'" *is* the generic, it *is* society as a whole. The Third Reich's propaganda machine emphasized that the German people were *Das Volk* (not *a* people, but *the* people), and the same tendency is at work in such concepts and phrases as the Han (*the* people) of China, the Jews as the Chosen People, Holy Mother Russia, the Manifest Destiny of the United States, and thousands of other examples of a specific group's perceiving itself as both the center of and the salvation for every other group, whether any other group likes it or not. This is the heart of nationalism and the oldest excuse for empire. Consequently, Campbell's arbitrary (and ethnocentric) labeling of Moses as "local" hero and Jesus as "universal" hero is misleading, particularly since Jesus (and Muhammad, and Gautama Buddha), whether historical figure or mythic archetype, was *self*-perceived as being "local" and bringing salvation or liberation to his own "folk." Which leads us to Campbell's second misperception, that universal heroes, unlike those local boys, bring about a greater and overarching sense of community. The Crusades, the Jihads (Islamic holy wars), and millennia-old religious strife on the Asian subcontinent certainly imply that the respective followers of a Jesus, a Muhammad, and a Buddha understood their leaders' message of *tribal* loyalty, even if Campbell, in his own humanism, yearns to ignore that. The last but most important misperception of all, the one upon which the previous two in fact depend, is Campbell's *andro*centricism, revealing itself in both the letter of his language and the spirit with which he accepts the concept of conquest: the "lord of the universe" to whom all "men are brothers." With one stroke the chthonic mystery of the cosmos dwindles to an object of conquest, and half the human souls longing for salvation and liberation are wiped invisible.

Campbell is careful to state that the hero may be male or female, although more than 90 percent of his examples from myth, legend, and folk tales depict the hero as male. What Campbell does not see is that even the token female hero is an imposter in a realm created and defined by male consciousness and reinforced by male power; she is no more a true representative of most women than the airbrushed *Playboy* centerfold is a true representation of most women's bodies. This enforced invisibility of the real, and enforced erasure of the female, are intertwined with *un-noticing,* and lie at the very core of patriarchy. The dangers, the search, the empowerment, the conquest, the lordliness, the brotherhood, the terms themselves—none of them are from us or from our female experience, for us or for our experience; none of them are ours.

It could be said that the male hero and his quest are not representative of most men, either. But then it must be asked whether most men notice and realize *that.* Do the little boys, playing with purchased or makeshift toy weapons, tanks, battleships, bombs? Do the young men, war-dancing in puberty rites or hanging tough on street corners or doing the privileged version thereof in fraternity houses? Do the adult men, frenzied at their football or rugby games, their boxing matches and hockey skirmishes (called relaxation) as a break from jockeying for power in the company or church or government or academic department (called a career)? Do the men who kill animals for sport? Do the men who voluntarily join armies or let themselves be drafted? Do the men who "only obey orders"? Do any of these men comprehend that the hero is a figment of the lack of their own imagination, that they could breathe free of his impact on their simple mortality? Or does each, secretly or openly, identify with him? And how is it possible for a male human being *not* to identify with him, when power—not necessarily heroic power, but everyday power in myriad forms—accrues to that male human being merely by his having been born male in the patriarchy? The dangers, the search, the empowerment, the conquest, the lordliness, the brotherhood, the terms themselves, are from and for *his* experience; all of them are his.

The hero is only the average man writ large, in turn continually holding out that promise of inflation to the average man. He makes good his overall promise often enough for it to remain tempting, and he makes good one part of his promise every moment—in the bait of male power over the female—sufficiently to keep the average man in thrall. A daily dose of power over someone else's life (no matter how utterly subjugated to other men a man may be himself) is rather addictively heady. And power *over*, as differentiated from power *to*, is now so enmeshed with world culture as to be thought human nature, when it more accurately reflects male human dynamics. But "human nature" sounds conveniently unchallengeable, and comfortingly "natural." Sexism therefore becomes a perfectly normal, invisible state of affairs—even in the private lives of liberal men who make (heroic) public shows of denouncing it. Keep this normality in mind while recalling that the overwhelming majority of terrorists are male. And keep it in mind while recalling Martha Crenshaw's statement that "the outstanding common characteristic of terrorists is their normality."

Armored with these insights, we can ride out to meet the mythic hero, where he merges with god, king, god-king, warrior, liberator, and savior. He has been invented, after all, by mere mortals—the collective (male) unconscious—and he has been gradually constructed or reconstructed over eons. Listen to Sir James Frazer describe that onerous task of invention in his great study of myth, *The Golden Bough:*

> Certainly no men ever had stronger incentives . . . than these savage sorcerers. To maintain at least a show of knowledge was absolutely necessary; a single mistake detected might cost them their life. This no doubt led them to practice imposture for the purpose of concealing their ignorance; but it also supplied them with the most powerful motive for substituting a real for a sham knowledge. . . .[9]

Is this not a logic perfectly adaptable to testing nuclear bombs, with demonstrable threat and pursuit of knowledge as double justifications?

The hero wears, as Campbell puts it, a thousand faces. But he has more or less a single profile, which varies in minor detail but remains substantially the same from culture to culture. He is usually fatherless, the father slain or unknown (Oedipus, Abraham, the Irish Cuchulainn) or a mysterious god (Theseus, Herakles, Jesus). He comes of noble lineage yet falls into obscurity while an infant (Oedipus, the Hindu Chandragupta, Siegfried, Jesus) or he is raised by a noble house but chooses poverty as a youth (Moses, Joseph, Buddha). He is nonetheless highly educated and / or skilled in physical prowess, which he demonstrates early by amazing deeds. He is severely tested while young, narrowly escapes death (the Flight into Egypt, the baby Herakles strangling the serpents in his cradle, the Finnish hero Väinämöinen straining to be born over a period of centuries), and establishes a record of prodigious achievement. His call-ing—to save or avenge his family, clan, or people—comes upon him while a youth (Oedipus at the Sphinx, Jesus preaching in the temple, the Hindu Krishna and Cuchulainn and Siegfried accomplishing wondrous feats while still boys). Aware that he faces an early death if he assumes his heroic destiny (Orpheus, Jesus, the Egyptian Osiris, the Germanic Wotan, the Welsh Bran, the Babylonian Adonis), he finds courage through human and / or supernatural aid, learns to subjugate himself to a higher force / cause / leader / god, and pursues his mission and his fate. The land is purified by his blood. The crops flourish. Through his death, the people are purged in a ritual catharsis, and are thus resurrected.

As Campbell describes it:

> This death to the logic and the emotional commitments of our chance moment in the world of space and time, this recognition of, and shift of our emphasis to, the universal life that throbs and celebrates its victory in the very kiss of our annihilation, this . . . love of the fate that is inevitably death, constitutes the experience of the tragic art; therein the joy of it, the redeeming ecstasy. . . .[10]

The hero's strength, then, resides in his dying first to "the logic and the emotional commitments" of a simple joy in existing; his power is rooted in his emphasis on "the very kiss of our annihilation"; his charisma is dependent on his "love of the fate that is inevitably death." Valorous, abnegating his own selfhood and severed from that of others, disconnected from a living logic and the pathos of emotional commitments, recognizing only the redeeming ecstasy of a tragic death, *the hero already lives as a dead man.* As a dead man he is fearless, because as a dead man he is unconquerable by any life force.

But this is only the hero's background profile. He comes to maturation and the fullness of his powers by passing through ritual stages, each of them revelatory of male culture. Yet before we trace him through his rites of passage, we'll pause and glance at another profile.

Charles A. Russell and Bowman H. Miller drew a sociological profile of a terrorist, based on a compilation and analysis of published data involving over 350 individual terrorist cadres and leaders from Argentinian, Brazilian, German, Iranian, Irish, Italian, Japanese, Palestinian, Spanish, Turkish, and Uruguayan groups active between 1966 and 1976. They focused in particular on eighteen groups, examining the "modern urban terrorist," as opposed to the rural guerrilla fighter.[11] The groups included those engaged in transnational actions (such as the Japanese Red Army) as well as those involved locally and committed solely to ethnic struggles (such as the ETA, Euzkadi Ta Askatasuna, the Basque Fatherland and Liberty Movement). Their study is lengthy and detailed; their conclusions are educative.

Sex: "Despite minor variations among some groups studied, urban terrorism remains a predominantly male phenomenon."[12] Well over 80 percent of all "significant terrorist operations" were "directed, led, and executed by males"[13] during the decade under examination.*

---

* Notable exceptions to this pattern included the Tupamaros and the Baader-Meinhof Group, which we shall examine in greater detail further on. Yet the pattern holds for most cells and organizations. When women are involved at all it is as support personnel: nurses, couriers, safe-house hosts, and facilitators of false documenta-

Age: ". . . remarkably consistent from group to group . . . the usual urban terrorist was between 22 and 25."[14] (The Red Army Faction, better known as the Baader-Meinhof Group, was an exception to this, with an average age of 31.3; it also exhibited an unusually high presence—even in the leadership—of women.)

Social and Economic Background: "Over two-thirds came from the middle or upper classes in their respective nations or areas. In most instances their parents were professional people (doctors, lawyers, engineers . . .), government employees, diplomats, clergymen, military officers, or sometimes even police officials. Although these parents were part of the existing social and economic systems, many of them had been frustrated in their efforts to use them as vehicles for upward . . . mobility."[15] Clearly, terrorism reflects the old axiom that revolutions are made more by those with raised expectations than by those most severely oppressed. Only in the Provisional IRA is there a marked difference in composition, with many from a lower socioeconomic class.

Education or Occupation: ". . . two-thirds . . . are persons with some university training, university graduates, or postgraduate students."[16] The ratio rises to 75 percent among the Latin American groups, particularly the Tupamaros, the Montoneros, and the ERP (the Argentinian People's Revolutionary Army). Many were educated abroad and spoke a second language. Most of the Turkish People's Liberation Army members were Middle Eastern Technical University students or graduates. George Habash, head of the PFLP (the Popular Front for the Liberation of Palestine), is a medical doctor. Yasir Arafat,

tion, weapons storage, funding, etc. One of the hallmarks of the notorious "Carlos"—Ilich Ramirez Sanchez, the Venezuelan-born self-proclaimed terrorist currently associated with the European operations of the Popular Front for the Liberation of Palestine—is his use of female contacts across Europe in these support roles. At the other extreme, the Basque ETA strongly opposes women's participation because "their place is in the home" and "they talk too much, especially to their parish priest." (Robert P. Clark, "Patterns in the Lives of ETA Members," *Terrorism: An International Journal,* Vol. 6, No. 3 [1983], p. 427.)

who formally renounced terrorism in the 1985 Cairo Declaration of the PLO (the Palestine Liberation Organization), is a graduate engineer. Giangiacomo Feltrinelli, a millionaire book publisher, was a major figure in Leftist Italian terrorism. A sociologist founded the Italian Red Brigades, an economist led the Argentinian ERP, a lawyer created the Tupamaros; Ché Guevara was a physician, Andreas Baader an attorney. The Weather Underground, also called the Weathermen—all white, middle- or upper-class, and educated—followed this pattern as if it were a direct order. Again, the Provisional IRA is unique.

Marital Status: "The unmarried terrorist is still the rule."[17] Over 75–80 percent were single. "Some of the few married individuals involved in German terrorist activities (Mahler, Meinhof, and Luther) severed ties to spouses and children in order to pursue terrorist methods. Only in the case of the Uruguayan Tupamaros, a group that according to . . . Régis Debray may have made the greatest use of women [sic], were a significant number (still less than 30 percent) of the terrorist cadre in a married status."[18]

In the revised edition of her now-classic work, *Beyond the Veil: Male–Female Dynamics in Modern Muslim Society,* Moroccan sociologist and feminist theorist Fatima Mernissi offers a parallel analysis, the "anatomy of a fundamentalist." This is a subject of particular concern to Arab and Islamic feminists as religious fundamentalism threatens (and often manages) to roll back hard-won rights for women. Mernissi warns that the fundamentalist is neither uneducated nor uncultured. She cites Saad Eddin Ibrahim's in-depth study of thirty-four Egyptian Islamic militants, and his findings that the fundamentalist militant belongs to the middle class, favors scientific branches of knowledge, and performs exceptionally well, especially in medicine, engineering, technical military science, and pharmacy. In addition, most members come from "normal, cohesive families" but of recent rural background. The demographic factor—the "youthification" of the population—and such socioeconomic and political upheavals as sudden upward mobility and geographical transience, are other major ingredients.[19]

Age (as an acknowledged factor) and sex (as a less acknowledged one) are crucial elements. Dr. Rona Fields is a clinical psychologist based in the United States who has spent two decades working with children in Northern Ireland and in the Palestinian refugee camps of the Middle East. Over time, she re-encountered many of the children she had worked with, after they had become adults and, in some cases, had joined terrorist groups. Many of these children had survived the humiliation and powerlessness of childhoods in life-threatening daily situations. For them, a denial of death combined with chronic rage was characteristic, along with an inability to see any real way of advancing out of powerlessness for the rest of their lives. That this in turn created a flatly Manichean vision of the universe, as black or white, good or evil, should not shock us. Dr. Fields found that the only positive models, the only adults who appeared to control their own destiny and to act as if their actions made a difference, were those who belonged to terrorist groups: it was they who filled the children's hunger for strong, protective parents. Most of the children had already endured at least one close brush with death by the time they reached their early teens, either from illness or from direct attack. Some had already been imprisoned. This culturally affected the boys differently from the girls.

> The experience is a terrible blow to their identity as men, one which they redeem by joining these groups.[20]

Culturally, *powerlessness is not a blow to the girls' identity as females;* in a way, it's convenient training. Guilt at being a survivor, and revenge for wrongs done to one's family, are additional components that influenced the boys. Dr. Fields examined Palestinian children who survived the 1982 massacres at the Sabra and Shatila refugee camps in Lebanon. Before the slaughter, the boys had spoken with resentment against the military training they were encouraged to take from age eight onward, and were particularly angry at the Palestinian paramilitary forces that offered the training. But:

> After the massacre, the boys felt both grief and intense guilt about their earlier feelings of resentment. . . . they somehow felt responsible . . . and felt the only way they could make amends was by taking the place of those who had been killed. They were left with a monomaniacal obsession with revenge.[21]

So. The profile emerges. It is primarily of someone male, young, of "good" family, educated and cultured and skilled, showing precocity and accomplishment, uprooted and experientially mobile due to a period of upheaval, enflamed by the situation, and possessed by the suffering of his people. He is idealistic, brave, and self-disciplined, yet can find no way out of guilt, grief, and impotence until he encounters his mentor / leader / god. He then is made ready to follow a road of self-abnegation. He breaks all other human ties. He is aware of the risks, but his obsession to save or avenge his cause, together with his having contracted a love of his tragic fate, seal his doom. He takes up the gun.

Or the scepter. Or the staff. Or the tablets of law. Or the cross.

O weep for Adonis. For it's only now that the making of the hero really begins: his trials and testing, his rites of passage, the forging of him into a god.

Campbell will go with us and be our guide. He sees three major stages, each with substages. First, *the separation and departure;* this includes the call to adventure, the hero's attempt to fly from the task or calling, and the appearance of his mentor, guide, recruiter, or helper. Second, *the trials and victories of initiation;* this stage embraces hazards and dangers, the hero's encounter with the *Magna Mater* (the mother figure or "good woman"), his avoidance of the Temptress (the sexually free and self-empowered "bad woman"), and his atonement to and synthesis with the figure of the lost father. Third, *the return and reintegration into society,* which can occur in two ways: either by the hero's death / dismemberment / dispersal throughout his people—in which case his martyrdom provides and inspires them with cannibalized energy—or through his triumph, in which case his spiritual teachings and example (or his temporal victory and secular power) liberate them. Either way, Campbell tells us, "The effect of the successful adventure of the hero is the unlocking and release again of the flow of life into the body of the world."[22]

I must digress for a moment here, to note that at the moment of this writing—and, for that matter, at the moment of your reading—one-third of a million women are in labor; 300,000 human beings are right now hunched over in contractions, screaming or whimpering or panting in pain. Most are anemic or malnourished, some are starving, most lack modern medical aid, some lack even village midwives, many are genitally mutilated by clitoridectomies or infibulations,[23] many will die in childbirth, many will give birth to stillborn or anemic or drug-addicted or diseased or deformed infants, some are mere children themselves, giving birth at age twelve, some are in labor with their fourteenth or fifteenth child. By this time tomorrow one-third of a million women—sweat-drenched, blood-streaked, exhausted, many only half alive, some dead in the effort—will have unlocked and released again "the flow of life into the body of the world."

This is not regarded as an adventure. This is not termed the mission of the hero. This is merely "natural."

But then we've strayed from heroism.

Return with me again to the ritual stages in the transformation of boy into man, man into hero, hero into god. Each stage in one fashion or another is a harrowing initiation into the process of dying and death. Along the way, the hero acquires greater skills and intensifies those in which he's already proficient. From Greek myth to Central African legend, there's the leitmotif of his encountering a fearsome guardian at every

threshold of his passage; only by besting the guardian in a contest of wit or brute strength can he win tools or secret knowledge. The hero must also usually be twice-born. This is crucial
to his severance from the mother; he must either give birth to
himself or find a powerful *male* figure to bear him: Dionysus
from the thigh of Zeus, the biblical Jonah and the Eskimo hero
Raven each swallowed by a whale but re-emerging stronger
than before, the Polynesian Maui and the Celtic MacColl
devoured whole by a monstrous creature but managing to kill
the creature and escape. Only when "born again" is the hero
ready to encounter the force of the female.

She has already appeared in various forms, and is frequently
the helper without whose aid he could not have passed earlier
thresholds. She is Ariadne offering Theseus the thread to the
Minotaur's labyrinth (he will later abandon her). She is Medea
saving Jason from her vengeful father (he will later betray her).
She is Dante's guide Beatrice, Faust's inspiration Gretchen, and
the Virgin Mary, source of intercession with the wrathful Father.
To the indigenous peoples of the North American southwest,
she is Spider Woman. She has already shown herself to the
hero as the Great Mother. But now she appears as a *being unto
herself*. Now she is not present solely as a source of support
for *him*. And now she is dangerous. Now she is the temptress,
the Medusa, the Wild Woman of Russian folklore, the Jezebel,
the Magdalen, the witch. If, before, she existed (in his eyes) as
a boon to be used and discarded, now she exists (in his eyes)
as a threat to be fled from or conquered. She is object; he is
subject. She is noun; he is verb:

> Woman . . . represents the totality of what can be known. The
> hero is the one who comes to know. As he progresses . . . the form
> of the goddess undergoes for him a series of transfigurations: *she
> can never be greater than himself*, though she can always promise
> more than he is yet capable of understanding. . . . The mystical
> marriage . . . represents the hero's total *mastery* of life; for *the
> woman is life, the hero its knower and master*. . . . the testings of

the hero . . . made [him] *capable of enduring the full possession of the mother-destroyer,* his inevitable bride. With that he knows that *he and the father are one:* he is in the father's place.[24] (Italics mine.)

For the hero, she is merely another stage en route to his goal of finding and becoming the father, and thereby attaining the state of death which he perceives as regenerative to his people. To accomplish it, he must use but "transcend" what she represents: "an umbilical point, an Achilles tendon which the finger of mother life has touched, and where the possibility of perfect knowledge [of the father] has been impaired."[25] Plainly put, *because she represents life, she is the ultimate destroyer of what he values most—death.*

But now at last he has arrived at the throne of the father, the heart of the labyrinth. Campbell, surely not realizing the full import of what he is saying, tells us:

> The problem of the hero going to meet the father is to open his soul beyond terror to such a degree that he will be ripe to understand how the sickening and insane tragedies of this vast and ruthless cosmos are completely validated in the majesty of Being. . . . He beholds the face of the father, understands—and the two are atoned.[26]

Has *this* been the fatal flaw in women's perception of the universe? That despite millennia-long trials and testings that dwarf the word "adventure," and despite eons of struggle that bleach pale the word "heroism," women still fail to perceive the cosmos as solely ruthless, women still regard life as something more than an obstacle to death?

The hero is undeterred by such puerile questions. Having now achieved atonement with the father, he can return to his people either as paternal emissary or *as* the father. There's only one catch: "The hero of yesterday becomes the tyrant of tomorrow, unless he crucifies *himself* today."[27]

In that one sentence we glimpse all of patriarchal history.

Frazer interpreted this pattern as reflecting the reasoning of what he called "the savage mind":

> . . . if the course of nature is dependent on the man-god's life, what catastrophes may not be expected from the gradual enfeeblement of his powers and their final extinction in death? There is only one way of averting these dangers. The man-god must be killed as soon as he shows symptoms that his powers are beginning to fail, and his soul must be transferred to a vigorous successor. . . . When the king first succeeded in getting the life of another accepted as a sacrifice instead of his own, he would have to show that the death of that other would serve the purpose quite as well as his own. . . . the substitute had to be invested, at least for the occasion, with the divine attributes of the king. . . . no one could so well represent the king in his divine character as his son, who might be supposed to share the divine afflatus of his father. No one, therefore, could so appropriately die for the king, and, through him, for the whole people, as the king's son.[28]

The man-god must be killed as soon as he shows symptoms that his powers are beginning to fail. No wonder Crenshaw tells us, "On balance, terrorism assists in the demise of regimes already distressed".[29] No wonder "terrorism appears to have strengthened the old order, [and] underscored the primacy of force in international relations."[30] No wonder, as Arendt perceives, "In a contest of violence against violence the superiority of the government has always been absolute; but this superiority lasts only as long as the power structure of the government is intact—that is, as long as commands are obeyed. . . . Everything depends on the power behind the violence. The sudden dramatic breakdown of power that ushers in revolutions reveals in a flash how civil obedience—to laws, to ruler, to institutions—is but the outward manifestation of support and consent."[31] No wonder it begins again from the start, over and over, tyrant unseated by hero, hero martyred by tyrant.

No wonder terrorist organizations and cells have initiation rites for new members—tests that require violating taboos or (literally or figuratively) "burning bridges" behind them.[32] No wonder Frantz Fanon saw this requirement—"that each individual perform an irrevocable action"[33]—as central to a solidarity that will literally come under fire.

No wonder, too, that glorified vengeance plays such a primary role as motivation: "The terrorists' willingness to accept high risks may also be related to the belief that one's death will be avenged. The prospect of retribution gives the act of terrorism and the death of the terrorist meaning and continuity, even fame and immortality. Vengeance may be not only a function of anger but of a desire for transcendence."[34]

The transcendence offered by life-affirming acts of love, birth, care for self and others and the planet, apparently cannot compete with the transcendence offered by vengeance; the ecstasy of "divine enthusiasm" must be less attractive than literal bloodlust. Women's cross-cultural "collective unconscious" (and collective conscious) vision of living apparently is at best a source to manipulate and to leech energy from, and at worst a wicked temptation away from the higher cause of murder and destruction. Martha Crenshaw notes that terrorists tend to exhibit an intense obsession with morality, in particular with sexual purity*—in the name of a "higher good."[35] It brings to mind the so-called Moral Majority (which feminists exposed as being neither). It also brings to mind the now-infamous marine lieutenant colonel Oliver North, who, from the offices of the National Security Council, coordinated the U.S. bombing raid on Libya, supervised the U.S. invasion of Grenada, oversaw the mining of Nicaraguan harbors, organized the Contra operations in Central America, and devised the Iran-Contra-diction of selling weapons to Iran. This is the man Ronald Reagan called "a national hero" (though North himself chuckled that "I have also been described as a terrorist" by others†). This is

---

* Our new concept of "the banality of good" would explain the obverse of this in contemporary (especially Western Left-wing) groups. The Weathermen, whom we shall later discuss at greater length, were fiercely and forcibly anti-monogamy.

† Testimony before Joint Senate-House Investigative Committee on Iran/Contra affair, July 8, 1987.

the man who has adventuristically waded through scores of illegal and covert murderous actions with a boyish grin on his all-American face. And this is the "born-again" Christian who states that he has "a personal relationship with Jesus Christ as a driving force" in his life. This is the anti-reproductive-choice zealot, one who is "pro-life" and whose car bumper sticker boasts "God is Prolif-ic."[36] None of this terrorist tradition is contradictory in the context of the hero. Life is death, death is life. Or, in the slogans George Orwell foresaw, "War is peace, freedom is slavery."

As if rewriting the Bible, the Torah, or the Koran, the manuals of terrorism all give the same guidance to the faithful.

The *Catechism of a Revolutionist,* written in 1869 by Sergei Nechaev, with the collaboration of Bakunin, chills the soul with the directness of this message.

> *The revolutionary is a doomed man.* He has no interests of his own, no affairs, no feelings, no attachments, no belongings, not even a name. . . . He is an implacable enemy of this world, and *if he continues to live in it, this is only to destroy it more effectively.* . . . All the tender and *effeminate* emotions of kinship, friendship, love, gratitude, and even honor must be stilled in him by *a cold and single-minded passion.* . . . Night and day he must have but *one thought, one aim—merciless destruction.* . . . no place for any romanticism, any sentimentality, rapture, or enthusiasm. . . . *He is not a revolutionary if he feels pity for anything in this world.* . . . he must face the annihilation of a situation, of a relationship, or of any person. . . . All the worse for him if he has family, friends, and loved ones; . . . he is no revolutionary if they can stay his hand.[37] (Italics mine.)

Almost a hundred years later, Carlos Marighella, a Brazilian who left the Communist party because of its insufficient militancy, wrote the *Handbook of an Urban Guerrilla.* It became one of the seminal (I use the word intentionally) books of the U.S. New Left, and has been called the bible of insurgent forces throughout the Third World. Marighella, with twentieth-century sophistication and public-relations style, flatters his subject in a manner that Nechaev would have considered sugary. To Marighella, the guerrilla is characterized by bravery, decisiveness, "moral superiority," initiative, mobility, flexibility, versatility, and a command of any given situation. He must also be an excellent marksman and a smooth liar. He must be able to endure rain, heat, hunger, and exhaustion. He must know how to hide, how to trust no one, how never to fear danger but never to act impetuously. He must "know how to live among the people and must be careful not to appear strange and separated from ordinary city life," i.e., he must be able to act *normally*. He must train "systematically" to gain "knowledge of and apprenticeship in professions and skills of all kinds."[38] As Christopher Dobson and Ronald Payne have observed, these qualities "amount to what used to be called in the British Army 'OLQ'—Officer-like Qualities."[39] Poised midway between the smiling hypocrisy of the British army and the bare-skull honesty of Nechaev, Marighella embraces both when he gets to the heart of his teachings: *"The urban guerrilla's reason for existence is the shot."*

Marighella did avoid becoming tomorrow's tyrant (although some of his followers have managed it). He opted for crucifixion of himself. He was killed in 1969. "His truth" goes marching on. He had gone to the heart of the labyrinth. He is revered by many as "the father of modern revolution."

But he's not the only father in this world of paternal power and fraternal struggle—power held and struggle waged in the name of the brotherhood of man. We hear his echo, as well as that of Nechaev (and of the Apache and Sioux elders, and Muhammad, and Moses, and Jesus) in these words: "In our country the individual knows that the glorious period in which it has befallen him *[sic]* to live is one of sacrifice; he has learned its meaning." This is Ché Guevara, in *Socialism and Man in Cuba*. Ché might have earned Nechaev's scorn as "effeminate" by disavowing terrorism per se, and claiming that "the true revolutionary is moved by strong feelings of love"—but he clarifies that as love of the *cause*. He goes on to hammer at a refrain we've heard before: "Revolutionary leaders are not often present to hear their children's first words; their wives must also share in their sacrifice if the revolution is to reach its goal; their friends are to be found only among their comrades in the revolution. For them there is no life outside the revolution."[40]

Let's try a little exercise in logic here—the logic to which Campbell's hero must be dead. Substitute the words "religious" and "religion" for "revolutionary" and "revolution" in the above quotation, and notice that it still makes unsettingly familiar sense. Now substitute the words "corporate" and "corporation." Now "military." Now "national" and "nation." Now "tribal" and "tribe." Now "professional" and "profession." It works terrifyingly well. (Revealingly, it does not work when the words "feminist" and "feminism" are substituted, precisely because of the integrative nature of female experience.) Most women will instantly connect what most men will not: that it's a rare man in any walk of life in any culture who's present to hear his child's first words; that the institution of "wife" itself, in spirit and legal contract, demands sacrifice to the husband's goal; that friendships, domicile, lifestyle, are determined and circumscribed by his career, work, politics, or calling, whether humble or exalted.* Guevara is not just describing the revolution. He is describing the institutions of religion, business, war, the State, and the family. He is describing the patriarchy.

In "The Cadre, Backbone of the Revolution," Guevara (who,

---

*Lieutenant Colonel Oliver North would have earned Guevara's respect. In his testimony before the Joint Senate-House Investigative Committee on July 8, 1987, North said that his only faint regret about all his activities when a member of the National Security Council staff was that "I abandoned my family for work." Betsy North, his wife (and mother of four children) filled us in on the behind-the-scenes reality in "A Man of Many Faces," a *Life* magazine interview (August 1987, pp. 12–17): "The children mostly just saw him weekends. . . . I rarely knew where he was going. . . . I used to complain, 'Why *can't* you be here?' I'd be real mad. . . . Then you think, 'This is causing friction. Be happy when he's here.' It wasn't anything about *him*. It was something that *I* had to work through. . . . He's been gone a lot of our married life, so he appreciates that I've done a good job with the children. I intend to work at some point. . . ." It isn't anything about him or his work. It's her problem, her neurosis. And she doesn't realize that she's been "working" all along.

by the way, had two wives and a number of mistresses, in "normal" Latin-male cultural fashion), preaches more self-sacrifice. He repeats that the cadre develops through daily tasks and rigorous training, and must be "constantly preoccupied with all the problems of the Revolution."[41] But even Ché—who demonstrated his own "capacity for sacrifice" through what Fidel Castro eulogized as "his heroic and glorious death"—never managed the tortured illogic of the following words from a little book that became the living *logos* for more than a quarter of the earth's populace:

> The immediate object is to destroy the enemy, but at the same time it is self-preservation. . . . *How then do we justify the encouragement of heroic sacrifice in war?* . . . Is this not in contradiction with "preserving oneself?" In fact, there is no contradiction at all. . . . *sacrifice and self-preservation are both opposite and complementary to each other.* For such sacrifice is essential not only for destroying the enemy but also for preserving oneself—partial and temporary *"non-preservation"* (sacrifice, or paying the price) is necessary for the sake of general and permanent preservation.[42] (Italics mine.)

No contradiction at all. This contorted reasoning, disturbingly reminiscent of the hero's being summoned into god-kingness via dismemberment for the sake of his people, is from the "Little Red Book": *Quotations from Chairman Mao Tse-Tung*. Mao taught that all political contradictions must be resolved—except, apparently, for this marvel, in which "non-preservation" is not suicide but the ultimate preservation of a self which has been abnegated to begin with. The feminist philosopher Mary Daly has aptly named this kind of illogic "patriarchal reversal."

Patria o Muerte: the Fatherland or Death. Whether from the Right or the Left, the direction is dizzyingly the same. If transnational insurgent groups use terrorist tactics to unseat the global power of their (tyrannical) economic and political fathers, so it can be said that local, nationalist, ethnic-separatist groups such as the Basque ETA and the Provisional IRA wage battle in order to carry on the work of their political and literal (martyred) fathers. In either case, a primary motive, as we'll recall from chapter 1, is to be *legitimized,* even when victory in itself is unattainable: what Luigi Bonanate terms "arousing an answer from the opponent."[43] Acknowledgment of and by the father means it's possible to become him.

Along the way, however, other types of legitimacy can serve as rewards, as well as further goads. Conor Cruise O'Brien, while granting that the terrorist does have authentic grievances shared with members of a wider community, writes that the terrorist also is "hauling himself up, by means of the grievance or oppression and the violence it legitimizes, to relative power, prestige, and privilege in the community to which he belongs."[44]

It is a male community.

Certainly power, prestige, and privilege have accrued to "Carlos," who takes pride in his panache, his love of caviar and fine wines, his identification with Robin Hood, and his exploits at evading capture and escaping when caught. As early as 1975, he could boast with some validity, "I am the famous Carlos." In December of that year, he led an audacious seizure of the Vienna headquarters of OPEC (Organization of Petroleum Exporting Countries), and held hostage some of the world's most powerful men, among them eleven oil ministers, including Sheik Yamani of Saudi Arabia. Apparently fascinated with each other, Yamani and Carlos engaged in a dialogue. The sheik asked him what was the *real* reason—beyond politics or adventure—for his terrorist career. Carlos must have recognized from the question itself that Yamani would understand, because he shrugged off all rhetoric and answered directly, man to man: "I want to be a hero."[45] After Carlos released him, Yamani reported the conversation in a tone of respect. (There's more than one way of becoming the father.)

But meanwhile, what of the woman? In his myths, she is the mother he rejects, the temptress he conquers, the wife he subjugates.

In the real world, she constitutes two-thirds of all illiterates and 90 percent of all refugee populations. She is the majority of the elderly as well as the primary caretaker of the elderly. In the developing nations, she contributes over 50 percent of all food production, and on the African continent, she is over 80 percent of all farmers—but her labor is invisible in the GNP and GDP. In the industrialized nations, she forms over 40 percent of the paid labor force but is paid only one-half to three-quarters of what men earn at the same jobs. She heads one-third of all the families on earth. Nowhere does her reproduction of the species count as "productivity." She constitutes the majority of the twenty million persons who die annually of hunger-related causes, and of the one billion who endure chronic undernourishment and other poverty deprivations. She suffers earliest and longest from toxic and nuclear waste, acid rain, chemical warfare, and deadly pesticides, because such lethal pollutants take their first toll as a rise in cancers of the female reproductive system, and in stillbirths, miscarriages, and congenital deformities. Wherever she exists, she labors: her work as homemaker or mother, as prostitute or nun, is erased because it's considered natural; her work in farm, factory, or office is marginalized because it's considered unskilled, transient, or migratory.[46]

In the real world, her feet have been bound to the size of three inches. She has been burned on the funeral pyre of her husband (the practice of *sati* has been on the rise again in India in the past two decades). She has been murdered while in infancy (the practice of female infanticide has risen again recently in China, because of the government's stringent population policy and the desire for sons). She was set on fire as a witch at nine million stakes during the Burning Time in Europe. She still suffers and dies from child marriage and polygyny and abandonment, from genital mutilation and gratuitous hysterectomies, from forced concealment in purdah and forced exposure in pornography. In some North American, African, and Asian tribal traditions, there are food taboos specifically denying her protein, reserving it for males. In hundreds of cultures, both "developed" and "developing," either by proscription or socialized politeness, she eats last, after the men—and only what is leftover.[47]

This is not called glorious sacrifice.

This is not called heroic martyrdom.

This is deliberately unspeakable.

Her existence as herself is unspeakable. It impedes the hero from his quest for himself, his search for disconnection from the life force of a shifting, chaotic, uncontrollable universe. She is less threatening only if he can forcibly disconnect her from *her*self, fragment her into the appendage-selves *he* defines, and sublimate those selves to aid him in his task—what Robert Graves, writing under the influence of Laura Riding in *The White Goddess,* deplored as "the male intellect trying to make itself spiritually self-sufficient."[48] When she does utter the unutterable and name this schism he has created, he will blame the messenger and call *her* the separatist. The only means by which she can hold him in any check is to deny herself. If she makes his quest her quest, his system her system, his mode of breathing death-in-life her mode, then she can be accepted (up to a point): the "good woman." Which means, ironically, she may then survive—but as someone she will no longer recognize.

And so the wife will excuse in her husband what she would not excuse in herself. And so the daughter will yearn after her exciting father, forsaking her mother's dreary life model. And so the mother will clitoridectomize her daughter—that her daughter may be marriageable and not starve to death. And so the "liberated" wife will become sole breadwinner, support her husband, and call it modernity. And so the mother will avert her eyes when her husband slips his hand between their daughter's legs, and disbelieve the daughter's cries. And so the mother will tell her sons that no matter how badly their father may behave at times they still must respect him. And so some feminists nonetheless hand over infant sons in barbarous initiation circumcision rites, to please allegedly "feminist" husbands. And so women batter children as they themselves are battered.

And this is called survival.

But there are myths older than the myth of the hero, artifacts of a conceived reality different from his, myths buried under centuries of patriarchal overlay. Volumes have been written on ancient religions that preceded the father-gods in every culture on the planet. She was the Cosmic One then, called by a million names. She was the Virgin, the Mother, the Crone. She became Astarte and Innanna, Erde and Aphrodite, Dana, Ngame, Demeter, Cerridwen, Brigit, Lucia, Morrigen, Astraea, Kali and Sarasvati, the Mexican Coatlicue, the Hebrew goddesses Hokhma and Matronit, the Polynesian Pele and Papatuanuku, the African Ala and Oya and Oshun and Oba, the Asian Ameratsu and Kwannon, the Christian Mary. She was Corn-Goddess and Grain-Goddess, Healer, Domesticator of Animals, Bringer of Fire. She was Shaper of the Word, Source of the Crops, Rhythm of the Sea, Arch of the Firmament, Creatrix of the World. Later, she was the mother of the god—and the sole means of his resurrection. As Ishtar, Cybele, and Au Set, or Isis, she sought and found the fragments of his shattered body, slain by brother or father or son, stitched them back together again, and made him whole. *But she was for and of herself.*

She has always been threatening him with life, she who could spill blood to bring forth not the dead but the living, she whose magic tool was herself.

What Frazer called "the savage mind" (as if it did not think through us still) believed that the soul or essence of a creature resided in its blood. If so, then she must have appeared even more awesome, for she could bleed but retain her soul. And if he, the hero, could not, then perhaps he could make another soul bleed and so increase his own powers by that other's blood: the sacrament, the war. *What she would spill for life, he would spill for death.* If her actions seemed effortless, then his must seem heroic. All things, including nature itself—the crops, the seas, the weather, the ozone layer—must come to depend on his effort. And "if the course of nature is dependent on the man-god's life," then he must kill and die, die and kill, as the sole way he knows of replenishing it.

Is it then so mystifying that those people most enamored of the fetus's "right to life" are usually the same people who support capital punishment, compulsory military service, and increased funding for armaments? To "the savage mind," the taboo at the core of all taboos is that blood cannot be cleansed except in the fire of male contest, whether for territory, wealth, power, fame, or souls. If her shedding of blood were to be respected as a life-affirmative process, his as a death-affirmative one would be negated. Her body, mind, spirit, traditions, *her authentic existence,* must be obliterated.

But he cannot totally erase her, for then who would support him?

What cannot be totally erased must be controlled.

So he made her his object, his thing. He reduced her to her relation to *him,* as consort or rib or offspring, as he reduced Athena from "she who is for herself" to a warrior-goddess daughter sprung from his brain.

And did she shrink with docility? In a preen of ego, the hero has left us records of her struggle. One is the Babylonian epic that depicts the overthrow of the Great Goddess Tiamat by her son Marduk, after she had created the universe from the flow of her menstrual blood, the residue of which became the Red Sea:

With lips that failed not she uttered rebellious words. . . .
Then the lord raised the thunderbolt, his mighty weapon,
And against Tiamat, who was raging, thus he sent the word:
"Thou art become great, thou hast exalted thyself on high . . .
And against the gods my fathers thou hast contrived. . . .
Stand! I and thou, let us join battle!"
When Tiamat heard these words,
She was like one possessed, she lost her reason.
Tiamat uttered wild, piercing cries,
She trembled and shook to her very foundations.
She recited an incantation, she pronounced her spell. . . .

To the fight they came on, to the battle they drew nigh.
The lord spread out his net and caught her,
And the evil wind that was behind him he let loose in her face.
The terrible winds filled her belly. . . .
He seized the trident and burst her belly,
He severed her inward parts, he pierced her heart.
He overcame her and cut off her life;
He cast down her body and stood upon it . . .
And with his merciless club he smashed her skull.
He cut through the channels of her blood. . . .
Then the lord rested, gazing upon her dead body, . . . and devised
    a cunning plan.
He split her up like a flat fish into two halves;
One half of her he stablished as a covering for heaven.
He fixed a bolt, he stationed a watchman,
And bade them not to let her waters come forth. . . .[49]

Marduk, the hero, revised the creation by re-forming the
heavens and the earth from her slaughtered flesh—so that he
could then create a new race: of heroes. In this perverse revisionism, Marduk represents order, Tiamat chaos. The vivid-
ness of language and imagery in the archaic poem stand
testament to his intense animosity toward her. It was not a
message she learned or one by which she was swiftly subdued.
It has taken him all of "civilization's" history to reinforce that
message, day after night, year after decade after century, life
after death after generation.

And she still refuses it.

Bound, hobbled, silenced, battered, raped raw, starved,
exhibited, bought and sold and traded, pedestaled or guttered,
derided, trivialized, dismissed, erased—*something there is in
her that refuses it.*

He has told her for eons that she has no self. Even when she
has believed him, she has not stooped to seek that self in his
ways of the hero. She may have sought it in the very churches
and temples which institutionalized her supposed lack of it.
She may have sought it in her children, only to lose it as they

grew away from her. She may have sought it in consciousness-raising groups or with therapists. She may have sought it in the anterooms and corridors of his palaces and legislatures and corporations, his juntas and courts and intellectual brothels. But *something there is in her that knows that she*—in her poverty of flesh, knowledge, means, at times even spirit—*has never lost that self.*

It's commonly held that impotence breeds violence—commonly held by men and commonly exemplified by men. Terrorist, Hero, or Everyman, he continually acts against the fear or the reality of impotence. As Jeanne N. Knutson put it in "The Terrorists' Dilemmas," "The difficulty for the terrorists is that government players *[sic]* are unaware that, behind the violent rhetoric, lies the pain of powerlessness, *a pain which only activity perceived as strength will assuage*"[50] (italics mine). And Lawrence Zelic Freedman, as if in agreement, writes, "These manifestations of unconscious psychic institutions arouse not only fear but also the sense of the uncanny; the terrorist is seemingly omnipotent."[51]

His powerlessness—that of androcentric son against patriarchal father—connects inextricably with his sense of impotence, his sense of a hollow self. For him the assuagement is not an authentic strength of self but a strength perceived as such by his adversary: it's a closed circle of male perception, male definition (of both potency and impotence), male conception of self as strength validated only by other males.

Her powerlessness (enforced and intensified by his) is not synonymous with impotence either in his eyes *or in hers.* He may have defined her solely as a sexual creature, he may have circumscribed her by his perceptions of her erotic and reproductive functions as mere resources for him, but she is after all human—and she has always known that the sum of herself is greater than genitalia and womb. The irony is that while he has defined himself as a multi-faceted being, *he* is the impatient entity ceaselessly operating in terms of his sexuality: fearing it, seeking it, demanding it, proving it, forcing and enforcing it.

His is an ejaculatory politics. Just as long ago he forgot what "self" truly could be, so he forgot what "power" really is.

Violence appears when power is in jeopardy, Arendt reminds us. If the son's violence appears when the father's power is in jeopardy, then what conclusion might we draw from the fact that both of them, throughout history, have been using violence as if it were their only course? Is it that both continually feel jeopardized, not only by each other in their male duet, but together, by something else, the target of their combined fear and misogyny? And why?

If she can give life, then he will give death. But much as he can conquer her, possess her, own her, kill her—*he cannot become her.*

He has made of his power what the Greeks termed *thanatos,* what the Buddhists call *mara:* the force of hostility, the magnetism of death. What she is making of hers the Greeks called *eros,* the Buddhists *kama:* the power of desire, the life force.

In both Oliver North and Carlos we can recognize the politics of Thanatos. But the politics radiating contrarily and chaotically through the phenomenon called "feminism" is evolving from a social process breathed forth by an indefatigable, affirmative human self. It's *that* politics women now reclaim, *that* politics men must engage to free themselves of tyranny or crucifixion. If we don't heed it, none of us will survive.

It is the politics of the twenty-first century. It is the politics of Eros.

CHAPTER 3

༶༶༶༶༶༶༶༶༶

THE LOVE-DEATH: RELIGION, PHILOSOPHY, AND AESTHETICS

I will send forth My terror before you, and I will cast into panic all the peoples among whom you pass, and I will cause all thy enemies to flee before you.   / Exodus 23:27

No creature can attain a higher grade of nature without ceasing to exist.   / ANANDA K. COOMARASWAMY

The death of a beautiful woman is, unquestionably, the most poetical topic in the world.   / EDGAR ALLAN POE

Religion, philosophy, and aesthetics are all means by which the human psyche reaches toward something greater than itself, to glimpse life's meaning and beauty. Ostensibly, this is their common purpose. Where all three accomplish the opposite is in their conceptualization and practice as patriarchal institutions, because they share a propaganda of toxicity: the love-death, abnegation of the self as the highest good. To all three traditions, consciousness is intolerable, ambivalence unacceptable. As a consequence, the delicate virtues of ambivalence—

hesitation and patience—are devalued. Connect this with the tradition that considers intuition and ambivalence "womanly traits," to be smiled at indulgently and then dismissed from serious philosophical discourse.

In his article "Religion and Terrorism" Moshe Amon spies such a connection, the tendency of spiritual and political ideologies to deal not with people but with concepts. He regrets that "it takes a philosopher, a scientist, or a lover to approach people individually and as individuals, not as abstractions."[1] He does not add "or a woman." Yet haven't women been pilloried for being supposedly incapable of "abstract thinking"? Since we know that women have demonstrated considerable competence in higher mathematics, philosophical and theological rumination, poetic creativity, scientific discovery, and other such abstract disciplines, may we not assume that the pillorying in fact was about a gender refusal on women's part, a refusal to revere abstraction for its own sake, a refusal to abstractify out of a terror of the specific?

That terror lies at the heart of "civilization's" darkness. All of history's messianic campaigns to impose a crisp, dry, linear "order" stem from that place. (That Mussolini's trains ran on time, for example, apparently justified their periodic cargo of Italian Jews to death camps in Austria.) It's a place that necessitates "un-noticing" because to *notice* is to realize the impossibility of being in absolute control of every detail of existence. And it's a place of fury at whatever cannot be controlled. Together, religion, philosophy, and aesthetics have functioned as the propaganda for that control.

Days of Wrath, Day of Reckoning

If we're to look more closely at the worldwide historical conspiracy of religious terror, let the woman reader be warned. You will have to cover your arms and legs, you will have to veil your face. You will have to wear bolts of cloth from crown to toe; you may not wear trousers, though your priests may wear skirts. You will have to cover or shave your head. You will be legally raped in wedlock. You will have to obey father, husband, brother, even son. You will have to become pregnant, whether you wish to or not, and carry the pregnancy to term, whether you wish to or not. You must figuratively or literally carve out your sexual organs. You must stay away from holy places so as not to contaminate such sites, or, if you are fortunate and permitted access, you may be forced to worship from behind a wall or a screen. You must learn that as God is to man, so Man is to you. You must "dwell in terror of the living God"—and of the living man. You must nod, bow, genuflect, kneel, kowtow, prostrate yourself. You must avert your eyes. You must labor for centuries to (only partially) win a questionable victory (in only certain faiths)—that of approaching the altar directly and of ministering to others. You may be told that you have no soul. You may be told that you can enter paradise only at Man's disposition, as his appendage, his rib, his odalisque. You will be excommunicated if you question. You will be declared lapsed, heretic, apostate, damned, doomed, hell's handmaiden. You will be tortured, flogged, stoned, hanged, set aflame.

If you contract your soul and sacrifice your body to this system, you will be honored as a living emissary who facilitates Man's entrance into the Kingdom of Heaven.

But, you ask, what have these rules to do with the vitality of spirit? What has this to do with . . . *awe?* The cell in division—a minuscule star in nova under the microscope; a fragile crocus shooting its wand greenly up through snow; the frog in the Kalahari Desert that neatly reconstitutes its buried, desiccated body in the first rain after long drought; vast black holes dense with energy and galaxies in whorls of dance with one another's iridescence—what have they to do with such rules? How does this system address undersea volcanoes erupting island after newborn island in chains as invisibly indivisible as the string theory, the most advanced hypothesis of theoretical physics? How does this system speak to and for the mystical uniqueness yet relatedness of each fingerprint, each shell, leaf, gene, snow crystal?

Religion speaks to none of these wonders. That is not its function. Religion is not about awe and joy, despite its purported proprietorship of them and its promise to eventually deliver what already lies around us every day, freely available for celebration. Religion is about something else. The etymology of the word itself, from the Latin, is related to being *bound by rules*. Religion is about terror.

> Jehovah . . . expressly forbade them from touching the fruit of the tree of knowledge. . . . But here steps Satan, the eternal rebel. . . . He makes man ashamed of his bestial ignorance and obedience, . . . he emancipates him. . . . God admitted that Satan was right [commanding]: "Behold the man is become as one of the gods; . . . prevent him, therefore, from eating of the fruit of eternal life, lest he become immortal like Ourselves."[2]

It would be fair to mistake that for an apocryphal biblical text, but it was written by Mikhail Bakunin—coauthor, you will recall, of *Catechism of a Revolutionist*.

In the balance between two figures—the jealous god and the satanic rebel whose bitterness equals the other's wrath—our lives swing perilously, and have swung so for centuries. The coming of the messiah has always meant revelations of the apocalypse: the end of the world.

Evidence of that messianic message of death has for thousands of years filled our libraries—and our cemeteries. But we can spot-check some examples, if only to place contemporary religious terror in its time-honored context.

The wrathful god of order and the insurgent messiah of rebellion afflict the entire pantheon of patriarchal deities. Zeus the Thunderer and Prometheus shaking his fist in revolt against the gods might be one place to begin. Or we could focus on the Western Judeo-Christian tradition, in which the theme of messianism is particuarly pronounced. To see the son, we might analyze the Sicarii and the Zealots who, through widespread terrorism, fostered mass uprisings against Rome as early as 66–70 C.E. The aim was to intensify Jewish lack of confidence in local Jewish authorities, and to incite such hatred between Jews, Romans, and Greeks that all negotiations would be impossible. This was accomplished by a strategy of terror: murders by stabbing with concealed daggers in broad daylight, especially at religious festivals, creating a climate of panic. Realizing that "a man is potentially most vulnerable when he considers himself entirely secure," David C. Rapoport writes in "Terror and the Messiah: An Ancient Experience and Some Modern Parallels," these messianic nationalists intended their assaults "to demonstrate that no circumstance or convention could provide immunity."[3] The uprising ended in the Zealots' mass suicide while besieged at Masada, an act still honored today as exemplary of heroic self-sacrifice chosen over surrender. What went unnoticed in 70 C.E. and still goes unnoticed is that the Jewish women and children at Masada were given no choice between enslavements: they were not consulted about either the campaign of terror or the mass "suicide," yet they too perished in a heroism defined by their men.

To counsel patience was to sell out. To hesitate was to betray. To be ambivalent was to be impure. To yearn toward the splendor of living was to show oneself a coward.

A "purity" enamored of such perfection, attainable only by death, is characteristic of the millenarian fantasy. For a fantasy, it has been acted on with alarming consistency. To see the perfect father, we might spend our time reinspecting the divinity of kings, or their divine right, from the pharaohs through the Bourbons to the contemporaneous Saudi house of Wahhabi. To see both the perfect father and perfect son, we might examine what the scenario "Luther versus the Pope" was actually reenacting. Or we might study the Puritan Revolution—including Milton's adoration of God but identification with Satan as the great rebel.

In the Eastern tradition, we would find more god-emperors, more rules, more sacred terrorism. We would find ornate controls inherent in Confucianism. We would wander the maze of the Hindu caste system and its political convenience right up through Gandhi's brilliant use of it for independence against the British in the twentieth century. We would study the Thugs, the Hindu sect whose members demonstrated their religious devotion with ritual murder, or Thuggee, garrotting performed on strangers. We would encounter pacifist Buddhism applied militarily in the fight for Burmese nationalism. We would examine persistent militance in Islam, from the eleventh-century Hassassins (source of our word "assassin"), who believed killing was the key to instant paradise, through the religious fundamentalist wave now sweeping the Islamic world. We would loathe the deranged thinking behind such language as *Jihad* ("Holy War")—but then wouldn't we have seen that same derangement at work in the "Holy Crusades," and heard the twentieth-century secular rationalization of it in the phrase "a just war"?

We might deplore the religious rites practiced by the Mau Mau before embarking on terrorist missions during the Kenyan campaign for independence. But we would recognize those as mirroring all the "conquests for Christ" practiced for centuries by European powers in their annexation of entire continents as colonies—the taking, selling, and holding of slaves (for Christianity's sake, to save their souls by forced conversion); genocide of Mayans, Incans, and scores of other indigenous populations; missionaries pouring across the world, crucifix in hand, right in the front lines of the armies of empire—bestowing upon those armies their ultimate justification.

Religious violence is the best marching beat men know. It's a dementedly logical development, if one's attitude toward the energy of the cosmos is terror in the first place. Adaptable, convenient, morally void, the message travels far: "If it is the will of God that it requires violence to recover our rights, who am I to defy the will of God?" That was originally spoken in the 1960s by the conservative former U.S. senator and former presidential candidate Barry Goldwater—but by 1987 it was quoted admiringly by the radical organizer Apisai Tora in defense of the anti-democratic coup in Fiji.[4]

We could spill out the entirety of our lives on the ground of this subject. Generations already have done so. But all we need do is look around us today.

In Sri Lanka, the Hindu Tamil populace, long discriminated against by the majority Buddhist Sinhalese, now adopts terrorist tactics in response.

In India, caste wars against caste, Hindu against Muslim, sect against sect. The separation of Pakistan was to have solved it, the separation of Bangladesh from Pakistan was to have solved it. Now the Sikh minority suffers, dies, and kills in terrorist acts, claiming that separation of the Punjab will solve it.

Partition of Ireland was also to have solved it, but Roman Catholic priests still hide fugitive members of the Provisional IRA—while the Protestant Reverend Ian Paisley incites his followers to keep terror ablaze. As Bernadette Devlin wrote, "There are very few Christians in Northern Ireland. . . . its people hate each other in the name of Jesus Christ."[5] God is on all their sides, and each side is afire with its own messianic glow.

On the most sacred day of the Islamic calendar, in the Haram at Mecca—the holy zone in which violence even to plant life is forbidden—402 people are killed, most of them women, in riots triggered by an Iranian demonstration. The Iranians are Persians, not Arabs, and they are Shiite Muslims, not Sunni like the other 90 percent of the Muslim world. The struggle is about identity, about visibility, legitimacy, ethnic animosity—and about geopolitical power, about economics, about oil. But the *rabidity* of the struggle dates back thirteen centuries, to a battle over which men of Islam would inherit the succession from Muhammad. The Shiites lost, becoming an underclass in diaspora throughout Islam, many nurturing revenge in a messianic fanaticism that emphasizes martyrdom. Each year, on the anniversary of the great Shiite defeat of 680 C.E., fundamentalist

Shiite men flagellate themselves, smashing rocks against their heads until they stand masked and shirted with blood in commemoration. "I want to die before my friends. They want to die before me. We want to see our God," explains one young man.[6] During the 1979 Iranian revolution, many men marching against the shah wore white burial clothing to signify their eagerness to die for their religio-political cause. In the Iran–Iraq war, youths volunteered for duty wearing crimson "martyr" bandannas and small "keys to heaven" around their necks.[7] At Mecca in 1987, demonstrators placed women in the front ranks; the men behind them carried banners declaring "Victory is made by waves of martyrs," hurled stones, and set fire to cars. Saudi security forces at the shrine moved in. Chaos ensued, and hundreds were trampled to death. In addition to the 402 dead, 649 people, including 303 Iranians, were reported injured, the violence lasting over five hours. Both Saudi and Iranian sources reported that the bloodstained ground was littered with women's slippers and veils.[8]

Sickened by the notion of "holy terror," Amir Tahéri, an Iranian journalist and newspaper editor now in exile, claims that "Islamic terrorism does not accept today's world; it seeks to destroy it. It has no interest in negotiating anything, even forcibly. . . . Islam is a political movement, not a religion. . . . Women are superfluous in this vision of the world. One of the prophet's proverbs says that if women did not exist, humanity would be able to worship Allah more perfectly because women keep men from performing their religious duties and are a source of evil. . . . Khomeini's motto is: 'To kill and be killed is the highest duty of every Moslem.' "[9]

Yet Islam, like Judaism, is a faith of interpretation, not of unified dogma: it has contributed its share of mystics, scholars, and peacemakers. So has every religious tradition had its exceptions who proved the rule (and were often declared heretics), individuals whose spiritual integrity transcended the system they nevertheless served. What is more to the point is that rather than being spiritual, *all organized religion*—and fundamentalist interpretation of religion in particular—*has always been "a political movement,"* consistently articulating a politics of Thanatos, and just as consistently targeting women as the worst impediments to that politics. The Arabic word *fitna* denotes both chaos and a woman's sexual power. The Confucian concept and Chinese ideograms for "woman" and for "slave" are the same. The central Orthodox Jewish prayer for a man is one thanking God for not having been born a woman.

It's been said that the Jewish people found their "manhood" with the creation of the State of Israel, not because they fought back against their oppressors but because of the violent manner in which they fought back. (The Israeli clandestine "counterterrorist" unit which conducted reprisals against Palestinian journalists and PLO officials in Europe after the 1972 Munich massacre of Israeli Olympic athletes was named WOG: Wrath of God.) Always there's a justification, no matter where one decides to enter the cycle of violence. The Jewish Defense League began in the United States in 1968; its stated objective was patrolling the streets of Brooklyn, New York, to protect its own community from street crime. But it quickly assumed a vigilante character, and JDL members began to organize, commit, and sometimes even take credit for terrorist acts. JDL members have been linked to at least six such incidents, including firebombings of cars and homes, assassination attempts, and the tossing of tear-gas grenades into a performance of the Moiseyev Dance Company at the Metropolitan Opera House in 1986, in which twenty persons were injured.[10] The founder-leader of the JDL is a rabbi, Meir Kahane. He also backs and reputedly leads the ultranationalist Kach movement in Israel. Kach is accused of attacks on Palestinian laborers, bombings of Islamic shrines, and support of yet another even more clandestine group, Terror Against Terror, or TNT (the initials of the group's name in Hebrew). TNT in turn is suspected of (or has openly claimed responsibility for) the murders of three West Bank mayors in 1980, an assault on Hebron's Islamic University in 1983 in which three Arabs were killed and thirty-three persons critically wounded, and a plot to bomb the Dome of the Rock, one of the holiest of all Islamic sites.[11] A rabbi, like a mullah, is a man of God.

So were the white Christian ministers who participated in or condoned lynchings in the U.S. South.[12] So are those who desecrate synagogues and Jewish cemeteries. So are the members of the new Christian Right, which includes such white-supremacist organizations as the Aryan Nations Church of Jesus Christ Christian. Supporters of this Idaho-based group have been connected to bombings of federal facilities; its leader, the Reverend Richard Butler, is under federal indictment on charges of sedition.[13] The Silent Brotherhood, the White American Bastion, The Order, the National Alliance, the Klan, the Posse Comitatus, and the Arkansas-centered congregation called the Covenant, the Sword, and the Arm of the Lord—all of them loosely affiliated Christian Right paramilitary groups—share a common theology, aptly named Identity.

Identity was originated in 1946 by Klan organizer and former Methodist minister Wesley Swift. Identity adherents will tell you that Christ was an Aryan, not a Semite, that the Jews are descended via Cain from Eve's mating with Satan, that the lost tribes of Israel were really Anglo-Saxon, and that the United States is the Promised Land—to be purged of all non-Aryans. From his Ministry of Christ Church in Mariposa, California, William Potter Gale, an Identity pastor, preaches: "Damn right I'm teaching violence! God said you're gonna do it that way! It's about time somebody is telling you to get violent, Whitey." But Gale is regarded as a bit of a wimp by Keith Gilbert, who served five years in San Quentin on conspiracy to explode 1,400 pounds of dynamite during a speech by Martin Luther King. Gilbert, who founded the Restored Church of Jesus Christ in Post Falls, Idaho, preaches that the prophet Elijah was reincarnated in the person of Adolf Hitler and that *Mein Kampf* is actually the last book of the Bible.[14]

These Christian soldiers forge onward, and recruit in the nation's prisons. George Stout, a Klan and Texas Aryan Nation leader, brags that the "prison network" is extensive: "In one Texas prison alone, more than 300 inmates are on the Aryan Nation mailing list." But lest we comfort ourselves with the thought that such a philosophy and tactic appeals only to what some would consider society's uneducated and impoverished *lumpen* fringe, we should realize that the Christian-Patriots Defense League holds training sessions at its 232-acre "survival base" in Missouri; its leader, Illinois millionaire John Harrell, recruits members who own airplanes toward the building of a Right-wing Christian air fleet.[15] Nor should we forget former Secretary of the Interior James Watt dismissing the alarm of environmentalists with the comment that nuclear-waste dumping and pollution didn't matter because Jesus would soon be here for the Second Coming. Or electronic Pentecostal preacher Pat Robertson, who in 1987 and 1988 conducted a serious, well-financed campaign for the presidency; while beaming steady anti-Arab "sermons" from a radio station in Lebanon (one of many which Robertson owns), he predicts that nuclear holocaust—Armageddon—is due within our lifetime, and that it should be welcomed because it will presage Christ's re-arrival to bring peace and to embrace those "saved" through conversion. Then there is Ronald Reagan himself, who has never disowned his remarks at a dinner in 1971: "It can't be too long now. Ezekiel says that fire and brimstone will be rained down upon the enemies of God's people. That must mean that they'll be destroyed by nuclear weapons . . . now that Russia has become communistic and atheistic, now that Russia has set itself against God . . . it fits the description."[16] When Armageddon is imminently anticipated and even invoked by a man with his finger on the nuclear trigger, the alleged separation of church and state is in danger of becoming terminally blurred.*

---

* Grace Halsell's book *Prophecy and Politics: Militant Evangelists on the Road to Nuclear War* (Westport, Conn.: Lawrence Hill, 1986) is a chilling consciousness-raiser for anyone who has laughed off the U.S. religious Right as an irrelevant movement or a temporary phase.

A longing for apocalypse is common in the Christian Right. William L. Pierce, a leader of the neo-Nazi National Alliance, with headquarters in Washington, D.C., wrote an apocalyptic novel and terrorist manual, *The Turner Diaries*, which deeply influenced a man named Robert Jay Mathews, another Christian militant. During the early 1980s Mathews built up a fund of over three million dollars from bank holdups and armored-car robberies; although he had managed to bomb a mere two buildings before barricading himself in a shoot-out to the death with FBI agents in 1984, he left evidence of detailed plans to attack and immobilize "the infrastructure and support systems of a major U.S. city." Mathews also had found himself through Identity.[17] So had two men caught in the California desert with the biggest illegal cache of weapons in U.S. history. So had the minister in Michigan who claimed he had resurrected the Albigensian* heresy.[18]

Undeniably, women are also involved in the Christian Right. Andrea Dworkin has devoted a highly intelligent book-length analysis to the hows and whys of their presence.[19] But they're not active in the terrorism of that movement. Perhaps they haven't truly discovered themselves in Identity? Or perhaps they're not to be entrusted with God's firearms, since women are such notorious vessels of the Devil.

Certainly the Roman Catholic church has been warning men about women's hellish talents for years; it's a candidate for the most reliably long-term gynophobia on record. During the witch persecutions, whole towns in Europe were reduced to male-only populations: all the women had been slaughtered.[20] As recently as 1976, the Associated Press carried the story of a

---

* The Albigensians were a persecuted body of accused heretics in the south of France from the eleventh to the thirteenth century. The papacy charged them with holding Manichean doctrines. Manicheism itself has been summarized as "the ultimate and extreme apex reached by antique, dualistic gnosticism." ("Mani and Manicheism," in *Encyclopedia of Religion,* ed. Virgilius Ferm [New York: Philosophical Library, 1945], pp. 465–67.) In its purest form, Manicheism held that all matter was evil, that nonexistence was the only route to the light.

twenty-three-year-old woman, Anneliese Michel, of Klingen-berg, Germany, who died after having undergone exorcism rites conducted by two Catholic priests. Civil authorities investi-gated the exorcism procedures, which were originally recom-mended by an eighty-one-year-old local priest who believed Michel was possessed of demons which sent her into violent seizures. With the permission of Bishop Josef Stangl, two exor-cists—Father Arnold Renz and Father Ernst Alt—were called in. Father Renz, not one averse to publicity, claimed during a television appearance that Michel was possessed by no less than six spirits, including Lucifer, Nero, Judas, Cain, and Adolf Hit-ler (how he does get around). The exorcism rituals continued for ten months; Michel's seizures grew more frequent and intense, and her weight dropped to seventy pounds. The priests called in no medical assistance. Finally she died, "of malnutri-tion and dehydration" according to the medical report. Bishop Stangl's diocese is Würzburg, where in one year alone during the seventeenth century more than three hundred women were burned alive for "trafficking with the devil." Medical back-ground uncovered after she died indicated that the mysterious seizures had been diagnosed when she was in high school: Anneliese Michel suffered from epilepsy.[21]

The cathexis of male identity, fascistic politics, woman-hatred, violence, and religious institutions is an infamous alliance. In the 1930s, the German National Socialists—the Nazis—agi-tated against employed women, contraception and abortion, and homosexuality, and revived the ideal of *Kinder, Kirche, Küche* (children, church, and kitchen) for German woman-hood. A working coalition of misogyny between the Nazi party and the religious establishment served long enough for Hitler to consolidate his power. Feminist groups and publications were closed down, as were contraception clinics. In 1933, the year Hitler became chancellor, feminists, along with "non-Aryans," were forced out of their jobs in teaching and other public posi-tions. Women were barred from political office and from the judicial bench. In 1934, abortion was banned and made a criminal offense against the State, punishable by hard labor or the death penalty.[22]

Ah well, shrug the Marxists, what do you expect? Religion is the opiate of the people. Religion can also be the opiate of the Marxists, a civic fervor complete with holy days and secular saints, showing itself not only in the devotions of a millenarian belief (however atheistic), but as plain old religion. It was Lenin who described the Bolsheviks thus: "We are the Young Turks of the Revolution, with something of the Jesuit added." Cast a sharp eye on the Christian Left as well as the Christian Right.

Kenneth Kaunda, the first president of Zambia, was an ardent advocate of nonviolence and passive resistance during Zambia's freedom struggle against the British. That struggle won in 1964, the young country then faced a protracted war in neighboring Zimbabwe (then Southern Rhodesia). Zambia became a refugee sanctuary and guerrilla base for the neighboring independence fighters, and also a target for white Rhodesian land and air strikes. At this stage, Kaunda, a devout Christian, revised his beliefs about violence, defending its present imperative and making of his Christianity an apologia: in effect, he emphasized that forgiveness after the fact was virtually the end which excused the means of violence. In his book *The Riddle of Violence*, he tortuously delineates this politico-theology:

If we are not acting to change things—which must evoke violence from those who will do anything to protect privilege—we are, *in our passivity*, throwing our weight on the side of the oppressor. . . . I ended up supporting armed struggle because I could no longer believe that anything is preferable to the use of force. I have been much taken with some words of a Victorian writer, Douglas Jerrold: "We love peace as we abhor pusillanimity, but *not peace at any price*. There is a peace more *destructive of the manhood of living man* than war is destructive of his body." . . . [We weighed] one form of evil against another and asked for God's forgiveness as we undertook to do what had to be done.[23] (Italics mine.)

I would instantly question why we are offered an either / or choice, as if violence and "passivity" were the only options. But an even more revealing aspect of this position is not that violence was adopted by the oppressed in a struggle for freedom, but that supposedly nonviolent Christianity could be (and was) applied *as a rationale*. I think this was less a matter of recutting the religious cloth to fit than of realizing that it fit perfectly to begin with. And the thread for securing it in place? Manhood. *Why is manhood always perceived as the too-high price of peace?*

In 1987, President Daniel Ortega Saavedra of Nicaragua addressed the United Nations. He chose to do so on October 8, the anniversary of the death of Ché Guevara. At his press conference afterward, Ortega compared Guevara to Jesus Christ, "in his selfless devotion to others."[24] As Ortega spoke, linking his gods in a hushed tone of reverence, the November issue of *Playboy* hit the newsstands. It was much heralded in sensationalistic terms for carrying seminude photographs of Jessica Hahn, a young fundamentalist Christian woman who had "brought about the downfall" of PTL ("Praise The Lord") televangelist Jim Bakker's financial and real-estate empire in a religious scandal nicknamed Pearlygate. Hahn claimed Bakker had raped her; Bakker claimed Hahn had seduced his manhood into sin. Much furor ensued—including some confused self-righteousness among women who had been supportive of Hahn as victim but now didn't quite know where to knot their politically correct line, since she had granted an interview and photos to pornocratic *Playboy* in return for a considerable fee. Few seemed to care that the same issue of *Playboy* also ran a long interview with Daniel Ortega Saavedra (serious politics, you understand). But to some of us, this was outrageous manhood politics as usual. Despite his protestations of being a male feminist (I wonder if genuine feminism can be said to decline in direct proportion to the number of "male feminists" around), Ortega had written a so-called revolutionary book of poems while jailed by former dictator Somoza. The book was entitled—without irony—*I Missed Managua in Miniskirts*. No one then criticized Ortega for his manly, revolutionary title. No one now criticized Ortega for appearing in *Playboy*. Either way, Daniel Ortega's acts were those of a revolutionary. Either way, Jessica Hahn's acts were those of a slut.

In *The Mass Psychology of Fascism*, Wilhelm Reich wrote that "Catholic Christianity, in particular, has long since shed its revolutionary character," and has debased itself by now asking "its millions of adherents to take war as 'fate,' as 'expiation of sin.' "[25] Again, I disagree. Christianity—and Catholic Christianity in particular, if you will—has retained every feature of its androcentric "revolutionary character," at the secret heart of which has always coiled the hiss of obliteration: a love of death as the pure, selfless, and sole means of expiation for the sin of consciousness. No wonder that woman, the incarnate affirmation of Eros, birth, and life, is such a damnable obstacle.

"Liberation theology" only confirms this. I am not speaking of those courageous individuals who have left their church after having glimpsed the extent of its self-interest and collaboration in human suffering, left to work and live and sometimes die among its victims in a daily affirmation of grace. I am, rather, speaking of those (also individually courageous) priests and nuns who, like their missionary colonialist predecessors, work, live, fight, and also sometimes die among the victims of the institution to which they still swear fealty. This is called having it both ways—and Rome is a master at that technique. The smoke screen of theological contention can be raised: the establishment church can claim that Caesar must be rendered what is due to Caesar, that political noninvolvement is imperative; the "liberation" church (harking back to Reich's interpretation) can insist on reviving the "revolutionary character" of Christianity *engagé*.[26] If Caesar in the person of the generals and their juntas wins, the cardinals will celebrate a mass. If Caesar in the person of the rebels (and *their* juntas) wins, the cardinals will celebrate a mass. Either way, the Vatican will retain its seat in the United Nations. Either way—across Latin America, in Spain and Portugal, in the Republic of Ireland and the Philippines—divorce, contraception, and especially abortion will be unacceptable. (And back at home in the United States, the Berrigan brothers equate a woman's right to abortion with the murderous might of the Pentagon.) "Faith and morals" issues, for which read women's human, sexual, and reproductive rights, will remain inviolate. Either way, the bargain is struck over the bodies of women. The old Caesars owe a debt for having been kept in power; the new Caesars owe a debt for being placed in power. Only the masses of women lose.

Perhaps the most astonishing trick of all is the regularity with which masculinists get away with this. Hitler invoked the "big lie," and prophesied that the bigger the lie, the more believable it would be. Orwell pegged it in *Nineteen Eighty-four,* and Mary Daly, as we've noted, termed it "patriarchal reversal." Yet it persists. "In life we are in death," drone the sermonizers. "Thou shalt find thy self through losing thy self," pronounce the theologians. For women to transform the world, much less our own lives, requires seeing through such systemic "truth" again and again, even if that process so lacerates the eye that only tears, again and again, can rinse away the scabs of our fearful longing to not see any more.

Then, perhaps, we might perform an authentic annunciation, to ourselves and one another: that *we* are a miracle.

A politics of ecstasy, here and now, even in the teeth of formerly unspeakable suffering, is one hallmark of feminist thought and action. Not abstract "life everlasting" as some promised dividend (*if* sufficient agony is invested today and accumulated over all our tomorrows). A quiet, immediate, *specific* affirmation of life *now.* You can hear it in the humor and the hurt of women comparing notes about their lives. You can see it in the ways mothers hide their sons—from mullahs, from revolutionary cadres, from superpower agencies. You can breathe it from flowers grown in cracked pots on the stoops and sills of urban slums and refugee camps. It is patient, conscious, ambivalent. But it is not passive. It is not unrebellious.

This gynarchical approach, you understand, is regarded as chaotic, impractical, and even conservative.

It is a form of action and rebellion totally different from the politics of ecstatic death that patriarchal religion celebrates and accomplishes, the double-duty feat of enshrining and solidifying the power of the god fathers while inspiring and justifying the rebel sons. That death-ecstasy is what you hear in the sermons preached by military chaplains of every army. You can see it as underground code in such slave-originated religions as Voudon in Haiti, and Candomblé, Macumba, and Obanda in Brazil. You can breathe it in the stench of flesh self-immolated by Buddhist monks, or corpses rotting after the Masada-like death of Jim Jones and his followers of the People's Temple.

This patriarchal approach, you understand, is regarded as orderly, pragmatic, and progressive.

This is a world turned inside out. This is psychosis.

Psychosis, whatever its other ingredients, always includes the element of terror.

If institutionalized religion has hypocritically masked its true message—a lust for annihilation—with ritualized lies, traditional philosophy and aesthetics have at least been more honest. Religion has claimed to love life while pursuing death—and has kept the rules in place by terror. Masculinist thought and art, on the other hand, have openly conceived, worshipped, and promulgated the "love-death."

The Poison Cup

Philosophy is secular religion, just as religion is sanctified politics—politics with "bells and smells." Because religion is more visible (which possibly explains its need for hypocrisy), philosophy appears to have less impact on people's lives. Yet men's *(sic)* search to obliterate the self they purport to be seeking

affects us all: it parallels and informs the traditional philosophies, Eastern and Western. Whenever passion is split into the
sacred versus the profane, each of those, in yearning after the
lost vitality in union with the other, becomes a means for *unat-
tainment*, in effect self-annihilation. A fragmented and exclusive vision of the universe must elicit a fragmented and exclusive
analysis of the universe.

Ah, but look. We've been offered an alleged bridge across
this artificially made chasm: "pure love" as the opposite of
profane lust and the alternative to divine rapture. It's neither
an opposite nor an alternative, and it's certainly not a bridge.
In popular culture (Hollywood movies, trashy novels, Hallmark greeting cards), it's used to trivialize and sentimentalize
the fierce, genuinely hard *work* of loving passionately—a labor
women carry almost exclusively in human relationships. In the
less popular but influential arenas of intellect and art, "pure
love" is linked with the *Liebestod* ("love-death") theme, as the
passion that blooms obsessively only in ill-fated lovers, flour-
ishes briefly, and ends in betrayal, chaos, murder, or suicide.
The ancient pagan* sensibility and gynocratic spirituality were
utterly different. They celebrated a combination of lust *and*
affection and acknowledged female sexuality (in all its expressions) as a vibrant force. But what the European witches called
the Old Way or Wicce (Craft of the Wise) was crushed by the
rise of patriarchal religious and cultural institutions—which
could more efficiently inspire and justify political violence.
Lustful affection has no place here. In compensation, we're given
pure, tragic lovers, like Romeo and Juliet, who ostensibly transcend such hostilities. But in social reality and social consciousness those models have *strengthened* cultural assumptions that
hostility is inevitably linked with violence and that love's only
escape is a liberation into death.

It's naive to assume this is a disease only of Western culture,

---

* *Pagan* meant "country dweller" (and *heathen* meant "heath dweller"). Because
the ancient goddess-worshipping faiths survived longest among peasants and country
folk, these terms came to be names for adherents to non-patriarchal spiritual beliefs.

or that the syndrome began with the Romantics. On the contrary, this theme was born, a Siamese twin, with patriarchy: earlier myths suddenly change shape and message in androcratic retelling. Lilith shifts from Adam's original mate into the serpent, the Harpies and Sirens become lethal, the Fates contort into the Furies, the Sphinx into a murderess. An identical change elevating cruelty occurs in African legend, in Native American folk tales, in Asian fables. The same kind of "holy" sadism, pornographic in tone, comes into play in the ancient Babylonian *Gilgamesh* epic, the Welsh *Mabinogion,* the Scandinavian Eddas, the Hindu *Mahabharata* and *Ramayana* and *Rig-Veda*—until finally, as Mario Praz phrases it in *The Romantic Agony,* "the identification of Lust with Death" is complete.[27] Woman, of course, is always the agent of lust.

Tristan, that primordial romantic hero, is avatar of this triple knot: passion, rebellion, and morbidity. The knight Tristan, you will remember, is sent to escort the Princess Isolde on her journey to meet and wed King Mark, but Tristan and Isolde unknowingly drink a fatal love potion and become lovers. After her marriage, the triangle descends to tragedy, with the lovers' attempted escape (and death) and King Mark's destruction. Even in its variations, the legend parallels the Lancelot-Guinevere-Arthur triangle. But earlier versions of the story, residues of Celtic and Teutonic matriarchal myth, give us an Isolde who is luminous with her own power. In some versions she's a priestess of the Goddess, in some a regnant queen. She is no one's consort. It is she who chooses her own lover. Her fate is in her own hands, and the love potion (not even present in some versions) is just that—a *love* potion. It is she who offers it to her lover, openly, an invitation to unambiguous bliss. Some of the earliest versions even have a happy ending (not necessarily a prerequisite either for art or for a feminist sensibility, but always pleasant when you can get hold of one). With the entrance of the new god, with the tension between the pagan world view and the Christian, with the fall of queens regnant and the onset of the Salic Law forbidding female succession to a throne, the plot shifts. Enter King Mark, jealous husband, jealous god. Enter a changed Tristan, now a rebel like Satan, a messianic martyr like Christ. Enter the involuntary and the poison cup of love, the drinking of which means transient tragic ecstasy awaiting inevitable punishment: lust, betrayal, guilt, possession, doom.

In an essay entitled "Models of Rebellion," Vytautas Kavolis hypothesizes that the Tristan legend for the first time "provides a model for man and woman to be equal fellow [sic] rebels," in conspiracy against King Mark. (That's all very well, but we are now aware that such "equality" in the later versions meant not her empowerment but her loss of power, not the humanizing of him but the elevation of him to hero.) Kavolis sees romantic love as the culprit: "At the roots of the [liebestod cup] 'alchemy' of romantic love is the transformation into a power-driven machinery, separated from consciousness, of that activated receptivity called emotion." He sees these "equal fellow rebels" as being chosen by their rebellion rather than choosing it, as pawns in circumstances from which they're forcibly alienated—and he sees in this alienation a precursor of modern forms of rebellion: "The Greeks have provided two mythological models for rebellion: a 'rational' rebellion for the privileged individual (Prometheus) and an 'emotional' rebellion for the underprivileged collectivity (Dionysus).* The modern European civilization inverts the equation: an 'emotional' rebellion for the privileged individual (Tristan) and a 'rational' rebellion, later on, for the oppressed collectivity (Marx). Dionysus has been individualized, Prometheus collectivized."[28]

Prometheus, Dionysus, Tristan—and Marx (who was the descendant, by the way, of messianic rabbis). All males; all male modes of rebellion. With the modern European "inversion," into which a real historical personage enters to take his place with the gods and heroes, the poison cup runneth over. A Tristanic mode of rebellion for a privileged individual man

---

* The god whose festivals were thought to inspire rampages of sexual abandon, blood lust, and chaos.

in the twentieth century *is* a form of self-sacrifice (and sacrifice of others, willing volunteers or no). Martha Crenshaw, writing on self-sacrifice as a terrorist motive, comments that many individuals "seemed to welcome capture because it brought release . . . and a sense of content and fulfillment." She quotes Meridor (a member of the Irgun High Command) as being in "high spirits" once he was arrested by the British, and she notes that Menachem Begin articulated similar sentiments: a jolt of elation on arrest, because the real suffering that was a hero's due could be experienced at last.[29]

The Marxian "rational" rebellion is not so literally suicidal. It's a different kind of death; it seeks centralized power: *The hero of yesterday becomes the tyrant of tomorrow, unless he crucifies himself today.*

Even worse, what happens when those who adopt the Marxian "rational" mode (acting, they claim, on behalf of the oppressed) are themselves motivated by the Tristanic "emotional" mode? Double-love-death. The privileged, fueled by guilt, seek absolution through martyrdom. And / Or the privileged, acting "for" the collectivity, seek absolute power through tyranny. *Each route is a flight from identity masquerading as a search for it.* The oppressed never stand a chance.

And this is called politics.

This is also called philosophy. It was the State that offered Socrates the poison cup; it was not Isolde (and it certainly wasn't Socrates's mother Phaenarete, who was a mathematician, or his "shrewish" wife, Xantippe, who was a midwife and healer). It was other men.

Nietzsche, who called George Eliot "a mere bluestocking" and George Sand "a prolific writing cow," who wrote, "Women are considered deep—why? because one can never discover any bottom to them. Women are not even shallow," also gave us such jewels as "Only excess of strength is proof of strength; strength is restored through wounding." He derided the spiritualization of love and called for the "spiritualization of enmity." But he was at his virulent best on freedom:

The value of a thing . . . lies in what it *costs* us. . . . *War is a training in freedom*. . . . For what is freedom? . . . That one is ready to
sacrifice men to one's cause, oneself not excepted. . . . Freedom
means that the manly instincts that delight in war and victory have
gained mastery over the other instincts, for example, the instinct
for "happiness." . . . The man who has become free spurns the
contemptible well-being dreamed of by shopkeepers, . . . cows,
women, Englishmen, and other democrats. The free man is a *warrior*."[30]

It makes you want to re-evaluate Englishmen. It also makes
you understand why his philosophy was so readily adopted by
the Third Reich, despite Nietzschean apologists who still claim
that it wasn't his fault and that the poor guy gets a bad press.

Granted, Nietzsche is an easy mark. But *androlatry* (fearful
worship of the manly, triumphant father) and *necrophilia* (death-
loving worship of the manly, doomed son) divide all masculinist philosophy between them. The more contemporary the philosopher, the more discernible their dual influence. The marquis
de Sade could be said to be the true father of modern philosophy, in that his writings (and practice) promulgated the pornographic political, intellectual, and aesthetic exercise of the
love-death. Sade is the ghostly ancestor of such revered existentialist moderns as Sartre, Gide, Genet, and Bataille—all of whom
are preoccupied with the futility of tenderness, and for all of
whom, as Deborah Cameron and Elizabeth Frazer note about
sex murderers, "the erotic is transgressive and transgression is
erotic."[31]

If transgression is erotic, then violation can be revolutionary. Possession equals Rape equals Ravishment. Noncon-
sciousness equals Obliteration equals Ecstasy. If death makes
one more intensely alive, then terror is a prerequisite for living.

The word "philosophy" comes from the root *philos,* one of
the Greek words meaning "love." Love of thought? Perhaps
we should rename this discipline "phobosophy."

Unlike Nietzsche or Sade, Albert Camus is not an easy mark.

As philosopher and novelist/playwright, he produced a rich body of work, all of it thematically yearning toward freedom.* In *The Just Assassins* and *The Rebel,* he recognized the terrorist who must risk or seek death as a means of salvation. In *The Myth of Sisyphus,* he named "the total gift and forgetfulness of self" as one of the forms of suicide.[32] He could see that his hero rebel was in thrall to the love-death, but he still didn't see that such a rebel would not limit himself to suicide, but would bring down with him the innocent—who might prefer a conscious self, a love-*life.* In *The Rebel,* he described that hero:

> The rebel is a man *[sic]* who is on the point of accepting or rejecting the sacred. . . . every question, every word, is an act of rebellion while in the sacred world every word is an act of grace. . . . *only two possible worlds can exist for the human mind:* the sacred (or, to speak in Christian terms, the world of grace) and the world of rebellion. The disappearance of one is equivalent to the appearance of the other. . . . *There again we rediscover the All or Nothing.*[33] (Italics mine.)

Why must we always rediscover the all or nothing? *Why* can only two possible worlds exist for the (male) human mind? *Why* can't an act of rebellion and an act of grace be the same? Not possible? Then tell me into which of those two categories the following images fit:

A woman is saying No.

Two people in their mid-seventies are making love.

---

* An active member of the French resistance during World War II, Camus bewildered French radicals and intellectuals by his refusal to join with Sartre, de Beauvoir, Malraux, and others in condemnation of French actions in Algeria. His apologists have claimed that his personal conflict over having been born and raised in Algeria as a *colon* was actually secondary to his growing repugnance for all forms of violence; they argue that by the 1950s this repugnance had so saturated his work that everything he wrote became an implicit denunciation of France, but he felt that to be more explicit was to encourage Algerian insurgent violence on the other side. This is a questionable defense. See Georges J. Joyaux, "Albert Camus and North Africa," *Yale French Studies* (special issue on Camus), Spring 1960, pp. 10–19.

A grown woman is learning to read.

A man is packing to go to prison rather than go into the army.

A child is asking, "Why *can't* I vote?"

A pair of lovers are lying at peace in one another's arms, limbs entwined, souls entwined; they are of the same sex.

A woman is realizing that she doesn't wish to bear a child she cannot love or care for; she picks up the telephone and dials the abortion clinic.

A nun is celebrating mass.

A woman is sending coded messages: she stitches them into a Chilean *arpillera,* she embroiders them onto a Palestinian headcloth, she metaphorizes them into a poem.

Acts of rebellion, acts of grace—or both at once?

The creation of art is always a simultaneous act of rebellion and of grace, as Camus should have known. But the politics of Thanatos cramped his thinking:

> Modern conquerors can kill, but do not seem able to create. Artists know how to create but cannot really kill. Murderers are only very exceptionally found among artists. In the long run, therefore, art in our revolutionary societies must die. But then the revolution will have lived its allotted span. Each time that the revolution kills in a man *[sic]* the artist that he might have been, it attenuates itself a little more.[34]

Think, then, what *every* so-called revolution has done, killing in men the artists of living they might have been, killing in women the artists of living they were, *killing the art of living.* No wonder each man-made revolution exhausts its allotted span in the instant it comes to power.

The killing of art can take many forms: direct and indirect censorship, isolation of the artist into irrelevance, trivialization, proscription of subject matter, commercialization, and— one of the most effective means—manipulation of art into a mode of propaganda. When this is done swiftly and blatantly, it's absurd enough to be recognizable. But when it is done steadily for eons, it becomes virtually inseparable from what we know as art, and is not so easily identifiable. The artist holds up a mirror to society; that's one of her functions. But the Demon Lover's soulless reflection by now is invisibly omnipresent. Aesthetically, violence has been so braided with our ideas about romantic passion and sexual power that terror has come to represent not only religious salvation and intellectual exploration but beauty itself.

L'Homme Fatal

Ravishment. As rape, as possession, as a ticket out of the state of consciousness, as an obliteration of the self—the theme of ravishment saturates phallocentric world art, literature, culture. It is the Demon Lover who stalks in beauty, like our nightmares.

We could pursue him through galleries and museums, or through the lives and leitmotifs of male composers, or across the stages and screens of performance. But literature's page— or even a fragment of it—will be sufficient to demonstrate the whole, just as one shard of a holographic plate is sufficient for reconstruction of the entire hologram.

Maybe because, like most women and some men, I like making lovely things as well as making things lovely, I've sometimes been mystified about the forms in which beauty is cast when we consider it "great art." Tragic beauty, virtually all of it. But comedy, now trivialized to humor or wit, was once considered the most sublime of all aesthetic modes. Ancient festivals of theater closed with the comedy *after* the tragedy, not to dismiss the audience with a saccharine happy ending but to leave impressed upon them the most difficult task of human consciousness: to celebrate simultaneously what one dares to understand and what one cannot comprehend. Yet today "comedic beauty" is a kind of oxymoron. What is considered most beautiful is (again) the doomed or damned, the rare and therefore precious (as opposed to the commonplace and therefore precious). What is beautiful must be transient, something to be valued because it is already lost or will be. Aesthetics is in a continual state of perceptive mourning, instead of a daily celebration of all we could see, know, love, *before* it's too late.

We've come to believe that if an image or subject is humble, humorous, or simple, it must be superficial; if it's stately, tragic, or perverse, it must be profound. An analogy begs attention here: just as women's art for millennia has been considered "craft" (because the quilt, the pottery bowl, the basket also have a daily *function*, to warm, to feed, to carry), so "fine art" is defined as something magnificently unuseful, thereby "pure," thereby a practice largely limited to men.

Like most women, I like to be useful. But I'm neither an academic nor a formal aesthetician. I'm a woman whose tools of art are the ordinary ones of our daily living—the same ones used in grocery lists and newspaper headlines, on street signs and cereal boxes, in children' songs, old people's stories, and the mutterings of the mad, in recipes and love letters: words. Perhaps the artist whose tools are less commonplace—the painter, sculptor, composer—finds herself more differentiated from others because her tools are more specialized. Certainly this would seem true of the performing artist, whose tool is her own body. But there it is—as a writer one must deal in words, which means attempting to rediscover and freshen their power, which in turn means noticing the manner in which they have been rendered stale and powerless, which in turn means noticing how that was accomplished and by whom.

All this, of course, is political. Since the living tools of language are shared with people all around one, from the homeless shopping-bag lady talking to herself on the street corner to the politician delivering his press-conference statement to millions, the mutual use of those tools demands an ongoing involvement with the human condition.

So (with a full awareness that men say women always talk

too much, and with an even fuller awareness that two-thirds of the world's illiterates are women who are kept from learning how to read) I'll focus our discussion of aesthetics on literature.

Here, too, the fatality of the female is a refrain—in primitive legends about *vagina dentata,* or through the sophistication of Aeschylus, or in the genius of Elizabethan dramatists like Marlowe and Webster. (For the Elizabethans, orgasm and death were equated in word play, with "to die" used as a synonym of "to come.") Woman is "La Belle Dame sans Merci," she is the Arabic houri, the Hebraic dybbuk. The historical Cleopatra and Lucrezia Borgia are reworked to fit this image. "Venus, who was the world's delight, now fallen, in Christian times, to the level of a sinister vampire," Mario Praz (mourning perceptively) notes.[35] *La femme fatale* is such a cross-cultural archetype that she has become a secular stereotype, to be used against real women in our painstaking and unheroic quest for our own humanity.

A far more dangerous archetype—because it's *un*acknowledged as translated into secular reality—is *l'homme fatal.* Yet he was there from the beginning of patriarchy. The same shift that brought us the terror of the Medusa reduced Dionysus from a figure of celebratory ecstasy to one of violent ecstasy, coarsened the early, cheerful, playful Pan into a rapist who bequeathed us the word "panic." *L'homme fatal* was the sly trickster turned malevolent (Loki in Germanic legend, Lugh in Celtic myth, hundreds of variants in the legends of Native Americans, Polynesians, and other indigenous peoples—the roguish Lord of Misrule becoming the humorless Prince of Darkness). By the late eighteenth or early nineteenth century, he *is* the vampire, the Demon Lover. By now, he symbolizes an immortal passion for what he defines as freedom, a passion so fierce it can be consummated only in the grave. As Praz puts it:

In the second half of the nineteenth century, the vampire [again] becomes a woman, as in Goethe's ballad; but in the first part of the century, the fatal, cruel lover is invariably a man; and, apart from reasons of tradition or race (the stronger sex [sic] remained such not only in name, until the time of the Decadence, when . . . the roles appeared to be reversed), there is no doubt that the sinister charm of the Byronic hero was an influence. . . .[36]

Praz shadows the Demon Lover through Goethe, Schiller, Flaubert, Shelley, Keats, Byron, Swinburne, and of course Baudelaire and Verlaine. He unearths the roots of "the Beauty of the Horrid" in such authors as Tasso, Marlowe, and Novalis. He also observes that female gothic novelists—Mary Shelley, for example—"fell under the influence of the masculine point of view."[37] A seemingly sympathetic statement, until we consider that Mary Shelley, and certainly Emily and Charlotte Brontë, actually wrote their way *through* the Demon Lover archetype. Each in her way acknowledged its attraction but *named* it as a monstrosity of male creation, an artificial erotic form *(Frankenstein),* or a savagely destructive force unless matured over generations by time and love *(Wuthering Heights),* or a plainly tyrannical personification that must be fled until human pain and inner sight can temper it *(Jane Eyre).*

To rescue erotic passion from thanatotic passion—and to claim the former while rejecting the latter—is not an easy task when one's culture shrugs that, as Oscar Wilde put it, "each man kills the thing he loves." Besides, history is a story of violence—public, legitimized violence (men's relationships with other men) and private, eroticized violence (men's relationships with women). Most of the ancient epics (*Gilgamesh*, the *Mahabharata*, etc.) already referred to in these pages are war stories. Certainly the *Iliad* is—and so is the Bible. In *Women and War,* Jean Bethke Elshtain devotes some analysis to the phenomenon that "novels numbered among the world's greatest—for example, Tolstoy's *War and Peace*—give presence, even nobility, to the genre." She notes that "men have long been the great war-story tellers. . . . The stories of women resistance fighters and soldiers have sometimes been told but have not attained the *literary* status of the great war novels by men—Stephen Crane, Erich Maria Remarque, A. P. Herbert, Ernest Hemingway, Norman Mailer, James Jones, Joseph Heller. . . ."[38] And Rudyard Kipling. And Siegfried Sassoon. And Robert Graves. And William Styron. And Thomas Pynchon. And Kurt Vonnegut. The list is depressingly impressive.

Although there is some notable war writing by women (Edith Wharton, Gertrude Stein, Willa Cather, Simone de Beauvoir, Marguerite Duras), Elshtain confirms that women not only have been less published on the subject but in fact have addressed themselves to it less (and differently) than men. Paul Fussell, author of *The Great War and Modern Memory*, wonders why: "[Women are] next to the permanently wounded, the main victims in war, their dead men having been removed beyond suffering. Yet the elegies are written by men, the poems registering a love of soldiers are written by men, and it is not women who seem to be the custodians of antiwar irony. This seems odd, and it awaits interpretation."[39]

Does it seem so odd? Is the male homoeroticism expressed most acceptably through violence really so mysterious? As for women, is it just possible that we don't get off erotically on war the way men do, that we actually might not like the subject? Let Gertrude Stein, in *Wars I Have Seen,* help Fussell out with the antiwar irony he awaits:

> It is true but of course women cannot suffer from it [war] the way men do, men after all are soldiers, and women are not, and love France as much as we do and we love France as much as the men do, but after all we are not soldiers and so we cannot feel a defeat the way they do, and besides in a defeat after a defeat women have more to do than men have they have more to occupy them that is natural enough in a defeat, and so they have less time to suffer.[40]

Quite a few of us have noticed that just as men, in the words of the Christian prayer, "are in death even in life," so men as a class are at war even when they are at peace. In her now-classic work *Sexual Politics*,[41] Kate Millett chose three literary heroes—D. H. Lawrence, Henry Miller, and Norman Mailer—as expressive of what I'm terming the thanatotic sensibility. One could analyze the major Japanese novelist Yukio Mishima in the same way, but Mailer, who has grown ever more feeble-mindedly male supremacist over the years, has saved us the trouble by providing worshipful writings about Mishima's obsession with manhood, militarism, and death, his contribution to the Mishima cult of necrophiliac androlatry that has sprung up since the latter's suicide. Still, we needn't rebreak our hearts and intellects by dwelling overlong on authors who have idolized violence. Even to list them would be an imitation of the phallic tactic of overkill, since it could be said that violence is *the* subject of patriarchal literature.

Terrorism per se has a smaller, more elite literary following, but of late the genre is growing. At least in this case the writers see certain patterns more clearly than the "experts" do.

Dostoevsky returned to the subject repeatedly. In *The Possessed, The Brothers Karamazov, Crime and Punishment,* and *Notes From the Underground,* he agonized over his perception of the central either/or: salvation through God (the father) or salvation through social action (the rebel son).

Joseph Conrad explored terrorism in a number of novels, particularly *Under Western Eyes* and *The Secret Agent.* In the latter, a character driven mad by the lack of concern of a depoliticized general populace wanders through the novel with explosives hidden in his shirtfront, eternally in search of the perfect detonator. His eagerness to kill himself *is* his means of identification; nothing can satisfy his identity but destruction. Conrad captures a quality of insatiability, the quest for a truly outrageous act requiring ever more spectacular devastation in order to be noticed—and most of all, in order to reach a satisfaction virtually orgasmic. It brings to mind Wagner's celebrated "Liebestod," that musical line straining onward and onward, unappeased and unappeasable. In a lateral leap of connecting, it also brings to mind Mick Jagger's frantic "I Can't

Get No Satisfaction," which was so popular in the 1970s (before we realized that women's so-called penis envy was probably a projection of men's envy of our capacity for multiple or serial orgasms).

Here is Mr. Vladimir, a character in *The Secret Agent,* trying to fix on a target that *would* be satisfying:

> A bomb in the National Gallery would make some noise. But it would not be serious enough. . . . But what is one to say to an act of destructive ferocity so absurd as to be incomprehensible, inexplicable, almost unthinkable, in fact mad? Madness alone is truly terrifying, inasmuch as you cannot placate it either by threats, persuasion, or bribes. . . . The attack must have all the shocking senselessness of gratuitous blasphemy.[42]

Here is real-life Hans-Joachim Klein, a German terrorist who was involved in the 1975 Vienna kidnapping of OPEC ministers, as interviewed in *Der Spiegel* in 1978:

> We asked ourselves . . . what would be an action that no one can disregard. . . . We looked for a focal point where everything would come together:* the Germans still wrestling with their past; the newly arising Palestinian problem; a starting gun for an urban guerrilla fight. Such an action could not be disregarded by anyone, from liberals to old Nazis. . . . We found it: a bomb exploding in the Jewish community house—on the very anniversary of Kristallnacht ["crystal night," in November 1938, when the Nazis conducted simultaneous anti-Jewish raids throughout Germany]. . . . Even though the bomb did not explode, this story went halfway around the world.[43]

Notice (as Conrad did) that the *political content is secondary or even irrelevant* to the hunger for a sufficiently outrageous, ferocious, *senseless* act. This goes beyond the perverse reverse

---

* Interestingly, the focal points of terrorist attacks are virtually never sports stadiums, massage parlors, men's clubs, or comparable places where sizable segments of the male population congregate.

of confusing freedom with violence. The excuse of freedom is no longer even used. This is "the pure act" itself—madness.

Henry James took terrorism for his subject in *The Princess Casamassima*. Possibly because of his good fortune in having Alice James as a sister, James was unusually sympathetic to female sensibility; his woman characters are almost always more developed and more memorable than his male characters. (Some male critics have faulted him for this.) In *Princess,* his idealistic male revolutionary, Hyacinth Robinson, is torn between a world of revolutionary violence to which he has already pledged himself, and a world of beauty and refinement to which the Princess introduces him. James engages all the issues of class oppression, but also, remarkably enough, of a male "world" versus a female "world." Robinson cannot fully make his peace with either: he kills himself.

Despite a self-described lifelong fascination with the cult of the hero, André Malraux also glimpsed an alternative politics, a politics of Eros, through his female characters in *La condition humaine* (a fine novel translated into English, irritatingly, as *Man's Fate*). But the glimpse was fleeting, and he let it pass. "It's not so hard to die when you're not dying alone," whispers one of his revolutionary terrorists, revealing the importance of taking others with you into the love-death. Another character "had strength left only for the pain that he could inflict . . . upon this woman: to abandon her by dying." Still another exults, "It was necessary that terrorism become a mystic cult," and then blows up his bomb—and himself.[44]

The late Julio Cortazar was one of the contemporary Latin American writers who attempted to reconcile terrorism, revolution, culture, and (male-defined) sexual liberation. He justified corruption as inevitable in the transition to the new world where a new man (yes, *sic*) can be reborn. In *Libro de Manuel* he writes of his kidnapper-hero, "One had to love in paroxysm the image of liberation . . . in spite of the inevitable worst options; the revolutionary's hands had to be stained by bile and excrement, like a surgeon's—in order to extract the tumor and give new life to the young man."[45] The young man is the State in need of paroxysmic curing. *L'état, c'est moi.* Again murdered and born again.

Graham Greene worked for years in the British Secret Service, as did John le Carré. Both have used terror and counterterror as subjects in their fiction. Greene is invariably and exquisitely poised between the cynic in himself, the love-death seeker, and another self who seeks a not always illusory grace. That tension alone makes his work unusual and appealing. Le Carré settles for a simpler tension, between the *habit* of death as a way of life and the surprise of encountering a desire to live otherwise.

In the past two decades, woman novelists have taken up their pens to write about this sword—and with a discernibly different approach. It is neither possible nor necessary to summarize their various plots here, but it is possible to note a similarity in their tone and thematic treatment of this subject. Despite a tendency to glamorize the lives of fugitives (in *Vida*) and romanticize the struggles of a youthful revolutionary underground movement (in *Dance the Eagle to Sleep*), Marge Piercy names and wrestles with the attraction the Demon Lover holds for her characters, male and female alike. Doris Lessing, in *The Good Terrorist,* engages in a more simplistic class analysis—her indulged young seekers after excitement find themselves in deeper than they planned. But Lessing, too, peels away the façade of love-death euphoria; her male terrorists are cynical, admittedly self-destructive types or posturing egotists; her female terrorists are variously made uneasy by the sloppy irresponsibility with which the group's actions are planned and executed, and by the results even when successful. Meanwhile, too, the women on both Piercy's and Lessing's pages try to continue life-as-usual. They clean up the squatters' slums in which the communes are located, they plant gardens and scrounge for cash and buy groceries and cook nourishing cheap meals and deal with police and bureaucrats *and* case targets *and* wire detonators *and* comfort their men. Meanwhile, the men swagger, argue political theory, and jockey over tactical and sexual advantages.

Interestingly, most of these fiction writers reveal what remains a mystery to terrorism experts. The sexuality of terror and of terrorism is crucial to the work of Piercy and Lessing, but also informs that of James, Malraux, Greene, and le Carré. All of these writers have depicted the sexual component as central to terror, as being what fatally attracts men to such action, what attracts other men *to* the men already committed to such action, and what attracts women to those men. The male writers (except Greene) see the pattern but don't particularly question it. For them, the fatal attraction, the sensualization of cruelty and death, has by now edged out most other expressions of sexual intensity between human beings. Antonin Artaud's "theater of cruelty" has become our daily entertainment, our daily reality.*
For the male writers, it's normal that men connive, murder, and get themselves killed as a bizarre form of fun, while women (either by joining them or by refusing to do so) in vain try to stop them. The male writers may deplore this situation, but they see it as chronic and epidemic in society, and most likely unchangeable. The woman writers may not (yet) be imagining alternative approaches, but they at least spy a qualitatively different rebellion, however small, in their woman characters. Furthermore, they differentiate between genuine defense and a violence gratuitous (and omnivorous) *because* it's felt as the thrill of sexual identity.

And so we return to identity.

In *Pornography: Men Possessing Women*, Andrea Dworkin writes, "The first tenet of male-supremacist ideology is that men have this self and women must, by definition, lack it. Male self . . . is entitled to take what it wants to sustain or improve

---

* Nehemia Friedland and Jeffrey Z. Rubin see terrorism as deliberately staged Artaudian political protest in a social setting jaded by the democratic political contribution: "Political terrorism is not likely to disappear from the stage. But viewing it as theater may help prevent mindless tragedies." ("Theater of Terror," *Psychology Today*, March 1986, p. 21.)

itself, to have anything, to requite any need at any cost. . . .
The self is the conviction, beyond reason or scrutiny, that there
is an equation between what one wants and the fact that one
is."[46]

Paul Wilkinson, in *Political Terrorism,* suggests that for some
terrorists "extreme violence is primarily undertaken as an act
of self-assertion and self-expression."[47] Jillian Becker goes a
step further; she comments on Wilkinson's theory, "This is certainly true of the terrorists I have studied, and I think it may
be true of all terrorists. The romantic tradition, with its stress
on . . . indulging passions . . . , and what Paul Wilkinson calls
the aestheticization of politics, so that politics is seen as a kind
of art form (which is the way Dr. Goebbels liked to think of it)
. . . is still alive and working in the terrorists."[48]

What Dworkin sees—and what neither Wilkinson nor Becker
notices (though Becker at least extends the analysis)—is the
importance of *who is doing the defining* of the self, and I would
add, of who is doing the defining of a romantic motive. The
culprit is not romantic love but a thanatotic interpretation of
romantic love. The issue is not the aestheticization of politics
but the masculinization of politics *and* of aesthetics. Passion—
and even the indulging of it—is not to blame, but rather the
depraved idea that *passion demands a victim,* a perfectly Sad-
eian idea blessed by men's religion, rationalized by men's philosophy, beautified by men's art, and practiced by men's politics.

Yet passion originally was about an intensity in *loving:* love
for another person (*that* would be a romantic rebirth), love for
the act of creating (*that* would be an aesthetic resurgence), love
for the play of ideas (*that* would be a philosophical renaissance), love for all life on this planet and for the biosphere itself
(*that* would be a political renewal), love for both the imaginable and unimaginable splendor of the universe (*that* would be
a spiritual resurrection).

Why must passion demand a victim?

In their superb work *The Lust to Kill: A Feminist Investigation of Sexual Murder,* Deborah Cameron and Elizabeth
Frazer write:

In love, the Self tries to escape from itself, and into the Other; but because the Other necessarily excludes the Self by virtue of its Otherness, love can easily turn to loathing and desire to destruction. In these coincidences of transgression and eroticism, sex and death, love and hate—and finally, therefore, freedom and death—we can see the possibilities for an existentialist account of sex murderers as the ultimate rebels, the ultimate actors-out of eroticism in its purest form.[49]

Cameron and Frazer point out two flaws in such an account. First, the transformation of love into hatred is a boringly conventional rebellion. (Not coincidentally, feminists have exposed the "sexual revolution" and "erotic liberation" that pornographers claim to promote as the most conventional kind of collaboration and conformity with the status quo. Just as tyranny and terrorism require each other, so do sexual repression and pornography. There's nothing revolutionary—or even new— about any of it. Or as Conrad phrased it in *The Secret Agent,* "The terrorist and the policeman both come from the same basket. Revolution, legality—counter moves in the same game.")[50] The second flaw is that this mode of "freedom" depends on someone else's servitude or even death. This is the situation feminists address in the phrase "There are no personal exceptions." Freedom can't exist in exclusivity or in a vacuum, in the face of someone else's suffering, and certainly not at the cost of that suffering.

Cameron and Frazer's analysis gives us a clue to why so many men are caught up in the search for a more and more "Exotic Other," and why this search is played out in various forms of racism, sexism, and child abuse. The Exotic Other is a staple in the international sexual slave traffic. Blue-eyed, blonde young women "disappear," via the so-called Minneapolis-pipeline prostitution routes, for export to African and Arab brothels, while African and Asian women are in high demand at the "Eros Centers" of West Germany and the Netherlands. One thing is certain: whatever cruelties men visit upon one another they have first tested and refined on women.

But the Other still "necessarily excludes the Self by virtue of its Otherness." Which means that the desperate attempt to escape from the self continues. All around us, the modern Demon Lover moves smoothly, with adaptable sophistication. Seduced by him, some of us try to escape through "mortifying the flesh"—denying it, repressing sexuality (the rules of the father). Others seek disintegration of the self in excessive alcohol or drugs (the revolt of the son). The father's pompous order is out of control and the son's rebellion is a conformity, but each does offer obliteration. Why should obliteration be pleasurable?

How can it not be pleasurable if there's no self to begin with?

If you were the Demon Lover and you gazed back along your trail, where not flowers but carnage sprang from each footprint, where the last messages of all your dead were daubed in frozen blood as signposts that you had passed that way, where your exhalations hung in the air befouling it with terror—would you not feel repulsion? Would you not long to forget, would you not wish at any cost not to remember, not to see any more?

Each of us does this every day. We call it survival. Sometimes we blaspheme language, and call it love. We drink it down to the dregs of the cup.

If for one instant we sense another way—beyond indifference or even indignation—he is prepared. This male assertion of self to disguise a lack of it is, as Dworkin writes, "indifferent to denial or challenge. . . . This self is not merely subjectively felt. It is protected by laws and customs, . . . documented in history, upheld in the distribution of wealth. . . . When the subjective sense of self falters, institutions devoted to its maintenance buoy it up."[51] So, should we contact in ourselves a different reality—*an energy responsible to joy*—he is ready.

He knew we would one day unmask him of his myths, religions, philosophies, pseudo-aesthetics. They always were to him useful but ultimately effete exercises. He must show himself more openly now? No more elegant, seductive games? Then so be it. He has constructed against this day an edifice he calculates to be invulnerable. It is from here he will defend himself, with a system so overwhelming as to be his terminal destination and, he intends, ours.

He calls it the State.

CHAPTER 4

⌐⌐⌐⌐⌐⌐⌐⌐⌐

OFFICIAL TERRORISM: THE STATE OF MAN

Great men, great nations, have not been boasters and buffoons, but perceivers of the terror of life, and have manned themselves to face it. / RALPH WALDO EMERSON

Terror . . . is a consequence of the general principle of democracy applied to the most urgent needs of the fatherland." / ROBESPIERRE

Every state is based on violence. / LEON TROTSKY

There is no way to begin it.

I sit in a small room on a quiet street in North America, in the middle of the night. My lamps blaze defiantly against the darkness outside, but to do that they must illumine the piles of evidence that surround me, stacks of paper collected and saved to prove—what? Reality?

This months's bulletin from Amnesty International cites torture in China, Kampuchea, Fiji, Brazil, Surinam, Burundi, Taiwan, the USSR, Somalia, Turkey, Vietnam, Libya, Ethiopia, Italy, Paraguay, Venezuela, Sri Lanka, Mexico, Chad.

The latest alert from UNICEF (the United Nations Children's Fund) finds world hunger still growing, and still having the most devastating effect on women and children. In 1985 and 1986 more children died of starvation in India and Pakistan than in all the forty-six nations of Africa together. In 1986 more children died in Bangladesh than in Ethiopia, more in Mexico than in the Sudan, more in Indonesia than in all eight drought-stricken countries of the Sahel.[1] Today's newcast reports a 100 percent crop failure in Ethiopia. Meanwhile, FAO (the Food and Agriculture Organization) notes that hunger is increasing even though food has never before been as abundant or cheap as it is today; in parts of the developing world, food production is continuing to grow faster than the population. But, FAO points out, countries like India and Indonesia now *export* vast amounts of food, even through increasing numbers of their own people cannot afford to eat. "Polarization in the global food system is continuing," says FAO Director General Edouard Saouma.[2]

I think of the obsession with scarcity, of a love-death sensibility killing the thing it loves and valuing the thing it loses, and find myself recalling a sentence of Herbert Marcuse's: "But the closer the real possibility of liberating the individual from the constraints once justified by scarcity and immaturity, the greater the need for maintaining and streamlining these constraints lest the established order of domination dissolve."[3]

I stare at the absurd piles of paper. If saving lives were as easy as saving paper . . .

A recent issue of *ANC News Briefing,* the newsletter of the African National Congress, calmly describes escalations of violence in South Africa—detentions, seizures, tortures, assassinations, trials, cripplings, evictions, riots, beatings, killings; *They Will Never Kill Us All* is lettered on a sign carried by a young black African woman pictured on its cover.

The current bulletin of the Palestine Human Rights Campaign calmly lists escalations in the Occupied Territories—detentions, seizures, evictions, trials, beatings, riots, killings . . .

Small slips of paper pinned to the wall shudder as a night

breeze from the window stirs them. Each has a name scribbled on it, to remind me: Idi Amin. General Pinochet. Shah Pahlevi. Duvalier. Jaruzelski. Trujillo. Marcos. Botha. On one is scribbled a quote from Stalin, his remark to a colleague before he personally signed almost forty thousand death warrants in four categories (military, secret police, general, and "wives of the enemies of the people"): "To choose one's victims, to prepare one's plan minutely, to slake an implacable vengeance, and then to go to bed . . . there is nothing sweeter in the world."[4] Another is a clipping from the *New York Times,* coverage of the 1987 French trial of former Nazi officer and torturer Klaus Barbie, the "Butcher of Lyons"; in acknowledging Barbie's employment by the U.S. Counter Intelligence Corps in Germany between 1947 and 1951, CIC officers described him as "honest," "violently anti-Communist," and "one of our best agents in Germany."[5] On still another is a quote from former general Iberico Saint Jean, governor of Buenos Aires Province, Argentina, under the military government: "First we will kill all the subversives; then, their collaborators; later, those who sympathize with them; afterward, those who remain indifferent; and finally, the undecided."[6] Tacked up beside that is a yellowing letter long ago smuggled out from one feminist to another: "How can I tell you. . . . Silently, they drift into the Plaza de Mayo each afternoon. One by one, alone, together, old women, ordinary women, they appear in the face of terror, each one wearing an apron or scarf or headcloth with the names embroidered on it, the names of her children, of her grandchildren, the 'disappeared.' If they're arrested, more come. Silently. There's no stopping them. No one, *no one else* in this whole wounded bleeding country has the courage to make any other protest, *no one*. These women are called 'The Mad Ones.' Who is mad, I ask you, my sister? Who is mad?"

My desk is littered with three-by-five cards. Numbers are jotted on them. Nine million—the witches. Three million—the Armenians. Six million—the Jews. Two million—anti-Nazi partisans. Seven million—the captives on the slave ships. The numbers are approximate. The numbers are competitive, meaningless; they overwhelm and understate. How many perished during the Long March in China? How many during the forced relocation of indigenous peoples in the New World? How many Aborigines in the "settling" of Australia? How many in the Ukrainian and Polish pogroms? How many in the past twenty-four hours in Lebanon?

A temporarily discarded notebook lies open on the floor at my feet, helpless, strangled attempts at a poem scrawled in it. The words snake across the white page with their own logic, their own invented etymology. *Terror. Terrain. Territorial. Terrestrial.*

There is no way to begin it.

Next to the notebook are strewn the file folders, virtually carpeting the room. *Nationalism,* one is labeled. *The State and the Family,* reads another. *The Economics of Terror,* a third. *Language and Euphemism of Terror. Hiroshima. Diplomatic Terror. The Nuclear State. The Environment in Terror. Atrocities (twentieth-century only).* Each file folder is thick, bulging—and incomplete.

There is no folder marked *Women.* Women suffer namelessly, scream soundlessly, and die invisibly through each clipping, each citation, each scrap of evidence. In *The Creation of Patriarchy,* the distinguished historian Gerda Lerner wrote, "It was only after men had learned how to enslave women of groups who could be defined as strangers, that they learned how to enslave men of those groups and, later, subordinates from within their own societies. . . . the enslavement of women, combining both racism and sexism, preceded the formation of classes and class oppression."[7]

There is no way to begin it. But there must be some way to end it.

"If the personality of the terrorist is to be a psychological-psychiatric rather than a legal-political concept, its study should include many statesmen, military personnel, police, businessmen (particularly armament manufacturers), scientists and technicians (particularly weapons designers) as well as skyjackers and urban guerrillas."[8] This was the reasoned approach taken by Risto Fried of the department of psychology, University of Jyväskylä, Finland, for the Berlin Conference on Terrorism. But the personality of the terrorist *is* a legal-political concept—all the more reason that its study should embrace the categories Fried mentions.

It's a cliché that those who win the battle get to write the history of it, which means (as we all nod, yawning) that truth becomes malleable. It means, too, that *the continuum of violence is deliberately ignored.*

Why do we ever trust leaders who were terrorists before the mantle of respectability descended on their shoulders (meaning that having won, they were legitimate): Hitler, Stalin, Mao Tsetung, both Menachem Begin and Anwar Sadat? Why do we not think it passing strange that many of the same torturers whom Shah Pahlevi of Iran employed in his dreaded SAVAK force still ply their trade, re-employed under Khomeini? What atomization of thought has been perpetrated upon us so that we regard the terrorist as someone with a fixed personality and world view while he is committing terrorist acts from a position of relative powerlessness, but then regard those acts as a "phase," now outgrown, once the same man attains power and can wield terror via the formal scepter of the State? Don't we understand that killing changes people in ways from which they can never quite recover?

This is the same atomization of thought that accounts for our shock at the high rate of battery in the homes of Vietnam war veterans, and at such predictable foreign-policy developments as the Iran-Contra scandal. We have been propagandized to *un-see* a world "diplomatic" process central to patriarchal power: the legitimization of terrorism.

"Legitimization" is the key. It's enlightening to connect political legitimization with familial legitimization: a "legitimate" child is one acknowledged by its *male parent;* the child acknowledged "only" by its female parent is still, in the statutes of most nation-states, "illegitimate." The leap from legitimate child to legitimate power is not so far. Legitimacy is an idea conferred and inferred by *men*. (The word "family," by the way, has as its root the Oscan *famel*, "servant" or "slave," a possession. "Father," of course, derives from *pater*, "owner" or "master." Hence, the Latin *pater familias*—"owner of slaves," "family man.")

Nor is legitimacy conferred by the State merely "represented" in the family as legitimacy conferred by the father. We are not talking in similes or metaphors. We are witnessing an actual pyramidal construct of power, using a repertoire of violence from denial to genocide, each stone of which rests upon the other. In discussing his work *The History of Sexuality*, Michel Foucault describes this pyramid: "The family, even now, is not a simple reflection or extension of the power of the State; it does not act as the representative of the State in relation to children, just as the male does not act as its representative with respect to the female. *For the State to function in the way that it does, there must be, between male and female or adult and child, quite specific relations of domination.*"[9] (Italics mine.) In other words, the effect is trickle-*up*, not the reverse. Alice Miller, in her extraordinary book *For Your Own Good*,[10] analyzes in detail Hitler's authoritarian patriarchal upbringing. She does so not in a simplistic psychologically reductive manner, but to expose just how much garden-variety patriarchal brutalizing of spirit and body occurs in average, normal families—and how that affects, supports, and indeed *makes inevitable* the State as we know and suffer from it all over the world today.*

* In this respect, feminists already have had more effect than the October Revolution and the Ten Days That Shook the World. Marxism-Leninism predicts an eventual withering away of the State. But it manages in theory and practice to keep patriarchal power intact by sanctifying "the family" in tones that would make the Reverend Billy Graham beam with recognition and agreement. Women, having noticed for some time that a narrow, male-defined form of "family" is inimical to the interests of both women and children, meanwhile have been quietly redefining "family" in myriad ways. This has created wide-reaching lifestyle changes in the industrialized world and a fresh recognition of traditional female modes of family

Legitimacy in the family rewards progeny who ensure the successful continuation of a paternal bloodline. Legitimization in the State rewards progeny who engage in terrorism successfully conducted, i.e., bestows power on the terrorist who wins. The perpetuation of the family and of the State is the paramount concern, no matter the cost. In the case of the family, the price for the legitimacy of children is marital ownership of the woman who is their mother—which means her obedience, her silence, and her acquiescence to the institution of the family. In the case of the State, the price for the legitimization of the terrorist is the abrogation of democracy itself, both as concept and as process—requiring a comparable obedience, silence, and acquiescence from the populace with regard to the institution of the State. The majority of the population in virtually all nation-states is female, and is forced by patriarchy *to* obey, be silent, and acquiesce—which means that "democracy" does not yet exist anywhere. What happens then, when that majority begins to refuse acquiescence and obedience, begins to speak? What happens when we realize that far from being a threat to the State, *terrorism is the means by which men under patriarchy judge one another fit to succeed?*†

Terrorism reinforces the State. If the terrorists fail, the current State is all the stronger for having put them down. If they succeed, then today's terrorists become tomorrow's statesmen (busily decrying terrorism).

in the developing world—all of which is met with shouts of alarm from the world's Statesmen. In the U.S., the USSR, and the Third World as well, male leaders are expressing alarm at the "destruction of the family." The withering away of the family as a patriarchal institution is a *prerequisite* to the withering away of the State as we know it. As usual, women aren't promising an eventual liberation. Women are doing it—spontaneously and synchronistically—*now*.

† Michel Foucault pinpoints this same process: "Controlled illegality is an agent for the illegality of the dominant groups. The setting up of prostitution networks in the nineteenth century is characteristic in this respect: police checks and checks on the prostitutes' health, their regular stay in prison, . . . the strict hierarchy that was maintained in the prostitution milieu, its control by delinquent informers, all this made it possible to canalize and to recover . . . enormous profits from a sexual pleasure . . . condemned to semi-clandestinity and naturally made expensive."(*Discipline and Punish* [New York: Vintage Books, 1979], p. 279.)

Martha Crenshaw comes close to saying this: "Terrorism appears to have strengthened the old order, underscored the primacy of force in international relations. . . ." She goes on to expose where the real power resides: "The major risk of international conflict perhaps lies less in revolutionary terrorism against the state than in the state use or exploitation of terrorism as an instrument of foreign policy."[11] As the gangster saying goes, "Make 'em an offer they can't refuse." Which leads us to the folder labeled *Diplomatic Terror*.

Coercive Diplomacy

"Coercive diplomacy" is a term Michael Stohl uses in the rather daring anthology he edited with George A. Lopez, *The State as Terrorist: The Dynamics of Governmental Violence and Repression*.[12] Stohl perceives coercive diplomacy as synonymous with overt state terrorism—the U.S. bombing of Cambodia in 1975, for instance, which was conducted not to gain military ground but *to convey a message of force,* and hence was literally a terrorist act.

The bombings of Hiroshima and Nagasaki are even more hideous examples. If the aim was to defeat Japan, why was the bomb not dropped on the emperor's palace or the center of government in Tokyo? Or if the aim was, as sometimes claimed, merely to give warning notice of this mighty new weapon, why was the bomb not dropped offshore, in the Pacific? Because the former would have destroyed the official State and all its machinery of bureaucracy (something not done by brothers-in-arms), and the latter would have instilled insufficient fear. *Terror* was required.

So, at 8:15 in the morning on August 6, 1945, a U.S. B-29 bomber unloaded its cargo with the explosive force of twenty thousand tons of TNT. The central city of Hiroshima vanished outright, incinerated within seconds. The immediate toll of charred bodies was incalculable. But we do know that within three months, 130,000 people had died. Over forty years later, almost 400,000 persons are still suffering and dying from the effects. The *hibakusha* (atomic-bomb victims) are mostly female. They have endured a high incidence of miscarriage and off-spring with birth defects, and they and their children suffer from myriad conditions resulting from radiation: leukemia and other cancers, decalcification, retardation, tumor growth, cat-aracts, etc.; they die early and painful deaths. Women have also been the primary caretakers of the sick and dying. Disfig-ured *hibakusha* women with ulcerated faces were abandoned by their husbands in the thousands, and are frequently still ostracized; their unemployment rate is triple the national aver-age. All this was, you understand, in the cause of peace. Despite U.S. Secretary of War Stimson's observation, before the atomic bomb's first test at Alamogordo, that it should be considered not "as a new weapon merely but as creating a revolutionary change in the relation of man to the universe," and despite the urgings of certain scientists working on the bomb's design and manufacture that it not be used first on a civilian target (the June 1945 "Report to the Secretary of War"),[13] precisely that was done. The justification was twofold—that the bombing was necessary to traumatize Japanese leadership (terrorism) and to save American and Japanese soldiers' lives which would oth-erwise be sacrificed in a prolonged war. One set of leaders got the message from the other set of leaders. Soldiers were saved. Women and children were expendable. Diplomacy was served. The terror worked.

For terrorism to succeed, amnesia must follow. We must be forced to forget, preferably that the event occurred at all, but at least that it was an act of terrorism. Consequently, the enforced invisibility of the *hibakusha,* and the subsequent min-imizing of the entire catastrophe in U.S. and—even more stag-geringly—in Japanese national consciousness. Within the past decade, the Mushroom Club—comprised of atomic-holocaust victims and generational survivors—and the Japanese Peace Movement, also with a female majority, have protested the diminution and offhanded treatment of the atomic holocaust in history textbooks. The Japanese government desires history to reflect only friendship in United States–Japanese relations. The U.S. government finds that most agreeable. It is all diplomatic courtesy. Besides, in the economics of today's world market, such revisionism is lucrative. The Mushroom Club women argue that this erasure ill serves the world's memory, and ill serves Japan, which of late has abandoned its postwar pacifist emphasis for a samurai-warrior tone, evidenced primarily in business dealings (see chapter 9) but also in a steady rebuilding of the military (Japan's defense spending is now the world's third-highest, surpassed only by that of the two superpowers). The Japanese women are ignored. When Elie Wiesel, chronicler of the Nazi death camps, visited Japan (at the invitation of the Japan Advertising Council) in May 1987, he was not ignored. Wiesel was a man, and a Nobel Prize winner. Besides, he knew how to play the comparison game of one-upmanship in human suffering. In a stunningly offensive statement which was met with applause, he said, "Auschwitz was meant to be the condemnation of the last Jew to death. Here, obviously, it wasn't meant to kill the last Japanese." That clarified, the official wreath-laying ceremony could proceed.[14]

This, too, is diplomacy.

The USSR has played the same game of coercive foreign-policy messages with "restrained interventions" in East Germany, Hungary, Czechoslovakia, and Afghanistan—force giving notice of further force, always justifying itself as being in the cause of peace. The rules were explained by John Stoessinger in *Henry Kissinger: The Anguish of Power,* where he reported that "Nixon's logic was that he was bombing for peace. . . . Both parts of Vietnam, Nixon reasoned, would be ready to sign with the United States once the shock treatment was over. By this reasoning, much of Hanoi and Haiphong was reduced to rubble."[15]

That superpowers are not the only ones to engage in coercive diplomacy is evident from actions like the Israeli "warning" air raids over Beirut, the India-Pakistan border "incursions," and the Morocco-Libya "skirmishes" in the western Sahara.

But should coercive diplomacy as the overt form of State terror not always be practical, there's the clandestine form. If terrorism's aim is to overthrow established governments by disruption, then most of the CIA's actions fit the bill. Samples would include CIA operations in Iran (1953), Guatemala (1954), Indonesia (1958), the Bay of Pigs, Cuba (1961), and Chile (1970–73). In 1976, the Senate committee on intelligence activities chaired by Frank Church revealed "officially sanctioned efforts" to kill Fidel Castro (unsuccessful) and Congo leader Patrice Lumumba (successful, in 1960).[16] Of late, a number of former "inside men" have decided to kill and tell, so we've been made privy to the out-of-court tales of Edwin P. Wilson, seduced and abandoned by the CIA; soldier-of-fortune Eugene Hasenfus; and former agent Philip Agee, who in *Inside the Company: CIA Diary*[17] describes the wide range of techniques operatives are taught. Investigative journalist Bob Woodward's 1987 book of revelations about the late CIA director William Casey is rancid with such examples.[18]

One of the more circuitous forms of covert official terror is what I would name "ventriloquist terrorism." Le Carré depicts it in fiction, Woodward has documented it in fact—a technique employed regularly by the CIA, the KGB, and the Israeli Mossad, among other secret State forces. This strategy consists of engineering an assault, assassination, or other act of terror in such a way that the other guy appears to have done it: you knock off some of your own (or your allies) and blame this savagery on the Other Side. Since you're already practised at knocking off your own when they're civilian and female, this is no jolt to your conscience. And the perversity of this exchange is that the Other Side, aware of the futility of protesting innocence in such "propaganda by deed" *sometimes proceeds to take credit for what it did not in fact do.*

Then there is what I would term "forward-looking, long-term, State terrorism." Alberto Franceschini, a founder of the Italian Red Brigades who is currently serving a prison sentence until the year 2020, has recently published a book detailing the history of the Red Brigades. He claims that his decision to abandon terrorism as a tactic was caused by disillusion at the way different governments used various terrorist groups as pawns in a larger geopolitical game. Franceschini recalls the visit of a messenger from the Israeli secret service, who offered Red Brigades members a deal: he would reveal to them the names of colleagues who had betrayed them, plus the names of two undercover police agents who were trying to infiltrate the group; in return, the Brigades must swear not to give up armed struggle. The reason? The Israeli government "wanted to keep Italy permanently destabilized so the U.S. would see Israel as its only sure ally in the Mediterranean."[19]

Reader, I am not making this up.

Sometimes covert, clandestine State terrorism *and* "coercive diplomacy" are required, consecutively or in tandem. Both, for instance, have for some time been employed regularly by the United States against Qaddafi's Libya—so much so that Qaddafi's own undeniable fondness for terrorism is pathetically reminiscent of an eager freshmen pledge trying to pass tests and gain admission to the fraternity during a prolonged hazing. After having covertly sold weapons, plastique, and other tools of the terrorist trade to Qaddafi via Wilson and his cabal, the U.S. then tried by clandestine means to assassinate or overthrow him. This effort climaxed with the U.S. bombing raids against Libya in the spring of 1986, carried out in hope of inspiring Qaddafi's domestic opposition to rise against him. "Not incidentally," Richard Falk noted in the *Nation,* "the raids provided an opportunity to test new weapons systems and interventionary tactics, such as long-distance night bombing raids."[20] Ostensibly, the raids were in reprisal for Libya's sponsorship of a discotheque bombing in West Berlin—which was found to have been more likely supported by Syria. With the U.S. unable to prove the Libya–discotheque connection, the official line nonetheless remained that the raid against Libya was—what else—to stop terrorism. However, since it's illegal to assassinate a head of state, Secretary of State George Shultz's pronouncement of intent—widely carried in the press after the bombing—was a miracle of double-talk. He said, "Qaddafi was not a direct target. We knew that that was his residence and that he perhaps might be there and members of his family. We were showing him that we could get people close to him, and this is the price he's going to have to pay for continued terrorism, and that's why members of his family were hurt during this thing." After all, it was only his infant daughter who was killed, and a few peasants and farmers. The wounded don't count. This is not called terrorism.*

Meanwhile, back at home, the FBI operates domestically, using a comparable variety of overt and covert techniques. The Bureau has a history of infiltrating and disrupting groups within the United States, primarily through COINTELPRO, its counter-intelligence program; at times it works fist in glove with organized crime in order to do so—another case of "illegitimate" and "legitimate" force shading into each other along the spectrum of violence.† It was once said that the hilariously tiny and ineffectual Communist party–U.S.A was so infiltrated that its membership consisted of nine FBI agents and the octogenarian labor activist Elizabeth Gurley Flynn. The Bureau established a new unit in the 1970s, SOARS (the Special Operations and Research Staff), "to apply the concept of a multidisciplinary team approach to the study of the terrorist threat and to make

---

* The members of the American public were not so confused as to believe Shultz, but their attitudes reflected the schizophrenia of their government: in a *Newsweek* poll taken one week after the U.S. raid, 71 percent were behind the president "personally," but 39 percent of those polled believed the raid would *increase* terrorist activity, 23 percent thought it would have no effect, and only 31 percent believed it would actually reduce terrorism. The question "Was the U.S. raid itself a terrorist act?" was not asked. (Richard Falk, "Thinking about Terrorism," *Nation*, June 28, 1986, p. 887).

† International organized crime was challenged in 1982 by the formation of an organization of Mafia widows in Sicily and Calabria—birthplaces of the original Mafia—"to oppose the culture of male violence and female submissiveness." This astoundingly courageous act, in the heart of ultra-masculinist territory, went almost unnoticed in the world press.

its services available on both a national and international basis."[21] Also at the national and international junction, President Richard Nixon in 1972 established the Cabinet Committee to Combat Terrorism, chaired by the secretary of state, and consisting of the secretaries of defense, transportation, and the treasury; the attorney general; the directors of the CIA, FBI, and National Security Council; the U.S. mission to the United Nations; and the president's domestic counselor. Concurrently, Nixon created "the working group" of the Cabinet Committee, which by 1977 represented twenty-six departments, agencies, and bureaus.[22]

This appropriation of taxpayers' dollars for the bureaucratization of "national security" activities seems more accurately to be an appropriation of funds for one huge therapeutic encounter-group program on impotence. Richard J. Barnet in his book *Roots of War: The Men and Institutions behind U.S. Foreign Policy,* describes what in the Kennedy-Johnson era was unashamedly termed "the hairy chest syndrome" at the Pentagon, State Department, White House, and CIA:

> Toughness is the most prized virtue. . . . The man who is ready to recommend using violence, . . . even when he is overruled, does not damage his reputation for prudence . . . but the man who recommends putting an issue to the U.N., [or] seeking negotiations . . . quickly becomes known as "soft." . . .
> Bureaucratic *machismo* is cultivated in hundreds of little ways. There is the style of talking to a subordinate—the driving command, masked by superficial informality—or to a superior—fact-loaded, quantitative, gutsy[—] . . .[the development of] machine-gun delivery[,] . . . speed-reading[,] . . . crisp, uncomplicated, usually mechanistic analysis of a problem because in a militarized bureaucracy that is the easiest to sell. . . . The man who agonizes about taking human life is regarded by his colleagues at the very least as "woolly."[23]

This power circle is a virtually *all-male society:* between 1940 and 1967, of the more than four hundred people who have been national-security managers, only one was a woman. Today, twenty years later, the State Department has only five female assistant secretaries (all with "soft" portfolios, such as Consumer Affairs, Communications, Protocol, and Narcotics Matters). Only three women have scrambled up anywhere near the real power circles and then just to the outer rim: Anne Armstrong, Jeane J. Kirkpatrick, and Clare Boothe Luce, now deceased, were, as of October 1986, members of the President's Foreign Intelligence Advisory Board.[24]

George A. Lopez, characterizing techniques common to the State as terrorist, lists four approaches—information control, law enforcement/legal, economic coercion, and outright life threatening (including kidnapping, disappearances, torture, etc.). He argues with unusual acumen that all four are entwined with the dynamic of patriarchy: "The emphasis on masculinity demands the assumption of warrior-hero characteristics: a proclivity for violence, an aura of the fighter, and an explicit rejection of those characteristics associated with the frail and womanly aspects of human beings: sensitivity, pity, emotionality, tenderness toward others, and so on."[25]

He's right—but the truth is even worse. The phallic malady is *epidemic and systemic*. It's too easy to imagine the power concentrated in a series of rooms, with ten or even a hundred high-level would-be-hero bureaucrats raving toward Armageddon for one another's approval. The more frightening reality is that *each individual male in the patriarchy is aware of his relative power in the scheme of things*. A few may be distressed at that power, many may claim innocence of it, most may deny it or pretend to ignore it, and some may blatantly delight in it—but all are aware of it. As a consequence, there's no need to issue specific instructions to the individual torturer in, say, Santiago or Ankara or the Gulag. He knows that his actions are supported by the twin pillars of the State of man—the brotherhood ritual of political exigency and the brotherhood ritual of a sexual thrill in dominance. As a devotee of Thanatos, he is one with the practitioner of sado-masochistic "play" between "consenting adults," as he is one with the rapist. He is one with the "head-hunter" corporate executive, one with the Green Beret, and one with former U.S. Secretary of Defense Robert McNamara yelling at anti–Vietnam War protestors at Harvard, "I was tougher than you are in World War II and I'm tougher than you are now!"[26]

Nowhere does this ejaculatory politics show itself more clearly than in language itself. We're by now familiar with euphemisms, obfuscations, and reversals so pervasive as to make Kafka's portrayal of the rhetoric of the State seem one of charitable minimalism. Phrases like "soft targets" (unarmed civilians), "surgical strikes" (air bombings and strafings), "defensive offense" (initiating attack), "war games," and "battle simulation training games," are so common as to constitute an ongoing *daily* disinformation campaign, so dulling to our ethical neurons that we have lowered resistance to disinformation campaigns of outright factual lies by the time they are announced. We read about research and development for a neutron bomb which will not damage property, will "only" kill people and animals and, because it will be low in fallout, is "perfectly clean." We learn the new acronym NEWOT—for "non-essential workers without transportation" in evacuation plans for a nuclear emergency; NEWOT is in effect a synonym for "women and children." Have we become too atomized to make the connections?

Item: "I'm not in the habit of questioning my superiors, and I have no trouble with that."—Lieutenant Colonel Oliver North, in testimony to the Joint Senate-House Investigative Committee on July 9, 1987.

Item: "I was only obeying orders."—Adolf Eichmann, at his 1961 trial in Israel for crimes against humanity.

Item: "It was necessary to destroy the village in order to pacify it."—widely quoted U.S. soldier in Vietnam, 1968.

Item: "We must level the system in order to save it."—slogan of Baader-Meinhof Group/Red Army Faction, 1970s.

Item: "The morality of altitude" is a term of art used to

describe the callousness which must be trained into bombardier pilots, to develop in them the remoteness necessary if they are to "distance kill" with effectiveness "multiple soft targets," and to overcome what might otherwise be guilt at killing from a position in which one is not threatened oneself (as one would be in ground hand-to-hand combat, for which, by contrast, a "self-defense" morality is fostered).

Item: As discussed in the 1987 Joint Senate-House Committee's investigation of the Iran/Contra affair, the United States provided "humanitarian assistance" to the Nicaraguan Contras in addition to "lethal assistance." The former consisted of boots, fatigues, food rations, tents, and field materiel—as well as Christmas toys for Contra children, medical supplies for the wounded, and shrouds and coffins for the dead. The latter consisted of weapons and ammunition.

Item: During the same investigative hearings, on July 21, 1987, Senator William S. Cohen (Republican, of Maine), addressed Rear Admiral John Poindexter about the semantics used by the Reagan administration:

> Language is as important in politics as it is in literature, because it helps define what our values are. And I must tell you that I find it troubling when you say that "I withheld information from Congress but I did not mislead it." Or that the Administration's support for the contras was secret activity but not covert action. Or that the United States acquiesced in the initial shipment of TOW weapons [to Iran] but did not authorize it. . . . And that we did not trade arms for hostages, even though Mr. Hakim and General Secord arrived at a formula of one and a half hostages for 500 TOWs. . . . And I would respectfully suggest that if the Administration would like to regain the strong support of the American people . . . it has to stop insulting their intelligence.[27]

Previously Admiral Poindexter had defined his managerial style as one good at "compartmentalizing action."

Language as a tool in the State's arsenal is at its most revealing in terms of specifically sexual politics. Feminists have noticed this for some time. Charlotte Perkins Gilman was one, earlier in this century. More recently, Helen Caldicott's book *Missile Envy: The Arms Race and Nuclear War*[28] has contributed a vital analysis of the subject, and Carol Cohn has furthered that analysis in an article titled "Sex and Death in the Rational World of Defense Intellectuals."[29] But the brazen practice continues, and the men who engage in it are unabashed at what they're revealing about themselves.

The July 1987 issue of *Air Force Magazine* (every page of which could frost the brain) carried a typical article, "Missiles and Targets," which pleaded for retention and expanded production of the ICBM, the intercontinental ballistic missile. Peppered with such terms as "kill capability," "thrust ratios," "hardened silos," and "erector launchers," the article approved of the "timely development of deep earth penetrators to put at risk Soviet superhardened targets." We were told about warning-and-response "couplings," and reassured that the focus is on a design optimized for packaging a *"rigid* deep earth penetrator,"* that "even more potent penetration aids are in the works," and that ASMS (the Advanced Strategic Missile Systems program) is providing direct support for the Peacekeeper missile program through PADS (Penetration Aid Deployment Systems). A single "Peacekeeper" MX missile is up to four hundred times more destructive than the bomb that destroyed Hiroshima. The article compared the Minuteman system with the Peacekeeper system, eagerly anticipating the new generation of weaponry, including "the son of Peacekeeper II," and exulting that "Peacekeeper is seventy-one feet long and ninety-two inches in diameter and weighs 195,000 pounds."[30]

Wow.

In the same issue of *Air Force Magazine,* a full-page advertisement* by Rockwell International ("where science gets down

---

* For the activist reader who appreciates knowing which corporations to boycott, the following is a partial list of associate contractors in the Peacekeeper projects: Boeing, General Electric, Honeywell, Lockheed, and Westinghouse. The next time you buy a plane ticket, a refrigerator, or a toaster, try to un-compartmentalize— and enjoy the integrity of doing so.

to business") stated its commitment to the national defense, pledged itself to "defend the European Theatre and other Theatres around the world from an attack—conventional, chemical, and/or nuclear," and listed its contributions to "state-of-the-art hardening techniques . . . through a combination of active and passive system designs." The ad boasted that "Rockwell has been an integral part of the Peacekeeper missile development team . . . [working on] guidance and control, navigation, launch control, nuclear hardness, and survivability." (If you think survivability refers to life forms, you're wrong. It means the survivability of missiles when under attack by other missiles.)

I am not making this up.

The UNICEF publication *Action for Children** was not making it up either when, in 1986, it reported that "there has been a massive arms build-up in the toy industry of the United States. The majority of best-selling toys are weapons or action-figure [military] dolls. . . . War-toy sales jumped from an estimated US $325 million in 1982 to nearly US $1 billion in 1984."[31]

The atomic bomb that obliterated Hiroshima was affectionately named "Little Boy."

A whole new generation has been readied—hardened little boys who will be fanatic about rigid deep-earth penetration. We've met them before, the *patri*ots. The Germans of the Freikorps movement, World War I veterans who were precursors and early members of the burgeoning Nazi party, are one subject of *Male Fantasies,* a book by Klaus Theweleit, a West German writer. In it, Theweleit devotes some study to the images of liquidity and dirt in the fascist imagination. It seems that the

---

* The same issue of *Action for Children* reported on a column of fifteen thousand Iranian boys as young as nine years old marching off to fight against Iraq, chanting, "Plunge on, plunge on, those who step on mines will go to Paradise." The female children? In 1984, sixteen thousand prostitutes were working in the five hundred bars and massage parlors that serve the U.S. military base at Subic Bay, in the Philippines, the majority of them between the ages of twelve and fifteen.

Freikorps literature was obsessed with the idea that communism was a flood or a tide, and had a vision of woman as bifurcated into the Red Woman (whore, communist, engulfing force of dangerous sexual ecstasy) and the White Woman (mother, wife, nurse). The Freikorps members were antagonistic to "all of the hybrid substances that were produced by the body and flowed on, in, over, and out of the body . . . *the warmth that dissolves physical boundaries*"[32] (italics mine).

How great it must be—the terror of dissolving physical boundaries between frail human bodies, between illusory national borders! How treacherous the soft must seem, the liquid, the enveloping, the unstatic uncontrollable *movement* of history, of life processes, of existence itself! Everything must be employed against such treachery. Everything must be used— invented, devised, distorted, reversed, and pressed into service—to shore up the fantasy.

Order. Delineation. Barriers.

Language must be made to lie. Brains must be bleached to forgetfulness. Religion must beatify this hardness, philosophy must ennoble this rigidity, art must elevate this dryness. Laws must condone it, rules must enforce it, economics must make it profitable, education must propagate it. And each cost exacted, each price paid, each act committed, must be for one purpose: *to solidify and perpetuate* (even by ritual overthrow) *the phallocratic state.*

For this purpose, even adversaries in a masculinist world can cooperate.

For this, German Right-wing terrorist groups establish contact with munitions networks in Left-wing Lebanon and Algeria.[33]

For this, Israel trades with South Africa (its largest single customer for armaments as of 1980),[34] and both the United States and China sell weapons to Iran and Iraq for their war against each other.

For this, direct telephone lines are set up to connect the interior ministries and security forces of all European countries, in what commentators are calling "an anti-terrorist Common Market."[35]

For this, the world can afford an annual military expenditure in excess of U.S. $110 for each woman, child, and man on the planet, exceeding world spending on health by 28 percent; world spending on military research and development can equal one-quarter of the entire world expenditure on research and development on every other issue and subject. If you spent U.S. $1 million a day for two thousand years, the total would equal one-half of the U.S. defense budget from 1983 to 1988—while according to the National Advisory Council on Economic Opportunity, the entire poverty population of the U.S. will be composed of women and children by the year 2000. For this, more than 20 percent of the planet's qualified scientists and engineers can be engaged in work for the military; the twentieth century can have endured 207 wars in which 78 million lives were lost; two-thirds of all nation-states (with 97 percent of the world's population) can have been involved in at least one war in this century; 93 new versions of the state can have been created—most of them violently—between 1945 and 1985.[36]

For this.

"Maybe a case could be made for terrorism as a positive contribution to society; at least it should not be overlooked. . . . Who has considered terrorism in society from the perspective or model of a predator-prey relationship?" That is a question coolly put by Dr. F. Gentry Harris, who in the same paper also writes, "Motivationally, elements such as masculinity, depersonalization, intimacy, and magical thinking play a role [in terrorism]."[37] And Antal Deutsch, in "On the Economics of Terrorism," hypothesizes that terrorist acts fostered by one superpower (or its surrogate) against another (or *its* surrogate) are more cost-effective than outright major confrontation between the giant states themselves. Terrorist attacks on or thefts from tactical nuclear warheads of one side, for example (and ensuing counterattacks, to be sure), are more "peaceable." They inflict a loss of face, but are more in the interests of each state than the formidable use of the weapons themselves would be. Deutsch argues that a loss of face is, after all, preferable to nuclear war.[38]

Quite so. But this kind of thinking still ignores the *spectrum of violence*. The face (saved or lost) is connected to the head— and to the body.

Nuclear terrorism lives along a direct line between the State-that-is and the State-that-would-be (in the persons of insurgent terrorist statesmen). In the not-distant past, nuclear power and weaponry were the sole property of the State-that-is. Now they are becoming available to the State-that-would-be. Between the superpowers, the process of stockpiling spiraling amounts of overkill capacity to equal, outdo, and again equal each other is called "nuclear deterrence." The situation is also called, liter-ally, "the Balance of Terror." However, as with coercive diplo-macy, smaller states can play at this game, and the proliferation of nuclear weapons is becoming "democratized." Certain smaller states deny the possession of these arms. Some broadcast it to the hilltops. And some play with it in ventriloquist terrorist fashion. When Mordechai Vanunu leaked news of Israel's secret nuclear arsenal, Israel denied it. He was then kidnapped by the Mossad, brought by force from Rome to Jerusalem, tried for endangering State security, and found guilty (in March 1988) of treason, aggravated espionage, and transferring secret infor-mation useful to the enemy. The Bertrand Russell Peace Foun-dation has nominated him for the 1988 Nobel Peace Prize. Yet his attorney noted that "the main feature of a nuclear arsenal is deterrence" and suggested that the Israeli government might have actually wished Vanunu to talk to the press. After all, the attorney argued, "If someone presented evidence that Israel *didn't* have nuclear weapons, *that* would be a threat to Israel's security."[39]

Thefts of nuclear materials—for reasons of profit, ideology, or coercive diplomacy—are on the rise. The 1980 Rand Cor-poration Report warned of a continuing escalatory trend in these "nuclear incidents."[40] In November 1987, the Pentagon delivered a report to Congress expressing alarm that terrorist opportunities for stealing "civil plutonium" may increase as a result of plutonium's increased commercial use.[41] (It's estimated that by the 1990s, up to three hundred shipments per year of separated plutonium for waste-processing plants will travel by air to nuclear facilities in Europe and Japan in commercial trade deals.) For the Pentagon this material takes on the malevolent characteristics of a radiological hazard only when in the hands of the State-that-would-be as opposed to the State-that-is.

Any mother can tell you that once a toy exists, it will be marketed; once marketed, obtained; once obtained, played with. Five years ago, one of the worst fears of airline pilots was the invention of a plastic handgun that would elude airport metal detectors. This weapon now exists. So the same industry that developed the gun unveils a new X-ray scanner that purportedly can detect it. Nevertheless, the ante gets upped. Forty-two percent of the U.S. stockpile of chemical weapons is housed at Tooele, in the western Utah desert. In 1987, representatives of the USSR were given a guided tour of the installation, as part of tentative reciprocal inspections of chemical munitions on both sides. Both superpowers agree that it is "overly optimistic" to think that a treaty to ban such weapons can be easily reached. Still, the Soviet delegates (in between hearing the Mormon Tabernacle Choir and being treated to banana splits) were shown such weapons as chemical rockets and "GB," the most toxic of all chemical weapons, which causes "nausea, vomiting, cramps, and drowsiness, leading to coma, convulsions, and death." Chemical weapons, one U.S. expert said, do present a special danger because "they're cheap and easy to produce—they can be a poor man's monster weapon."[42] In 1986, the Rand Corporation released the results of a survey of three hundred "terrorism experts" from twenty-five different nation-states. Almost 70 percent of those surveyed said "it was likely that terrorists will ultimately possess chemical or biological weapons." And almost 40 percent said that terrorists may obtain nuclear weapons.[43]

Nuclear properties—whether power plants, weapons, or waste—are likely to bring about the withering away of the State more swiftly than Marx envisioned. Unfortunately, not only the State will perish. This surely is the ultimate toy for a hardened little boy and one that is inevitably a weapon, whether used for "peaceful means" or not. First, the continuum of violence is just that: it refuses neat compartmentalization. Second, nuclear accidents are becoming more common than male masturbatory fantasies of penetration. Third, if we still trust the word "peace" emanating from mouths of either Statesmen-who-are or Statesmen-who-would-be, we are suicidal fools. (Brazil is building underground nuclear installations beneath the Amazon region. In doing so, it is destroying one of the world's greatest rain forests, which alone produces over one-quarter of the planet's oxygen. The nuclear installations are, the Brazilian government swears, only for peaceful means. It just happens that the installations are under the control of the military.)

There must be a way to end it.

There is. The 1980s witnessed many revealing examples of female process in its own form of (soft, flowing, engulfing) confrontation with the State. One—operating along its own circuitous route in a dimension utterly different from the continuum of violence—has substantially affected world nuclear politics.

As early as the 1950s, women in the Pacific Island countries began to experience radiation effects from U.S. test bombings in the Marshall Islands. They coined the term "jellyfish babies" to describe the children being born to them—children without eyes, arms, or legs. They were ignored. They began to mobilize. Lacking funds, power, and communications technology, they had to move slowly. By the 1970s they were involved in a steady stream of small protest actions; in 1974, for instance, the National Island Women's Association in Tahiti demonstrated against the dumping of radioactive waste in the Pacific; women blocked roads used to transport the waste materials. By the mid-1970s, scientists were finally confirming what the women had been saying for two decades—that there was a causal relation between nuclear testing (primarily, at that time, by the French), and the incidence of stillbirths and abnormal births, miscarriages, female cancers, and radiation sickness.[44] (Incidentally, the French assign female names to the craters they have created by their tests of "deep earth penetrators" on Mururoa Atoll.) The Nuclear-Free Pacific movement dates its inception (among the approximately twenty thousand Pacific Islands) to that time—when men became involved. By the early 1980s, the movement was visible, vocal, and perceived as threatening to the nuclear State in its various national guises and geographical locations around the globe. In June 1984, the National-party government of New Zealand fell—over the issue of whether to permit nuclear-powered or -armed vessels into that country's harbors. A snap election had to be called, and the opposition Labour party was swept into power—on a nuclear-free platform. The United States responded to its ally first with threats and eventually with dissolution of the ANZUS (Australia–New Zealand–U.S.) treaty. (In the May 1985 issue of *Air Force Magazine,* retired U.S. Air Force general T. R. Milton expressed outrage that the United States was being "spurned" by "New Zealand's nuclear virginity."[45]) But New Zealand's mouse-that-roared approach was spreading, as other small countries began to express open reluctance or refusal to host superpower bases, nuclear installations, or nuclear dockings.

Now, much of the above is familiar to anyone regularly in touch with a newspaper or newscast. But what has been less noticed in this otherwise widely covered story is that *it was women* who mobilized the Nuclear-Free Pacific movement in the first place. *It was a feminist woman* parliamentarian (Marilyn J. Waring, then thirty-one years old) who withdrew from the government caucus of her own (National) party regarding this issue, thus precipitating the fall of her party and of the government. *It was women* in the new Labour-party government who forced the new prime minister to stand by his campaign pledge of nuclear-free harbors as well as nuclear-free land.

A year later, in July 1985, the international environmentalist Greenpeace ship *Rainbow Warrior* was bombed while at anchor in Auckland harbor; a crew member was killed. It was only a matter of weeks before investigation made it clear that the bombing team was composed of State terrorist agents on assignment from France to destroy the *Rainbow Warrior* before it commenced planned anti-nuclear sea demonstrations in the Pacific. *It was women* who facilitated the speed of the investigation. All but one of the French male agents had heavily frequented "relief massage" parlors and bedded women at every opportunity; in all other respects, the team kept a low profile, but in sexist behavior they left a clear trail. Once captured, the only member of the French terrorist team to exhibit "unhardened" behavior was a woman, Dominique Prieur. Michael King, author of *Death of the Rainbow Warrior** and an authority on the case, has hypothesized that this was because Prieur might not have been told that the mission involved the risk of taking human life, and might have refused to take part had she known.

By mid-1987, the French government finally had been forced to acknowledge its State terrorism (although it persists in its nuclear testing in the Pacift†), "reparations" were made, and all the Statesmen involved seemed eager to put the matter behind them. The Labour government of Prime Minister David Lange floated a rather draconian bill on international terrorism emergency powers—which would have given the government the

* Michael King's analysis of Dominique Prieur's behavior was communicated to me in a personal conversation, after publication of his book by Penguin Books in 1986.

† In 1988, France announced plans to abandon Mururoa Atoll as a no-longer-safe testing site, since the island's foundation is fragmenting and the French don't wish to expose their own personnel to the extremely high radiation levels. At the same time, the French government—while disowning responsibility for Mururoa—declared that it would move its nuclear-testing operations to another of its colonies or territorial "possessions" in the Pacific region.

right to censor or restrict press coverage in (what the State deemed) an emergency; the bill also contained several other far-reaching emergency powers which could be used in infringement of domestic civil liberties. Perhaps the State assumed that the people, still traumatized by a first brush with terrorism in the *Rainbow Warrior* affair, would rally out of fear in support of the bill. But the press mobilized, civil-liberties groups mobilized—and so did the National Council of Women of New Zealand. (At this writing, the bill is back under revision—without the censorship clause and with a drastic reduction in the sections curtailing civil liberties.)

I do not mean to imply that there were not some principled men of conscience involved in this entire process. There were. I also do not mean to imply that there were not some women who worked in support of the politics of Thanatos. There were. I *am* noting that the history of the Nuclear-Free Pacific movement, and the press coverage of a government's fall, of the dissolution of ANZUS, of the swift capture of the terrorists, and of New Zealand's revision of its anti-terrorism bill, *all have focused on men.* Pacific Islands *men,* New Zealand *Statesmen,* Greenpeace crew*men* (although the crew included women), etc. I *am* focusing on the hidden variable, the overlooked factor which has meandered, flowing softly but steadily: *women.*

Women, the State assumes, are too irrelevant to make a difference. Besides, the State assumes, women don't understand matters of State—and aren't interested anyway. In 1985, Donald T. Regan, then White House chief of staff, made one of his more infamous remarks in a career already notorious for racist and sexist utterances. At the Geneva summit meeting between President Reagan and Soviet leader Mikhail Gorbachev, Regan chortled, "Women are not going to understand throw-weights" or other national security issues. The remark still rankles Assistant Secretary of State Rozanne L. Ridgway. A woman admittedly loyal to the State of man, Ridgway hopes for women's advancement on those terms, and holds "a deep belief that there is no women's view on national security—deciding numbers of troops, numbers of missiles, what is an appropriate rate of growth for the defense budget. . . ." Confessing the real reason for her "deep belief" in a recent interview, however, she added, "To the extent that a woman in the field says, 'As a woman, I think . . . ,' she is going to find that the doors on the corridors of power are closed to her."[46]

The debate over whether women would govern differently from men continues, like a sideshow entertainment while Rome burns. But Marian C. Diamond, a professor of neuroanatomy at the University of California (Berkeley), writes, "It is only a matter of time before technology allows us to measure precisely the differences in the structure of male and female human brains. Animal studies clearly indicate that such differences exist. With different arrangements of the nerve cells between the sexes, there are undoubtedly different kinds of behavior that are inherent. That females would govern unlike males is a real possibility."[47]

Understandably, feminists are made uneasy by such a biological analysis: all we have to do is look at the way it has been used against women in the past.* But that was actually *biological materialism*, and again, it wasn't women who were defining or interpreting "difference." Nor was it women who were conceiving a *constructive practice* which might be possible in terms of options that "difference" offers for us all. We are *not* the

---

* Or in the present. On December 18, 1987, the Bundeskriminalmt staged thirty-three raids in cities throughout the Federal Republic of Germany. Heavily armed police burst into the homes and workplaces of women's-rights activists—feminist critics of genetic and reproductive technology, surrogate motherhood, sex predetermination, genetic engineering, and abuses in amniocentesis and in-vitro fertilization. The coalition of groups working on these issues stretched from the radical Red Zora to the Housewives' League. Among those arrested were medical doctors, social scientists, and journalists. The women were strip-searched, and the materials confiscated included papers for educational seminars, lists of those attending the seminars, and private address books. The police claimed the assaults were justifiable under the law's Paragraph 129a: "possible support or membership in a terrorist organization." See Gena Corea and Cynthia De Wit, "Current Developments and Issues: A Summary," *Reproductive and Genetic Engineering: Journal of International Feminist Analysis*, Vol. 1, No. 2 (1988), pp. 183–203.

same as men. The "same" is a standard defined *by* men—and is as aberrant as any standard defined by only a part declaring itself to be the entity.

Whatever the case or cause—inherent or socialized, biological or traditional—the reality is that *women as a group* historically do not share the phallic excitement that confuses toughness with strength and so produces State mechanisms of terror under the pretense of "national security."

What does that ridiculously empty phrase—"national security"—mean in the age of ozone depletion, the greenhouse effect, Chernobyl, Bhopal, Love Canal? Disaster doesn't need a visa. What does the phrase mean within a country's own borders, for that matter, if natural resources there are so pillaged that their "security" is a sick joke? *There is no such thing as "national security"* in a world where one State can reduce another to ashes within minutes, and where air, land, and water (which *move, shift,* and *flow*) are—for better or worse—shared.*

The State of man seems bent on ignoring this as long as possible in its rush to an ultimate, controlled, thanatotic, orgasmic climax. Norwegian feminist theorist Berit Ås put it succinctly: "A patriarchal state is one which is either rehabilitating from war, is presently at war, or is preparing for war."[48]

We live in it, this "State of War." It saturates our lives. The whole vast grotesque State of being in which we are forced to survive is a State of emergency, a State of terror. To keep naming it as such is to invite scorn, to be called excessive, alarmist. To puncture the smooth, featureless façade of this terror is to be disruptive of order—a defined, linear, brittle order. "A vio-

---

* For alternative visions regarding "national security," see "If Women Had a Foreign Policy: A Roundtable Discussion with Bella Abzug, Patricia Derian, Marcia Gilespie, Perdita Huston, Robin Morgan, and Gloria Steinem," *Ms.*, March 1985. See also Richard Falk's excellent pamphlet "Nuclearism and National Interest— the Situation of a Non-nuclear Ally," Annual Peace Lecture (Auckland, New Zealand: The New Zealand Foundation of Peace Studies, 1986). For an exploration of the legal rights of natural resources, see Christopher D. Stone, *Earth and Other Ethics: The Case for Moral Pluralism* (New York and San Francisco: Harper and Row, 1987).

lent order is disorder," the poet warns, and "A great disorder is an order."[49]

They came for us in the middle of the night . . .

At sixteen, she's the youngest inhabitant of death row . . .

Preventive detention is legal under certain circumstances . . .

Less than 35 percent of the eligible U.S. electorate voted in 1980 . . .

Today martial law was declared in . . .

Thirteen thousand children imprisoned in South Africa . . .

He put the cattle prod into my vagina. "Talk to me," he said . . .

My only child. I don't know where they took him . . .

Poverty is the greatest killer of children in the United States . . .

The summit leaders were unable to agree on further nuclear-arms reduction . . .

I sit in a small room in North America. Dawn leaks a metallic gray light across the city streets outside my window. The walls and floor are littered with notes, reminders, testimonies, facts. Scraps of paper. Scraps of flesh. *There must be some way to end it.* In the death grip of such panic and pain, such vulgar official stupidity, such sexual misplacement and legitimized cruelty—and so little time left—*surely,* we think, *anything that can change this State is worth doing. Anything. No matter what.*

The Demon Lover is here before us.

"There is a way," he whispers comfortingly, "a way that offers hope—and a euphoria beyond the thrill of stately power. See it, moving soundless in the underbrush, crouching on rooftops, crying out to the suffering people, massing in the hills and in the streets? Isn't it beautiful, exhilarating, irresistible? It's a festival, a conflagration. It's what the world needs. It's your own most secret desire. It's Revolution."

CHAPTER 5

⌖⌖⌖⌖⌖⌖⌖⌖

WARGASM:
THE REVOLUTIONARY HIGH

Whenever I put on my face-mask, I feel the heat of the proletariat.
Nor does the eventual risk offend me: it fills me with a feverish
emotion, as if I were waiting for a lover. . . .
/ Italian self-proclaimed terrorist TONI NEGRI

This is my rifle,
This is my gun.
One is for killing,
One is for fun. / U.S. Army training song

We declare a Wargasm in America!
/ Weathermen, Chicago (1969)

---

*A*n old friend and I are sitting at dinner. She is a white, middle-
aged American of Irish descent, a feminist, a lifelong pacifist.
She is also a sensitive and intelligent human being. The food is
well prepared, the wine mellow, the conversation stimulating.
With the obsessive absorption of the writer entangled in her
current book, I maneuver the subject around to terrorism. She
is quick to understand, and helpful. In concert, we mourn epidemic violence. She teases me lightly: she remembers a time
when I dismissed her pacifism as bourgeois liberalism, when

she worried that her morning newspaper headlines would pro-
claim my death in a shoot-out with the FBI or my arrest on
some sabotage charge that would mean a life behind bars. I
volunteer that now she has every right to say "I told you so."
We laugh, and the talk continues. We've been talking politics
for two decades. In concert, we bemoan the mounting power
and terrorism of the State. In concert, we express alarm at Right-
wing vigilantism and we mourn Left-wing loss of a humanitarian vision.

"The *humiliation* of being oppressed," I hazard, "informs
every aspect of the suffering—the humiliation that one's behavior
is totally dictated by the oppressor." She nods. I am hardly
saying anything new. "But then . . . well, the frightful thing is
that revolutionary behavior itself also has been dictated by the
oppressor. Somehow, women are outside that images-in-the-
mirror-unto-infinity pattern. Somehow, maybe we can leap free
of that mode of imitative rebellion entirely."

She stares at me. I've lost her.

"You're not saying, you can't be saying . . . look, this is a
problem bigger than sexism. You can't be simple-minded about
this. I mean . . . surely you're not including national-liberation
struggles in that pattern!" She says this incredulously.

I begin to stammer. I hadn't thought I was saying anything
particularly outrageous.

"Well, uh, yes, I am," I mutter. "And I don't think it's necessarily simple-minded to believe feminism may be uniquely
capable of addressing the problem. I do feel it's a problem . . .
uh, of men. I mean, I *do* think that national-liberation movements—however just, and however many women are involved
in them—have been demonstrably male-led for male purposes
with male tactics and male definitions of power. Incidentally,
they've all betrayed women after 'liberation.' Surely that's not
new. So national-liberation movements carry the seeds of their
own blood-lust, their own corrupt—"

She interrupts me, horrified. "You can't *possibly* mean *all* of
them. Maybe the Iranian revolution, yes. Or some of the Latin

American or African ones, those that settle for being mere *coups*."

I feel we're on dangerous ground, but I still don't understand why. "Yes," I mumble, swallowing hard, *"All* of them."

"That's crazy!" she says, her voice rising. "That's reactionary!" She is shouting now. "You can't lump them all together like that! *The Irish are different!"*

———

Somebody's always different. These circumstances, this time. The people who are always being different are always the same. They are male people. The other people, who are busy trying to prove that they aren't different, that they're really just the same (i.e., the same as men, i.e., human), must defend the male people. They must do so because others' perception of them *and* their perception of themselves *and* their objective behavior—are different. They are female people.

But god forbid we should be simple-minded about this.

As a corrective to our intellectual vacuity, then, let's thrash ourselves through some patriarchal revolutionary thinking. This exercise is always a challenge, because such thinking has for centuries tried to kill us—either by outright murder or by boring us to death.

It's fancy footwork, a familiar dance of death, that tries to justify the actions of the Revolution (the State-that-would-be) as differentiated from those of the State-that-is. The generals, Statesmen, and "experts" cited in chapter 1 used the same justifications—of exigency, of the need to meet force with force—in their case, to the benefit of the State. Similarly, Sergio Panunzio, one of the major ideologues of fascism as a political philosophy, offered a cognitive "differential" between "force" and "violence":

Normative, material, or coercive *force* manifests itself via socially sanctioned ("legitimate") instrumentalities: the communications media, the schools, rule-governed codes of conduct, entrance criteria into the professions, the legal system, the armed forces of public security, and the institutions of detention and punishment, among others. *Positive law* holds all of this together. . . . *Violence,* in turn, is the perfect analogue of force except that its activities do not possess established social sanction and its behaviors do not represent positive, but *potential, law.* . . . force represents the interests of the present social system, while violence is the cutting edge of an alternative system.[1] (Italics mine.)

What *would* one do without the other as its rationale for existing? Sometimes this is flatly admitted. Former Baader-Meinhof/Red Army Faction member Hans-Joachim Klein, in a 1978 interview in the French journal *Libération* declared that the RAF believed "it is a question of sharpening the contradictions of the system in order to emphasize latent Fascism. In order for the masses to move, the situation must become more serious."[2] This was also the reasoning of the Communist party in Germany before World War II. The contradictions decidedly got sharpened—and the Communists got smashed. (Is it only an interesting aside that anti-State terrorism seems to emerge most violently in those countries where, a generation earlier, acute State terrorism and literal fascist philosophy was the rule, e.g., Italy, West Germany, and Japan?*)

The polarization approach—which some of us embraced in the 1960s and 1970s—can serve as a moral justification for those (rare) moments when the less powerful State-that-would-be folks actually perform acts that approach the savagery of the State-that-is, or even (more rarely) try to go the State one better. It requires an adjustable logic: Violent acts against the State will inspire, rally, and mobilize the populace (for which read the workers, the proletariat, etc.—automatically visioned

* All three can also be seen as examples of Luigi Bonanate's blocked societies: "West Germany with a nonexistent Communist Party and working-class movement; Japan with a model of capitalist labor organization which tends to be more and more clustered; and Italy with a very solid ruling class [which] . . . absorbs any innovation." (Luigi Bonanate, "Some Unanticipated Consequences of Terrorism," *Journal of Peace Research,* Vol. 16, No. 3 [1979], pp. 205–6.)

as men). If the populace doesn't in fact rise up, the State *will*, in repression, and then at least the populace will have become "radicalized." If this also doesn't happen—if the hard-hats, for example, come out on the side of the police—why then clearly organizing the "masses" (automatically visioned as the masses of men) is at that moment historically impossible, which is all the more justification for desperation, and for committing violent acts. Or, as Hegel wrote, "Die, and become what you are." Circular reasoning. The word "revolution" *means* that: a turning of the wheel, an upside-down reversal. *But the wheel that spins is the same wheel.*

And what about that "desperation" that surfaces when polarization for the sake of radicalizing and mobilizing fails? Is it really desperation? I think not. We know the State defends its terrorism as necessary for national security or domestic order—and that those excuses are cover-ups for the retention of power. Just so, the Revolution justifies its terrorism as necessary for mobilization, or if not, then for radicalization, or if not, then as born of desperation. But this "desperation" is not constituted of suffering or even impatience. If it were, it would have the energy of an emotion that makes imperative the conception of *innovative* tactics rather than one that settles for going round the wheel again. Just as the violence never was really about "security," "order," "mobilizing," or "radicalizing," so it's also not about "desperation." Albert Camus named what it *is* really about without realizing the full import of his metaphor: "Resentment is . . . an autointoxication—the evil secretion, in a sealed vessel, of *prolonged impotence*"[3] (italics mine). Well aware that revolutions serve to sustain or rejuvenate the State, he also wrote, "The strange and terrifying growth of the modern State . . . nevertheless gave birth to the revolutionary spirit of our time. The prophetic dream of Marx and the . . . predictions of Hegel or of Nietzsche ended by conjuring up . . . a rational or irrational State, which in both cases, however, was founded on terror."[4] Admitted, with equanimity.

To break this pattern, the "revolutionary" would have to

reject *revolving* in it. But then he would have to dare abandon his most basic idea of what power is, and his notion of who humanity is. So long as the son retains the father's idea of power (and judges himself human by that very identification), so long will the insurgent settle for the power of the incumbent. Both Marx and Engels acknowledged that women's labor—in producing the labor force itself (reproduction) and in maintaining it (housewifery and motherhood)—was the underpinning of all economic activity. Having noted that, they went on to ignore it and to concentrate all hope in their narrowly defined "labor force"—for which read men. Had they done otherwise, they would have wound up with a very different vision of the proletariat. Again and again, revolutionary male thinkers have proceeded blind to this insight, as they are blind to the female majority of humanity—its needs, its pain, and its silenced solutions.

These thinkers, you realize, constitute the unsimple-minded finest political theorists of our century. Paulo Freire was one. In *The Pedagogy of the Oppressed,* he bumps up against the insight, then swerves safely around it. Denouncing the "lovelessness which lies at the heart of the oppressors' violence," he calls for the revolutionary to create himself *(sic)* differently:

> But almost always, during the initial stage of the struggle, the oppressed . . . tend themselves to become oppressors, or "suboppressors." The very structure of their thought has been conditioned by the contradictions of the concrete, existential situation by which they were shaped. Their ideal is to be men, but for them, to be men is to be oppressors. This is their model of humanity, . . . their model of "manhood." . . . As long as [the oppressed] live in the duality in which *to be* is *to be like,* and *to be like* is *to be like the oppressors,* this [transformative] contribution is impossible. . . . Functionally, oppression is domesticating. . . . there is only one way for [revolutionary] leaders to achieve authenticity: they must "die" in order to be reborn through and with the oppressed. . . . Sectarianism, fed by fanaticism, is always castrating.

Freire's solution is that men (and he does mean *men*) must enter a "dialogical communion" with one another, risk "the act of love" for one another, and thus create a new model. He never notices that the model for *being without being like* already exists in front of his nose: the female people whose oppression has been most "domesticating" and "castrating"; the female people who have been in a "dialogical communion" not only with one another but with their menfolk for centuries; the female people who have risked, and risked, and risked again "the act of love."[5]

Sooner or later we must deal with Frantz Fanon. This is hard for me, harder than I anticipated. I first read Fanon in French, in the early 1960s—and his impassioned works, in particular *Les damnés de la terre (The Wretched of the Earth)*, deeply marked my emerging political consciousness as a woman in her early twenties. Throughout those years, and even into the founding years of this feminist wave, Fanon was my most cherished revolutionary voice. Long after I had discovered the words of Elizabeth Cady Stanton and Margaret Fuller, and broken free of Albert Memmi and Ché and Ho and Mao and all the other boys, I still quoted Fanon. I titled one of my earliest articles on feminism "The Wretched of the Hearth." It was Fanon I read myself and other women *into*—that sleight of hand we're accustomed to—inserting one's own existence between the lines of a text that uses (and acutally means) the generic male pronoun throughout. It's taken me over two decades to divorce Fanon.

Consequently, only now do I realize that though I read all of Fanon, I focused on the parts of his work that magnetized others of my New Left generation. One essay in particular, "Concerning Violence," in *The Wretched of the Earth,* is in fact what Fanon is best known for. Most readers manage to overlook (as we did) the fact that his explanation of violence as a purgative act does not summarize his total position on violence. He was a physician after all, a psychiatrist. Born in Martinique, he headed the psychiatric department of Blida

Hospital in Algeria in 1952, as the Algerian independence struggle against France was intensifying. What he saw and named was the "mental disorder" produced in the oppressed by colonization. But whom did he identify as "the oppressed"? Toward the end of *The Wretched of the Earth,* there's a section called "Colonial War and Mental Disorders." Fanon cites such cases as "impotence in an Algerian following the rape of his wife—who had thereby 'dishonored' him," "marked anxiety psychosis of the depersonalization type after the murder of a woman—while temporarily insane," "a European police inspector who tortured his own wife and children after working as official torturer," "accusatory delirium and suicidal conduct disguised as 'terrorist activity' in a young Algerian" (who kept chanting, "I am not a coward, I am not a woman, I am not a traitor").[6]

The raped, tortured, and "cowardly" women did not attract Fanon's attention. He treated the men, and attributed their actions to colonization. He lists fourteen sample cases variously categorized under four different headings and twenty-two subcategories, but he mentions women as patients only three times. One is the case of the "neurotic attitude of a young Frenchwoman whose father, a highly placed servant, was killed in an ambush." (Her "neurosis" consists of an inappropriate "lightheartedness over the death of her father," and a misplaced sympathy with her Algerian contemporaries.) The second mention involves "puerperal psychosis—mental disorders which occur in women around childbirth." Algerian women, Fanon writes, especially those who are refugees, suffer "agitation, . . . deep depression, tonic immobility, . . . attempted suicides; . . . [express] tears, lamentations, and appeals for mercy; . . . [experience] delusions of persecution . . . [and] the impression of imminent death, in which the mothers may implore invisible executioners to spare their child." (After a one-sentence clinical description of how this psychosis can occur in *all* puerperal women, Fanon attributes its appearance in his cases to colonization.) The third mention of women as patients occurs in the section "Psychosomatic Disorders." I quote the passage in its entirety: "Menstruation trouble in women. This pathology is very well known, and we shall not spend much time on it. Either the women affected remain three or four months without menstruation, or else considerable pain accompanies it, which has repercussions on character and conduct."[7] Despite this "pathology" being "psychosomatic" and "very well known," he attributes it, in his cases, to colonization. In any event, we need not spend much time on it.

What does humanity need to do, standing before his eyes— raped, tortured, guilty of the cowardice of sympathy, appealing for mercy, imagining its pain, frantically waving its scarves with the names of disappeared children on them, banging its cookpots, weeping, lamenting, pleading—*what does humanity need to do in order to be seen?*

Fanon's diagnoses, his analysis, his *perception,* were totally circumscribed by his gender. Ironically, his prescription for a cure, while assuredly addressed to men, groped toward a different way. Seeing that "what is madness to the Father Country is sanity to the colony," he recognized the colonial world as (his words) *"a Manichean world."* He feared what he foresaw: that "the pitfalls of national consciousness" were many and mortal, that domestic corruption, tribal warfare, and economic neocolonialism would follow in the wake of independence—unless some means other than violence could be found to induce freedom. Still futilely addressing his circumscribed audience (his *fellow* Algerians) and still holding out hope of the wrong cure (manhood once again), he pled, "Come, brothers, . . . humanity is waiting for something from us other than such an imitation, which would be almost an obscene caricature. . . . we must work out new concepts, and try to set afoot a new man."[8]

Humanity continued to wait.

Humanity would wait even longer, if it were up to another (unsimple-minded) major male thinker, the man through whose filtered interpretation Fanon had his greatest impact on the West.

In his famous Preface to *The Wretched of the Earth,* Jean-Paul
Sartre riveted his and our attention totally on the issue of violence as a purgative act and, even more, as a generative act of
manhood:

> Make no mistake about it; by this mad fury, by this bitterness and
> spleen, by [the colonized's] ever-present desire to kill [the Euro-
> pean], by the permanent tensing of powerful muscles which are
> afraid to relax, they have become men; . . . this irrespressible vio-
> lence is neither sound and fury, nor the resurrection of savage
> instincts, nor even the effect of resentment: it is man recreating
> himself. . . . no gentleness can efface the marks of violence; only
> violence itself can destroy them.[9]

I do hate to be simple-minded, but what is Sartre doing here
in lieu of cogitation? If man can only violently recreate himself
to escape violence and if no gentleness can efface the violence
and if violence itself is the sole cure for violence then when how
why where does he expect the cycle to end? *Does* he expect it
to end? Does he hope it *won't* end, so that man will perpetually
be recreating himself? This is pure twaddle. This is also the
foremost political philosopher of our time. I do not understand
why Simone de Beauvoir, upon reading those lines in manuscript, did not tap Sartre sharply on the head with one of his
beloved (hard) sausages, to save him from public embarrassment. (Perhaps she tried—and he ignored her advice, as he often
did.) She was later to say that Fanon had harsh words for Sartre,
whom he blamed for having insufficiently expiated the sin of
being French. Poor Fanon. Between his white male oppressors
and his white male friends, he never stood a chance. He never
perceived the authentic constituency, the truly wretched of the
earth.

Alien as they were to one another, Fanon and Sartre shared
a brotherhood, one that spanned the State-that-is and the State-
that-would-be. They shared, too, the manly virtue of blindness
that permitted them to see and address only one another, and

they shared the understanding of how much each might misunderstand the other.

Again and again, power changes hands but does not alter definition. Again and again, this is done *for the sake of, in the name of, on behalf of, from, over,* "the people," "the masses," "the proletariat," "the workers," "the farmers," "the populace"—none of whom are perceived as female. *Visible power exchanged between visible antagonists for the sake of a never-perceived or never-acknowledged invisible humanity will always perpetuate the cycle.* And they wonder why their revolutions have not "worked."

Political scientist Harry R. Targ, one out of hundreds of such unsimple-minded wits writing today, hypothesizes that terrorism occurs more in preindustrial and post-industrial societies than in industrial ones, in those "more likely to have a plurality of their work force in agriculture . . . [or] a plurality of workers in service occupations."[10] Targ doesn't notice that most of the agricultural workers in the world are female. Women constitute over 80 percent of all farmers on the African continent alone. And who are the workers in "service occupations"—the formal labor-force category, not even counting that massive service industry called "the home"—if not women? Is it then possible that the "mass-based political participation" that Targ sees as necessary to preclude terrorism (and that he sees as possible only in industrial societies) is, in fact, mass-based *male* political participation? Is it possible that men in an agrarian context *and* in a post-industrial context can act in terrorist fashion because they're working even less than usual and so have more *time,* as well as more technology, for violence?

Again and again, the erasure of women permeates the theory and practice of so-called political change—and thus leaves the political structure inherently intact. We've seen it in every revolution (perhaps more accurately termed "revolvement") to date. We see it still in Third World liberation struggles—complete with the expectable token woman "heavies," and with most other women *desperately* trying to find strategies alternative to violence. It persists in the ongoing lack of concern (or in concern restricted to lip service) with "women's issues" as defined by both incumbent and insurgent leaders.

Three short examples from recent history give evidence of the pattern.

The civil-rights movement in the United States began as a female-oriented and female-organized network, based in the black churches of the U.S. South. That far-reaching affiliation of women's groups, deaconesses' meetings, and ladies' clubs was rooted in turn in three centuries of Afro-American women's activism. It had been an amazingly courageous resistance and protection system for their families, even under the suffocating proscriptions of slavery. It had created, among other resistance tactics, the Underground Railroad. Foremothers indeed. Michele Wallace, in *Black Macho and the Myth of the Superwoman*, wrote:

> There has been from slavery to the Civil Rights Movement a thin but continuous line of black women who have prodded their sisters to self-improvement. . . . Day to day, these women, like most women, devoted their energies to their husbands and children. When they found time, they worked on reforms in education, medicine, housing, and their communities through their organizations and churches.[11]

The civil-rights movement is usually said to have been born on the day in 1955 when Rosa Parks, of Montgomery, Alabama, refused to move from her seat in the front of the bus—because she was tired. Meanwhile, Fannie Lou Hamer was the political dynamo for equal rights in Mississippi, and thousands of other black women were doing the same organizing, prodding and working throughout the country. As the "movement" emerged, however, it did so with male leaders, although its nonviolent tactics were influenced for years by the women who had given it birth—and those same tactics were articulated by the preacher-men whose charisma had been bestowed by those women. With the emergence of Black Power came "manhood" (much hailed by Normal Mailer). Wallace again: "The headlines about the Black Muslims in 1964 left me with the impression that a resurrected Hannibal was marching upon New York with an army of seven-foot Watusis to eat all the whites alive. The press—white men as sexual beings reacting to black men as sexual beings—was clearly swept up in that 'new hysteria' Mailer had described."[12] Daniel Patrick Moynihan diagnosed the "Black Matriarchy" as having ruined the black family. Stokely Carmichael proclaimed that "the only position for women in SNCC is prone." Eldridge Cleaver declared, "We shall have our manhood or the earth will be leveled by our attempts to gain it." After Malcolm X was assassinated, he was eulogized as having been "our manhood, our black, living, manhood." The descent into violence had begun. It was to end in shoot-outs between the police and the Black Panthers, the police and the Symbionese Liberation Army, the police and the Black Liberation Army. Ever since then, black women have been picking up the pieces. In 1979, Michele Wallace was attacked by black (and white) male intellectuals for her "man-hating" book that merely told the truth about black women's lives. Almost a decade later, Alice Walker had to endure the same attacks (from the same quarters) for having told another part of the same truth in her novel *The Color Purple*.

Notice the pattern. The environmentalist movement was in fact begun by Ellen Swallow, who founded the scientific discipline of ecology and was the first women admitted to the Massachusetts Institute of Technology. More popularly, it's thought to have been begun by Rachel Carson, with her germinal book *Silent Spring*. Those were the days when ecology was a "soft" issue; men were more concerned with organizing to save their own skins—burning draft cards and opposing the war in Vietnam (eventually doing so in startlingly warlike fashion, for pacifists). But in the past decade, working on environmental issues has become manly. In the interim—while women populated the marches and sit-ins and staffed the little offices—the men's tactics became increasingly militant. By 1985, "ecoter-rorism" has made its entrance. At first the acts mainly took the form of sabotage against property, as in the blowing up of power lines to the Krummel nuclear reactor on the Elbe River in West Germany. But an apparent alliance with what remained of West Germany's Red Army Faction soon followed. And then came the Molotov cocktails, and a carelessness about endangering human life. Anti-nuclear militants attacking the customer-ser-vice office of Hamburg's nuclear-power facility jammed a door leading to twelve private apartments above the office; they fled when an alarm went off, but left two fire bombs behind. The bombs were defused in time; the people upstairs narrowly escaped death.[13]

Notice the pattern. The welfare-rights movement in the United States has from the first clearly been a movement about, by, of, and for women. Yet the original grass-roots leaders—women who themselves were or had been welfare clients—were dis-placed by men who thought them insufficiently aggressive. Women were good enough to raise the issue, to "feel deeply" about it, to be "victimized" by it—but *action* had to be male-determined and male-led. Theresa Funiciello, one of those early organizers, was criticized because although her brilliant theo-retical analyses and passionate speeches could stir people to action, she refused to urge women and children into tactical situations where they would get hurt. To this day, she says, "I won't do with other people's children what I wouldn't do with my own." The National Welfare Rights Organization peaked in militance—and was destroyed. Years later, Funiciello and other women like her are still picking up the pieces, still orga-nizing, still working on an issue that is no longer considered glamorous. The male leaders have moved on to the cushy jobs in the social-work bureaucracy.

Those are only three examples. One can look in any direc-tion where "the revolution" beats its chest and howls, and see the same process. Given minor variations, I would delineate that process in ten steps.

1. Women notice a problem, compare notes about it, name it, decide to do something about it.

2. Women move from the daily resistance that informs their lives (hiding children from slave masters or armies, secreting food for their families in famine, writing protest letters, etc.) into a loose linkage of action with other women (parent groups, church affiliations, "good works" associations, neighborhood action committees, market women's guilds, etc.). These are all voluntary. The groups are informal, fluidly structured, filled with a sense of hope and good will.

3. These groups urge, cajole, and guilt-trip ("nag") men to become involved: agribusiness is taking over the farm; the corner needs a traffic light; a toxic-waste dump shouldn't go in next door; this village needs a well. I would characterize this phase as *"Please*, Herman, come *with* me to the meeting. It's *help*ful. Honest, you'll *like* it."

4. The men finally become involved. The issue is now Important because it is no longer a "women's issue." The men assume leadership. The women permit this because they are relieved that the men are now concerned and active at all, they know that the men will be Taken Seriously, and they know that the men won't return to future meetings if they're *not* the leaders.

5. Because men's time is valuable, the leadership positions can no longer be voluntary; the men must be salaried. Funds must therefore be raised. The women raise the money through more voluntarism (making and selling baskets, bake sales, etc.).

6. The men regard the women as tangential to the issue because the issue is now Political. (Tautologically, if it's a women's issue, it's not important; if it's an important issue, it doesn't concern women.) Because of their self-serving myopic definition of women's issues, the men exclude the women as a political constituency. The men say that prior to this time, the group was "masturbatory—merely talking to those already convinced." Now, however, the men will build a *real* 'movement,' i.e., the men will confront other men.

7. A fatal shift in tone occurs—a slide from moral and spir-

itual integrity (now regarded as sentimental, idealistic, *womanly*) into self-righteousness. If the previous activism was church-oriented, for example, the shift is likely to be from a spiritual basis to one of religious fanaticism. Fragmentation of the practical from the metaphysical occurs—with the former then being lost in materialist fundamentalism and the latter being lost in religious fundamentalism of various sorts.

8. The consequence of this fragmentation is the emergence of the "higher good" fallacy, leading to an ends-justify-the-means attitude. As abstractions proliferate, the original issues are likely to be forgotten entirely. Unease expressed by the women at this point is dismissed as conservatism, cowardice, liberalism, or divisiveness. Acceptance of this situation separates the girls (the tokens) from the women.

9. The combination of a circumscribed constituency, self-righteousness, and the concept of an abstract higher good introduces manhood as the real issue. Manhood identity now depends on waging the struggle. Rhetoric, "turf," tools and weapons, uniforms, become fetishes of that manhood identity, as in Frazer's concept of contagious magic to the savage mind. The result is a dead end: the shift from living for a cause—e.g., fighting to enhance the quality of living—to *dying* for a cause now locks into place. Violence. Those who question are traitors.

10. A politics of hope has become a politics of despair. The goal is now too abstract and absolute to be attainable, nor can manhood be satisfied by less. Cynicism sets in, as does the strategy of provocation and polarization. What once aimed for a humanistic triumph now aims for a purist defeat. Martyrdom. The State obliges.

The politics beneath the politics was manhood.

One way to see this absurdity in perspective is to reverse the reversal and imagine people boasting about killing and dying in "womanhood struggles." That women have indeed been robbed of a self-defined womanhood ought to be obvious by now, but women don't seem to feel that supertoughness and murder will suffice to recreate the self or engender that womanhood identity. However enraged we become—and however much an individual woman may act (classically) in defense of her children or (lately) in defense of herself—*women as a group do not mobilize for our own rights through violent means*. Too patient? Too hesitant, having considered too many variables? Too held back by the virtues of ambivalence? One thing is certain: men of the State-that-is *and* men of the State-that-would-be share form as well as content; as the State increasingly adopts terrorist means, so the terrorists increasingly adopt State structures of organization—"playing State," so to speak. They become mirror images admiring each other. And men of the State-that-is and of the State-that-would-be also share a peculiar intoxication. It permits them to call up armies, attach electrodes to living flesh, justify the invention, testing, and stockpiling of world-destroying weapons; it also permits them to "knee-cap" informers with electric drills, purge "incorrect" colleagues by literal crucifixion, and eventually to consider the political reasons for doing these things as secondary or irrelevant to the mere doing of them as creative acts. *Such men suffer from a lack of ambivalence.*

Here is an image of the lack of ambivalence:

When a bomb tore through a Naples–Milan express train [in 1985], killing fifteen passengers and injuring more than 150, everyone from the neofascist Black Order to the Left-wing Red Brigades to an Islamic guerrilla group claimed credit for the act.[14]

A lack of ambivalence must be fostered:

There were emotional scenes and huge demonstrations in Iran today as 50 more coffins of the Iranian dead arrived. . . . They were paraded . . . and then carried to the Cemetery of the Revolutionary and War Dead south of the city, marked by a bright red "fountain of blood."[15]

A lack of ambivalence must be made to seem pleasurable:

It is only in the context of Terrorist Chic that it becomes permissible, even appealing, for *Penthouse* magazine to offer the *bon mot* "Fucking and killing are the same" to its three and a half million readers.[16]

A lack of ambivalence must be made to seem honorable:

The self-esteem afforded by terrorism is a renewed sense of masculinity. The "chivalric courtesy" of skyjackers has been widely noted. . . . the pilot's attempts to deal with the situation only escalate the danger, [it is] perceived by the skyjacker as a challenge. The flight attendant* is more likely to be effective . . . than are male passengers or members of the crew.[17]

A lack of ambivalence must flaunt a mystique:

I am an evil spirit which moves only at night. . . . I will ignite a huge fire in the Middle East. . . . I am Abu Nidal.† Not even my eight-year-old daughter, Bissan, knows who I am.[18]

A lack of ambivalence remains firm even when self-contradictory:

Régis Debray, author of *Revolution in the Revolution*, former friend of Ché Guevara and comrade of the Cuban Revolution, served a prison term in Bolivia for taking part in an insurrection which Guevara led. Today, although he says that "I maintain my revo-

* The author of this statement, Abraham Kaplan, writes in the same article, "If [punishment] is to serve as a deterrent for the male terrorist, it should be labor which he will perceive as degrading, especially as unmanly. . . . There is less deterrence in . . . hard labor than to what he sees as some sort of 'women's work,' . . . kitchen aide or hospital orderly." ("The Psychodynamics of Terrorism," *Terrorism: An International Journal*, Vol. 1, Nos. 3/4 [1978], p. 247.)

† Abu Nidal is the public name of Sabri al-Banna, head of the Fatah Revolutionary Council, which split from Yasir Arafat's mainstream Al Fatah, and which claims responsibility for most if not all "Palestinian militant acts." These have included (by Abu Nidal's count) more than a hundred such acts in countries around the world—and have also included murders of Palestinian "rivals" or "adversaries." Arafat is on his hit list.

lutionary position on Latin America," he serves the French government as Secretary General of France's South Pacific Council—
overseeing such exploits as French nuclear testing [see chapter 4]
and policy in crushing anti-colonial struggles in New Caledonia
and other French colonies and territories in the Pacific. He sees no
contradiction.[19]

A lack of ambivalence recognizes its brothers across political
differences:

Kozo Okamoto is a self-proclaimed terrorist member of Sekigunha
(the Japanese Red Army). In an interview after his capture following the 1972 Lod Airport massacre, he expressed admiration for
the heroic Kamikaze suicide pilots of World War II, and for the
suicide of Japanese author Yukio Mishima: "Even though Mishima and other Japanese suicide heroes believed in anti-revolution-
ary or reactionary ideologies, their emotions were the same as those
of revolutionaries."[20]

A lack of ambivalence is the manly form of transcending
class and nationalism in one brotherhood:

The Italian neofascist terrorist Stafeno Delle Chiaie (also known
as the Black Pimpernel and the Black Bomber) went on trial in
1987 for his role in the Bologna massacre. He has worked in Fran-
co's Spain (against the Basque nationalists), in Angola (as advisor
to Savimbi's UNITA forces), with anti-Castro Cuban terrorists, for
Chilean dictator General Pinochet, in Santa Cruz (in association
with ex-Nazi Klaus Barbie), and was implicated in the shooting of
Pope John Paul II in 1981. In this "vast informal web of Right-
wing violence," Delle Chiaie has been directly and indirectly protected by Michael Ledeen, a consultant to the U.S. National Security Council and a close associate of Colonel Oliver North.[21]

A lack of ambivalence never flinches from judgment:

In 1972, the Japanese United Red Army (Rengo Sekigun) purged
itself. Half of the group sentenced the other half to death for

"bourgeois deformities" and "absence of revolutionary zeal"; among the charges were bearing a child in wedlock, "fornicating," and wearing earrings. Fourteen Rengo Sekigun members, mostly female, were found dead, their bodies tortured, mutilated, stabbed, and staked out crucifixion-fashion in the snow, left to die of exposure.[22]

A lack of ambivalence cannot tolerate complexity or compassion. A lack of ambivalence is the hallmark of leadership—in the State-that-is as well as in the State-that-would-be. Indeed, the State-that-is *trains* its sons in this lack. Sometimes the sons fight for the State and sometimes they fight against it, but either way they reinforce it.

Here are two brief histories of men suffering from a lack of ambivalence—two U.S. veterans of the (undeclared) Vietnam War:

The first man is named Dennis John Malvasi. He was born in 1950, his mother's seventh child. She had her first baby at age fifteen and bore twelve children by three different men. Until age twelve, Dennis lived in a Catholic orphanage; then he came home to Brooklyn, New York, to a slum neighborhood of racial warfare between whites, blacks, and Hispanics. He enlisted in the Marines at age seventeen (lying about his age), was shipped to Vietnam, and conducted 505 patrols, 214 ambushes, and eight extensive sweep-and-clear operations around Da Nang. He took heavy fire and relished it: "I felt really alive, really wanted. The baddest people I knew were in front and they came shooting at me. I felt kind of honored." After his discharge in 1970, he became an itinerant actor on Manhattan's Lower East Side, was involved in street crime, charged with assault, sentenced, put on probation, arrested again, and wound up serving two years in jail. When he was released, he drifted through various odd jobs—as mailroom clerk, paramedic, licensed pyrotechnician. He joined the Vietnam Veterans Ensemble Theatre Company, but persisted in shady extralegal activities. He became a fugitive in 1985 on a six-weapons felony charge. "Stuff like that doesn't bother me," he said. "Actually, I don't feel good unless I have someone hunting me down. It makes me feel alive. It makes me feel wanted." He became involved in a Roman Catholic cult with a particular dedication to Saint Benedict and a fanatic aversion to abortion. In May 1987, after a two-year manhunt involving three hundred Federal agents and city detectives and a public appeal by Cardinal O'Connor, Archbishop of the New York Catholic Diocese, Dennis John Malvasi turned himself in to stand trial on the charge of bombing the Manhattan Women's Medical Center (December 10, 1985), the Eastern Women's Center (October 29, 1986), the Queens Women's Medical Office (November 11, 1986), and a Planned Parenthood center (December 14, 1986). The bomb in the last attack—made with fifteen sticks of dynamite and a sophisticated assembly of blasting cap, timer, and battery—was defused at the last minute, but was potent enough to have collapsed the entire façade of the building and to have broken windows blocks away. Tucked in with the dynamite was a medal of Saint Benedict. Malvasi spoke of abortions as "kills," in Vietnam troop parlance, and was indignant that "when I came back from Vietnam, they called *me* a baby-killer." His defense hinged on whether his wartime experience "warped him to the point of insanity." He pled guilty and was sentenced to seven years, a reduced sentence because of his promise to Cardinal O'Connor "not to take part in bombings again."[23]

The second man was a Vietnam hero who could display six rows of ribbons on his chest. He was called "the ultimate marine [who] wants to step forward and take the spears in his own chest."[24] He was bitter after Vietnam; a fellow platoon leader recalled that his "clear feeling was that we were winning but the press was portraying our victories as defeats."[25] He came home to teach war at Quantico, Virginia, in the Marine Corps officers' training school, and began to "act out"—he taught classes dressed in jungle fatigues and battle paint, and he accidentally injured a student by spraying a room with blanks from an assault rifle. He was transferred to Okinawa to direct a marine training camp. There he was known as the workaholic who had hung a banner over his quarters reading "Lead, Follow, or Get the Hell Out of the Way." Back in the U.S. in 1974, he apparently suffered some sort of breakdown and spent three weeks recovering at Bethesda Naval Hospital. Unconfirmed marine lore claims that a fellow officer found him running naked through the streets of his suburban neighborhood, waving a .45 pistol and screaming "I'm no good, I'm no good." In 1981 he was given full security clearance to join the staff of the National Security Council of the White House of the United States. The name of this lieutenant colonel is Oliver North.[26]

A lack of ambivalence must be trained into a man. Can it ever be trained out of him? The war toy, the rigid penetrating missiles, the dynamite and the blasting cap—these are at first only symbols of the message he must learn, fetishes of the ecstasy he is promised. But he must *become* them before he is rewarded with what the lack of ambivalence promises him: a frenzy, an excitement, an exhilaration—an orgasmic thrill in violent domination with which, he is taught, no act of lovemaking could possibly compete. This is the Sadean "high" trained into the heart of manhood, the father's legacy to the son. One terrorism "expert" oversimplified it as follows: "Rebellion can be traced ... to the human being's [sic] secret love of violence, which people [sic] often deny exists and which they tend to repress, but which becomes manifest in activities as diverse as lynching, boxing, and football. ... Violence and the ecstasy of violence can become indivisible."[27] Given the deplorably common use of the masculine noun and pronoun for the generic, it's fascinating that in this case the author uses "human being" and "people" when he actually means *men*.

The revolutionary high—which is the intoxication of believing you will revolve to the top in victory or else attain the ultimate orgasm of violent death—is the bond between members of the State-that-would-be. Their styles may differ (the Italian Red Brigades emphasize kidnappings, the Japanese Red Armies prefer direct armed assaults, the West Germans are jacks-of-all-trades specializing in high-tech bombings, and the IRA Provos focus on low-tech bombings but don't engage in hijackings—probably because their lesser-financed working-class coffers can't manage airplane tickets*). But however the styles differ, the bond of exhilaration has been expressed and romanticized at various times by all of them. They have become extrahuman beings, immortalized in their impending mortality. They feel themselves transformed into living weapons.

In *Terror and Resistance*, Eugene V. Walter describes an African society in which the men designated as the king's agents of terror are named "the king's knives."[28] *This is the transition of identity that makes possible (and inevitable) acts of terror.* If manhood is perceived as localized in a hardened penis, and if the penis is perceived as a weapon, then *manhood itself is the means by which male human beings must (and do) make of themselves weapons.* From the Pentagon's pride in nuclear hardness to Eldridge Cleaver's roars of manhood, from the dropping of "Little Boy" in an ejaculation of death over Hiroshima to Jean-Paul Sartre's hymn to violence as man's way of recreating himself, the obsession is consistent.

> [Ecstasy] literally means "to stand outside oneself," that is, to stand outside the limits of ordinary consciousness or to stand free of the restraints and limits of everyday behavior. Terrorism—whether of the established regime or the revolutionary left—is characterized by this ecstatic element. . . . Special uniforms, masks, sunglasses in Haiti, white robes and hoods for the Ku Klux Klan—all these devices emphasize the distinction between . . . the everyday world and the consecrated activities of those who . . . justify and apotheosize a dreadful violence.[29]

That passage was written by William F. May in his article "Terrorism as Strategy and Ecstasy." It's quite an essay, because he comes so near to the crux of the issue and yet remains so far from it. He sees that "the brush with death relieves men of that

---

* In this, at least, the Irish *are* different.

other death—boredom." He understands that when terrorism moves from "selective and discriminate action" (assassination of power figures) to random attacks on civilians, the terrorist has begun to associate himself "with those [arbitrary] powers that already beset the psyche and command the headlines. The terrorist seems in alliance with [the capricious] universe itself." May even sees that such violence is redolent of the religious festival, the sacramental ritual that comes to have meaning in and for itself.[30]

What May fails to see is that the deity with whom the terrorist merges ecstatically is a *male* deity, the system that kills by boredom and then offers violence as the alternative is a *male* system, the descriptions (from D. H. Lawrence to Norman Mailer) of the penis as a separate member, an ethos which will literally "stand outside oneself," represent *male* perceptions, and the *identification of oneself as a weapon* with which to pierce, penetrate, probe, and explode is a *male* identification.

H. H. A. Cooper has written, "The key to female terrorism undoubtedly lies hidden somewhere in woman's complex sexual nature."[31] So busy are they at defining women solely in terms of sexuality that it never occurs to these "experts" to examine their own: *the key to male terrorism undoubtedly lies hidden somewhere in man's complex sexual nature.* The king's knives are all around us.

If one is a weapon, how can god not be wrathful?

If one is a weapon, how can power not mean dominance?

If one is a weapon, what is one to do with oneself but kill or be killed?

If one is a weapon, how can sex not be murderous and murder not be sexual?

If one is a weapon, how can women be other than targets?

If one is a weapon, how can death not bring ecstasy?

———

Contrarily, if one sees a human being—vulnerable living flesh, blood coursing warmly through delicate veins, muscles knotting and releasing to coax sinews to lift intricate fragile bones in response to the wonder of electric impulses leaping across each synapse and traveling from brain to nerve to tissue, a human body that can dance, can laugh, can kiss, sing, sleep and wake, can touch and be touched—if one sees such a miracle, and finds that such a human being believes himself a weapon, how can one not try to stop him? How can one not try to stop him by thinking love will release him from the weapon of himself?

Because women are the other side of the story.

On April 17, 1986, there was an attempt to plant a high-powered plastique bomb aboard an El Al jet bound for Tel Aviv from London's Heathrow Airport.[32] The explosives were found in the carry-on bag of a thirty-two-year old chambermaid named Anne Marion Murphy. She went into shock. The bag had been given to her—packed with "surprise gifts" to open when she landed in Israel—by her lover, the man she thought was going to marry her, a thirty-one-year-old Jordanian-born Libyan, Nezar Nawaf Mansur Hindawi. He had said he would meet her in Israel in a few days.

She was pregnant with his child.

He was already married. He had deserted his Polish wife and their four-year-old daughter, but had never been formally divorced. His brother, it appeared, had been involved in an earlier bombing of a West German discotheque. The brother, too, had a girlfriend, a German woman, and she too was stunned; Heiderose Pohmer, age thirty, described her lover as "completely unpolitical, a gentle lover, and an excellent cook." She worked as a cleaning woman in a nursing home. The brothers came from a family that had lived in various parts of the Middle East, had fled Palestine when Israel was declared a state, and had settled in Bakura, in northern Jordan. There, their home was destroyed by an Israeli raid—which in turn was a retaliation for guerrilla attacks on Israel—which in turn were retaliation for . . . which in turn . . . which in turn . . .

Are further details necessary? Surely we can fill them in by now. They sicken us with familiarity, these details—of hatred, grief, revenge. What we don't know, we can imagine.

But we cannot so easily imagine what goes on in the brain

of a no-longer-young, not-very-pretty woman who works as a chambermaid, a woman who falls simply and gratefully in love, who thinks he will marry her. A woman who carries his child under her heart, and who now realizes that he—knowing these things—put into her hands what would make of *her* a weapon, make of her who carries life a walking carrier of death for four hundred passengers on an airplane—and a walking carrier of death *for herself, and for their child.* What we cannot so easily imagine are the shapes of pain into which her mind melts, the shapes of memory, of hope, of trust, of disbelief, an endless repertoire of shapes grotesque in their betrayal.

As she was led away for intense interrogation at Heathrow, she reportedly murmured over and over, as if she were saying a rosary:

"I loved him. I *loved* him. *I loved him.*"

Anne Marion Murphy—and, for that matter, Heiderose Pohmer—were the innocent ones, the women who never even knew it was the Demon Lover asleep at their sides after love. Like millions of other women, they saw in their lovers ordinary men, nice men, gentle men who even took a turn with the cooking and who promised to marry them. Just like the guys next door.

What then of the other women—the ones who intuit, suspect, or even know who the lover really is?

What of the women who stake their sanity on their ability to love him into being human?

What of the women who understand that he is beyond their saving—and who deliberately, in their own approximation of his sexualized death ecstasy, fling their life into his arms and onto his funeral pyre?

And what of the women who vow to incarnate him in their own female bodies, trying to become the weapon that he desires, the weapon that he is, the weapon whose definition is to him "human"?

Are they so different from the rest of us, the women who court him, dance for him, imitate him?

These are the women we must face next.

CHAPTER 6

꧁꧁꧁꧁꧁꧁꧁꧁

TOKEN TERRORIST: THE DEMON LOVER'S WOMAN

Anyone who knows anything of history knows that great social changes are impossible without the feminine ferment. Social progress can be measured exactly by the social position of the fair sex—the ugly ones included. / KARL MARX

Women should be divided into three main types: first, those frivolous, thoughtless, and vapid women whom we may exploit as confused liberals; second, women who are ardent, gifted, and devoted, but who do not belong to us because they have not yet achieved a real revolutionary understanding; and finally there are the women who are with us completely, who have been fully initiated and who accept our program in its entirety. We should regard these women as the most valuable of our treasures, without whose assistance we cannot manage. / SERGEI NECHAEV

Kiss me with your blood
before the next war.
Kneeling before you
I see the sabre medals mirroring
tortures to come, prisoners to hunt.
I am then
the silence that shall be.
Kiss me, nail me against you
and allow a new cataclysm of death,
of civilizations,
to whirl. / ISEL RIVERO

*P*atricia Hearst and I talked together in the visiting room of the "progressive" Federal Correctional Institution at Pleasanton, California. It was a chrome-and-formica environment presided over by matron and guard, offering only vending machines and lavatories in the way of relief. The architecture was campus-style: modern colleges and prisons come more to resemble each other all the time. There, for almost four hours one warm California winter morning in 1978, Patricia Hearst and I tried to establish a sense of sisterhood.

In case you have forgotten the details, Patricia—an heiress to the great Hearst fortune—was sentenced to serve a seven-year prison term for, in effect, having been kidnapped when she was nineteen years old by the Symbionese Liberation Army. She was held captive and, according to her testimony, tortured and forced to participate in a bank robbery, a shoot-out, and the SLA's fugitivity. She was later captured by the FBI, charged with acts involving collaboration in terrorist activity, analyzed, hospitalized, indicted, tried, convicted, sentenced, imprisoned, bailed out while her case was appealed, and then re-imprisoned when the appeal was denied. She already had served almost two years in jail when I met her. She was not yet twenty-five years old.

She sat across from me—a smallish, slender young woman with the brown eyes and light-brown hair familiar from a thousand photographs and television newsclips, dressed in a manner that seemed to combine low-profile clothes functional for prison with a tackiness practiced by rich kids who can afford designer fashions and so avoid them: faded blue jeans, a slightly soiled baby-blue sweater, and what my dear departed aunt used to call hooker shoes, platform wedgies of raffia and cotton with open toes and ankle strings. A chaste gold cross hung from a chaste gold chain around her throat, and what looked like a costume-jewelry band with a peeling finish encircled the fourth finger of her left hand, presumably in lieu of the real engagement ring the prison wouldn't permit her to wear. She was everything I expected. She was not at all what I anticipated.

My own preconceptions require exposure. They comprised a mixed bag, one I thought I was bending over backward to carry with a sense of fairness. I'd come to feminism out of the New Left, having discovered that "radical" men could be as sexist as any other, and I was approaching Patricia Hearst with a feminist analysis: I recognized a Blame-the-Victim game, and knew that the daughters and wives belonging to rich men almost never wield power in their own right. Being a survivor of the violent late 1960s and early 1970s, I no longer had any illusions about the glamour of terrorism or of being underground, and I had myself been jailed, and had corresponded and visited with many incarcerated women, so I had no romantic attitudes about prison. I knew that the media had distorted many things about Patricia. But I also knew that it's almost impossible to describe San Simeon, the vast Hearst estate spread out along the California coast, or to exaggerate the wealth that built it. And I confess that I happen to be able to quote from memory whole speeches from Orson Welles's *Citizen Kane*.

More specifically, I knew some things about Patricia from the correspondence that had preceded our meeting, including the fact that she in turn knew something of me (she had read some of my books). I knew that she disliked the trivializing nickname "Patty," and that she had a wry sense of humor: "If you can read my handwriting, you're halfway there. We aren't allowed to have typewriters here. The prison apparently feels that we may commit suicide with them."

I knew that her hope for release had become concentrated on the possibility that President Carter would grant her clemency, reducing her term to time already served. It was to that end, to arouse public opinion on her behalf, that she was for the first time giving select interviews. I had flown to California to interview her for *Ms.* magazine[1]—but I was also there as a woman and a feminist in support of another woman. I can't swear that I wasn't a bit on my guard: I knew about the campaign of petitions and letters to the White House and Congress, the T-shirts that read "Pardon Patty" on one side and "Being Kidnapped Means Always Having to Say You're Sorry" on the other, and the strange-bedfellow notables who were calling for her release—from Left-wing Cesar Chavez to Right-wing William F. Buckley, Jr., with almost fifty members of Congress somewhere in between. I had heard that she wanted to add feminist supporters to that list, and so I was cautious, not wanting the women's movement callously exploited. But I had also heard that she'd expressed a genuine desire to work for the Equal Rights Amendment. I carried a mixed bag of pre-conceptions, indeed.

As for our conversation, I wasn't interested in rehashing the gory details of her past ordeal, and I knew the futility of asking any prisoner—especially an educated or "privileged" one—to reveal much of a current prison experience without endangering herself further from other inmates *and* prison authorities. What I was interested in was Patricia Campbell Hearst the woman—her thoughts, plans, politics. Nonetheless, I had braced myself to be prepared for a lack of self-image; after all, this was a human being who had been shaped and reshaped—by the Hearsts, the SLA, the FBI, lawyers, psychiatrists, chaplains, media interviewers, and the U.S. prison system itself. After that many brainwashings, one's brain might well feel a bit shrunk.

But I'd come so to trust the energy of feminist communica-tion that I simply was not prepared for the persistence of ste-reotype between us, or even more for the gulf of style. The urgency that electrifies so many interchanges and overrides so many differences among women today had seemed to buzz with promise through our letters. In our actual meeting, however, it kept draining away into polite listlessness. I kept thinking of the F. Scott Fitzgerald lines from "The Rich Boy": "The very rich . . . are different from you and me. They possess and enjoy early, and it does something to them, makes them soft where we are hard, and cynical where we are trustful. . . . Even when they enter deep into our world or sink below us, they still think that they are better than we are. They are different." That tone echoed in Patricia Hearst's voice as we sat in conversation—a voice resonant with no ethnic vibrancy, no middle-class eagerness, not even the self-congratulatory huskiness of the recently rich. It was, rather, a thin, nasal drawl, pitched high from the towers of generational wealth. Nursemaids and a convent education may have further muted its colors, until it was almost monotone. It was the voice of a woman bred to please. I also had a sense that Patricia found it difficult to be curious or feel very deeply about anything; that she was barely listening (to her own words as well as anyone else's); that she was utterly preoccupied yet unacquainted with herself; that she had turned inward but somehow got no further, as if afraid of finding nothing there. Women of the powerful are trained for precisely such vapidity. But survivors of concentration camps also mouth descriptions approximating such emptiness; rape victims have recurring dreams of themselves melting away like wax. How to know which of her experiences, or how much of each, was responsible for such loss of affect?

Egotistically, I tried over the hours to evoke some real emotion, some shock of intellectual communion. But such arrogance on my part was worn away by what felt like an arrogance of indifference on hers, by the blandness of even her direct answers. We talked as if through a Carmelite grille, as if we were two women sleepwalking our meeting at the bottom of the ocean, conversing dreamily over a silver tea service but refraining from vulgar mention of the creatures swirling around us.

We talked about her case, the labyrinthine legal motions and hearings and the "Free Patty" campaign—everything we said formulaic and predictable. Then we talked politics. Yes, she was for the ERA, and believed in reproductive freedom. But she didn't like women being "shrill," and thought men shouldn't be confronted too much or "put down." She disapproved of affirmative action because it could amount to "reverse discrimination." That was it for feminism. We left political discussion behind us.

We didn't fare a lot better on the subject of her personal philosophy. My probings got deflected to standard religion. I had solipsistically high hopes, I confess, for books as conversational bait. But Patricia said she didn't read much, preferring to embroider samplers. Sisterhood can be difficult. Then she did shyly admit an addiction to gothic novels. "Don't apologize!" I said, smiling and eager to identify with her interest, I enthused about the Brontës. It was a mistake. Patricia meant that she liked *modern* gothics, "bodice rippers," though she couldn't recall any in particular. So much for literature.

I can't remember whether it was from a brief discussion of the feminist campaign against pornography or from the mention of embroidered samplers that we drifted into talk about marriage. Patricia was engaged at that time to Bernie Shaw, a police officer eight years her senior. They had met when he was one of her bodyguards.

There was a gleam of feminist consciousness in her views on marriage. Perhaps because Bernie was recently divorced and the father of two children, there had been discussion of simply living together, but Patricia had had quite enough of that with Steve Weed (her fiancé at the time of the kidnapping). "I've had to bring in lawyers over getting furniture back from Weed," she snapped; "a woman has less protection outside of marriage." I passed along the feminist aphorism that in free love with a man it's usually the woman who pays. She agreed, almost with a sign of energy. A possible sampler motto, I suspected.

Bernie Shaw seemed an odd fiancé for a woman like Patricia Hearst. He was a former longshoreman and a black belt in karate. He had been quoted as saying that he loved Patricia very much—because she was cute, had beautiful skin, and remembered birthdays. It struck me that, for her part, Patricia was drawn to Bernie because, like Everest, he was there. But that wasn't the whole story. When I asked her about the ironic pattern I had noticed—a number of women who were former political fugitives and prisoners gravitating romantically toward men who worked in law enforcement—she shrugged that she hadn't thought about it much: "That's all I had around me, lawyers and bodyguards. My old boyfriends couldn't comprehend what I'd been through." She said that she also knew Bernie loved her because he got on well with her guard dog, Arrow, a German shepherd who seemed the most valued being in her life. She told me she "adored animals," and could imagine herself becoming an animal trainer, although not a vet—too much studying. But the future seemed as remote to her then as to any other prisoner. In jail you plan one day—or hour, even—at a time. Your hopes may reach beyond that, but your sense of reality can't. As for Patricia's love of animals, I wondered aloud if this was enhanced by their reacting to her as a human being and not a symbol. She glazed out again and replied that she didn't know, hadn't thought about it.

This self-preoccupation without insight was a peculiar combination, particularly since the most constant theme in our conversation, returned to obsessively by Patricia, was violence. Not the transcendence of violence (as in what she'd termed those "gloomy" Brontës), but violence itself: graphic descriptions of how guard dogs like Arrow are trained to attack, go for the jugular, sink in, and hang on; how strong the recoil is on the right kind of rifle used to kill deer; how bone-crunchingly rough the touch football games at San Simeon could get; how interesting it was to hear Bernie talk about his job as a cop. Quite verbose now, she rattled on, her eyes glowing, about how only recently he had gone on a police call that turned up a body which had been dead for some time, and she excitedly repeated his description of the color and texture of the corpse's globulating skin. Going rapidly globulate myself, I asked whether this might not present a problem—Bernie relating details of His Day to a wife who herself had survived such violence. No, Patricia thought it was "fascinating." Besides, she felt it was important for a woman to express interest in her man's work, or he might "grow away from her."

I suddenly glimpsed the sexual and emotional force with which violence still operated in this woman's life, not as an abstraction, but as a reality that had threatened her for so long as to become inseparable from daily living.

Perhaps someday, I thought, when she's been out of prison a long time and the future seems less enclosed by bodyguards, guard dogs, and fenced-in estates, when the cranks and the justice system and the Establishment she "deserted" and the Left she "betrayed" are less out to get her—perhaps then she may not come alive most when talking of death. But at the time, she was like a wraith rising to the subject as if summoned by a spell to her master—enthralled and unknowing. It wasn't pleasant to witness. I had to remind myself of her trial testimony—that this was the woman whose eyes had been unable to endure any light after almost two months in a closet, who had been stuffed into a garbage can for the moves from one SLA hiding place to another, whose menstrual periods had stopped from pure fear, whose hair had been forcibly cut by SLA women to less than a one-inch length, who had been made to urinate and defecate while her kidnappers watched and laughed at her, who had been raped and beaten, and who had narrowly missed being burned alive during the shoot-out between the SLA and the Los Angeles police. This was also the woman who had issued statements of solidarity with the SLA, who had refused to testify against her "comrades" for a long time after their capture, who had said that she was in love with their leader and that she had never been so free as with her kidnappers, who had posed with a defiantly raised fist after *her* capture by the police.

Our culture now acknowledges that a prisoner of war can be the victim of brainwashing. That same culture is less understanding and even less forgiving when a woman's brain and life are at stake—whether such a woman is abducted into prostitution and sexual slavery and "seasoned" by forced drug addiction and brothel beatings, or is Patricia Hearst.

In that context, the only wonder was that Patricia spoke intelligibly at all, rather than gibbering or falling catatonically silent. One had to admire her acknowledgment of her own focused will to survive—even when that focus sometimes was expressed in superficiality.

Attention to surface and avoidance of substance may, after all, be survival tools. Patricia clearly took pride in not having given other inmates, prison officials, the press, and the public, what she thought they wanted—for her to "break down." Had she shown stronger emotion in front of the jury, in fact, its members might have rewarded the performance with a more "grateful" verdict. The mask (if it was one) made her less likable, less trustable in a world of cheap emotions; but then, what had that world done for her to inspire *her* affection or trust? Even Patricia may no longer have known whether her persona was created by some long-ago mother superior or necessitated by SLA men, whether her stiff spine was a product of upper-class posture or a corrective to huddling in that dark closet.

I began to appreciate what an asset a stiff spine can be when her father arrived to join the accumulating set of lawyers and friends toward the end of our visiting-day conversation. "Randy" they called him—and his version of such pride, if he ever had it, appeared to have been shattered. He could have been ill, but he seemed to me a destroyed man. He was polite, even hearty, through his slurred sentences, but just as not much seemed to emanate from the daughter, so not much seemed to register with the father. He kept repeating the same questions, statements, small talk. The warmest interest father and daughter showed one another was expressed in the gift he brought—a drawing specially done for her by a cartoon artist. This was the man whose family at one time controlled most of the newspapers in the United States, and who still commanded a massive financial empire.

When power and wealth combine with ignorance and an unsteady hand, the result is societal violence, making almost inevitable—in the patriarchal pattern—the enforced ignorance and terrorist violence of groups like the SLA. Horribly, the two come to deserve each other. It's the people in the middle, mostly women and children, who get crushed. Randolph Hearst apparently had sufficient power to be viewed as a "corporate enemy of the people" that is to say, what he *owned,* including his women, was coveted. The men of the SLA had sufficient power to entice a few women into helping them commit hideous acts on another woman, for male approval. The FBI and the Los Angeles police had sufficient power to burn some of them to death, and to immure the survivors. Nowhere did the women have such power—except as addicts of men who functioned as conductors of violence between men.

As for Patricia Hearst, her "initiation," her "seasoning," began when she was born—as female and as Hearst. That brainwashing predated the SLA's, and may have outlasted theirs. Patricia sometimes sounded like a heroine reliving her gothic horror story over and over, but in the format of a Disney cartoon. Maybe that simply proved she was essentially American. Maybe it proved she had a case of the Galloping Shallows. But it was frightful that someone might go through what she had and still seem to know so little about the human heart.

Still, I was left judging myself for having dared judge her. And I was left facing certain internal temptations in writing up the interview. The first was to patronize her, as many of her supporters had done, to inspire easy sympathy by failing to portray her as honestly as my admitted subjectivity permitted, warts and all (hers *and* mine). The second temptation took me by surprise with the intensity of its pragmatic hiss: to say only nice things, so that maybe the Hearsts would donate desperately needed money to the women's movement; we couldn't afford to criticize and make new enemies. Falling for that lure would have been the ethical equivalent of holding Patricia for ransom again. The third temptation was a poignant one: I just didn't want to hurt her feelings (my arrogance again, perhaps, in thinking that I could?). And I didn't want to mistake the symbol for the woman, although I had to confess doubt about my own capacity to separate them out.

I did want to respect Patricia by taking her seriously, which meant telling the truth about what I had seen and heard in her. That's why what stays with me most is our parting. We embraced—but that, too, was a ritual. I turned to go. Then she put a hand on my arm and held me back. Almost out of nowhere it came.

"You know," she pleaded softly, "there's a scene in this movie—*Cool Hand Luke*, I think it is—where they're beating up this guy and he falls down and gets to his feet and keeps getting knocked down and keeps coming back for more. He's all broken and dazed, and they yell at him, 'Why don't you just lie down, you stupid bastard? Just lie down and give up and we'll leave you alone.' That's what they want from me. If I'd only lie down and give up, they'd leave me alone."

She had said it too late and she had used a he-man metaphor and any fool could guess it might be a standard emotionally manipulative farewell—and I couldn't have cared less. I turned full around again to face her, and to mutter fiercely, "Don't you ever give up, Patricia! Don't you *dare* lie down!"

Through somebody's embarrassingly womanish tears (mine? hers?), I saw her grin.

"I won't," she said firmly.

And this time the embrace felt real.

Ten years have passed since that meeting. Patricia Hearst is long out of jail, her sentence having been commuted in 1979 by President Carter. Her 1982 book, about the kidnapping and aftermath, has formed the basis for a movie. I wish her well, and only regret that I was unable to really connect with the woman who had written, in 1978, "What happened to me happens to women all the time. I've been kidnapped, held prisoner, threatened, beaten, humiliated, raped, battered. I've been lied to and lied about and disbelieved. The only difference between what happened to me and what happens to other women is that mine was an extreme case."[2]

When Patricia Hearst wrote those words, she had sensed and named the presence of the Demon Lover. Yet his hypnotic spell re-worked its magic on her in the shape of a handsome young man who was a crack shot, who could hunt deer and humans alike, who could tell tales of death.

Reader, she married him.

It could be said that hers was an extreme case, the heiress turned (forcibly?) terrorist, turned (forcibly?) heiress again, turned (forcibly?) housewife. What about the women who choose militant involvement ostensibly of their own volition? Surely they are "real" women terrorists.

How many "extreme" cases does it take to make a norm?

Cherchez l'Homme

It always happens when women become at last the subject and not the object: in order to define what women, or a group of women, or an individual woman are/is, first one must define what this subject is *not*. So thorough is the stereotyping, the perception of female as Other, the deliberate misinterpretation of motive, that the lies must be peeled away before a female reality can even be approached.

Perhaps the most common misapprehension is the one that blurs together women who participate in general uprisings and "terrorist" women. For the record, then. Women taking to the streets banging pots and pans during food-shortage riots are not engaged in terrorist activity. Women marching in a public demonstration against a colonial government are not engaged in terrorist activity. Peasant women agitating for land rights, squatting on their small sharecropped farms, are not engaged in terrorist activity. Honduran campesino organizer Elvia Alvarado speaks indignantly about such calculated miscategorization:

> The military has started accusing us of . . . being Sandinista terrorists, . . . of working with the Salvadoran guerrillas. . . . I don't know anything about Nicaragua, . . . I don't know what's gong on in El Salvador. Hondurans have to worry about what's going on *here*. . . .

They always try to say we're part of some big conspiracy, when we're just a handful of poor campesinos. . . . Before, when we used to try to recover the land, we were charged with damaging private property. Now we're still charged with that, but also with being terrorists, . . . you can't even get out on bail. . . . Where do they get off calling us terrorists just because we try to recover the land? We don't want to hurt anyone. We don't even have weapons. So why do they call us terrorists?[3]

A second kind of predictable analysis bases itself on that old stand-by, Blame the Victim. Who is responsible for intensified violence in terrorist groups? Women. J. K. Zawodny writes:

This problem has never been publicly aired for fear of . . . being charged with antifeminist bias. . . . [Women] do produce tensions within extralegal organizations. . . . it is inevitable (although never admitted formally) that there is conscious or unconscious competition for them . . . affecting relationships among the men. Women's ability to manipulate the membership of the organization on an informal level is another problem. . . . Men who compete for women try to "outdo" each other, often initiating violence first; looking for a formalized excuse afterward. The fact that the women observe the actions as direct participants is quite an incentive. In this type of cultural setting, the presence of women within a terrorist organization is a psychological inducement to violence that is constantly present on all organizational levels.[4]

As an afterthought, Professor (of International Relations) Zawodny adds, "On the other hand, in some cultures, [women's] presence may serve as a brake on violent actions."[5] But he says no more about *that*—for fear of being accused of a profeminist bias?

Moving right along from blaming all women in general to blaming some women in particular (and don't forget that male terrorism is the fault of the terrorists' mothers), authorities not infrequently cite feminism as the culprit in female terrorism. A rare voice does disagree—but for the wrong reasons. Vera

Broido, in her book *Apostles into Terrorists: Women and the Revolutionary Movement in the Russia of Alexander II,* sneers, "To assign to revolutionary women the narrow partisan role of feminists is to distort their position in the revolutionary movement and to diminish their contribution to Russian history."[6] (That silly, narrow, partisan role again, selfishly addressing itself to the majority of the human species.) Most of the terrorism "experts," however, when they decide to examine women's participation at all, claim a direct connection between feminist foment and female violence. Daniel E. Georges-Abeyie is a special favorite of mine. In an article entitled "Women as Terrorists," he reviews the literature on women and criminality, from Cesare Lombroso (criminal women exhibit primitive traits, considerable body hair, lower intelligence), to Freud (they're anatomically inferior, attempting to be men), through Otto Pollak (the rising female crime rate is the result of sexual emancipation), M. Rappaport (female criminals are psychological misfits), J. Cowie, V. Cowie, and E. Slater (there is a chromosomal explanation: such women are more masculine than the normal female), H. C. Vedder and D. Sommerville (they show maladjustment to the normal feminine role), F. Adler (they're a side product of the women's liberation movement), and R. Simon (women's violence is created by a shift in patterns of sexual inequality and the rise in female labor-force participation).[7]

Georges-Abeyie himself does not agree with all of the literature. In fact, he finds some of the conclusions "laughable." He is a modern scholar, rational, one of the "honorable men." But he does feel that "there is some merit to a less extreme interpretation of some of the correlates to these and other theories of this specific form of female criminality [terrorism]." He even adds some correlates of his own, focusing on such Northern American groups as the Weatherpeople and the SLA, with "sizable numbers of female cadres [who] proselytized female homosexuality and bisexuality as well as pansexualism and feminist ideology."[8] His empirical research apparently did not include the later public statements and writings of women previously involved in such groups, to wit, that pressure for rejection of monogamy and for lesbian acts (but never for *male* homosexuality) as forms of "sexual liberation" emanated *from the male leadership of those groups as direct orders.* Rejection of monogamy was to make the women available to all the men, and lesbianism (under male direction and control) was thought by the men to be titillating.[9] Georges-Abeyie notes that "various social-control agencies" today share the assumption that woman terrorists have masculine psychologies and even body types, and (contradictorily) that most of the acts committed by such women are "emotive rather than instrumental, i.e., emotional rather than well-thought-out acts with a rational program of action not tied to a love interest, such as an attempt to free a captured husband or lover." (Masculine psychologies but feminine emotions: this is called eating your analysis and having it, too.) These "social-control authorities," according to Georges-Abeyie, are certain that female terrorists are much more likely than men to commit acts of "senseless or nongoal-oriented violence"—as opposed to sensible and goal-oriented violence, I presume. For himself, he theorizes that we can expect a further increase in women's participation in terrorism, because of "changing role-sets" for women in general; the influence of feminism in raising women's expectations of society; and the likelihood that "women who lack the characteristics . . . that society considers appropriate [gentleness, seductiveness, physical attractiveness, etc.] . . . may seek success in some non-feminine realm, by displaying aggression, unadorned faces and bodies, toughness, or other masculine qualities."[10] (Run for the Revlon, quick, before the shoot-out.) He anticipates that the women in this rise will be seen integrated into national-liberation and socialist struggles, "and not as autonomous legions of Amazon-oriented warriors"—yet he does not ask *why.* Being a good liberal, he feels it imperative to factor into his hypothesis the influence of feminist demands "both logical *and* irrational"; he will decide which is which.

Well. It's difficult to know where to start, with such a barrage of imbecilities. So why not start with feminism? Need it
be said that Georges-Abeyie (and Vera Broido, too) would not
recognize feminism were it to appear and introduce itself in
person? An even more tragic truth is that women who become
involved in terrorist acts wouldn't recognize it either, despite
claims on their part that they are acting as "liberated" women.
How and why feminism eludes them—or, rather, how and why
they elude it—is a story unique to them yet familiarly parallel
to the story of every woman.

As we've seen, all women share the cross-cultural burden of
being viewed as the repositories of (male-defined) morality.
Therefore, women must never be wrong doers. To encroach
beyond preset boundaries—to trespass, disobey, transgress—is
a far more censurable act for a woman than for a man. It's the
old double standard, as in sex, drinking (a male drunk is a jolly
good fellow; a female drunk is disgusting), drug abuse, and
prostitution (in the statutes of most countries, the male buyer
goes free, while the female seller is jailed). If, then, transgression for a woman is made into an unthinkable act, or at least
one for which she knows she will pull down much more oppro-
brium than a male, *she must transgress via a man.* She believes
she has no access to transgression by and for herself. She must
try to androgynize herself, combine herself with him. "Wow,
what a trip!" reminisced Charles Manson "family" member
Susan Atkins while in prison. "I thought 'To taste death, and
yet give life.' "[11] As with everything else in her vicarious existence, her rebellion can be conceived by society *and by her* only
through him, his modes, his means.

It wasn't a historical coincidence that the nineteenth- and
twentieth-century waves of feminism in the United States were
born out of the abolition and civil-rights movements respec-
tively. Women, black and white, were in the forefront of those
movements, their rebellion always in the context of altruistic
struggle for the good of the whole, for the suffrage rights of
their men, and later for the rights of *manhood.* All of which

was a historical prerequisite to their articulating the smallest revolt on behalf of their own female predicament.

Just as the structure of the male corporate world is the means for a woman to rise in our economy (playing the game by following his rules), so is the structure of a male revolution the means for a woman to rebel (overthrowing the rules by playing his game). The knowledge that she is exchanging one form of male leadership and style for another is not always tolerable, certainly not at first—and then, suddenly, it can be too late.

The "revolutionary" woman has bought into the male "radical" line, as articulated from Nechaev through Castro. She has learned that in order to be a *real* revolutionary, she must disassociate herself from her womanhood, her aspirations, her reality—and most of all, from other women. She must integrate into herself the alarm and disgust with which such men regard "women's issues." Two cases in point: Nadeshda Krupskaya, Lenin's wife, was in her time and fashion a feminist and an advocate of women's sexual freedom—as was his mistress, Inessa Armand. Both have been virtually erased from the official canons, though these two, together with Clara Zetkin, created the idea of International Women's Day (March 8). Lenin was appalled when Armand wanted to write a pamphlet on female sexual liberation; he worried that she was promulgating "adultery" and "freedom from child-bearing."[12]

So the woman who wishes to rebel learns yet another of man's realities. As wife, sister, and mother, she has mouthed his patriotism during national wars, carried his flags, waved at his parades, driven his ambulances. She has tried for millennia to demonstrate her loyalty, to win his acceptance; Jean Bethke Elshtain has thoroughly documented that fealty in her book *Woman and War*. All the while, though, she has been petitioning, pleading, organizing—for peace. (Is this one reason why his approval has never been forthcoming?) And when her rage at his ignoring her reaches a certain point of necessary expression, she finds again that the only model for it is a male one: *his* revolution.

"By God, I shall exceed my sex," are words attributed to Jeanne d'Arc. They are the words required of the woman who would "succeed" in the man's world (his State or his State-that-would be). *She may not rise with her people.* She must abandon them, abandon her own experience, and, more important, her own intuited, envisioned possible transformation. If she wants power, she must learn that power is synonymous with *his power*— and *his means* of seizing it. If she wants freedom she must learn that this too is synonymous with *his* definition of it and his struggle for it. Neither will save her. Both will destroy her. *But she has found a way to transgress which is acceptable.* She has entered the harem of the Demon Lover.

Her own psychology, ethics, desires, and truths, go underground in her soul. She must deny and deny and deny them. Listen to the court testimony of Vera Zasulich, who in 1878 shot and wounded General Dmitri Trepov, the governor of St. Petersburg, in reaction to hearing about the torture of political prisoners: "Such degradation of human personality should not be allowed to be inflicted. . . . *I could find no other way* of drawing attention to what had happened. . . . *But it is a terrible thing to lift one's hand against another human being.* . . . I fired without aiming [she instantly threw the gun away] . . . I was afraid it might go off again. . . . *I did not want this.*"[13] (Italics mine.) (Zasulich, by the way, was described in the press of the day as being a "spinster" of noble birth, twenty-eight years old—and plain-looking.) In her later life a critic of Lenin, Zasulich wrote in 1892 that "terrorist acts cannot make a movement more powerful, no matter how popular they may be. Terrorism is too morbid a form of struggle. However great the delight it sometimes arouses, in order to carry out terrorist acts all of one's energies must be expended, and a particular frame of mind almost always results: either one of great vanity or one in which life has lost all its attractiveness."[14]

Vanity and despair could comprise an excellent description of patriarchy.

The woman trapped in this position must not only pledge her fealty but defend her commitment—and defend her denial of herself—with a vehemence sufficient to convince her own troubled soul as well as her vigilant male colleagues. So the great Rosa Luxemburg suffered indignities from her long-term lover Leo Jogiches, and insults for being "the last man in the German Social Democratic Party." Luxemburg was torn all her life between a relentless political activism and her yearning for a contemplative life of writing, thinking, and caring for plants and animals; torn between her own insistent pacifism and the cynical prowar position of her own party; torn between what she herself saw as her dependent need for men and her knowledge that the need was self-destructive; torn between her friend Clara Zetkin's feminist influence and her own decision to oppose women's suffrage as diversionary to the workers' cause. Though her courage never failed her (she denounced Lenin as practicing a "Tatar-Mongolian savagery"), the resolve to use that courage on her own behalf and that of other women did.[15] Similarly, Emma Goldman denounced women's suffrage as a joke and a diversion, and sublimated her radical transgressions under the banners of male politics. When Goldman gave us the audacious phrase "If I can't dance to it, it's not my revolution," did she think she would exceed her sex and be dancing only with her brothers?[16]

What we glimpse in the life-loving personal temperaments of Luxemburg and Goldman—the longing for peace and for joy—shines like silver streaked through caverns of a so-called revolutionary male politics grimy with hatred and revenge, with manipulation, petty ambition, and violence. But their lives of torment have been bequeathed to the women who still dance in the Demon Lover's revolutionary State-that-would-be.

"We are becoming the men we wanted to marry" is a consciousness-raising phrase some of us coined in the early 1970s, as women began to look at their own potential instead of gazing vicariously at life through a male-imposed scrim, began to pour into law and medical schools, began to found small businesses, start magazines, break into nontraditional jobs. It was a useful phrase for its time. In retrospect, it has a built-in danger: the *terms* of our "becoming" remain defined by the men we may (or may not) want to marry. For the rebel woman, who is "becoming" the man she wanted to follow through the revolution, there's no time to question that the role she dons was cut like a uniform for him, not for her. In the act of donning it, she not only delays her own revolution, but in fact *obstructs* it: she reinforces both his priorities and his means.

It's certainly understandable why Nechaev considered such women "treasures." They will dare more, fight harder, work longer, and try to prove themselves to their comrades more than any man will (and more than any man needs to). And the men will exploit them ruthlessly—in the name of the cause the *men* have defined.

During the Chinese Revolution, the single most controversial issue was women's right to divorce; the most persecuted cadres were women trying to organize against foot-binding, wife-beating, and rape. In the 1927–30 purge of Communists by Chiang Kai-shek's Kuomintang, thousands of young women were identified as "radicals" because of bobbed hair, and were accused of "sexual license and free love" politics. Many were wrapped in cotton wadding, doused in oil, and burnt alive.[17]

> Not all were communists, some were bourgeois, and there were many students. . . . I think the brutality of the killing has no parallel in all the world. . . . When girls [sic] were arrested in Hunan they were stripped naked, nailed on crosses, and their noses and breasts were cut off before they were killed. . . . [After beheading] their heads were put into men's coffins and the gendarmes said "you have your free love now." . . . [18]

And in the wake of the sacrifice by women cadres? In 1942, Ding Ling, China's greatest novelist and herself a revolutionary, loosed a scathing criticism of the Communist party's betrayal of women in her famous "Thoughts on March 8, International

Women's Day." Women, she claimed, were still being subjected to the old oppressive treatments, new ones had been
added, and to boot women were being told they were now
emancipated. For this cry of truth, she was publicly attacked
by Mao, accused of being a reactionary, and sentenced to two
years of "thought reform." In and out of official favor for the
rest of her life, Ding Ling continued to speak her mind *and* her
feminism. In 1956, she was again charged, this time with the
crime of refusing to accept party supervision; she had been
fighting literary censorship and speaking publicly about wom-
en's oppression. The following year, she was denounced by the
official writers' union, denied citizenship, expelled from the
party, and sentenced to a term of hard labor in Manchuria—
where she remained for almost twenty years. "Rehabilitated"
and brought back into public favor after Mao's death (when
she was seventy-seven) she lived out her last years without
bitterness—still writing, and still calling on younger women to
free themselves—until her death in 1986.[19]

The "revolution in the revolution"—to borrow and give new
meaning to Régis Debray's phrase—does not always take such
a long-term or principled form. Sometimes it's simply a cry for
immediate help. On May 8, 1972, a Sabena Airlines plane over
Yugoslavia was hijacked by a four-person Palestinian team, in
what would be a failed attempt to free some prisioners being
held in the Israeli prison at Ramallah in the Occupied West
Bank. Brought to trial in Israel, the defendants were charged
with terrorist acts as well as with the crime of being members
of the outlawed Al Fatah. Two of the team were young women,
and both pleaded the "defence of constraint," under an inher-
ited British statute then still on the Israeli lawbooks. Their
attorney argued that they had been constrained to carry arms
under threat of death, and had been involved in the hijacking
against their will. One of the women was an addict whose drug
dependency had been used to force her participation; the other
pleaded that she had been kidnapped by the guerrillas and had
been unable to escape. At the trial and later at the appeal, these

defenses were rejected and both women were found guilty.[20] In the Sharia (the legal code of Islam) as well as in the Halacha (the legal code of Judaism) women are legally "irresponsible"; in the former, a woman's testimony is rated at half the value of a man's, and in the latter women are considered unreliable or illegal signatories to legal documents. Yet when the State-that-would-be and the State-that-is wish it otherwise, suddenly women are legally responsible for their views and their acts.

The coercion is not always so direct. Equally pernicious and far more common is the use of sex and "love" to enmesh women—and, in turn, the use of women's sexuality to further the cause. This form of coercion—recruitment by romance—is, after all, what the Demon Lover's message is about.

Colin Smith's biography of Ilich Ramirez Sanchez, *Carlos: Portrait of a Terrorist,* is one long saga of Carlos's proud seductions of women into the stable of his revolution:

> One of Carlos's greatest joys was that he was able to claim an energetic sex life as a legitimate working expense, part of the important business of establishing cover and hide-outs. . . . he was quite capable of ruthlessly exploiting his sexual conquests, . . . [at one point] he had four regular girl friends, two either side of the [English] Channel, whose homes he sometimes used as safe-houses to hide arms, explosives and false documents. They were also places of sanctuary, somewhere he could be assured, without warning, of getting a bed for the night—preferably a warm one."[21]

Most of these women wound up serving jail sentences, while their Lothario has not yet been caught. That Carlos was notorious among these women for his acutely masculinist attitude toward cooking and housework (he never helped) will strike some readers as amusing, considering the circumstances. That he lived the life of a *bon vivant*—enjoying gourmet food, Napoleon brandy, imported cigars, and designer clothes—often supported by these women, may seem more distasteful. That in country after country—in the Middle East, Turkey, Greece,

Germany, Italy, France, England, Scandinavia—he literally recruited women from his bed onto his battlefront, at last seems serious. (Yet all three stages are common, and are related.) Many of the women came in time not only to hide the documents but to smuggle them, not only to secrete the weapons but to shoot them, not only to store the bombs but to plant them. Some of these women are dead. Some are in prison for life. Some are still in hiding. Some are still dancing to his tune.

Each one was certain she was his true love.

Sometimes the Demon Lover pimps for the cause. The use of women as "Mata Hari" sexual bait is by now a cliché. (A subtle form of this was the slogan "Girls say Yes to Boys Who Say No" during the 1960s New Left campaign to encourage draft resistance. Change the letter A to R and color it scarlet for Revolution.)

Possibly the most famous contemporary case of a woman as sexual lure is that of the late Nora Astorga, the young, beautiful Nicaraguan attorney who was in sympathy with the Sandinista insurgents against the tyrannical Somoza dictatorship. General Reynaldo Perez Vega—called "El Perro" ("The Dog")—a ranking officer in Somoza's notorious human-rights-violating National Guard, had been pursuing her. Finally, in March 1978, she invited Perez to her home, dismissed his bodyguard, brought him to her bedroom, and undressed and disarmed him. Guerrilla men, hiding in her closet, then jumped out and slit his throat. They left his body, draped with the Sandinista flag, behind them when they fled. Astorga disappeared into the revolutionary ranks, leaving behind the message "I want it known that I participated in the operation of bringing to justice this bloody henchman." Later, she would revise her version of the event, claiming that the plan—merely to kidnap and hold Perez Vega for ransom—had gone awry when he attacked the guerrillas.[22] Whatever the real story, the State-that-would-be in this case won. The Sandinistas formed a revolutionary government. Possibly because there had been rumblings of discontent from too many women in Third World revolutionary ranks, it was

decided that Astorga need not meet the fate of such forerun-
ners as Haydee Santamaría of Cuba, a liberation heroine who
was relegated to a minor "cultural" post and who later committed suicide; or Nguyen Thi Binh of reunited Vietnam,
assigned the traditional female portfolio of minister of education and the young. The women were getting restless. So Astorga
was rewarded with a rare token position of power: Nicaraguan
ambassador to the United Nations, a post she handled with
intelligence and dignity, while carefully presenting herself,
nonetheless, as a beautiful and chic woman. When I met her in
1987, I couldn't help noticing how her self-discipline overrode
what was clearly great fatigue. I didn't know at that time that
she was seriously ill with cancer, but was remaining at her post
like a "good soldier"; she kept her illness a secret until a few
months before her death, in the spring of 1988. So, in person,
I merely expressed my solidarity with Nicaraguan women. That
elicited a sharp response: "Not solidarity with the Nicaraguan
people?" "Women," I responded politely, though perhaps a bit
wearily, "are my priority." There was no way to ask why solidarity with the majority of the Nicaraguan people—women—
was insufficient, why specific solidarity must be expressed for
the minority—men—in order to prove one's revolutionary
mettle. And there was no way to ask about the rumors of the
special man, for there had been one, whom she had loved and
whose rebellion she had made her own.

Cherchez l'homme. He is there, one way or the other. In a
study of Italian woman terrorists done by Leonard Weinberg
and William Lee Eubank, more than two-thirds of the case histories showed women who had become involved because they
were married to terrorist men, and in most of the other cases
the woman had become involved via a male sibling. A signifi-
cantly higher number of the women than of the men had had
prior blood- or love-relationship ties with terrorists; for those
few men who were involved because of family ties, the connections were fraternal or paternal rather than marital or romantic. Furthermore, the men had a history of political involvement

predating their terrorist activities; most of the women did not.[23] In effect, the men became involved because of politics and the women became involved because of the men. That too is "political."

The women became involved because men constituted the sole route of transgression available against a system the women knew enough to oppose (though not to oppose *enough*). That rebellion shows itself in the numbers. The study examined terrorist groups of the neo-Fascist Right as well as of the Left: the former had "little allure for women," who were to a significant degree more drawn to the revolutionary Left. In another survey of Italian terrorism, Vittorfranco Pisano found that women's "organizational abilities" were in high demand among Leftist terrorist groups, in particular the Brigate Rosse (Red Brigades).[24] Margherita ("Mara") Cagol was reputedly a paragon of such abilities. Her husband, Renato Curcio, is considered to be the founder of the Red Brigades: *cherchez l'homme*.

Mara Cagol and Renato Curcio are one pair among many in what I would term "couple terrorism." Another is Jean-Marc Rouillan and Nathalie Menignon of Action Directe, a couple known as the Bonnie and Clyde of French terrorism. There are Alexander Yenikomechian and Suzy Mahseredjian of ASALA (the Armenian Secret Army for the Liberation of Armenia) and, also with ASALA, Hratch Kozihioukian and his wife Siranouche Kozihioukian. In the United States, there were Sam Melville and Jane Alpert, and at the pinnacle of the Weather Underground Organization Central Committee, Bernardine Dohrn and Bill Ayers. The Weather Underground Organization could also boast of Kathy Boudin and David Gilbert, among other pairs, but in that case the woman apparently coupled with the wrong man. Gilbert never rose to a position of power with the Weatherpeople and, as one WUO faction later charged, "In an organization dominated by male supremacy, how a woman got to be a leader was to line up with the Central Committee men, on the backs of women." Consequently, Boudin's "relationship with Gilbert kept her down."[25] She may therefore have felt the need to prove herself all the more keenly: she is currently serving a twenty-years-to-life sentence for second-degree murder and first-degree robbery in a 1981 attack on a Brink's van.

These women would have died—as some did—rather than admit that they acted as they did for male approval and love. It takes, time, perspective, and courage to hazard such an admission. In 1987, after thirteen years of forced exile from her native Chile, Carmen Castillo was permitted home for a visit to her ailing father. When she had been sent into exile, she was recuperating from bullet wounds and was seven months pregnant with a child fathered by her lover, Miguel Enriquez; he had died at her side in a shoot-out with General Pinochet's military-intelligence forces. It has taken Castillo over a decade of suffering, and of learning to live again, to be able to say as she does now that although she still opposes Pinochet's bloody regime, she would not stoop to bloody means of contesting. "All that I did back then was for love," she says simply. "It had a logic, and the logic was love."[26]

Carmen Castillo is one of the lucky ones. In a different way, so is Anna-Karin Lindgren. A college graduate, she met Norbert Kroecher at a 1972 New Year's Eve party in Sweden. He was already married, as well as involved with two other women back in his home city of Berlin, but she didn't know that. She fell in love with him. He moved in with her. He had no job, so she supported them both by working as a teacher. Sometimes he came and went without explanation. As Lindgren's friend Pia Lasker testified at her later trial, "Kroecher was a genuine male chauvinist who did not do anything in the home but only exercised Anna-Karin. . . . Often he lay sleeping until late in the afternoon. He had a room of his own at his disposal in Anna-Karin's apartment." Kroecher "easily grew angry and he often snapped at [Anna-Karin]. Probably he found her irritating. One reason for this was certainly that he was very dependent on her. . . . Anna-Karin herself was not politically attached to any particular movement and her relationship with Kroecher was not marked by any political will or idea, but was exclusively of an emotional character."[27]

Kroecher was a fugitive from West Germany and a former fringe member of the circle of people around the Baader-Meinhof Group, the Movement 2 June, and the SPK (the German Socialist Patients' Collective).* Now, in Sweden, Kroecher was building a new terrorist group. Over the following five years, his gang robbed banks for funds, planned several bombings, and plotted Operation Leo, an abortive attempt to kidnap a Swedish woman cabinet minister. A number of Swedish men became involved—all of them pulling in their girlfriends. Gradually, some of Kroecher's German friends appeared and became active (along with *their* girlfriends), as did Armando Carillo, from Mexico (and *his* wife, Maria). But in the midst of their activity—after five years of paying for it and committing crimes she never understood—Lindgren was purged, ostensibly for political reasons. In reality, Kroecher had found himself a new woman. "Kroecher was not satisfied with Anna-Karin, who had shown passive resistance against his plans. . . . Their relationship had progressively worsened. . . . [At the meeting] it was said that Anna-Karin was unreliable and unpolitical. . . . there was some kind of voting. Nobody was against the decision. Anna-Karin wondered what they were doing but she did not ask since she felt there was no point in asking."[28]

The women who recognize their own powerlessness in such

---

*The German Socialist Patients' Collective was the bizarre brainchild of Dr. Wolfgang Huber, who in 1969 alchemized the theories of R. D. Laing and David Cooper into his own political dreams. He began organizing his patients at the Psychiatric Neurological Clinic of Heidelberg University into "working circles"—one on radio transmission, one on judo/karate, and one on explosives. His wife, Ursula Huber, headed the explosives group. The point of the SPK was that "The System has made us sick. . . . there must be no therapeutic act which has not been previously clearly and uniquely shown to be a revolutionary act. . . . Let us strike a deathblow at the sick system." ("Patient Info No. 1," pamphlet by the SPK, quoted in Jacob W. F. Sundberg, "Operation Leo: Description and Analysis of a European Terrorist Operation," *Terrorism: An International Journal*, Vol. 5, No. 3 [1981], p. 203.) In 1971, the SPK was raided by the police, shortly after announcing its merger with Baader-Meinhof.

a context are "simple-mindedly" more intelligent than those who cling to the illusion that they exceed their sex. "Unpolitical," passively resistant Anna-Karin Lindgren is at least still alive.

Ulrike Meinhof is not.

The Baader-Meinhof Group / Red Army Faction is sometimes cited as unusual both for the number of women involved and for their presence in leadership positions. Less attention is paid to subtler facts. The group was actually begun by two men—Horst Mahler and Andreas Baader. Baader and his woman, Gudrun Ensslin, were members of German SDS. After an attempt was made on the life of their colleague, radical organizer Rudi Dutschke, Baader began calling for violent action against the State, and he and Ensslin adopted the name Wetterleute (Weatherpeople) for themselves in imitation of the U.S. group. Ensslin previously had been calling herself an evangelical pacifist.[29] Ulrike Meinhof, also a declared pacifist, had been Dutschke's lover. They had worked together at *Konkret,* a "revolutionary pornography" magazine owned by Meinhof's husband. After the shooting, Dutschke dropped out of politics entirely and left the country—and Meinhof. She then joined Ensslin and Baader, to forge a "guerrilla" group that would, according to their propaganda, expose the contradictions of the Federal Republic of Germany and force the State to show its fascism openly. The Red Army Faction called for terrorism to accomplish this purpose. Ensslin became the operational commander of the group (because of her "organizational abilities"), but Meinhof had led a successful and highly publicized attempt to free Baader after his arrest in 1970, and the Red Army Faction informally came to be named after the two of them. From its founding in 1968–69 until 1972, by which time the original members had been mostly killed or captured, the group carried out bombings, arson, kidnappings, hijackings, and assassinations. It sometimes worked with Carlos (at Entebbe and in the assault on the OPEC ministers), and is also thought to have had links with the Japanese Red Army, the Italian Red

Brigades, the Dutch Red Help cells, the Palestinian Black September faction, and Wadi Haddad's breakaway PFLP. At Entebbe, Red Army Faction member Brigitte Kohlmann, together with her man and teammate Wilfried Bose, was killed by Israeli commandos. Ulrike Meinhof committed suicide in her prison cell, as did Ensslin (some factions of the Left in Germany claimed the suicides were murders by prison authorities). Today, the group has fragmented, but some "second-generation" members are thought to be still working throughout Europe, in isolation or in periodic contact with other self-proclaimed terrorist groups.[30] One former member, Beate Sturm, claims in retrospect that the Red Army Faction members were "naive and incurably romantic" with regard to the role their terrorist acts played in furthering world revolution.[31] Anna Mendleson, formerly of the Angry Brigade in the United Kingdom, takes a similar view: "It hasn't changed anything. It hasn't changed anything at all."[32] Dismissing such statements as standard recantations of aging radicals would be easy, except that they have the ring of disillusion uniquely voiced by women betrayed in love.

Whether as troops or as "leaders," these women were followers. Their "rebellion" for love's sake is classic feminine—not feminist—behavior. Ulrike Meinhof was no more of a rebel than Sheela P. Silverman, who took the name of Ma Anand Sheela in the community headed by Indian guru Bhagwan Shree Rajneeshm. The guru, infamous for his 64,000-acre thirty-million-dollar Oregon ranch and his fleet of eighty-five Rolls Royces, was charged in 1984 with election fraud: he had imported thousands of followers to the area in an attempt to take over control of the county. He is now comfortably back at his ashram in Poona, India, having paid a fine. Sheela Silverman, however, is serving a federal prison sentence for wiretapping, attempted murder, and "causing a salmonella epidemic by tainting salad bars, poisoning more than 750 people in Waco County." Silverman has said that she acted "as the fall-guy" for the guru's machinations—but she still reveres him.[33] Sandra Good, a Manson "family" member, still apparently revered *her* guru (who had seen his name as a pun on "Man's Son") even after ten years in prison. In March 1986, she refused her first parole because it was conditional on her not visiting Manson, who is still serving a life sentence.

Of the so-called independents—women who appear unattached to men—the two most famous are probably Fusako Shigenobu and Leila Khaled.

Shigenobu allegedly heads the "Arab Committee" of the JRA (Japanese Red Army, Sekigun faction); she has worked closely with Carlos and with Wadi Haddad of the PFLP, and has been shuttling back and forth to Beirut since 1971. Born in Tokyo only a few weeks before the atomic bombing of Nagasaki and Hiroshima, she is the daughter of a shopkeeper who, in his own youth, was a member of the Blood Oath League, an extremist Right-wing group pledged to "cleanse" Japan of corrupt politicians by selectively assassinating them. Shigenobu wanted to write poetry and fiction but was forced to end her education after high school because the family couldn't afford college tuition. She married a Left-wing radical and cofounder of the JRA, Tsnyoshi Okudaira, and at one point supported him by working as a topless dancer in the Ginza red-light district. Of this period, she wrote, "I hated the men who pawed me and used my body to satisfy their lust. . . . I had murder in my heart. But I smiled, for I saw every kiss turn into a rice ball for the Red Army."[34] When Okudaira, one of the JRA terrorists involved in the 1972 PFLP attack on Lod airport, killed himself with his last bullet rather than surrender to the Israelis, his widow moved up into the leadership echelons of the JRA. Since then, it is rumored that the "marriage" between the PFLP and the JRA was "quite literally consummated when [PFLP leader] Habash, who is a good-looking man in a Thirties matinee idol sort of way, and Shigenobu became lovers."[35]

Leila Khaled burst into world headlines on August 29, 1969, when she led the Palestinian hijacking team that commandeered a TWA jet and force it to land in Damascus. She was young, she looked like Audrey Hepburn, and she was the first "female terrorist" to hit the news in mid-action; the press had a field day. Khaled came from a middle-class background; her family had fled Haifa in 1948 and settled eventually in Tyre, in Lebanon. She attended the American University in Beirut and later taught at an elementary school in Kuwait. She joined the PFLP as it was about to splinter from Arafat's more mainstream Al Fatah, in 1967. Her 1975 autobiography, *My People Shall Live*,[36] was ghost-written by George Hajjar, a member of the PFLP's political think tank,[37] which may explain why the book avoids details of her own life and hews more to a line of political rhetoric. In early interviews, too, she would say only, "I am engaged to the Revolution." This was not totally true: she was also engaged to a man, an Iraqi Palestinian militant, whom she subsequently married and later divorced. At the 1980 Mid-Decade United Nations World Conference on Women in Copenhagen, Khaled was lionized by the press, to the dismay of the entire Palestinian delegation. The men, who headed the delegation even though this was a women's conference, were furious that so much attention was being paid to a woman. The women expressed irritation (off-stage and unofficially in private conversations) because Khaled never spoke about *women*. But her reasons came out a year later in an interview with a German feminist newspaper. She displayed the elite disdain for which PFLP commandos are notorious—a contempt for the *fedayeen* who make lowly border raids on Israeli kibbutzim—compounded with a double message about being female:

When I speak at an international conference, as in Copenhagen, *I represent Palestinians, not women.* . . . Although in Arab society to be married and have children is very important, in my case, nobody wonders about it. A woman who fights politically is respected. . . . *The organizers and organizations would not take us seriously if we were to begin speaking about it* [women's rights]. They would say we wish to be like European women . . . *and they would reject us.* So we try instead to say that honor means more than virginity, that there is honor in recovering our homeland.[38] (Italics mine.)

Khaled has survived assassination attempts by the Israeli secret service, survived prison and release (in a hostage exchange), survived being married and divorced. Of late, she seems to have disappeared into the PFLP bureaucracy, her much-photographed face now making her a liability on terrorist missions. One wonders what that means to her. For she has not survived being female. It's clear in the interview: even for the unattached women, the gestures of obeisance, the protestations of denial, must be made. The woman who rebels via the male mode can do so only to the point where her own rebellion might begin.

Feminist writer Andrea Dworkin is one woman who embarked on that rebellion in the midst of what she had thought was going to be "the revolution":

I married an anarchist, an ex-Provo,* a proven urban guerrilla. I woke up three years later and the total substance of my concern was housework. I was virtually catatonic; I didn't know who I was anymore. "Love" turned to violence and abuse. Some revolutionaries, after all, have to fight all the time—if not on the streets, then in the home. When one loses all hope of ever changing anything (which he did), one must live out the despair somehow. Some commit suicide, some commit assault. I finally recognized myself as a woman: . . . I had been a victim, of a particular man, of a whole sexist system, of my own illusions. . . . my marriage taught me, much as prison had, the nature and dimension of oppression—in my own body, where I learn best.[39]

---

* The Provos were a loose movement in the Netherlands in the late 1960s, a mix of counterculture lifestyle and "revolutionary" militant tactics. The first issue of a magazine they published was confiscated because it carried a recipe for making bombs. As Dworkin wrote, "The idea was to make the information available; the idea was to provoke the police." ("Whatever Happened to Provo or The Saddest Story Ever Told," unpublished essay written in 1968, quoted by the author's permission.)

That insight came at the beginning of what would be a long journey toward self-discovery, self-invention, self-affirmation. Back in 1972, though, her voice was still tentative; she was still reaching out to understand him, still comprehending his motivation, his despair, more than her own.

For how long must our voices hover in the tentativity of that insight?

We pose the insight, as did the collective voice of the Portuguese writers "the Three Marias," in rumination:

> I wonder whether the *guerrillera* who battles side by side with her brothers . . . is fighting side by side with her real brothers, or whether these brothers may not still bear within themselves the roots of treason, both in the dialogue of the present struggle and in the future City.[40]

We pose the insight, as does the insurgent Association of Salvadoran Women, in a question:

> The parties and movements of . . . the Left have, in general, not dealt with the problems of women with the same consistency with which they confront other social problems, . . . [but] conceived of women's liberation . . . as technical and private, . . . becoming collective and social only *after* the exploited sectors have won their liberation, that is to say, in some distant and unpredictable future. . . . Will the people's organizations be capable of focusing on the specifics of daily life, or will they leave this to the mercy of the dominant ideology?[41]

More and more, we dare to pose the insight as fact. Inevitably, that daring has come from Third World women who are themselves veterans of liberation struggles. Marie Angélique Savané of Senegal has termed all contemporary governments—of the Right and the Left—"phallocracies."[42] Fatima Mernissi of Morocco has written about nationalism having repeatedly betrayed women.[43] Lidia Falcón has exposed how the Spanish Communist party first capitalized on and then jettisoned the feminist movement.[44] Ama Ata Aidoo of Ghana writes, "If, as a woman, you try to flex your muscles as a revolutionary cadre where your comrades are predominantly male, you can hit the concrete wall with such force that you might never recover your original self. . . . And don't be shocked if—when victory is won—they return you to the veil as part of the process of consolidating the revolution."[45]

To pose the insight as *action* is most difficult of all.

Elsewhere and at length[46] I've constructed a detailed analogy between women and colonized peoples, observing that colonization requires at least three elements: first, control over the land, so that it can be mined for its natural resources—in the case of women, the "natural resources" of our bodies, in sex and in reproduction; second, the enforced alienation of the colonized from their own territory by a system based on exclusion and mystification—in the case of women, alienation from one's own flesh (lack of reproductive freedom and freedom of sexual preference) and alienation from one's own self-defined existence; and third, a readiness on the part of the colonizer to meet all demands for self-determination with a repertoire of repression, from ridicule through tokenism to brutality—in the case of women, a repertoire spanning derision, individual cooptation, and the more blatant forms of response: rape, battery, *sati,* purdah, erasure, prostitution, and other such means of enslavement.

I would now add a fourth element. The colonized are an invaluable resource (veritable "treasures") in the colonizers' wars *against one another:* in fact, this is one of the reasons for and conveniences of an empire. The examples are many: the all-black division (in a segregated army) fighting for the United States in World War I; men of France's Pacific Island colonies battling for France in the Indo-China War; thousands of "Gunga Dins" supporting the British Empire; the fierce, much-acclaimed Nepalese Gurkha troops in the Indian Army—commanded by British officers—fighting in Britain's wars; the New Zealand and Australian troops massacred at Gallipoli, for the sake of the British Empire; the colonial and Commonwealth nationals used by that empire in the Boer War ... one could go on and on.

Some of the colonized served in their masters' armies reluctantly. Some were drafted and had no choice. Some enlisted voluntarily. Some served in order to learn how the master wages war, the better to someday wage it against him. Some fought willingly out of an ironic but undeniably powerful *identification* with him, since to be him was to be human. (And they stood a chance of becoming him, after all, since they were men.) The frantic desire to prove oneself loyal to the colonizer has shown itself like a pathetic refrain. Men of color have fought and killed and died for the white man in the hope of winning his approval and respect—and their freedom.

Is it any wonder, then, that women identify men's interests as their own? All women, at some time or other, in one way or another, are forced to do so. The rebel woman in a male-defined State-that-would-be is merely acting out another version of the party woman running for office in the State-that-is. And the terrorist woman is doing the same thing, writ large in letters of fire.

I can hear her now, in furious rebuttal: "To say that my revolutionary struggle is a male-defined one is to trivialize me the way you feminists claim men trivialize women. You refuse to take me, my politics, my militance, seriously as my own. You treat me as a pawn in a game between men. Is this your support? Is this what you call sisterhood?"

And I would reply: "*Yes.* Trying to name the truth, however painful, to one another is the highest respect sisterhood can offer. To dance with the Demon Lover is only to dance oneself toward the false liberation of death. To rebel on his terms is only to rebel against the challenge of living on your own terms."

He tells her (he tells us all) how women's issues are narrow and marginal. Sometimes he tells us that these issues are already solved and we are greedy and spoiled to complain. Sometimes he tells us that these issues can never be solved and we are countering "nature." Sometimes he tells us both lies at once. Always he tells us that our freedom depends on his. So long as she (and we) believe that feminism concerns solely what he defines as women's issues—reproduction, pay equity, child care (however vital each of these is in itself)—she (and we) will remain in conflict. Not until she, and you, and I, fully comprehend the enormity—that all issues are women's issues *to be defined in women's ways and confronted in women's ways*—can any of us break free and refuse to settle for rebellion within his deadly context.

The woman who lies in terror's arms is clasped in an intricate emotional bondage. One cord, coiled around her brain, is her own justifiable human indignation at the suffering of her people, her country, or her planet. This anger has never been taken seriously, since being female, she is expected to be altruistic, and besides, she is less than human anyway. So another bond slips into place—her rage at being a woman in what appears to be a male universe of perception, thought, and action. There is, too, the silken rope of what Nechaev termed "initiation," the bond of her own lust for approval, respect, an acceptance which might mean (as it did for Khaled) relative freedom and power; it loops around her spine. In his world, the elite are those who claim to fight and sacrifice on behalf of those *beneath* them; to confront on your *own* behalf means the humiliation of acknowledging your own oppression, as well as the risk of being accused of selfishness. So she who lies in terror's arms clutches for another bond of reassurance, and it is waiting to curl and knot around her loins: charisma. The men will initiate her and she will be (almost) one of them; other women will look upon her with awe. The charisma attaches because of her intensifying proximity to death: she becomes even more of a treasure to him, since she will be lost to him and since he loves only what he can lose or kill. How well this skein meets now around her throat with another—her well-fostered nurturant "mothering instinct," which longs to interpose her between death and others. At best, then, she believes he can free her by annihilating the subhuman female persona she has worn. At worst, she will still be released from that old non-self. If she is to be consumed in his fires they will grant her her version of his definition of ecstasy—a "standing outside of" the self he never permitted her to have. In all this she is allowed to feel that she is heroic, altruistic, noble—and an exception to her sex. And the final bond, pure satin steel the color of blood ruby, is knotted tight around her heart: it is, in almost every case, her own personal passion for an individual man.

And will she struggle now? Not likely. The combination of promised rewards—from rebellion through respect, charisma, relative freedom and power, requited love, and becoming in his terms nearly human—is one she finds irresistible.

From Marx through Nechaev to Ortega, they have used her and acknowledged it. They have proclaimed aloud their exploitation of her, written it out in print, denied it and then reaffirmed it, practised it, and practise it still. *They have made it plain: they need women. They cannot do it without women.* The State-that-would-be will never become the State-that-is without our aid. The State-that-is cannot sustain itself without our support.

If they cannot do it without us, then what will happen if we turn from them, turn to our own definitions, means, and energies?

Such a message of selfhood and sisterhood is more than terrifying. It takes time for that message to filter through the thick hangings that curtain terror's bed, time we have less of each day. The women there are literally *in terror* of hearing it. The women there lie, not fully living yet undead as Dracula's legion of brides, in the Demon Lover's embrace, trusting him, trusting his love, trusting his promise of immortality, trusting their own lies that they have chosen this. And somewhere, in the deepest recesses of her soul, each one suspects otherwise.

I know these women.

I was one of them.

CHAPTER 7

꒝꒝꒝꒝꒝꒝꒝꒝

LONGING FOR CATASTROPHE: A PERSONAL JOURNEY

I am pregnant with murder.
The pains are coming faster now,
and not all your anesthetics
nor even my own screams
can stop them. / ROBIN MORGAN, "Annunciation" (1969)

And I will speak . . .
more and more in crazy gibberish you cannot understand:
witches' incantations, poetry, old women's mutterings,
schizophrenic code, accents, keening, firebombs,
poison, knives, bullets, and whatever else will invent
this freedom. / ROBIN MORGAN, "Monster" (1972)

*I*t was neither the best of times nor the worst of times, despite claims to both contraries. It was the late 1960s through the mid-1970s. Political simmer in the United States was rolling to a boil. Decades of nonviolent civil-rights activity were exploding into black rage, black manhood, Black Panthers. Television screens bled full-color Vietnam carnage each evening onto the dinnertime news. The U.S. government was napalm-bombing and spraying Agent Orange throughout Vietnam in what was called a legitimate act to save lives, yet when college students back home set fire to the U.S. flag in protest against the war, that was termed "violence." Rap Brown was declaring that violence is as American as cherry pie, and the nation was still reeling in the aftermath of the assassination of John F. Kennedy, the eighth presidential victim of such an attack and the fourth to die of it. The ghettos were afire with poverty and powerlessness, the campuses afire with guilt and idealism. Even the staid *New York Review of Books* ran a recipe for making Molotov cocktails, and Leonard Bernstein hosted a fund-raiser cocktail party for the Black Panthers, an act that came to be known as "radical chic."

It didn't feel chic to some of us. I was one of many women who had put in years of activism in the civil-rights movement and the antiwar movement, one of many who bore bruises from police night sticks, sprains and torn ligaments from tramplings by mounted officers of the TPF (Tactical Police Force). My police mug shots of the day show a young woman whose eyes gleam with exhaustion and whose jaw is set firmly in defiance. My days were filled with juggling an editing job, housework, and street demonstrations that ended in acrid clouds of tear gas; my nights were filled with meetings, more demonstrations, stolen moments of writing—and fearing the knock at the door. Only five feet tall, my body was honed by karate training, my language salted with expletives, my spirit incensed at the injustice done to others. I had signed petitions, organized voter registration, picketed, marched, written pamphlets and press releases and leaflets and appeals, made phone calls, raised funds, raised bail, raised hell, been beaten up, been arrested, been jailed, been released, and been afraid—for years. I was white, educated, and married at the time. I lived with my husband—also a writer and also a radical—on New York's Lower East Side, then a fringe-slum neighborhood and a hotbed of political ferment. I was in my late twenties, and I was not the only one convinced that I would most likely be killed before I turned thirty-five. I was also not the only one convinced that the second American Revolution was imminent, and I was not the only one who vowed to bring that revolution about—by any means necessary.

Let me indulge briefly in a caveat and then be done with it. Although the New Left was terminally diseased with sexism and toxic with characteristic U.S. arrogance and impatience, there are things I do affirm about that period loosely called "the sixties." Today, when I encounter people—women *or* men—of my generation who managed somehow to sit out those years unaffected, I wonder about their lack of moral vitality. When I encounter those who were in the streets and on the barricades against war, racism, and poverty, but now are cozily settled into the establishment niches of a Reaganized America, I also wonder. The latter sometimes ask me, with a bemused smile, "How come you're still trying to save the world?" I can't answer that, except with the question "How come you're not?" For me, a severe critic of the New Left, the problem was never one of retrenchment from a radical analysis or from fighting to stop the suffering caused by the State-that-is. It was, rather, that the Left did not go far *enough,* in analysis, vision, or practice. To which, of course, my erstwhile revolutionary brothers reply that I was going *too* far.[1] What I can still affirm about those days, however, was our idealism and innocence, our justifiable rage, and our energy. That energy at times expressed itself in an insouciant humor, at times in creative organizing tactics, and at times—with the impending demise of our naive and impatient sense of hope—in violence.

Some years later, I was one of a number of radical activists who applied for access to files which the government had kept on our activities.* Some of my files are being held back even today; the claim is that they are classified. But for the rest, well, it was educative (and offensive to me, as a taxpayer) to see how wrong they were. The FBI and CIA were so hilariously off the mark that their operatives deserved being fired not only for infringement of civil liberties but also for incompetence. First, they filed me (labeled *a.k.a.,* "also known as") under both my

* This was made possible by Bella S. Abzug, then a congresswoman, who as chair of the House Subcommittee on Government Information and Individual Rights, pushed through changes in the Freedom of Information Act.

own surname and my husband's surname, as if one of the two were a code name. But I didn't use my husband's name, in or out of the movement. This confused them utterly. Second, their surveillance managed to place me frequently where I never was and rarely where I actually had been. Third, they were certain that telephone conversations (referring to editing jobs, or books I was reading or writing, or errands being done) were all secret signals for militant actions—as if one were dense enough to discuss such things, even in code, over a home telephone so tapped that the static crackled jolly as chestnuts in a holiday fire; it was a family joke that we frequently had to ask, "May I have an outside line, please?" through the hum of their tape recorders. It was also educative that files were assembled on me not only by the FBI and CIA but also by the White House Secret Service. I was apparently on the Secret Service list of dangerous radicals to be tailed whenever the president journeyed to New York, and on a list of people eligible for being picked up without charge and held in "preventive detention"— which was illegal. Even more absurdly, the air force had a file on me. To this day, I can't figure that one out. Possibly they felt I was convening an Amazon Airways fleet, that thousands of women would darken the skies, zooming in over the Pentagon in perfect formation astride their brooms. I confess I find the idea enchanting. But whatever their surrealist assumptions, there were real men who read and clipped, who eavesdropped and recorded, who sat in unmarked cars watching, who followed me and others like me through the streets of our lives, who infiltrated meetings, functioned as agents provocateurs, reported and analyzed. And who most of the time got it wrong.

In my research for the book you now hold in your hands. I scanned an anthology entitled *The Violent Women,* edited by Norman Hill. It was the amusement of the day. Hill had cast quite a wide net for his subject. Included were articles about such violent women as Charlotte Corday (assassin of Marat during the French Revolution), the nineteenth-century temperance leader Carry Nation, the Nazi Ilse Koch, such contemporaries as Angela Davis, Weatherwomen Bernardine Dohrn, Cathy Wilkerson, Kathy Boudin, and Diana Oughton, Manson followers Susan Atkins and Patricia Krenwinkel—and me. I apparently got included because of having counseled women to learn self-defense techniques against rapists, and because of having written "extremist" statements calling for "secretarial sabotage against white male power gone mad."[2] Bless that anthologist's pointed little head. If Hill had had any idea of what else I had done, he would have gone screaming into the night the way Byron did when Mary Shelley first told him the outline of a story she would later title *Frankenstein*.

Feminism already had begun trickling into my life by the mid-1960s. But I continued to be torn for almost a decade between my emerging feminist priorities and my allegiance to the male Left, even in its violent period. I was not a college student at the time, and never was a member of SDS (Students for a Democratic Society) or its offshoot, the Weather Underground. I was, however, involved in small nameless pre-Weathermen groups that believed in "armed propaganda." The period fixed by the statute of limitations for incrimination regarding certain acts is up now; regarding some others, not. I place little trust in "my" government. Consequently, I cannot write this chapter the way I might write it years from now—if the planet, much less myself, is still around then. Furthermore, unlike some activists of that time who in their eager political recantations veered so far to the Right that they chose to volunteer other people's names in an orgy of confessional writing, I do not intend to make vulnerable even persons I no longer trust or respect. At least as much care is needed in writing as in handling volatile materials. Yet the basis of all ideology is the experiential perspective. As a feminist, I know that the personal *is* political, and that an affirmation of subjectivity is the mark of an honest and humane politics. So it seems important here to explore some of what I did—and why—when I was a woman of the Demon Lover.

Context is important. Women had comprised the rank and

filing cabinet of the civil-rights movement, and continued to do so in the antiwar movement. For years, we had run mimeograph machines but not meetings, made coffee but not policy. In the civil-rights movement, the confluence of sexism and racism had produced the "Gimme some of my civil rights tonight, baby," syndrome in some black men—with some white women acquiescing out of guilt and that old lust for acceptance; meanwhile, black women got the worst of both worlds.* "Look out Whitey, Black Power's gonna get your Momma" was a threat from one set of men to another, a message about a shift in ownership of female human beings. For the white male Left, such issues as rape, abortion, sexuality, child care, and even poverty and peace, were insular and bourgeois when compared to the issues that were "universal"—like the draft or GI rights. The so-called counterculture was even worse regarding women. At the glorified Woodstock festival, unsuspecting women were fed LSD in soft drinks, and then gang-raped. Misogyny blared in the language: one gang of "street-fighters" in New York named themselves the Motherfuckers; a militant Puerto Rican political group was called the Young Lords; and a bit later, the Weathermen—despite a subsequent name shift in an attempt to co-opt their critics—remained at heart Weather*men*.

Radical women like myself were still a long way from identifying *as women:* we were chicks or birds, we addressed each other "Hey, man," in imitation of street rapping, and we were generally classified in three categories. There were the earth mothers, who exuded ultra-gentle, passive, I-belong-to-the-commune nurturance; they cooked endless pots of stew for the mass demonstrations, rolled joints for their men, and never said anything. Then there were the revolutionary right-on broads, who marched endless miles of demonstrations, rolled joints for their men, and never said anything. Last, there were the few token heavies, who by sheer persistence and by making some unique contribution managed to force themselves onto the var-

---

* *But Some of Us Are Brave*, ed. Barbara Smith, Gloria Hull, and Patricia Bell Scott (New York: The Feminist Press, 1982) is a poignant and courageous documenting of black women's experience of the period.

ious central committees of what posed as nonhierarchical groups. Such a contribution might take the form of paralegal or par- amedical skill, or might simply involve providing the money to fund a project. Most often, a woman got into the inner circle in the traditional manner: by being attached to a man who was there. I was damned if I was going to cook soup, march miles, and say nothing, and I deliberately rolled loose, raggedy joints. And I was damned if I wasn't going to gain admittance in my own right. The skill I bargained with was communication, the spoken and written word.

Some of the skills I was to study in turn, I would come to wish I'd never learned.

Those years now seem to me an exercise in deliberate *non*-connection. The whirl of events, the lack of analysis, the chronic panic, the self and mutual delusion that we were on the verge of bringing down the State, in retrospect reveal a lack not only of strategy but of substance. After more than fifteen interven- ing years of encountering complexity and patience in the wom- en's movement, I find it difficult to cast myself back into that former mind-set. When I try to get at the *why* of some of my actions, what rises is not a distinct pattern but a sense memory, a series of vivid, discontiguous moments.

———

I am one of seven women—three of us white—in the office of CORE (the Congress of Racial Equality); at a joint meeting with SNCC (the Student Nonviolent Coordinating Commit- tee). More than twenty men, black and white, are present, run- ning the meeting. Three civil-rights workers—one black man and two white men—have disappeared in Mississippi, and the groups have met over this crisis. (The lynched bodies of the three men—James E. Chaney, Andrew Goodman, and Michael Schwerner—are later found, tortured to death.) Meanwhile, the FBI, local police, and the National Guard have been dredging lakes and rivers in search of the bodies. During the search, the mutilated parts of an estimated seventeen different human bodies are found. All of us in the New York office are in a state of shock. As word filters in about the difficulty of identifying mutilated bodies long decomposed, we also learn that all but one of the unidentified bodies are female. A male CORE leader mutters, in a state of fury, "There's been a whole goddamned lynching we never even *knew* about. There's been some brother disappeared who never even got *reported*."

My brain goes spinning. Have I heard correctly? Did he mean what I think he meant? If so, is it my racism showing itself in that I am appalled? Finally, I hazard a tentative question. Why *one* lynching? What about the sixteen unidentified female bodies? What about—

Absolute silence. The men in the room, black and white, stare at me. The women in the room, black and white, stare at the floor. Then the answer comes, in a tone of impatience, as if I were politically retarded. "Those were obviously *sex* murders. Those weren't *political*."

I fall silent.

———

My white skin disgusts me. My passport disgusts me. They are the marks of an insufferable privilege bought at the price of others' agony. If I could peel myself inside out I would be glad. If I could become part of the oppressed I would be free.

I must do something, something more confrontative of the system than I've done so far. Besides, I believe the oppressed are going to win—and I want to be on the winning side.

I do not yet understand that guilt politics is a convenient paralysis, a moral suicide, a contradiction in terms.

I do not yet understand that I am already part of the oppressed.

I do not yet understand that I am already on the winning side.

———

As the black movement becomes more militant, whites are told to go and organize in their own communities. This some of us begin to do. But the white men want to imitate the black men's style, and the white women want to imitate the white men's imitation. (No one wants to imitate the black women, who are at the bottom of the heap, trying to imitate the black men and meanwhile keeping it all together.) In the white movement, the peer pressure is intense. The momentum is toward armed struggle. A new rallying cry of the peace movement is "Bring the war home." Not many dare to point out the irony in that. The few women and the rare man who argue against this trend are derided as cowards, liberals, or that horror of horrors—*bourgeois*. (In retrospect, this pressure to conform is of a piece with that described by former national security adviser Robert McFarlane in the 1987 congressional hearings when he testified that to speak out against aggressive schemes, no matter how harebrained—schemes such as the Iran-Contra deal—was to risk having someone stand up in a National Security Council meeting and brand you a Commie.*)

I am told that the We-Did-It communiqué sent out after the last action was incorrect. It was too impassioned, too emotional, insufficiently filled with the acceptable rhetoric of the genre: "imperialism," "fascism," "capitalism," *isms*. I am also told not to write and certainly not to publish anything of my own for a while. I am told my style is too individualistically identifiable. It will make me a security risk. I try to make the next communiqué as acceptably fulminating with jargon as possible. I am praised for it.

I continue to write poems. I do not tell them that.

Friends are going underground—some by choice, "to build a people's army," and some as fugitives from the law charged

---

* See chapter 5 for Richard Barnet's examples of this pressure as institutionalized in the power circles of the State-that-is.

with actions perhaps committed and perhaps not. I am sitting on an isolated grassy knoll in the park, together with four men and one other woman. I am euphoric at being included. We are, depending on the parlance, an "affinity group," a "cadre," or a "cell"—though a cell of no larger organization. There is a heated debate going on in lowered voices: whether or not to give a warning call to the building—a bank or draft-board office— in which a small bomb may be placed that night. Both women urge the call, all four men oppose it. The men argue that even from a phone booth it's an unnecessary risk; the building will be empty anyway, the night watchman takes his break right when the device is timed for detonation, nobody can get hurt. The other woman talks about the principle of the thing. She is disregarded. Pragmatist, I raise the subject of cleaning women who may well be in the building at that hour. The men fix me with that familiar contemptuous stare.

"If you're so preoccupied with lifesaving, go be a lifeguard," one says.

"The cleaning women are very likely black or Hispanic," I add, pointedly.

Suddenly, their attitude changes. As females, the cleaning women are irrelevant. As blacks or Hispanics, however, they deserve to be warned—because *race, ethnicity, is a quality women share with men.*

It is agreed that a warning call should be made. I am relieved.

In the midst of my euphoria at being included, I feel a quiet gladness about a different politics, one I cannot yet name.

———

A number of men have tried to teach me to shoot a rifle. They give up in disgust. They say that I am too small-bodied, that I keep squeezing the trigger and my eyes shut at the same time, that the recoil literally knocks me off my feet.

I am determined to learn.

In a single afternoon, a woman teaches me how to shoot. I find I can begin to learn as soon as she says, "Look, no matter what the guys tell you, this hurts. It's heavy as hell to lift and hard to aim. It's also like an explosion right against your ear and a sudden blow to your shoulder. I mean, I dunno why they get off on it. It's no fun. But we gotta know how, too."

We gotta know how, too.

I believe her. I no longer feel a failure for being unable to locate the fun of it all. I'm grateful to her.

I learn how.

———

My then-husband and I are being criticized for refusing to throw away our books and our battered old typewriters. We are warned to be wary of our bourgeois tendencies. One of our affinity group growls that the only revolutionary use for a typewriter is dropping it out of the window onto a cop's skull. We still refuse.

———

"This is the circuit wire, this the battery. This is the timer. Do you understand?"

I understand. I want to understand. I don't want to understand.

"Do you know how to solder? Do you know how to use a soldering gun?"

I nod.

My hands are trembling. I force them to stop by an act of will.

I nod.

———

I hear myself talking all the time. In speeches, at meetings, in communiqués. I talk to myself. If my skill is communication, what are these wires doing in my hands, what are these strange sticks taped together like paper-wrapped beeswax candles of a dark and final flaring?

These are a form of communication, I repeat to myself.

These *end* communication, I answer myself. These sticks can open the throat not to words or song. These sticks can open the throat in strings of muscle, in splatters of blood, in charred patches of flesh.

I try to talk to others about this.

No one here speaks my language.

I must be wrong. I must be mad.

———

I like none of these men. Secretly, I loathe them. Secretly, I congratulate myself that I am already "taken," married, safe—and that my man, although a revolutionary, is drawn to street surges rather than to this kind of cell activity. Some of what I do he doesn't even know about and vice versa; it's best for security.

I watch how the women are traded between these men. The men themselves do not attract me. What they *do,* what they *are,* what they *stand for* attracts me.

Risk. Skill. Power.

I don't want these men. I don't want to be these men. I do want to be what these men are. But I don't like what these men are.

Meeting after meeting, at some point I go to the bathroom and vomit—quietly, with the sink water running or the toilet flushing repeatedly, so no one can hear. Then I rinse my mouth, wash my face, and return to the meeting with an air of studied calm.

I loathe these men. But there is something about them that I want. I want their confidence in their own right to seize power.

———

I like these women. But I pity them, too. Because of their men. I think myself better off, safer. I refuse to join one cell because of its rule that each new woman must go to bed with every man in the group, for "security bonding." They say I am, again, bourgeois. I walk out. I tell myself that I am different from these women, I am safe. It makes me cling to the marriage. If there is pain in my marriage, there is also love, there is commitment. At least we have each other against the world. But these women—I pity them.

I also respect them. I fear them. I like making them fear and respect me. I like the way I am not here as a man's appendage, but on my own. It is intoxicating.

Let it be done. Now. Once and for all. Let it be over with. Let them catch me, let them kill me. Let it be finished.

I'm horribly afraid, every minute, every day.

I cannot live in this fear. The feverish impatience to act is an impatience for it to be finished, done with, simple.

It's a fair bargain: if I will do their dying for others, let others do my living for me.

I see the world around me as lacking in sanity, tenderness, humor. I think those who will do my living for me get the worst of this bargain.

I want it to be over with.

I realize that I do not want other women here. I want to save them from this.

I also *want* to be the token.

I want to be the only one.

Meeting after meeting, I go to the bathroom and vomit. I tell myself it's the stress of revolution.

Sex to this point in my life has been trivial, at best a gesture of tenderness, at worst a chore. I couldn't understand the furor about it.

But this—the hands shaking, the throat dry, the heart pounding, the brain in a blur of excitation, the body poised, exhilarated, the risk of being swept into obliteration, the aphrodisiac in demanding power—*surely this surpasses whatever they mean by sexual joy.*

—

There is one particular woman. I imagine that we share a language. I estimate her a peer in energy, intelligence, capacity for risk. But I am revolted by the way she cowers these characteristics away in the presence of her man. I find him a dullard of egotism, loose-tongued in his security, slovenly in his discipline. I cannot understand their relationship. I believe my marriage is different.

It is *her* I am a little in love with, not any of these men. This doesn't occur to me at the time. It doesn't occur to me that loving her is a way of loving myself for what I am doing.

—

Credentials accrue in an escalation of one-upmanship to martyrdom. It's better to have been beaten than tear-gassed. It's better to have been arrested than beaten. It's better to have been sentenced and jailed than to have got off and walked free. It's better to riot in prison than to organize in the neighborhoods. It's best of all to die—in a prison riot, in a shoot-out, in a mistimed explosion.

Being dead is the ultimate way of being politically correct. Only then is one beyond criticism.

One day I burst out against a friend, "But my God, don't we want to *win* this thing? *Don't we have to live to do that?*"

—

I become pregnant. This is a conscious decision jointly taken by my husband and myself, this is a wanted child. Friends say we're crazy. I continue in karate class up through the fifth month, but taking no front falls. I am involved in a women's group, but still see "women's liberation" as one wing of the Left, a sort of radical ladies' auxiliary. Though most are Leftists like myself, the women in my group know nothing of my other activities. Yet I infect the group with my imported style. They all begin taking karate. I try to organize a "women's skills camp." Six weeks of basic training in firearms, self-defense, motor vehicles (how to drive and repair), basic emergency medical techniques, ham-radio communications, basic "tactical chemistry" (odors, poisons, antidotes), Morse code and semaphore signals and cryptology, basic bivouac and survival techniques, basic electrical skills (how to wire lamps, appliances, etc.), and basic "tactical electronics" (how to wire "other things," how to detect and dismantle bugs, etc.). In a stray life-affirmative moment, I add to the curriculum basic carpentry and plumbing, paraprofessional abortion techniques, conversational Spanish, and basic printing skills.

When I bring the idea to one of the early women's conferences, other women are not enthusiastic about six weeks of basic training.

At the time, I can't figure out why women aren't interested.

———

"I refuse to plant the device in the ladies' room."

"You're the only woman in the group, you're petite, you can look innocuous, you'll be less suspicious a presence than any of us."

"But why does it have to be in the ladies' room?"

"Because you can't get into the men's room, idiot. And because a lavatory's the best place to leave it undetected."

"But it's secretaries who'll get hurt or even killed when it goes off in the goddamned ladies' room! *They* don't have any power!"

"It'll go off *after* hours, for chrissake!"

"What if somebody's working late and goes to the ladies' room?"

"Look, dammit! It's a multinational corporation! Whoever

works there deserves what they get. Don't be so fucking squeamish!"

"I will not place the device in the ladies' room."

———

SDS splits into antagonistic factions; RYM (the Revolutionary Youth Movement) is born, then RYM-I and RYM-II, and finally the Weathermen. The Weathermen (including the women who call themselves that) soon loom over the whole New Left movement with a larger-than-life charisma, since they are white "revolutionaries" calling for domestic war. Swaggering and strutting, the Weathermen dominate meetings, define priorities, regard all unarmed struggle as irrelevant or even reactionary. The women are placed in high-profile pseudo-leadership to deflect criticism from the rapidly growing feminist movement. I am one of many women who disbelieve the power of women in the Weather organization; we are denounced as shrill and divisive. The rhetoric of violence intensifies. There is a glorification of Charles Manson's "family" and the murders they have committed. In a public statement at a "national war council," the Weathermen express admiration for the Manson murder of pregnant movie actress Sharon Tate: "Dig it: first they killed the pigs, then they ate dinner in the same room with them, they even shoved a fork in the victim's stomach. *Wild.*" One Weatherwoman, on noticing my pregnant belly, asks if the father is black. No, I reply, it happens that the father is white, and my husband. I am informed that I am carrying a pig child. I walk out on the meeting.

———

Something is ticking, so loudly it drowns all other sound.

The clock.

Something is ticking, so relentlessly it constricts all silence between the bars of its rhythm.

The timer.

Something is ticking. I long for sounds I remember, miss, have no time for. The scream of a gull. A cat's purr. The click of pressed harpsichord keys before music. The click of pressed typewriter keys before a poem.

Something is ticking. *The clock? The timer?*

I long for sounds I have never yet heard. The first cry of the child I'm carrying. My own words murmured in code to myself in my sleep. My own unrecognizably joyous laughter in love-making.

Something is ticking.

My heart?

———

The particular woman comes to me with a tempting offer. She and her man have obtained some "high-grade plastique, beautiful stuff." They want to hit a draft board or recruiting station. They need me. Will I join them?

I am still strongly drawn to this woman—an uneasy blend of yearning to mother her and a titillating erotic *frisson* of fear. I want very much to work with her. But I mistrust her man, and I have begun to mistrust her politics.

I lack the courage to say an outright No.

I make a counter-offer, one with which I cannot lose. If she declines, I'm safely out. If she accepts, she and her man will be trapped in a commitment—in their own tactical terms—to the seriousness of feminism.

"I'll work with you on a target of your choice, but only if you'll reserve some of the stuff and work with me to hit a target of my choice."

"Groovy," she grins.

"The Playboy Club," I add.

She looks at me as if I were a madwoman. I know she knows she can never get that demand past her man. "What a crazy waste of the goods!" he'll roar.

I'm safely out.

———

There are about twenty of us in the holding tank, waiting for arraignment. We share cigarettes, tampons, stories.

Jeddie works as a prostitute. Her nine-year-old son has a harelip and needs an operation costing big money. Her pimp said she was stealing from him and so he slashed her with a razor. She wears a livid white scar on the blue-black sheen of her face, from temple to jawline. Did she try to get even, to slash him back, to do anyth—? She laughs and calls me a child. "Child," she says affectionately, "that's the way to get dead. I don' wanna get killed. I'm dead enough as it is. 'Sides, even *could* I be him, I don' *wanna* be him. I want me and my baby to *live*. So I jus' sneak around him, hide a little dollar here, a little dollar there. I find a way. Get it? *I sneak around him.*"

Mrs. O'Meara is seventy-three years old. She says she's been beaten up "just like clockwork" every Friday night for fifty years. Friday's the day her husband gets his paycheck, gets drunk, gets mean. On her golden wedding anniversary, she picked up the frying pan and let him have it. Then she walked to the nearest precinct and reported what she'd done. He's in the hospital with a concussion, she's in the holding tank with an assault charge. Why did she turn herself in? "Didn't want the bastard to die, you know. Didn't want to kill nobody. Just wanted him to stop. Stopped him, all right. Didn't want to hurt him, though. That's *his* way, *his* craziness."

We share cigarettes, tampons, stories. We wait to be called into court.

———

On March 6, 1970, a Manhattan townhouse which some Weatherpeople have been using as a safe house blows up, because of carelessness in the manufacture of a bomb. Some Weatherpeople are killed, others disappear underground. I think of all the times when the men have been careless with materiel, when they've accused the women of being "prissy," "skittish," and overcautious—about dynamite.

It takes nine months for the Weather Underground Central Committee to declare that the townhouse explosion was caused by adventurism and "military error." By 1973, the weather has changed again, with a renunciation of "armed propaganda" and a new emphasis on "organizing the working class." By 1977, Bernardine Dohrn, still underground, offers a public self-criticism: "For seven years, I have upheld a politics which is male supremacist."

By that time, I am long out of the Left and at home in the Feminist Movement.

The particular woman is indicted, along with her man and some of their friends. It seems that her man bragged about his bombing exploits—to an FBI informer. He is denied bail, but she is granted it. She jumps and goes underground. She turns to me for help.

For the next four years, it will feel like a sexual high when I hear from her, see her, speak with her. Because I am married and because she is heterosexual, I am safe from thinking myself in love, I am safe in preserving my marriage. I can love her and attribute my hammering pulse to the danger of the situation. When, periodically, I visit her in her fugitivity, I am dismayed at her lax security, her own repeated self-exposures, particularly to any man who takes her fancy. She confides to me mournfully that she is "a man addict," the more dominating and dangerous the man the better. But I, a feminist Pygmalion blinded by affection, believe in the flowering of her own feminism, believe in her growing sense of self, believe that her self-destructiveness will end.

Eventually she surfaces, plea bargains, is sentenced, serves time. I stand by her, find her attorneys, rouse women's movement support, show up for regular prison visits, write many letters, help maneuver her transfer to a co-ed minimum-security prison. We survive a bad scare: she thinks she may be pregnant—by a male inmate with whom she managed to have sex in the prison. It turns out she isn't pregnant. She finally walks free. We celebrate.

Now she finds herself attracted to the FBI agent who, years

earlier, had arrested her. It is the first time I notice the Demon Lover pattern. Now she says she isn't that interested in the women's movement anyway. Now she thinks she "isn't political" after all.

Have I imagined her, her fire, her feminism?

Our relationship, which had once been challenging, then exultant, then heartbreaking, has become merely boring. We drift apart.

It will take some years for me to comprehend that *she* functioned as *my* Demon Lover, and that my investing her with those qualities permitted me to keep my marriage free of them—for a while.

———

In 1968, I am one of the founders of a women's group we call WITCH—an acronym for Women's International Terrorist Conspiracy from Hell. The name is half in humor (for guerrilla theater) and half in earnest (for guerrilla actions). I am still trying to find a compromise between my growing feminist consciousness (and tactics) and my need for gaining the acceptance of Leftist men by showing them how tough I can be in their terms and tactics. By 1977, I am able to name that conflict and write about it.[3] In the interim, I have studied the lives of women who were actually called witches, who were massacred for being worshippers of the Old Religion.

Some were simply healers and midwives.

Margaret Jones, midwife, hanged 1648.
Joan Peterson, veterinarian, hanged, 1652.
Isobel Insch Taylor, herbalist, burned, 1618.
Mother Lakeland, healer, burned 1645.

Some were accused of the sin of being sexually alive.

Nicriven, condemned for lasciviousness, burned 1569.
Barbara Gobel, described by her jailers as "the fairest maid in Würzburg," burned 1629, age nineteen.
Ilse Dumler, boiled to death in hot oil, while pregnant, 1630.

> Sister Maria Renata Sanger, subprioress of the Premonstratensian
> Convent of Unter-Zell, accused of being a lesbian; the docu-
> ment certifying her torture is inscribed with the seal of the
> Jesuits and the words *Ad Majorem Dei Gloriam*—"For the
> Greater Glory of God."

These women were not terrorists. These women fought for
life, not death.

The Women's International Terrorist Conspiracy from Hell
begins to seem a superficial response.

———

Bernardine Dohrn, speaking for the Weather Underground,
comments approvingly on the SLA kidnapping of Patricia Hearst
in a letter to the *Berkeley Barb* dated March 1, 1974: "The
guerrillas have kidnapped the daughter of a rich and powerful
man . . . [and] unleashed . . . a leap in everyone's consciousness."

———

A year later, Susan Stern, a former Weatherwoman, publishes
With the Weathermen,[4] the story of her years in the organization. She confirms the worst suspicions and rumors of virulent
sexism: the occurrence of "politically necessary for the collective" rapes by the male leadership, beatings and purgings of
women who refused, perks and semi-leadership positions for
women who agreed and even handed over other women to the
men. Stern writes of herself as a damaged person. Her personal
testimony includes heavy drug-taking, turning tricks, suicide
attempts.

But at the end of the book, she is still looking in the same
direction for the same qualities in the Right Man.

A few years later, she is found dead in a Jacuzzi, reportedly
from a fatal combination of alcohol and drugs.

———

I pause in front of a street poster, my baby balanced on one
hip. The poster shows an enlarged photograph of a former

comrade's face. The text is a quote in which he proclaims himself the last pure leader, proclaims himself betrayed by everyone, proclaims the catastrophes to come with a joy so fearful it smears the print: world famine and world war, devastation, destruction, apocalypse. *The hatred that already burns in the hearts of millions is going to spread and deepen,* his text exults, *so let's go out and let's not only die—*

"But let's live?" I murmur to the poster.

—but let's kill to make revolution.

My child nuzzles my ear, laughing. I am on my way to a women's meeting. I have books to read, still on the shelves, never discarded. I have books to write, still inside my head, never discarded. I pass the poster and move on.

———

The more public my feminism becomes, the more danger seeks me out quite without my seeking it. I am fired from my editing job. The hate mail increases. I am burned in effigy. A man tries to throw acid in my face. Threats arrive about my child, my husband. Bombs are placed in auditoriums where I am booked to speak. Fraternity jocks carrying flaming torches encircle me after a speech at a midwestern campus. Two separate assassination attempts are made on my life, by knife and by gun. The Right accuses me of being a Communist. The Left accuses me of betraying the revolution.

The marriage is under strain.

———

I read about the Pankhurst women in the British suffrage movement. Careful acts of select damage only ever against property. No harm to life. Mass demonstrations. Humor (red-pepper "bombs" thrown at the king in procession). Hunger strikes while in prison. Militance without a lust for death. I read about Alice Paul and the U.S. version of Pankhurst tactics. I read about, hear about, talk about, write about, dream about, ordinary women's ordinary lives, ordinary revolutions. The enormity of this politics, this task, dawns on me. It is difficult, transfigurative, without any blueprint or model. It requires a deeper patience and stubbornness, a higher risk than any endeavor I've yet known. I realize I will not live to see its conclusion. It has no conclusion. It's about everything. This politics is awesome, but not terrifying. This is an utterly different euphoria.

I begin to face what, by any means necessary, I have resisted—that I have been keeping all the risks carefully external. The struggle is brought home. Feminism at first informs and strengthens, then exposes, tenderizes, weakens, agonizes, frays, and finally explodes the marriage.

I don't want to die, after all.

———

By 1979, I can actually write it in a poem:

> Surely, this time, I am done with
>   professions of love
> between taking aim, surely done with
> the beauty of sin, dying, death. Oh let me be
> done with all revolutions that long for
> catastrophe, done with this crawling
> along the rockface, with training
> my heart to live in love, killing for it,
> coming undone.[5]

———

The Female High Security Unit of the federal prison at Lexington, Kentucky, consists of a series of subterranean cells. There is no daylight. The inmates have no fresh air except for one hour of exercise daily, in the walled prison yard surrounded by razor wire, while bound with handcuffs and waist chains. Behavior-modification and sensory-deprivation techniques are utilized. Prisoners are not permitted to put up any photographs or pictures on the high-gloss white walls, may not have access to the prison library, may read only approved books and periodicals. Visits are restricted to family members, once a month, through a glass panel; a fifteen-minute telephone call with an attorney is permitted once a week. As of June 1988, seven women were imprisoned in the FHSU, which can "house" up to sixteen inmates. Civil-liberties attorneys and Amnesty International have been trying to publicize the unit and the effect of this cruel and inhuman punishment on the women there. The Bureau of Prisons claims it will eventually close this "experimental" facility, when a new maximum-security prison for women is built. No one can say when that will be. Meanwhile, the women wait. All of them are incarcerated for having committed supposedly violent crimes. Three of them are "politicals" in the traditional sense: Alejandrina Torres was sentenced to thirty-five years for involvement with the FALN of Puerto Rico, the charges being seditious conspiracy and possession of explosives; Susan Rosenberg is serving fifty-eight years for possession of arms and explosives and a never-proven connection with the 1981 Brink's robbery (neither has been convicted of actually committing acts of violence, and neither Torres nor Rosenberg had a criminal record); Sylvia Baraldini was convicted of racketeering and conspiracy in connection with the Brink's robbery, ostensibly in league with the Weather Underground.[6]

There is more than one way of moving from the clutches of the State-that-would-be into those of the State-that-is. In 1980, after more than ten years as a fugitive, Bernardine Dohrn turned herself in, surfacing in Chicago along with her man, later her husband, Bill Ayers, also formerly of the Weather Underground Central Committee. Because of legal technicalities, federal charges against her were dropped; she pled guilty to two counts of aggravated battery and two counts of bail-jumping dating from the 1969 "Days of Rage" demonstrations. She was fined $1,500 and given three years' probation. No charges at all were filed against Ayers—whose father is former chairman of the Commonwealth Edison Company and one of the most powerful men in Illinois. Dohrn resumed her law studies, apparently cultivated her father-in-law's friends, and—with the support of former federal judge Harold R. Tyler, Jr., a deputy attorney general in the Ford administration—by 1986 was clerking in the New York branch of a prestigious Chicago law firm. Tokenism in a male system is apparently a movable feast. She is now the mother of two sons, and is also raising the son of Kathy Boudin and David Gilbert, both of whom are still in prison. She has passed the New York bar exam but has been refused admittance because of her former activity.[7] Funds, supporters, and press have been marshaled to contest the bar's decision.

The women in the FHSU wait.

The elite on both sides of the barricades can recognize each other well enough. Brian Jenkins, the Rand Corporation's authority on terrorism, has said that groups like the Weathermen haven't survived because of the "enormous co-optive capacity" of the American system.[8] But neither Jenkins nor Dohrn yet has understood what really went wrong with homegrown terrorism, or where the authentic political energy went. Neither can comprehend why and how the women's movement has changed demography, the labor force, and the structure of the family itself in ways more radical than the Left ever dreamed and the Right ever feared.

Still, they walk my nightmares, those women who pace encircled with razor wire. I missed being one of them by what split second, what series of discontiguous, incremental, changes?

Certainly the fortuitous timing of the birth of my child was one factor. Still another was the spell of a magic healthier and, in my case, older than the Demon Lover's—a passion for words on the page. But it was feminism that provided the politics and the way.

This is not to say the Demon Lover doesn't sometimes haunt the feminist movement in disguise. Whenever I see power-and-purity ploys, correct-line tyrannies, rigid hierarchies, charisma acquired by trashing others, a pecking order of "toughness," or sado-masochistic sexual theories masquerading as feminism, I know whose brand of power is operating. It's not the kind of power most women in the world want, need, or envision. It's certainly not the kind of power that can transform society. Yet beneath those games, when played out between women, intense interdependence still vibrates, as well as the denied or acknowledged erotic attraction between women, an attraction that can be as much about intelligence, spirit, or trust as about a specifically defined sexuality.

For me, despite those periodic games, women—both in my own country and internationally—still articulate the most grounded and life-affirming politics I've encountered in any movement. It was that politics that drew me out of the Demon Lover's orbit.

For years, I have remained agnostic about the involvement of other women in violent actions, particularly when those are Third World struggles or (despite my revulsion for nationalism) battles for national liberation. Being white and the citizen of a superpower hardly offers one a valid perspective from which to estimate, much less judge, other situations accurately, no matter how hard one may work against ethnocentrism.

So another decade would have to pass before, in 1986, even that agnosticism would change. This transformation, too, had to wait until women taught me otherwise. In this case they were the last women in the world from whom one would expect to learn a profoundly new kind of feminist anti-violence.

They were Palestinian women in the refugee camps of the Middle East.

CHAPTER 8

᠅᠅᠅᠅᠅᠅᠅᠅᠅᠅

"WHAT DO MEN KNOW ABOUT LIFE?": THE MIDDLE EAST

Put two Israelis together and you have an argument. Put three Israelis together and you have a fight. Put four Israelis together and you have a riot. Put five Israelis together and you have the Knesset. / Israeli men's proverb

Myself, my brother, my father, and my cousin against the world. Myself, my brother, and my father against my cousin. Myself and my brother against my father. Myself against my brother. / Palestinian men's proverb

To whom do I appeal when the executioner is my judge? / Middle Eastern women's proverb

---

*H*uddled beside the azure waters and powder-white sands of the Mediterranean Sea is the Gaza Strip—a ribbon of land ten miles wide and less than twenty-nine miles long. Twenty-four hundred Israelis live here in nineteen heavily subsidized and lavishly irrigated settlements using 96 percent of the water and one-third of the land. Yet in 1985, Gaza surpassed Hong Kong as the most densely populated, poorest place on earth. Over 650,000 Palestinians, some in their third or fourth displacement, also dwell here; 460,000 of them are *officially registered* refugees.

2 4 3

Of the sixty-one refugee camps served by UNRWA (the United Nations Relief and Works Agency for Palestine Refugees in the Near East), Rafah Camp in Gaza is acknowledged to be the worst of the worst. Shelters are jammed up against one another, with tiny passageways between. No streets, no actual addresses. In early June, the sun is already intense by 6:30 A.M. The stench—of sweat, rotting garbage, open cookfires, the press of humanity—hits like a fist in the face; within hours, one will no longer notice it. The sound—mullahs wailing prayers, men shouting, women calling to one another, children crying, the roar of a population violently condensed—slams louder than the surf a few miles away; within hours, one will no longer notice it, either. The usual shelter in Rafah Camp is a concrete hovel approximately nine by thirteen feet: it houses an average family of fifteen members. The women wage a daily battle against filth. They sweep the dirt and sand floors. They trudge back and forth to the nearest communal water spigots, balancing pots on their heads. They try in vain to keep their children away from the open sewage channels that artery the camp. The children sit in the sewage, play in it. The visitor gets accustomed to omnipresent clouds of flies, accustomed to occupying one hand continuously in brushing them away from eyes, nose, mouth.

Zahra* welcomes me into her shelter-home. We sit on the sand floor—she, my female interpreter, and I—while Zahra's twelve children hover and tumble around us. Dressed in assorted ragged but clean hand-me-downs, they range in age like stair steps—one a year, down to the baby in her lap. The eldest, a girl about fourteen, looks eight or nine, so undernourished is she. Zahra's husband sits in the center of the one room, on its single threadbare carpet fragment. We three women hunch together, whispering, in a corner. Zahra's husband is immaculately dressed in a cheap white caftan, wears a wristwatch, and chain-smokes cigarettes. He is certified medically as unem-

---

* I have changed the names of camp residents for their protection.

ployable; he has been diagnosed as depressed. Since she has no support, Zahra qualifies as a Special Hardship Case, which means she is eligible for bimonthly food rations (four small tins of meat, some flour and wheat, some sugar), used clothing if available, blankets, and the equivalent of two U.S. dollars per person per year. Zahra is in her mid-thirties—ten years my junior—and looks as if she were ten years my senior. She is pregnant.

In a generosity of confidence I found startling but came in time to learn was characteristic of Arab women's culture, Zahra volunteers that she no longer knows where to turn in her despair. Her husband hasn't held a job in seven years. No, he never helps with the children, even though he's home all the time. Instead he beats them. When she interferes, he beats her, severely. He beats her even while she's pregnant, which is most of the time. She wants no more children, but he will hear none of it. Especially because he lacks a job, his manhood resides in fathering many offspring. "Look at them!" she whispers frantically, gesturing at the children who cling to all three of us where we sit, their fingers aimlessly picking at our sleeves, their huge black eyes liquid with hunger. "They keep coming and coming. What can I do? I can do nothing."

Yes, she went to the UNRWA clinic—in secret—to inquire about "spacing." (Since abortion and contraception per se are opposed by religious mandate—by the local mullahs in their interpretation of Islam *and* by the Rabbinical Courts of the Israeli Occupying Authority—UNRWA can neither perform abortions nor advocate birth control. The most it can do is urge "spacing" of children, via the Pill or the IUD, for the sake of the health of mother and child. Tubal ligation is forbidden, and vasectomy a laughable option in these cultural conditions.) Zahra had breakthrough bleeding with the IUD and couldn't take the Pill because she is acutely anemic. The clinic doctor prescribed iron to build her up so that perhaps in time she might be able to take the Pill—but Zahra never returned to the clinic because her husband discovered she was going and beat her badly.

As if he's overheard our whispered confidences, the husband suddenly rises. All three women react identically out of a mutual instinct: Zahra, a nonliterate refugee; Christiane, the interpreter, a Christian Palestinian who has endured a lifetime of triple abuse, as woman, as Palestinian, and as member of a religious minority among her own people; and me, the feminist, the journalist, the Westerner. All three women react to his rising with terror. All three women instantly reach for the children—to embrace them, to cover them, to protect them. In the glance we exchange no translation is necessary.

But he is rising only because he has seen my camera. He wants his photograph taken with his children. It is best to oblige. He poses, grinning, his arms outstretched beneficently around the brood of hollow-cheeked children and wife with swollen belly and dull eyes. Then he returns, unsmiling, to his place at the room's center. Zahra follows Christiane and me outside, trailed by the children. Suddenly she seizes me by the shoulders. Her sentences burst forth rapid-fire, punctuated by sobs through which Christiane tries to catch up: "You're from the West. You know about these things. Tell me, *tell me* how not to have another child. It's killing me. I'll die. I'll die of it. I'll do anything. I don't care what they say. What do men know about life? I don't care about the Israelis, I don't care about the PLO, I don't care about the mullahs, I don't care about my husband, I don't care about *God!*"

Three women stand weeping in one another's arms, amid a cloud of flies and a swarm of children.

This was only the first of literally hundreds of such scenes from which both the local interpreter and I would stagger away, shaken. No one had talked with the women in this way before, or had worked with woman interpreters, or had elicited these responses. In Zahra's case, we were able to arrange a special home visit from the clinic, to follow up on the iron regime for her anemia. Perhaps, then, in secret, the Pill. It was too late to save her from this pregnancy, but maybe from the next. . .

I had been told that Palestinian women had no understanding of or interest in feminism.

"What do men know about life?"

———

It had taken a year of delicate negotiation with UNRWA after their initial invitation to me to journey to the camps. My somewhat unorthodox requests, which at first had been received with a bit of shock, gradually and graciously were met: I would go alone, not as part of a journalists' group bussing from camp to camp as if touring zoos; I would focus specifically on women and children; I would view a minimum of buildings or health and educational installations but would be free to wander through the camps and talk with women; I would not be bound by UNRWA or other official contacts or schedules, and could avail myself of extra-official contacts and referrals acquired through networking with feminist activists in the Arab world. Most important, I insisted on woman interpreters, knowing that the kind of intimate communication I hoped to inspire would be impossible through male interpreters. Fulfillment of this last request appeared impossible: UNRWA had no female interpreters. The trip seemed futile in such circumstances. In time, however, UNRWA did manage to find Palestinian women among its own personnel who, although employed as educators, medical staff, or social workers, were able and eager to translate, never before having been given the opportunity.

UNRWA was established in 1949 with a purely humanitarian (and "temporary") mandate. It is now the largest single employer, apart from governments, in the Middle East. Its staff of over seventeen thousand people, most of whom are in the field, is almost as large as the staffs of all the other UN agencies combined. Yet it has a lower budget, relying on voluntary contributions from governments and the European Community for almost 94 percent of its annual revenue; only about 4 percent comes from the UN budget, and voluntary organizations and intergovernmental agencies provide the remaining resources. It ministers to 2.3 million registered Palestine refugees, of whom 349,388 are school pupils; it runs and staffs 633 primary and preparatory schools (most on double shifts) and eight vocational and teacher-training centers, ninety-eight health centers, and ninety-two supplementary feeding centers. It receives almost six million patient visits annually, provides prenatal, natal, postnatal, and pediatric services, dental services and immunization programs, and subsidizes 882 hospital beds. It operates fifty-six sewing and women's activities centers. It has more than ten thousand teachers in the field. It awards almost four hundred university scholarships annually. It offers special training to handicapped refugees, organizes co-ops, community self-help, and youth activity centers, and provides support for some fifty voluntarily run special play centers for preschoolers. It ministers to 135,375 Special Hardship Cases. It serves midday meals six days a week to some 29,000 children, and regularly provides 120,000 refugee mothers and babies with extra nutrition. It also provides potable water and essential sanitation services in sixty-one camps. It does not administer or "run" the camps however; that power lies in the hands of either the "host country" (Jordan, Syria, Lebanon) or the "Occupying Authority" (Israel in the Occupied Territories of the West Bank and Gaza). The curriculum in UNRWA schools must follow the local curriculum (Jordanian in the West Bank, Egyptian in Gaza), yet UNRWA students consistently test higher than the nationals in the countries where they reside. Palestinian women have the fastest growing literacy rate of all women in the Arab World.* The Agency is headed by a staff of "internationals," approximately 150 professionals. But the body of the staff in the field (now approaching 17,500 people) is composed of Palestinian

---

* Only in my own first-generation Ashkenazic Jewish mother and aunts have I encountered such a hunger and reverence for education as I found among Palestinian women. In a diaspora where nothing is rooted, knowledge is the only portable wealth. It is also a nonlethal means to identity. It is a Palestinian obsession—and the record of education is UNRWA's special and justifiable pride.

refugees— and most of them appear to be women. Statistically, the personnel of UNRWA is only 36 percent female, yet everywhere one looks in the field—in the maternal-health clinics and other health facilities, in the nutrition centers, on the clerical front, in the primary schools, the preparatory schools, the vocational training centers, the teacher-training centers—women. It struck me that they constituted the real government of the Palestinian people—not in the visible sense, like the Palestine Liberation Organization, but in that these women are preparing the substructure of what they trust will be their people's future: training the workers and technicians, teachers, professionals, artists, and politicians. They do this against almost insurmountable odds. As women, they face sexism-as-usual, inside and outside the Agency. As UNRWA personnel they share in the Agency's diplomatic vulnerability: UNRWA at times suffers slings and arrows from Israel (for helping the Palestinians "too much"), from the Palestinians (for not being partisan and "political"), and from the Arab states (for both those reasons, in concert or alternation).

There is a sign in the Jerusalem headquarters of UNTSO (the United Nations Truce Supervision Organization) that reads: *If You Think You Understand the Middle East, You Have Not Been Properly Briefed.* It's true.

One UNTSO officer—an old Middle East hand—advised me to ignore the statistics, the analyses, the sophisticated propaganda barrage from all sides, and to trust my own impressions. He himself, an Englishman who seemed to have materialized directly from the pages of a Graham Greene novel, was a rich source of stories. Witty and cynical, he could nevertheless still evince an impassioned concern, whether for his own staff, or about the machinations of Arab states in their repeated betrayals of the Palestinians, or about the erosion of morality in the Israeli government. It was he who told me, "The two best-educated, most secular peoples in the region are the Israelis and the Palestinians. Were they to reconcile, they would control the entire Middle East. The Arab countries know that, the Soviet

Union knows that, the United States knows that. Do you understand now?"

I was to take his advice about trusting my own impressions, and it is those impressions that I set down here. A large carton sits at the side of my desk, filled with background materials, statistics, photographs, official accusations and official rebuttals, thick documents proving atrocities on both—no, all—sides. The history of Zionism. The Balfour Declaration. The abandonment of European Jews by the West during the Holocaust and after World War II. The history of Palestine. The abandonment of Palestinians by the East and the West. The founding Constitution of the PLO. The Great Powers' creation of Lebanon and fabrication of Jordan, impositions of a Western-State format on lands charged with ethnic differences and tribal enmities. The 1967 Six-Day War. The 1973 Yom Kippur War. Meron Benvenisti's in-depth West Bank *Data Base Project Reports*. Oil. Citrus crops. Tourism. Theocracy. Religious fundamentalism—Jewish, Muslim, and Christian. The lineage of the patriarchs.

The data in the carton is available elsewhere, in libraries and embassies. However tempting it is to try to tell the "whole story" of a story that cannot ever be told whole, I shall ignore that carton for now. There is another story to tell, a more important one, the story my notebooks and taped interviews preserved; the story entrusted to me by women of that region. It is a story that has not yet been told anywhere.

This story, too, is a montage of images and emotions distilled and sealed in the brain and heart. But unlike the images from the sixties, these run fresh blood everywhere. And unlike the others, these seemingly disparate moments form a distinct pattern, one neither of my former experience nor my imposing. I went to the Middle East not to propagate feminism but to learn, not to talk but to listen. I went expecting to be disliked as an American, mistrusted as a "Western feminist," and disregarded as a woman. Those stereotypes are expectable: part of my responsibility as an internationalist feminist is to earn different responses. I went anticipating that I might not find an indigenous feminism among these women, particularly among the nonliterate women struggling to survive in the camps.

I should have known that in a region proud to actually call itself the Land of the Patriarchs I would find otherwise. This part of the world blares male history perhaps more than any other: the Tomb of Joseph, the Tomb of Abraham, the Tombs of David, Elijah, Jesus. God and His Son. God and His Prophet. In Egypt, I had felt suffocated by that history, Cairo is ringed by the Necropolis, an ancient city of the dead, in which almost a million people dwell, the living dead, squatters in the tombs. The museums, the galleries, the Luxor ruins, all stutter friezes repeating one message: how the Assyrians swept over the Hashemites, the Heberu smote the Philistines, the pharaohs marched, pillaged, took captives, the Persians rose and fell.* That history is malignantly alive today. Syria versus the Hashemite Kingdom of Jordan. Israel versus Palestine (the Palestinian pronunciation of "Palestine" is "Philistina"). It's alive on every highway in Israel, where one periodically sees a burned-out Egyptian tank by the side of the road, or a shot-down Jordanian plane—intentionally left standing by the government to commemorate its victories and remind the vanquished who won. The politics is not only that of the State-that-would-be against the State-that-is, but also that of the Tribes-that-were against the Tribes-that-still-are. The politics is one of ancient and undying enmity. The politics is the essence of patriarchy. It is as if the region were sacred to the Demon Lover. I should have known that in such a place, I would find not just women's suffering and endurance but women's resistance and rebellion.

What one hears from women in this region is dramatically

---

* The tomb of Hatshepsut, the only woman pharaoh, is a startling exception. One gasps to find one's politics so confirmed. No towering columns or mega-statues here, but low curved lines cut into and blending with the hills, ramps and small temples—and murals depicting women in joyful procession, the dance of freed captives, and the celebration of opening trade with former enemies. The images of Hatshepsut herself have been defaced by subsequent pharaohs.

different from what the male leadership on all sides *(and the token women of that male leadership)* would have us believe.

There are two well-fostered stereotypes of the Palestinian woman: she is a grenade-laden Leila Khaled, or she is an illiterate refugee willingly producing sons for the revolution. Yet I was to meet Palestinian woman doctors and nurses, dentists, midwives, social workers, educators, researchers and professors, architects, engineers, lawyers. I was to sit for a privileged afternoon with Saba Arafat in her small apartment in the Old City of Nablus in the West Bank, rooms filled with exquisite art treasures created, she smiled wryly, "by ignorant Arabs." It was she who founded the Ramallah Women's Training Center in the West Bank, the first vocational training center for women in the entire Middle East. "Sometimes I thought I'd go mad," she murmured, "traveling up and down the country, trying to sell the idea—to UNRWA, to Jordan, to Israel, to Palestinian men." Now in her sixties and retired as UNRWA's Field Education Officer, she winked at me, "I was so busy, I forgot to get married."

So Palestinian women care nothing for feminism?

I was to meet victims and survivors, women who by their mid-fifties were already great-great-grandmothers, women who bear the societal scars of having refused to marry at all, women who dare to love other women. I was to meet Palestinian women whose sole means of resistance is to wear keys on strings or chains around their throats, keys to homes bombed or razed forty years earlier. I was to meet principled Israeli women whose lives are committed to peace, reconciliation activism, and feminism. I was to meet highly educated Palestinian women, sophisticated in the ways of patriarchal politics, who had risen as far as possible with the PLO only to hit the glass ceiling of male supremacy.

But the focus of this journey was the women in the refugee camps, who suffer from the sexuality of terrorism with every breath they inhale. It was in their lives and voices I saw and heard the indomitable human spirit of hope and affirmation, a politics I call feminism. This is their story.

———

At the southernmost border of the Gaza Strip, the environs of the Rafah Camp have been severed by the "border" with Egypt. In these areas, called Brazil Camp and Canada Camp after the UN troops that were stationed there, all that seems to grow in the desertlike landscape is barbed wire. It stretches between watchtowers where Israeli soldiers sit manning machine guns. The camp, with a population of fifty-one thousand, was virtually split down the middle by the Camp David agreement between Israel and Egypt. Families were arbitrarily separated. Refugees on each side of the border have neither the money nor the papers to cross the hundred or so yards on visits. (In 1986, Gazans still had no official papers. Jordan-based Palestinians could obtain Jordanian passports, while Palestinians in Syria and Lebanon could obtain Syrian or Lebanese travel papers, which listed their nationality as "Palestinian." But Israel and Egypt each claimed Gazans' papers were the other side's problem, with Israel issuing Gazans ID cards listing their nationality as "Undetermined.")

The women come to the border every afternoon. Carrying and trailing their children, shuffling their feet through the sand in cheap rubber clogs, they approach the barbed wire. Beyond it, a few yards of sand. Beyond that, the paved Israeli patrol road. Beyond that, more wire, then more sand, then a dirt and gravel road for the Egyptian patrols, then more wire, then Egypt—and women and children on the other side. The women press their bodies against the wire, they squint in the sun, they recognize their relatives. They wave, they call out across the desert and the walls of wire, across the soldiers and the watchtowers. News is exchanged. They shout in the pauses of a wind that otherwise would carry their voices unhearable away. They hold up babies to be seen. They tell the children to wave. They repeat the same phrases over and over. "I miss you," the interpreter relays it. "I love you." "How is our mother?" "Have you got rations yet?" "I have not been well."

One woman suddenly lurches back from the wire, puts down the toddler she has been carrying, collapses to her knees, crying. Her head veil slides off and she twists it like a rope in her hands. She pounds the sand with her fists. She lifts her face to the white desert sky and keens. The interpreter reaches for my hand, holds hard. "She has just learned that her daughter on the Egyptian side died last night, in childbirth."

———

At the northernmost part of Gaza is the "border" with Israel. Here, each dawn, forty thousand refugees cross north to work in Israel. Some have formal work permits, most do not. One-third of those crossing over are women. Both women and men take whatever work they can get. The men work primarily as day laborers in construction, sometimes building the Israeli settlements beyond the Green Line in the West Bank, or they work in factories, sometimes in Israeli armament factories. The women work as charwomen or, more frequently, in the fields—often fields where they themselves grew up when their families owned the land as farmers. Some must seek different work each day.

We go while it's still dark to watch this exodus. The refugees include Palestinian professionals who can get no employment in Gaza; one with whom I talk is a medical doctor working as a manual laborer. The women and men wait, sitting separately. The men travel in rented busses, or piled in cars and trucks. Those without work permits are permitted to cross anyway: as illegal labor, they provide the Israelis with an even cheaper work force than those with permits. Because of a regulation reminiscent of South Africa, the workers, with or without permits, must—unless they have special permission—be out of Israel by nightfall or risk jail. Most of the women have no papers and no means of transport except hitchhiking or haggling for whatever space is available for a fee in the men's busses or trucks.

She says her name is Najat. She is thirty-five, has ten children. Her husband abandoned her. She lives in southern Gaza in Khan Yunis Camp, along with thirty-six thousand other refugees. Her mother cares for her children there. Najat rises each morning at two and travels to the northern border to be there by four. Then she travels another three hours to work in the fields near Jaffa—where she was born. Then she repeats the travel in reverse, getting home past ten at night. For this, she earns the equivalent of five U.S. dollars per day. Two of those dollars are spent on transportation. She has been doing this, six days a week, for six years.

This is neither the first country nor the first situation where I have been told that "here the women don't work." I see them working everywhere all the time. I see them working in the fields while men sit idle in the village coffeehouse. I see them employed in the lowest-paying jobs, and always, in addition, doing the nonpaying job that isn't even considered "work": the life-sustaining labor of bearing, feeding, caring for children, the keeping of homes even when there are no real homes to keep. I see them hauling water and balancing bales on their heads; scrubbing clothes under a thin stream from a communal spigot; lifting, pulling, carrying, chopping, cooking, sewing. I see them in sweatshops in the Strip, where Israeli cloth imported by the Occupying Authority for this purpose is cut and sewn into clothing by cheap labor, then carted back into Israel for sale at higher prices than Gazans can afford.

I see women in skill-training classes run by other women in UNRWA: learning how to sew, how to knit, how to embroider, how to type. Such skills to the Western eye may seem drearily "feminine," but in the context they are keys to a minuscule economic survival. The UNRWA women must convince the refugee men to allow "their" women to learn these skills— and then to use them—fighting a daily battle against traditional male hegemony. (The Agency also offers women training in nontraditional skills: as land surveyors, architectural and engineering draftspeople, construction technicians, radio/TV mechanics, lab technicians, etc.) The Israeli policy on such education blatantly represents traditional male bonding across cultures:

> Israel's policy to the employment and training of Arab women has been sensitive to their tradition and social obligations. The Ministry of Labour offers vocational training programmes and subjects for which there is a demand by the population and in the labour market. These courses are offered free of charge, and the graduates have no obligation to use their newly acquired skills by taking a job, if the latter goes against the wishes of the woman's father, fiancé, or husband. . . . For reasons of tradition . . . many families prefer to send their women folk to work in Israel through a *Rais* (local contractor), who is held responsible for the girl's honour. The *Rais* contacts employers directly and usually pays the woman's wages to male members of her family.[1]

It comes as no shock that the women prefer to learn their skills from other Palestinian women in UNRWA, and then to apply those skills toward gaining some dignity in their lives. As if in a collaborative response to Israel, the government of Jordan in 1968 published a population and labor-force survey including the following statement: "The traditional social attitude of the people [sic] considers the wife who is helping her husband in his agricultural work as being economically non-active and leads, therefore, to her exclusion from the members of the labour force in agriculture. The same attitude applies to all female family members helping men in agricultural work."[2]

So Palestinian women do not work?

———

Sameeha is one of 27,000 residents in Nuseirat Camp, in the Strip. She is a refugee, a traditional midwife who has also learned modern practical nursing through UNRWA, and now works with its local health center. She performs many home visits. She fountains a furious energy. "Year after year, a few of us women try to get on the camp council.* The men are scared of us, and won't let us on. But somebody has to *do* something. Work out better policies, demand better sanitary conditions. UNRWA can't do it all. The Occupying Authority has to do *more*. The *men* have to do more. Now drugs are coming into the Strip; every day more of our young men are in a daze of drugs. You know how the drugs come? From the sea, smuggled. Three groups of men aid this, by direct support or by closing their eyes: the smugglers, the Israelis, *and the mullahs*. The smugglers gain money, the Israelis gain a drugged-out male population, and the mullahs gain power and dependency by being the connections. This must stop! And the women are the ones who will stop it!"

This is one of hundreds of encounters that end with tears and laughter, with embraces, with exchanged addresses, with the Arabic phrase here transliterated as *"Bahibbik ya ukhti—* which means "I love you, my sister."

———

The terrain of this "land of milk and honey" is bleak. It's not a piece of real estate warranting such contest. The earth is a uniform beige and ocher, clotted with sullen yellow rocks and stones. What little green there is—the native cactus, the olive trees—is a harsh steel-green. The eye thirsts for color. A visitor's gaze rivets to the rare soft peach of a cactus flower or the blue, white, and gold of a mosque, shades that cool and refresh the eye.

In camp after camp, like flags of semaphore or banners of survival, the laundry is hanging out to dry—miles of it strung above and between shelters, bleaching white in the Mediterranean sun. In camp after camp, to my amazement, there are the attempts at gardens. In a two- or three-foot square of rocky sand beside a shelter—a garden. The women grow subsistence

---

* Camp councils settle internal conflicts in the camps and try to negotiate with the Occupying Authority, but have no objective power. They do have stature within the camp community, however.

food in this tiny space: a stalk or two of corn, some squash or zucchini vines, a tomato plant, a few cabbages. Sometimes a makeshift trellis with a grape vine curling up it. And always at least one flower—a crimson hibiscus, a fuchsia plant, a bougainvillea.

Aziza shows me her garden in Beach Camp. It is miraculous what she manages to grow, so densely, in this ridiculous space and inhospitable soil where forty thousand people are compressed. She has no tools, and water is a precious commodity in the camps. Sometimes, when there has been camp unrest, the Israeli soldiers deliberately urinate in the water supply in revenge. Why, in such circumstances, devote any of the precious space and water to flowers? "Because," Aziza grins and pokes me as if I'm teasing her, "*you* know why." She laughs, "The soul—it needs to be fed, too."

———

The genius of male collusion pretending to be enmity is fascinating. Palestinian secular resistance is forbidden (the Palestinian flag is illegal, displaying the colors of that flag is seen as provocative, and the use of the word "Palestine" itself is regarded by the Israeli government as an insult to the State). But "religious freedom" is much trumpeted. Is it surprising, in such conditions, that hitherto secular Palestinian resistance begins to merge with Islamic fundamentalism? There is only one university for Palestinians in the Gaza Strip. It was founded in 1978 by the Saudi Arabian government and is fundamentalist; Al Azhar University in Cairo—the greatest seat of Arab and Muslim learning in the world—refuses to accredit it. This fundamentalist school was welcomed by the Israelis. But when a group of Palestinian scholars in Gaza wanted to found a secular university there, that was not permitted. Women attending the fundamentalist university must wear the full *hijab,* not only the head veil but the complete body veil, and must cover their faces and wear gloves. There is no other source of higher education in the Strip. So the women go, like movable bolts of cloth, and each day as they leave, they peel off the veils and gloves.

———

The Gaza Women's University Graduates Association—all five members—receives me. They are refugee women in their late thirties and older, women who got their degrees in Egypt before the Camp David accords. Since then, Egypt has reduced its scholarships for Gazans from 1500 per year to about forty— almost all now awarded to men. These Palestinian women, highly educated, with excellent English, are what is left of a four-hundred-member association. Some years earlier, the Palestinian colors were used in decorative streamers at the fortieth birthday party—a private celebration—of one of the members. Two of the women were hauled in under "administrative detention" for six months each. The membership suffered considerable attrition, the intended effect. Now the five intrepid remaining members still meet in their tiny office crammed with Arabic and English books about women. Only one wears a head veil and a dress; the rest wear slacks. Two are historians; one is an expert in Arabic literature, especially poetry; one is a pharmacist; one is an archeologist.

The pharmacist divorced her husband because she refused to permit him to censor what she read. She says, "You get depressed all your life. The Israelis say No. Your parents say No. Your husband says No." She is the only one of the group who has a paying job at what she's trained in; unemployment in the Strip runs high—and highest of all for Palestinian women professionals. The pharmacist is the sole support of her mother and eleven siblings.

But it is the archeologist who is most poignant. Zeinab is the kind of scholar afire with a lifelong obsession about her work. When she speaks about ruins or talks about a particular stone's carbon-dating, her eyes dance with excitement. To suppose that Zeinab—a female Palestinian archeologist in the Gaza Strip without papers—could find work for which she is trained, is a sick joke. Never mind; she would do anything to be near her precious artifacts, to teach others about them—she would even, despite three graduate degrees, work as a tour guide.

This is not permitted: she might make a reference to the history of Philistina.

She speaks softly, restraining tears: "I have been privileged to have an education. I don't wish to complain or seem ungrateful. But there is no way I can use that education. There are women in the camps who still cannot read or write, and older women who never learned and now never will. I am, by comparison, fortunate. But—" her voice breaks, "I am a bird in a cage. In some ways, it's harder. To have the door opened, to glimpse the outside. And then to live for the rest of your life staring at the door shut again in your face."

———

The patriarchal contortion of language: The Occupied Territories are under the control of the Israeli Civil Authority for Administered Areas. One sees the signs of the ICA everywhere, on the watchtowers, the military installations, the prisons. Beneath the large words proclaiming "Civil Authority" are the small letters *IDF* for "Israeli Defence Force."

The patriarchal jokes of history: One not infrequently sees Palestinians with blue, gray, or green eyes, and red hair. Khitam, at one of the preschool centers in the West Bank, explains it. "The Crusades," she shrugs. "All those Plantagenets and their troops. Perhaps a few marriages—but mostly rape." Ayisha, the nutritionist who works with her, adds with a bitter smile, "Maybe it's one reason the other Arabs resent us so much—light eyes, light hair. Racism, or racism in reverse, it's all the same. It usually comes down to rape."

———

Yusra Barbary grants me a visit. She is now in her eighties, a wire of a woman, frailty, strength, white hair, eagle's eyes. She has been a Palestinian women's leader for years and still heads the network of women's groups in the Strip. She is of the old guard, organizing women to wrap bandages and send clothing to men in prison. She speaks of Palestinian youth with concern and, it strikes me, some confusion (over half the Palestinian population of Gaza and the West Bank is under age nineteen). She expresses disapproval of the younger women's thinking too much about their own freedom as women and not enough about the whole Palestinian people. Yet when I ask her what she sees as her greatest success over the decades, she answers without hesitation, "Rising literacy in our women." And the greatest obstacle? Surprisingly, not the obvious—the occupation. Instead: "The fragmentation in Palestinian leadership. The jockeying for power. As if we had time for that. Fighting. Killing. Idiots! All of these men are idiots." Would women be different if they held leadership? She blinks, looking at me as if I were another idiot. "Of course!" she snaps. "That's obvious. That's why the men won't let us have it."

As I leave, she embraces me, gives me a piece of embroidery, looks into my eyes, and laughs, "Remember now, I'm no feminist."

———

The shelter had been bulldozed within the previous hour. Inam's nine-year-old son was thought to have been one of the boys who threw stones at a passing Israeli convoy of trucks and tanks. Often, the response in such a case is to punish the family: with one hour's warning, their shelter is destroyed. Inam is a widow, raising fifteen children. She was able to complete only five years of schooling but had hoped to return for adult education. Now she stands dry-eyed amid the rubble of what was her home. Neighbors cluster, gawking, whispering. The garden is a heap of torn vines, leaves, and petals crushed under concrete chunks. Her cookpots are scattered, her laundry is strewn, ripped and filthy, on the sand. One of her daughters is trying to rescue a dollhouse built with discarded Coca-Cola cans and matchboxes. The younger children are screaming, clinging to her skirts. She must split up the family now, lodge some of the children with relatives in this camp and other camps. The Israeli policy is that UNRWA may not rebuild the shelter, because the camps are crowded anyway and need more "spaciousness." Inam has no place to go. She rummages through the rubble, picks out a small plastic plaque with something written on it in Arabic. I ask for a translation: *If you cannot be a star in the sky, be a lamp in a chamber.* She dusts off the sign and begins to make piles of her belongings.

———

Wherever I go, the women extend warmth, generosity, hospitality, and an unexpected trust. Lacking telephones and mail service, the women seem to have a mysterious swift line of communication from camp to camp. Somebody's cousin's friend's sister lives here but works there or knows someone or met somebody. All I know is that the word spreads—from the southernmost tip of Gaza, within one day, to the northernmost tip of the West Bank, where a woman will approach me and say "Jamila in Rafah says to trust you. She says you are the American woman with an Arab woman's heart. She says talk to you."

Wherever I go, in shelters where rationing is severe and coffee a rare luxury, the tiny cracked cup of strong coffee appears. By now I have fleas, lice, double menstrual periods, and dysentery. The last thing I want is Arab coffee. I long to decline, to say that the coffee is precious and the woman should save it, not waste it on a a guest for whom it is currently disastrous. But to decline is to overlook the tradition of hospitality. From time immemorial, to offer the traveler a drink from the oasis meant a welcoming trust; to accept meant a comparable trust that the drink was not poisoned. So she spends her valuable coffee as the coin of her dignity and I accept with respectful gratitude, privately reconciling myself to the fact that one portion of my brain is now specializing solely in sphincter control.

She is pleased when complimented on her coffee. It's worth it to see her pride.

———

The average UNRWA clinic doctor in the Gaza Strip must treat about 150 patients per day. Meanwhile, over two hundred trained Palestinian physicians in the Strip cannot find employment, nor has UNRWA the funds to hire them. The entire UNRWA budget for health amounts to an average of ten U.S. dollars per person per year. Yet because of the Agency, infant mortality dropped from 90 per 1,000 in 1975 to 30 per 1,000 in 1987.

Most of the patients are female. One-third of their illnesses are caused by poverty (malnutrition, parasites, diabetes, anemia, chronic dysentery); one-third, by multiple pregnancies; and one-third (blindness, especially) are genetic, due to the tradition of cousin marriages.

All of the health facilities are immaculate, though some are housed in decrepit buildings. Women by the hundreds wait to be examined. They squat, barnacled by children, in the courtyards. Inside, the women of the medical staff call across the babble of children's voices. Somehow, they smile—at each other, at their patients, at a visitor—through an unspeakable fatigue.

———

Shock upon shock. This is the first place I have ever been where no woman thinks it strange that someone can be both political and a poet. There is a long harem tradition in the Arab world of major woman poets—bards—who affected the politics of their time.

Shock upon shock. Fat'ma is in her late forties, a refugee, a primary-school teacher for UNRWA in one of the West Bank camps, which shall be nameless. With no fear or embarrassment, she volunteers that she is not married, never will be, has no children, never intends to, has a woman lover. This is the one question I have been warned by my Palestinian woman interpreters not to ask. In camp after camp, I have inquired, via their delicately phrased questions, about rape, battery, child molestation, intimate health details, women's attitudes toward their men. These are all subjects camp women had never been asked about by a foreigner, possibly by anyone, though they clearly discuss such things among themselves. But this question, I have been warned, is too incendiary.

Fat'ma smiles. She speaks in a halting but sound English. "I acknowledge it not to be a popular subject," she says, "but we do exist. I do not imagine me." She tells me an Arab proverb I have heard before: "When a woman loves a woman, it brings no shame to her father and no swelling to her belly." She adds dryly, "This is not the favorite proverb of Arab men." She specifically asks that I tell the women I write to and for that she exists. Not as openly as she would like, she murmurs, then gives me a long look. "But I was fortunate to study for one year, when I was younger, at university in your Colorado. It was not very open or acceptable there, either. Is it so very different for a lesbian woman anywhere?"

I do not imagine me.

Bahibbik ya ukhti.

Tell them I exist.

———

Sewing centers. Immunization centers. Kindergartens and crèches. Maternity centers. Embroidery centers. The first women's co-op to sell this exquisite work, at Kalandia, in the West Bank.

Embroidery is *the* great Palestinian art—and it is a women's art. By the pattern, the type of stitch, the juxtaposition of geometric or floral shapes, it is possible to tell immediately whether the artist is from Hebron or Haifa, from Jenin or Gaza. It becomes a cloth code, a mute articulate communication. Mats, front panels in long dresses, wall hangings, cushion covers, tablecloths. The preferred threads happen to be green, red, and black against white—coincidentally the colors of the banned

Palestinian flag. Most of the women in the camps cannot afford to wear their own embroidery anymore, even if it is their national dress. They wear—sometimes under a veil—flimsy synthetic fabric clothing with labels revealing manufacture in Taiwan. Taiwan is infamous for its garment industry: other sweatshops staffed by other women.

———

Jerusalem, the holy city, is for me an uncivil hell. In a smoldering populace, factions barely coexist by ignoring one another, repressing one another, or avenging themselves upon one another. Three different currencies are in use, whole sections of the city are shut down on different days each week (for the various religious holidays), a babble of every conceivable language is trying *not* to communicate with any other.

Small riots, clashes, street friskings, car bombings occur each day as matters of no consequence.

The secular Israelis are at civil war with the *Haredim,* the ultra-Orthodox Jews. The latter have been torching bus-stop shelters postered with "pornographic" bathing-suit advertisements. They've also been fire-bombing movie theaters that stay open on the sabbath, attacking and throwing stones at Israeli women wearing slacks, and gaining seats in the Knesset. Some secular Israelis have responded by bombing an Orthodox synagogue.

Christian feuds with Christian. Each Friday, representatives of the major Christian faiths (Roman Catholic, Greek Orthodox, Armenian Orthodox, Russian Orthodox) come to ritual blows about whose dedicatory lamp will hang closest to the Holy Sepulchre slab on which Christ's body supposedly was laid.

Muslim fights with Muslim—the liberal reformers versus the fundamentalists, the followers of Haddad versus the followers of Arafat.

There must be something in the water.

Everyone preaches "brotherhood."

The city seems lugubriously full of veiled women.

The *Haredim* women follow their men through the streets, a reverent pace behind. The *Haredim* women are always pregnant, with a train of stair-step children in their wake. The *Haredim* women must wear their own version of the veil: their shaven and *sheitel*ed (wigged) heads must be fully covered in public, their long skirts and sleeves must conceal whorish, temptress, Jezebel-like wrists and ankles.

The flocks of Christian nuns also go veiled.

The Muslim women wear mostly black, the *Haredim* women wear dark colors, the nuns are chiaroscuro penguins. The children crusting the bodies of the Jewish and Muslim women are their own; those clinging to the nuns are their pupils or orphanage charges.

None of the men wear veils or children.

The men wear guns.

The tourists wear Bermuda shorts and cameras.

This makes it easy to tell them all apart.

Jerusalem is the only place in the region where I encounter street sexual harassment—and it is from Israeli soldiers, catcalling and making remarks and sucking sounds dismally familiar from the streets of New York. It would seem that sexual harassment declines in direct proportion to the rise in religious fundamentalism: the choice partriarchy offers women.

In the camps I was not afraid, yet in Jerusalem I am afraid. The city is a grid of compartments. I am frisked by Israeli soldiers. I am glared at by Arab men. To wander too near the Orthodox Jewish section is to invite being stoned or beaten. The suburbs boast homes that are walled compounds. West Jerusalem is Israeli, a cross between old-world Vienna and modern San Francisco. The T-shirt shops display wares that read: "Don't Worry, America: Israel Is Behind You," "Peace Through Superior Firepower," "Fatah-Busters." On the front of one shirt: "Peace with Arabs is an Idea Whose Time Has Past"—and on the back: "Like Fucking a Virgin."

In the Old City, a sub-world with sub-sub-worlds lurks behind the walls. The Jewish quarter. The Arab quarter and the *souk* (open marketplace). The Christian quarter. The African quarter. Kodak Film stickers plaster the Via Dolorosa, Royal Crown Cola signs flutter around the Dome of the Rock. At the Wailing Wall, women are separated from men. The women's side (one-quarter the size of the men's) is crowded with baby carriages, strollers, toddlers. The women approach the Wall, pray, then peer through the lattice divider at the larger section where the men pray, converse, and dance in a huge circle celebrating themselves and their god.

The city is ringed with vast settlements nicknamed "the Jerusalem Fortress." Modern co-op housing developments (into which, by law, no Palestinian can buy) can each house up to 400,000 people. These are all built behind the Green Line and are therefore illegal. The State officially condemns such practices—yet offers subsidized housing in these settlements for Israeli citizens. Some in the government openly call for formal and permanent annexation of the West Bank.

Samahat is in her sixties, has raised seventeen children, is a widow. She refused to give up her small farm near Jerusalem for "compensation." Now she lives in a trailer on that land. Her home was razed after the land was forcibly requisitioned. Settlement construction is going on all around her. Some Israeli woman attorneys are helping her argue her case in the courts. Meanwhile, the Black Jews—newly arrived from Ethiopia, half-starved, innocent, simply glad to be here—are callously lodged by the State in some of the outermost settlements; they suffer daily knife attacks by Palestinian men on whose land they unknowingly live. Me'na is a Black Jew, still skeletal from near starvation. "I'm afraid to be here," she says. "I was afraid to be where I was. Where can I be where I won't be afraid?"

The *Jerusalem Post* carries a front-page story seriously inquiring why agoraphobia (fear of leaving one's home) is on the increase among Jerusalemites.

A Palestinian academic at Bir Zeit University tells me she now specializes in oral histories, because "in another ten years, we won't even have grandmothers who can tell us what peace tasted like."

———

Knesset Member Shulamit Aloni receives me at the Israeli parliament. She is a founder of the Civil Rights and Peace Movement party, which holds four parliamentary seats. A feminist, a crusader against the Rabbinical Courts' control over women's lives, a secular activist, and a peace and reconciliation leader, she is in her late fifties. She has chronic ulcers and has survived two heart attacks. She keeps going because "someone has to stand up and say these things." When the prime minister warns that Israel is being out-populated by the Palestinians and urges each Israeli woman to bear at least four children, it is Aloni who leaps to her feet in the Knesset, roaring that instead of a sensible political solution, such as relinquishing the Occupied Territories, the government wants to "nationalize women." Shulamit knows that Israeli women are not the focus of my visit this time, but she briefs me anyway.

"We are going backward in terms of legislation, but forward in terms of consciousness. The Orthodox religious lobby finally has become so violent that it brought about a liberal backlash and some support for what we feminists have been saying all along. Israel is at a turning point as far as democracy is concerned. It can follow the tedious, sick process of many newly independent states—liberation, then corruption, then fascism, then liberation, then finally normalcy—or live up to its ostensible vision of a humane, democratic, socialist country. The two-state solution *would* be possible if Israel made some gesture—regarding the West Bank, for instance—especially now, when the Palestinians feel so betrayed by the Arab countries. But the men in this government will not make that gesture. On the contrary, some of them talk about formal permanent annexation. They have a siege mentality. Even the synagogue here at the Knesset is underground—and at its dedication, I had to sit behind the *mehitza* [partition]. Well, women have more stamina. We're more willing to fight peacefully and creatively, no matter how long it takes, rather than feed our ambition and our ego. I'd like somehow to reach Jewish women all over the world, whether they're religious or not, to urge them to *exercise a moral vote:* influence, pressure, write letters to this government and to their own governments, lobby to change and humanize the Israeli state—on racism, on peace, on women, on orthodoxy. *I'd like them to let this government know that it may not, must not, do these things in the name of Jews."*

Tears. Laughter. Embraces. She tells me I'm too skinny, that I should eat properly. "Dysentery?" she asks. I nod. She sighs, "I was afraid of that. Try to get some rest." "Look who's talking," I retort. More tears. More laughter. More embraces.

—

Dheisheh Camp, with almost seven thousand people, is south of Jerusalem in the West Bank, near Bethlehem. It has a history of uprisings—stone-throwing at Israeli patrols, strikes, protest marches. Consequently, it is now a sealed camp. All exits and entrances but one have been blocked by the Occupying Authority: concrete blocks and barbed wire circle the camp, and Klieg-type lights beam down from dusk until dawn. An armed watchtower looms over the camp. Long-promised work on sewage has been stopped by the State as punishment; new unconnected pipes rust in and alongside still-brimming open channels. In Dheisheh I am stopped by the Authorities from taking photographs. It is not the first or last time I am questioned or harassed as a journalist visiting the camps. But this time there are paratroopers on the scene and they are more hostile. I have the proper permission, I am accompanied by an interpreter, I am here at UNRWA's invitation. The captain, jauntily sporting a paratrooper's red beret, must ring up headquarters to find out what to do with me, since I refuse to let him take my film.

While he is gone, I engage one of the young soldiers in conversation. He is a *sabra,* a native-born Israeli, shy about his

English. I learn he is just eighteen years old. My son is about to turn eighteen, back in the States, I tell him. He asks about my son. A musician? Wants to be a composer? His eyes are hungry, yearning. He always wanted to be an artist, he says, a painter. As soon as his military service is up, maybe . . . Then he won't re-enlist as a career? He shakes his head. He looks around to be sure his superiors can't overhear.

"I don't like what I—what we—what happens. I—I—"

My son is almost his age. I can't help reaching out to touch his hand, lightly, his gangly adolescent hand that rests on the butt of his Galil rifle. His dark eyes fill. "I—we do . . . bad things, lady," he whispers, "bad things. And we're—I'm scared. I'm scared all the time."

His commanding officer spies us, strides over, chews him out for talking with a journalist. I intervene, try to take the blame. Red Beret reappears, sullen: he is to let me go. "Are you Jewish?" Red Beret asks, suddenly curious. "Yes," I reply, "but not religious." "Even so, a Jew and an American, why do you care to go into the camps? You should be on Israel's side!" I cannot talk to him, I cannot reach him, and he will not let me talk with the boy who is almost my son. I cannot ask these men what they think of the growing Israeli resistance movement, boys who are almost my sons who refuse military service entirely or who agree to serve in the army of defense but refuse to serve in the army of occupation.

Now, as I proceed through Dheisheh, the residents withdraw from me. Whether because they mistrust me for speaking with the soldiers or because they understood I was being detained and are now afraid to be seen with me, I cannot tell. But the children still run alongside, smiling, pointing to the camera and gesturing to have their pictures taken. Everywhere the children do this. One little girl about eight years old wants to practice the bit of English she is learning in the UNRWA school. Her name is Iftikar. She is lovely, with onyx eyes and a grin to gladden the soul. She tells me she wants to be a doctor when she grows up. No, she will not marry; she shakes her head saucily, her hands on her hips. She has twelve brothers and sisters. Her father has two wives. She will *not* marry. *She* will be a *doctor.*

Bahibbik ya ukhti.

She giggles and corrects my pronunciation.

The little boys her age run off. I turn a corner and see them again. They have crude wooden guns and are playing a different game.

———

For days I crisscross the West Bank. North to Nablus, to Jenin. It was in Jenin and Araba in the spring of 1983 that 250 schoolgirls in five different schools suffered dizziness, headaches, breathing difficulties, tremors, fainting spells, and acute cramps. The Occupying Authority attributed the incident to "mass hysteria." The epidemic spread. In three other northern areas of the West Bank and in Yatta (south of Hebron), 943 cases were reported—70 percent of which were adolescent girls. No one died. Israeli civil-liberties groups and Palestinian organizations accused the State of a poisoning attempt, marshaling evidence—a rash of gas "leaks" and chemical "spills" in the schools. The U.S. Centers for Disease Control and the World Health Organization mounted investigative teams. At this writing, the investigations have been shelved for diplomatic reasons. The Jerusalem Center for Development Studies continues to pursue the case, claiming recent new information about Israeli agents who planted the toxic chemicals. Meanwhile, the girls and young women "face a social tragedy. Their marriage is refused on the ground that they are poisoned. Rumors have spread claiming that the girls are deprived of fertility."[3] In a culture where marriage can mean economic survival, this could be a death sentence.

North again, to the Ramallah Women's Training Center, an oasis of sanity and hope. Both vocational and teacher training are done here. The dorms and classrooms are spotless, the buildings are beautiful, the grounds spacious. Young women (288 vocational students, 350 teacher-training students) sprawl on the grass with their books, reading, picnicking, talking animatedly. They might be college women in New England. From this place will go forth the next generation of Palestinian women, to teach others, nurse them, doctor them, tell them about "spacing," give them visions of a life beyond the camps. This was Saba Arafat's dream.

The students walk proud and beautiful, arm in arm, some in the full *hijab*, some in jeans and T-shirts, chatting and laughing. In the well-stocked library (with books in Arabic, English, and Hebrew) is a prominent sign: *Ignorance Is Not Bliss*. The principal welcomes me and glows with pride as I show delight in her school. "The only tragedy," her face darkens, "is when they must leave, return to the families in the shelters, to their fathers and brothers who resent what they have learned. If we could somehow prepare them for that . . ."

I sit on the grass in the sun and talk with the students, as I have talked with lower-school female students in every camp. Over and over, the refrain:

I do not wish to marry until much later.

I do not wish to have more than two children.

I do not wish to marry at all.

I do not wish to have any children.

All children are mine, what do I need with my own?

And the questions I have heard repeated almost verbatim in the girls' schoolrooms and the social-activity centers and courtyards of camps for weeks now:

Who gives more, who can contribute more, to her people? The woman who has ten or twelve children and cannot plan one hour beyond their survival? Or the woman who gives birth to herself and is free to help her people and the world?

Almost verbatim. Almost as if an invisible network of woman educators had communicated this message to an entire generation of younger women.

———

Fadwa is in a typing class in Kalandia Camp, in the West Bank. She is sixteen and radiates a fierce intelligence. The other young women are learning this skill in the hope that their fathers and brothers will permit them to take clerical jobs. But Fadwa says she is learning for an additional reason, because she wants to be a writer, a poet even. One of the other girls says that a poet is no use to her family, no use to her people. "It is a use to *me*," Fadwa flashes in reply, "and if a people has no artists it has no soul."

———

The crossing into Jordan takes an entire day. It is a journey over only a few miles, a rickety bridge across a trickle of Jordan River, and an abyss of difference. It is also a surrealistic experience in denial. The Israelis call the bridge the Allenby Bridge, the Jordanians call it the Hussein Bridge. Two passports are needed, since Jordan doesn't recognize Israel's existence and will not permit entry if a passport has been stamped in Israel. Yet soldiers on both sides talk with one another across the chasm, arguing about sports and sharing jokes about women.

Multiple checkpoints. Special permits. Vehicle searches. No photographs. UNRWA personnel, who make this crossing regularly, warn me that no one can predict how long it will take. Anything or nothing can happen. More checkpoints. More barbed wire, for miles. Stretches of parched hilly landscape in that same brittle metallic gray-green and sickly yellow. Signs posted on both sides of the road, in English and Arabic: *HEAVILY MINED.*

———

Jordan hosts ten camps, some dating from 1948 and partition. These are veritable small cities; one houses 57,000 people. Baqa'a Camp is in fact the second largest city in Jordan, a runner-up to Amman, the capital. But then almost two-thirds of Jordan's 2.8 million people are Palestinian.* Forty percent of

* On July 31, 1988, King Hussein announced that he was severing Jordan's legal and administrative ties to the West Bank (which had been ruled by Jordan from 1948 until Israel occupied it in 1967); Hussein then abolished Jordan's Occupied Territories Ministry and laid off over five thousand Palestinians working as Jordanian civil employees in the West Bank. He claimed this step was being taken in

UNRWA's operations are in Jordan; 17 percent of the school population is in UNRWA schools. Established camps like Suf, Irbid, and New Camp have roughly paved roads (laid by the residents themselves), some sewers, some electricity. There are little shops, a few glass-fronted. And there are cemeteries. Two generations of refugees have already lived and died here.

Deen'a has given birth to twenty-eight children, of whom twenty-five are living. She wanted to stop after the fifth, she says. Her husband was incensed at the idea. She plotted in secret for years. Finally she found a doctor who was willing to lie, to vouch that she had cancer of the uterus, to give her a hysterectomy. When her husband learned what had been done, he railed at her and beat her. It didn't matter then, she tells me. The interpreter begins to weep as she relates the reasons why: "He could beat me, he could even kill me. But he could no longer make me do what I didn't want to do. My two eldest, both of them sons, had been killed, you see. Angry, always they were angry. I'm angry, too, but I don't kill. Their anger made them killers. And they were killed in turn. No more sons, I thought. But he wouldn't let me stop. Now I have forced him to let me stop. I will not give birth only to see my children kill and die. *My body is not a weapons factory.* It is *my* body."

———

The insistence on working with woman interpreters has yielded an unplanned bonus: it turns out to be a whole new way of organizing. Each new interpreter is nervous as she starts off— nervous about translating, about daring to focus on women, about working with this strange Western feminist. By the end

deference to the PLO as "the sole legitimate representative of the Palestinian people" and to support 900,000 West Bank Palestinians in their demand for autonomy and an independent state. ("Excerpts from Hussein's Address on Abandoning Claims to the West Bank," *New York Times*, August 1, 1988.) As of this writing, it is impossible to know whether this tactical move on Jordan's part is substantive or cosmetic, whether it is an act of support, challenge, or abandonment, and how far-reaching its political impact will be. Only one thing is certain: it will further intensify confusion and hardship in the daily lives of many refugees.

of the first day, each new interpreter wants to talk privately—
at her home, at my quarters, over coffee, or even in the little
UNRWA car or jeep—about what she has heard and translated, and about her own life as a Palestinian woman. It is
apparently impossible to go through these hours and days, asking these kinds of questions, hearing and having to repeat these
kinds of replies, without major upheavals in one's own consciousness. Each interpreter winds up confiding resentment and
rebellion about *her* father, *her* husband, *her* brothers. My
vocabulary in Arabic improves, albeit selectively. I learn many
words for "anger." And my pronunciation of *Bahibbik ya ukhti*
becomes almost perfect.

———

In Amman I meet with Isam Abdl Haddi, president of the General Union of Palestinian Women, the "official" PLO women's
organization. I meet with Haifa' Al Bashir, president of the
Jordanian Women's Union but herself a Palestinian. I meet with
Suha Eid, liaison officer for the Palestinian Bir Zeit University
in the West Bank. All are extremely cordial. All are in different
ways highly sophisticated, Western-educated, politically canny,
articulate women. The higher I move into the female leadership—that is, women approved by the male leadership—the
louder I hear an echo of the men's rhetoric that Palestinian
women can best serve the cause by bearing more and more
children. It is identical with the rhetoric of the Israeli prime
minister denounced by Shulamit Aloni.

Respectfully, I submit to one of these women that the desire
to have more children is not what I have been hearing from
most women in the camps. I am told that yes, there is resistance, particularly from the younger women, but this must pass.
Perhaps the better-educated ones, those who manage to train
for professional careers, can contribute via brain more than
womb, but the average woman refugee must make her contribution through children. As politely as possible, I ask whether
that isn't a rather familiar class differentiation and an odd one

for revolutionaries to adopt. Yes, I am told honestly enough, but it is necessary for the liberation of Palestine. Yet when I ask this same woman leader if she thinks she—so near and yet so far from the PLO Central Committee—will ever make it onto the committee, she drops her gaze. "Never," she mutters. Then, as if anticipating my next question, "And yes, my dear, yes. It does make me bitter."

———

Rada has just turned thirty. She lives now in an established camp which I will not name, in Jordan. She has no right arm; it was blown off by a grenade. She was formerly a guerrilla fighter, she says. She speaks a little English, and we talk alone, without the interpreter, at Rada's request. She works now as a medical orderly in a health facility, and hopes someday to complete her schooling and go on to formal medical training. She wants to heal people. Her story is simple and she tells it in an understated manner.

"I was eighteen. Three of my brothers had died as guerrilla fighters in border raids. Another was in prison here in Jordan. My mother mourned all the time. My father had arranged a marriage for me, but I didn't love the man. I loved one of my brother's friends, also a guerrilla. When I did what I did, I—it was a way of avenging my brothers, fighting for my people, and defying my father, all at the same time. Then I saw that the action I was in had wounded a child. But it was my turn to—the man I loved, he yelled at me to throw it, throw the grenade, *throw it*. I loved him more than my own life. But maybe not more than that child's life, I suppose. I couldn't throw it. It exploded. We escaped, but he never spoke to me again. I had shamed him in front of his comrades. So I have lost him. There are some other women, it seems, who can do it, but I—I am more like the most of us who have to find a different way. I would like to be a surgeon." She laughs. "A one-armed Palestinian refugee woman surgeon, who heard of such a thing? So I will find some other way.

I would like to heal my people, to heal any people. I would like to heal."

———

Zahira Kamal is one of the new generation of grass-roots Palestinian woman leaders. No men appointed her to a formal post she gladly does not hold. She is proud to be a feminist, and also proud that her work is not of the kind done in the women's charitable societies, like those headed by Yusra Barbary—of whom she nonetheless speaks with respect. Her work is markedly different. The WWC (Women's Work Committee) was begun less than a decade earlier by herself and five friends, all educated women. Slowly, they built a network of more than nine thousand women in over seventy groups across the West Bank and the Gaza Strip. Unlike the women of the Red Crescent Society, they have no Arab-donated funds. They have no center to which women must come: "You see, such a small percentage really can come. Their fathers, their brothers, their husbands, forbid them and beat them if they disobey. The police use our own traditions against us; they call on the husband or father, report on the woman, and tell him, 'Keep her at home.' The men collaborate with each other. So we go out *to* the camps, the villages, *to* the women." They hold small informal women's meetings. "In a segregated culture, this part is not difficult." They ask the women what is most needed in this camp, this village: Literacy classes? Sewing classes? Knitting? Embroidery? Typing? "The women must take the responsibility of organizing themselves. We will not do it for them. They must find the one woman among them who can already read, or sew well enough, or who knows how to use a knitting machine, and persuade her to teach them. Then we will provide the books, or the sewing machines or knitting machines, the cloth, the yarn. In turn, they must spread out and teach other women."

No "dependency" on any political faction, funder, or man: self-sufficiency. No organization or central office for the

Authorities to target and shut down. Only a fluid, semi-visible, dynamic network. And only the most painstaking and intimate of organizing techniques: "If a woman doesn't show up for a meeting, we visit her where she lives. We prod her, gently, to find out why. Usually she is being beaten and is ashamed to tell us. But it comes out. We talk together with all the women in her family, to build support for her—and we suggest ways in which the women might tactfully argue with the men. For instance, if the men use traditional koranic texts to justify beating women, we suggest that the women begin to question whether the teachings have been correctly interpreted. We never try to pressure women to reject Islam or the family, because that would be counterproductive and would backfire. But we do try to get women to challenge the power structure in the family. *And they do.*"

Once a month or so, the WWC rents busses and brings the women of several different villages or camps together for a day at the seashore. "For most of these women, it is the first day off they have had in their lives. We carefully do it on some holiday when we know the men will be with their male friends, so they won't get jealous. We bring the women and their children to the beach for a picnic. We provide child care off to one side, so the women can see their children but not have to tend to them. All they have to do is sit. And talk." Her eyes sparkle with mischief. "They talk. *They compare notes.* For the first time ever, maybe, they are meeting women from outside their own village or camp. Perhaps one group has finished literacy training and feels content. But then the women of that group learn that the women in the other group are learning how to type, or how to set up an embroidery co-op, or a co-op for processing and selling food. Marketing training. Lifting women's skills always performed free within the family out into the visible public world. Money to be earned from it—for themselves, for their children. For their own independence. Suddenly they are no longer content with literacy or socializing. Now they thirst for more." She beams. "Just one day at the beach, that's all. We bring them together and let them compare notes. They do the rest. We provide the machines and materials. They do all the rest."

Zahira Kamal was under town arrest for six continuous years, charged vaguely with "working against the State." She could not leave Jerusalem between sunset and sunrise and was required to sign in twice a day with the military authorities. She is still refused travel papers and cannot get permission to leave the country to attend international women's conferences.

This is a woman, now in her mid-thirties, who is the eldest of seven sisters and two brothers. Her father was twenty-seven years older than her mother, a not uncommon occurrence in a culture of arranged marriages. "My father was fairly liberal, but still . . . I saw the situation of my mother and refused to repeat it." At age sixteen, she went on a hunger strike for four days when her father wouldn't let her go to college in Egypt. She won, and studied physics at Ain Shams University. After her father's death, she supported the family by teaching and giving extra tutorials—and also sewed all of the family's clothing. This is a woman who has put all of her younger sisters through school and college. She lives with her mother, but says that when her mother dies, she will live alone, a dramatic step for a Palestinian woman in the region.

"My mother still longs for me to be married, but I shall not marry. Men are afraid of strong women, and my work and my self are too important for me to give them up now. Each woman must face that, must struggle for her own sake. She's no good to any one or any cause unless she is first good for herself. Here we women struggle for self-determination, for ourselves and also for our entire people. But it is the struggle of women all over the world, each for herself, that gives us together the strength to free women."

Laughter. Tears. Embraces. *I do not imagine me.*

"So there are no Palestinian feminists, eh?" I tease her.

"Sure," she answers, "believe that and you'll believe Israeli women are running the Knesset."

———

Three generations of women sit on the shabby sofa in their shelter in Suf Camp. Young girls, the fourth generation, bring in trays of the omnipresent devastating coffee. The great-grandmother is spitting out an infuriated speech through the interpreter.

"I blame myself. I never learned to read. I didn't stand up for my rights as a woman, as a mother. I didn't educate my sons properly to respect women as people. I blame myself. Now my granddaughter pays the price. She has a fine record, excellent grades, scholarships. She worked for two years as a teacher in the Gulf. A decent salary. Freedom from the camps. Now she cannot go back. And she cannot get work here. Look at her, she sits and wastes herself. It is the fault of my sons—and how they raised *their* sons. Because in order to return to the Gulf, she needs her brother to accompany her. Saudi Arabia will not let a woman into the country to work unless she is accompanied by a male relative. Her brother doesn't want to go back to the Gulf. He is a lazy man, a fool, he wants to be here. He wants to spoil her chances because she had a better job in the Gulf than he did. All of us here"—gesturing at her daughters, daughters-in-law, granddaughters, and great-granddaughters—"we understand, we want her to go. I'd let her go *alone,* if the Saudis would permit it. She's a good girl, I trust her. She is responsible and moral. She prizes herself. But her brother will not go with her, and his father, my son, will not force him to. I yell at them"—her voice rises with emotion—"I *yell.* And I hit him, my son, *I hit him in his face.* But he will not order my grandson to go. I blame myself." She strikes her chest with her bony veined fist, "I blame myself."

———

Latifa is twenty-five and has three children by a first marriage. Widowed, she was then betrothed by her brothers to a seventy-two-year-old widower with no children. Now, she complains, he says she is barren because she has borne him no children. He beats her every day for this, he rapes her every night for this. She says it right out, no shyness. Then she murmurs through the interpreter as we rise to go, "Don't worry for me, American sister, don't cry. He is old. I can outwait him. He will die, and I will live. And no matter what my brothers say or do to me, I will never, never, never marry again."

———

Lebanon is unspeakable, a living apocalypse, a world hallucinated by Hieronymus Bosch. On both sides of the border, houses, farms, fields lie in ashes, devastated by grenades from U.S.-manufactured grenade launchers on one side, from Soviet-manufactured Kalishnikov grenade launchers on the other. Concrete-block barrier walls. Troop convoys. Watchtowers.

Here Hizbollah (the "Party of God") pays starving refugee women the equivalent of ten U.S. dollars a day to wear the full *hijab,* then claims fundamentalist Islam is on the rise. Here one learns to disbelieve everything one has heard, everything that is reported in the press, everything that pretends chaos is not the norm. The Amal ("Hope" in Arabic) army has leaders, uniforms, weapons—yet it doesn't really exist as an entity: in some areas, Amal is Syrian-backed; in others, individual Amal fighters are actually on the side of Hizbollah—which is sometimes Iranian-supported and sometimes not. Near Tyre and Sidon, some Amal groups are even Palestinian, though elsewhere Amal fights against the Palestinians. Sometimes Amal men overlap Christian forces or fight on behalf of independent mullahs whose fanaticism makes Khomeini look like a moderate. Hizbollah also varies from place to place, from payer to payee in this mercenary game, from mullah to imam. One street banner at Tyre has Amal colors and slogans on one side and opposing Hizbollah colors and slogans on the other. Arafat's mainstream faction of the PLO is the only thing that approaches having a structure, and evoking permanent loyalty; this reveals genius in a situation where merely to stay afloat is a triumph.

In all of this, the Druse men bide their time. They're a minority, and though renowned for the ferocity of their fighting they do best in rural warfare. Sometimes they help Fatah / PLO by selling "free passage" through certain corridors they control, but the corridors change every day. The Christian Phalangists seem to control East Beirut and Mt. Lebanon, the Syrian Army much of the southwest, and Israel makes periodic land, air, and sea surges from the southern Galilee panhandle, as if in a patronizingly charitable gesture to remind all these folks who the real enemy supposedly is.

The camps here are in shambles, bombed, strafed, raided. In 1982, when Israel invaded Lebanon, the carnage resulted in an estimated 22,000 people dead, with an additional 30,000 injured and over half a million people displaced. During the 1985 siege of Beirut-area camps, Shatila Camp alone sustained damage to 529 homes, while 364 were totally lost—a 95 percent destruction rate.* Burj el-Barajneh Camp (population fifteen thousand) had a 75 percent rate: 1,416 homes damaged or destroyed. Mar Elias Camp also sustained damage; in addition, Tripoli-area camps lost 97 shelters during Israeli air raids in July of that year. In Mieh Mieh Camp, near Sidon, 184 homes were damaged and 80 destroyed; in the same area, at Ein el-Hilweh, 181 homes were lost. Reconstruction proceeds at a glacial pace, due to lack of funds.

Here UNRWA faces a staggeringly Sisyphean task. Between 1982 and 1985 alone, twenty-one UNRWA staff members in Lebanon were killed, fifteen were wounded, eight disappeared, and 422 were arrested or kidnapped. Alec Collett, UNRWA's information consultant, was kidnapped in March 1985 and has not been heard from since. A backup UNRWA office was opened in 1985 in Cyprus, so that administration and finance offices for Lebanon could maintain operations despite varying security conditions in Beirut. But the field staff remains, and wears

---

* Shatila had already endured the 1982 massacre by Christian Phalangists and Israeli assault; in 1986 its population was approximately seven thousand.

flak jackets to work. During the winter of 1986–87, UNRWA was dealing with almost fifty thousand displaced refugees. In 1987, after long negotiations in Beirut and Damascus, and after several UNRWA convoys had been turned back and one immobilized by gunfire, Agency staff finally managed to bring food and medical supplies to Amal-besieged refugees in the Beirut-area camps. By that time, the women and children in Shatila were catching and eating rats, and the twenty thousand refugees in Rashidiyeh Camp, near Tyre, had asked religious leaders for a dispensation to eat human flesh because people were dying of starvation.

Here all the UN agencies work together as best they can, overlapping their functions when necessary, cutting red tape to save lives. UNIFIL (the United Nations Interim Force in Lebanon) and UNTSO staffs spend days in precarious negotiation with one faction or another merely to effect body exchanges. UNICEF winds up staffing emergency orphanages as well as trying to continue an immunization program. The UNRWA teaching staff distributes food rations when the rations can be got in, and smuggles in potable water. The UNIFIL medical team of Swedish nurses helicopters into the camps, sustaining shelling as it lands.

"The Path of Death" is the name refugees have given to the route from Burj el-Barajneh. In March 1987, twenty-six women were killed as they hurried along that route to get food for their besieged families. Three other women died inside the camp. In the other five months of the siege, an average of about six women a month died. By the end of April, fifty-seven had been killed, and at least twenty-seven more were permanently disabled during the fighting around the camp.

There is no gasoline, there are no cars in which to flee, and there is nowhere to flee to. The roads are blocked, the corridors under fire, the routes under shifting control of different armies, factions, or mercenaries.

So the women scream, run, hide, mourn, and die. The women wail, all the time. At first one thinks it's the sound of the sea, or of distant sirens. But this unearthly arid music is made by women. A wordless keening as if the only life left in them were lodged in the throat, inarticulate, hopeless, a death rattle of the spirit.

In the summer of 1986, Lebanon experienced a strange phenomenon, which at first no one could understand. A spontaneous cease-fire started at about nine o'clock in the evening and lasted until almost three in the morning. People weren't being killed—and the silence itself was an incredible luxury to the ear. Was this miracle accomplished by any of the world leaders sonorously calling for peace in Lebanon? No.

It was the World Cup.

The World Cup soccer finals were being held. The televised games were broadcast live between 9 P.M. and 2 A.M. Furthermore, an Arab team, Morocco, was doing well. The men of all factions stopped shooting to find and cluster around television sets. The women used these vital hours to search for their children, to forage for food, to bury their dead.

One UNRWA teacher, a Palestinian herself, later told me she was not surprised. She added, with universal feminist gallows humor, "Perhaps the way to solve the Middle East torment is to give the men round-the-clock live male contact sports. Men are crazy, aren't they? But they pass for adults. They shoot things. They run the world."

———

Ghanima is a large-bodied woman. Her leathered face is tooled with lines. She has many missing teeth. I would have estimated her to be in her sixties, but learn she is only in her late forties. She and her seven remaining children have fled south three times now to escape the fighting—from Beddawi Camp near Tripoli to Dbayeh Camp north of Beirut to Ein el-Hilweh near Sidon to Rashidiyeh south of Tyre, near the border. The rest of her family, including eight other children, have disappeared or been killed. Two of her sons "called themselves guerrillas, said they were fighting for Palestine." She doesn't know with which faction they fought, which group. "It doesn't matter now anyway": both are dead. A Palestinian man eavesdropping on our conversation intervenes to pay her his respects as a "Mother of Martyrs." She wheels on him, shouting, "To what have you given birth? Who have you nursed at your breast? In God's name, I swear I will give you no more martyrs! *I am done with being a mother of martyrs!*"

———

Tahrir (her real name) is only fifteen, a refugee who has fled Burj el-Barajneh. She is proud of her English and her honor-student record at an UNRWA school. She thinks herself a good candidate for an UNRWA scholarship to university. "I want to teach," she says, "and also to write books, and also to travel." She is beautiful, a bud of young womanhood flowering into her own energy.

"I will help to end the killing and start the living. I hate death. I hate people being cruel." When I ask her, as I have asked so many others, what message she most wishes to send to women in the rest of the world, she thinks in silence for a long time.

These replies have formed a pattern. The women in male-appointed leadership say, "A Palestinian State." The women of grass-roots leadership say, "Self-determination." The women in UNRWA facilities say, "Help us. We want to push no one into the sea. All we need is space to breathe, some food, some medicine, education, *dignity.*" The woman refugees in the camps say, "Help us not to have more children; help us to save ourselves and the children we already have."

In one way or another, they all say, *Tell them we exist.*

And Tahrir, her eyes lustrous with intelligence, her smile a dazzle of optimism, has her own answer. "Tell them," she says carefully, "what my grandmother and my mother always told me—that it is women's job to save the world. In our *own* way, which isn't the men's way. Tell them," she says, "that whenever a woman anywhere fights for herself, she fights for me. My name, Tahrir, means 'Freedom.' "

Bahibbik ya ukhti.

Later I learn that the day after entrusting me with her message, Tahrir is killed by a shell.

———

There are many things I have not written of here. I have not written of meeting nomadic Bedouin women, hearing their nonliterate wisdom, watching their heavily tattooed faces. I have not written about Druse women who openly acknowledge their fear of their own men. I have not written about Galia Golan and other dedicated Israeli women who regularly organize marches, ten thousand people strong, in a mainstream Israeli peace movement to demand an end to occupation. I have not written about the Center for Women's Studies in the Arab World, still publishing its feminist journal, *Al Raida,* in what remains of Beirut. I have not written of the large and active Jordanian women's movement. I have not written about the valiant attempts of Syrian women and women's groups to gain my admission to that country, which ultimately denied me a visa.

In some ways, I will be writing about all these women for the rest of my life.

But for now, two grotesquely distorted human shapes rise and haunt my mind, each so common to my eye during that summer that I had to readjust my perceptions when I left the Middle East.

One has a torso bulging and jutting with objects: a rifle slung over the shoulder, a submachine gun cradled in the arms, ammunition belts and pistol holsters making the waist bulky. He is everywhere—on the streets, in the cities and villages, in the camps, on the roads, at the borders. He is usually in uniform, but he can and does change uniforms as he changes sides. Sometimes, as when he is a resident of a West Bank settlement, he is a civilian permitted to carry a rifle anywhere. He has hard eyes, but they can still sometimes fill with tears. He will do his job, though, no matter what. He is the Demon Lover. And he is almost my son.

The other form is also grossly misshapen. This specter has a protruding belly, and balances a bucket or basket on the head. Dark, cheap cloth shrouds the body, and smaller forms cling leechlike to every limb like growths on the flesh—children at the hip, thigh, calf, waist, breast, back, and neck. She is trying to refuse the job he requires of her. She is almost dying, almost surviving.

My body is not a weapons factory.

I am done with being a mother of martyrs.

I would like to heal.

The woman who gives birth to herself is free to help the world.

What do men know about life?

I do not imagine me.

Whenever a woman fights for herself, she fights for me.

My name means freedom.

Tell them I exist.

Bahibbik ya ukhti. She is ourselves.

CHAPTER 9

᚛᚛᚛᚛᚛᚛᚛᚛

THE NORMALIZATION OF TERROR: A NOTE PASSED BETWEEN HOSTAGES

Being alive was the hard part. / TONI MORRISON, *Beloved*

I have no way of knowing if this will ever reach you. I must try anyway. I must risk their intercepting this, risk their discovery of what I'm really attempting to communicate, risk whatever they will do to me then.

If this does reach you, it may help you feel less alone. I remember what it felt like. When I first realized I was in here, I mean. When I first stopped denying it, disbelieving it. The stunned days, hour after hour, my mind circling, trying to figure out why they had taken me, why they were holding me. The slow nights, staring into the darkness, trying to work out who they were, what they wanted of me. If I was worth a ransom, why did they treat me as worthless? If I was a bargaining chip, in what bargain? If I was of value to their enemy and they detested their enemy, why did they bother keeping me alive, unless they shared the same values as their enemy? But if they did, how could there be any real differences between them—

and what did that imply about my hopes for rescue? It made me a hostage to both sides—to all sides in fact, at least to all sides I could see. But then, of course, I lacked a vantage point. They reminded me of this at every opportunity. Still, my lack of their vantage point I've come to see in time as a vantage point in itself. But back then I was still questioning basics: How could I be a hostage to life itself, and what were the negotiating terms? What inconceivable ransom could buy my liberty? What would liberty feel like? Had I ever known it? Could I remember a sense of freedom with which to compare this? What was or would be freedom?

Oh yes, I recall the gradual dawning of that vast dull pain. The realization that I'd always been inside here, feeling this, not knowing I was here, not believing I was feeling this. That's why I must try against all odds to reach you with this message: it may help you feel less alone.

You think sometimes you're going mad. I understand. Try to trust my inadequate words. You may as well trust me, because you're beginning to glimpse the enormity of what you can no longer trust—all the familiar illusions that made you believe you were out there when you were in here right from the start. Better yet, trust yourself. *Try to understand: this is what it feels like to go sane.*

You too have been a hostage all your life. I know that's hard to comprehend. Humiliating. Ridiculous. Infuriating. How I came to comprehend it myself—well, it was by stages. First I began to realize I'd been a refugee all my life. That was back when I had begun to identify myself with *them*, you see—not that they were refugees. But I was trying to understand them, trying to fathom why they were holding me, trying to sympathize with their pain, which, they told me, gave them their right to power over me. My sympathy was a lie, of course. Underneath, I was hoping that they would notice me, adopt me, that my sympathy would make me one of them. But they made it clear: I could never ever be one of them. Strangely, I had never been one of them even on the other side, even when I thought

I was at liberty. You think me mad perhaps, you think I make no sense. You think these are the scribbles of a woman held captive so long she has lost her mind to solipsistic mutterings about freedom.

Perhaps you're right. I don't care what others think about me, ultimately. That particular not caring has taken me all of my life. To get to, I mean. It's a less simple place than you may imagine.

I do care what you think about yourself, though. That at least ought to interest you. I say this not because it may flatter you into thinking me less mad but because it may startle you into examining what you think is sane about yourself. And I say it because it's true.

I must stop now and hide this under the stone in the floor. Soon they'll be coming with the bread and questions. More later. If I can.

───

It's so difficult under these conditions. The light coming and going in this daze of time, the air so stale and foul. So difficult with the clarity coming and going inside my own blurry consciousness, the oxygen in my own spirit sometimes so rank and meager. But I must try. If this ever reaches you, you may be able to use it, take these feeble fragments of thought further than I am able, build something better from them than I can.

Think about yourself. Not in that obsessed old way—what have I done to deserve this captivity? where did I go wrong? how am I to blame for my own enslavement?—not in those ways. Those are the ways they keep you thinking yourself sane while actually you are mad; those are the ways you go mad for fear of appearing to be mad when you finally are going sane. Not those ways, believe me, I've done those ways to death for most of my life. Save yourself the effort. Think about yourself—in your own individual manner of course, which would be different from mine or any I could suggest—in other ways. Think about your life. That is, what up until now you called "my life."

Think about what you feared.

Leave aside for now the chronic fears, the ones with which we all grew so intimate that we no longer noticed the way we hunched our shoulders all day or clenched our fists in sleep all night. Leave aside nuclear attack—the sudden unnatural tornado, the bright blank horror. Leave aside rape—the subtle adrenaline leakage through your bloodstream when you walked the streets of your city or town, some part of you always on alert. Leave aside the fears that fitted so well you went gloved and shod in them.

What else did you fear?

Health? Was it illness, disease? Cancer perhaps, or AIDS? Perhaps you couldn't help knowing how high the odds had become on your contracting a terminal illness? Or had you tried not to notice or number the carcinogens—in your food, your water, your cigarette, the radon rising through your floor, the asbestos exuding from your walls, the poison in your blusher and eyeliner, the exhaust emitted by your car? Had you tried not to notice how casually many North Americans had begun to speak of having small skin cancers removed? Did you postpone going for a mammography, claiming laziness, knowing you were afraid? Or did you pride yourself on your eating habits and exercise, reassuring yourself that you somehow could manage without breathing air, trusting the word of bottled-water manufacturers, thinking you could avoid a sunlight no ozone layer had gentled? Was that what you feared? A fatal disease as the way it would end? And had you wondered why the research money was never sufficient, why somebody didn't *do* something? Had you thought: Who runs the agribusinesses that produce the food? Who manufactures and sells the pesticides, the insulation, the cigarettes, the cosmetics? Who then invents and markets the home water purifiers, radon detectors, remedies, solutions? Who? Had you let yourself be deflected by simplistic answers ("It's the capitalists' fault," or "It's the fault of the Commies," or "It's the fault of the Japanese trade war," or "It's just human greed")? Had you found thinking beyond that too frightening, too exhausting, too depressing?

Try now. After all, you haven't anything else to do, now that you've begun to realize where you are and what your options aren't. This time, though, push the thought as far as you can. *It's the one power you have.* This they cannot take away from you, once you begin to use it. So try.

Try to visualize the process, try to visualize the people who are killing us all—and even themselves. Not only the good, simple, ordinary folks who collaborate all along the way, but the originators and sustainers, the owners and leaders. Picture them. There.

Do you see women in the picture?

Wait, now. Go back to the beginning again.

Was it money that scared you—not finding a job, or losing the job you had? Debts? Being evicted for lack of rent? Losing the mortgaged home so precious to you? Who was the boss— not just the immediate superior, but the *boss?* Who controlled your industry? Who was the banker, the landlord? Who owned the mortgage? To whom did you have to appeal?

Or children, perhaps? You feared for your children? That the girls would be assaulted, or become pregnant as teenagers? That the boys would get into trouble, or wind up in some war? Did you worry that addictive drugs, including alcohol, would corrode their bodies and brains? That they might perish in an accident in some automobile that the auto company would recall as flawed two years later? Who committed the assaults? Who commanded the armies? Who designed and marketed the cars? Who oversaw the growing and refining and packing and shipping and selling of the drugs? Who pushed the drugs? Do you see them?

Are there women in the picture?

Was it aging you feared? Seeing the elderly in their shocking poverty and loneliness as they sat on park benches in a pale winter sun, stooped over, ignored, waiting to die? Who defined and circumscribed age? Who preached reverence for the old but eroded benefits, medical care, respect? Who built and owned nursing homes? Who assigned, funded, and used market research on the elderly as consumers? Who decided that older human beings have no sexuality, that they require no meaningful work, that they need no voice?

Or was your fear more specific, more immediate? That your husband or lover was angry with you, perhaps? Because you'd wasted so much time lately reading? Was the threat so imperceptible that you told yourself you were silly, petty, paranoid—the tiniest twitch in his jaw, maybe, or the way he fell silent and then more silent? Or was it not the silence but the noise you feared, the fights, the yelling, the insults, the irrational energy of hating someone you love? Did you fear that he might leave you, after all? You knew that the most secure middle-class married woman is still one man away from welfare. Or did you fear what would become of you if you left him? Did you fear that leaving would mean failure, that you couldn't love, be loved?

Or was it a different fear—that if you and your lover walked down the block arm in arm, eyebeam fixed to eyebeam in a wild jubilance of being in love, luminous with living, someone would spit in the gutter while looking directly at you, or mutter filth at you, or fall on you with fists, because you and your lover shared not only the same love but the same gender? Who so fixed the canon of love's forms?

Who was it you feared? Trace it, trace the fearing to a source. Not the mid-management collaborators, remember. Not those who only obey orders; just because the responsibility is everywhere doesn't mean that it's not somewhere. Trace it further, as far as you can. Scrutinize those in power behind the fear. Visualize them. There.

Are women in the picture?

I must stop. Someone's coming. Until later. I hope.

———

There is such pressure, all the time, isn't there? You know what I mean—or you will. I never know when they'll decide to move me. For security, they say. Some days they keep my hands tied and the blindfold on, and I can't scribble anything down here.

Some days they never leave me alone, not for a second, and I can't get back to this message either. Then there are the other times. You know them. When they don't come near for days. And one grows famished—for food, for a human face, even theirs.

Such pressure to write these things to you while I can.

Do you begin to see? That you were a captive before you knew you were a captive, I mean? Do you begin to remember how far you've traveled from whatever you originally dreamed, thought, swore your life would be? An origin you can barely remember except in some intangible dream like a key hung round your throat, a key to a door no longer closed or open, no longer standing at all? Were you a refugee in your own life?

What else did you fear, back then when you were so at liberty? Did you thank your gods you'd never been raped—but not count the times he wanted to and you didn't and you were afraid not to . . . ? Did you congratulate yourself on never having gone hungry—but not count the meals you denied yourself because of a standard of appearance you thought you didn't meet and you were afraid that . . . ? Did you feel privileged that you enjoyed religious freedom—but not count the times the priest said you'd be damned unless, the rabbi said you were unclean if you didn't, the minister said you'd go to hell because, and you laughed that off of course but sweated with fear that . . . ? Did you not eat forbidden foods, not touch yourself where you shouldn't, not think bad thoughts? Were you god-fearing?

Were you never afraid your god would punish you, your parents would punish you, your teachers would punish you? Did you never fear your siblings would resent you, your friends would betray you, your boss would fire you, your lover would abandon you, your husband would strike you, your children would hate you?

Back when you were free, I mean.

Did you never have fantasies of killing someone? More than one? All of them? Of mayhem, murder? What stopped you? What stopped those thoughts? What stopped those thoughts from becoming your reality?

Has your space always been your own? Have you always known where you ended and others began or where others ended and you began? Does your small cell now seem rather large in fact?

What kept you from recognizing you were in here all along?
For each of us it's different. Me, I thought to get off with recognizing parts of the whole, rationing out the pain of consciousness bit by bit, day by day. Like hoping to stave off the rest by acknowledging the segments, you know? I would try to build up a tolerance in myself, try to make myself immune by sipping a few drops of poison from each day's cup. I prided myself, too, that I could *reason* my way out of here (the here I denied I was in, that is). You recognize that one, I'm sure. How one doesn't wish to appear unreasonable! And it seems so unreasonable to stop even for one perilous instant and visualize who is defining what's reasonable, doesn't it?

In my case, I began to notice details. For instance, I would remind myself of how often men claimed they longed to transcend nationalism. I would try to dwell on how admirable their longing was, but then I would find myself wondering why they didn't do something about it. Then I would realize that men *had* actually devised not one but two ways to accomplish this goal, both of which they had already put into action. The philosophical way took the form of fundamentalist religion promulgated with missionary zeal, as in the spread of fundamentalist Islam or Pentecostal Christianity. The secular way took the form of multinational corporations, the one-world government of tomorrow. I found neither form reassuring—although I did find it interesting that the most powerful men, while already planning well beyond nationalism for themselves, were still selling that tired old concept to less powerful men in the Third World. Still, undeterred, I persisted in trying to reason my way through. I proved things. I made lists and organized categories. I saved quotations from things I had read. Some were grim, some incredibly funny. This was one of the ways I kept myself from going stark raving sane. This was one of the ways I kept the terror *out there*. To be looked at, stud-

ied, analyzed. It wasn't so difficult to do, but it was risky in its
own way because I sensed it would lead to absurdity, to this
place, to being in here and knowing it. I'll give you some
examples. If I have to stop short suddenly you'll know why,
but until they interrupt, well, these are the kinds of things I
began to notice.

Category: Terror

There is a small paperback book entitled *The Terrorism Survival Guide,* written by a gentleman named Andy Lightbody.
(I did not make this up. People often thought I was making
things up when I wasn't.) Mr. Lightbody is also the editor of
International Combat Arms, which calls itself "the Journal of
Defense Technology." *The Terrorism Survival Guide* promises
to "take away the fear and put back the pleasure in your traveling." It contains 101 tips, educating the reader about many
things. For instance, it warns the traveler never to assume, "It
can't happen to me." It lists the kinds of clothing and haircuts
not to wear: three-piece "power" suits, cowboy boots, Hawaiian
shirts, crewcuts (could mean you're in the military). It tells you
to update your last will and testament before you go anywhere
and to carry pictures of children—even if you have none—in
your wallet, so some terrorist may have mercy on you as a
parent. It says not to sit near airport or terminal windows, to
request a hotel room on a high floor and in the back, and to
leave the TV or radio on when you go from your room. It
instructs you to "sanitize" your papers, to carry no "incrimi-
nating" identification—for example, to *keep your real occupation hidden,* particularly if you are a corporate executive or
diplomat or aerospace official or member of the military. It
tells you not to have stickers on your luggage such as "Go,
Navy!" or "Boeing Aircraft Company," and not to be seen
reading "controversial" materials such as "gun magazines, religious books, anticommunist books, or *Playboy.*" It says lots of

other things too, among them that many terrorists are "first-timers" and are as scared and nervous as you are and that you should be comforted by that.[1] All in all, it is a remarkable little book, even if it does address itself totally to the businessman and doesn't have any tips for a woman traveling alone or a mother traveling with three young children or an elderly traveler or same-sex lovers or a disabled person or any person with skin pigmentation other than white; it says nothing about what they should do to "take away the fear and put back the pleasure" in traveling. Nevertheless, it promises to sell very well.

But then, as Brian Jenkins has commented, "a semipermanent culture of terrorism" is emerging. He is an expert, so he must know. Common sources of financing and weapons supply and overlapping personnel contribute to this, he says, as does a "global infrastructure" that is "institutionalizing terror." Noting that more and more governments designate a specific agency to study and combat (or establish relations with) terrorists, he observes that "like any bureaucracy, that agency competes for influence and budget, promises results, and resists dismantling. . . . the security measures taken against terrorism will . . . become a permanent part of the landscape [which] may be the most insidious . . . development in the coming years. Terrorism will become an acceptable fact of contemporary life—commonplace, ordinary, banal, and therefore somehow 'tolerable.' "[2]

Then again, none of this is new. Janet Aviad, an Israeli sociologist, has called it the "rhinocerosization" process. "Your skin just keeps getting thicker and thicker, year after year, until you just stop noticing things. Twenty years ago the shooting of a Palestinian student or the firebombing of a settler would set everyone here on fire. Now most people just accept it. Events happen. They are written on your memory but you don't let the feelings sink in. It is a terrible analogy, but I can't help thinking of what they said about the people who lived near Auschwitz. They just didn't smell the smoke anymore. We don't either."[3]

I used to read such things, I used to clip and save such things—
back before I knew I was in here. It was a way of trying, you
know, to get a handle on terror. But the trouble with the categories—well, they kept stretching. Their edges were never as
defined as I knew they ought to be in order to prove . . .

Category: Normalcy

Addressing terrorism experts, Dr. Martti Siirala of the University of Helsinki writes:

> Terrorism as a subject will make its entire phenomenological spec-
> trum resonate within each one of us participants as well as also in
> the relational process among ourselves. . . . Without caring con-
> sciously together for the realization of such a process, we [risk
> producing] dangerous trivialities—dangerous, because they come
> from experts. Conventional scientific ritualism in the signs of rep-
> etition compulsion may get the upper hand. . . . Inner areas of ter-
> rorist constellation will be found in each man, as there are family
> phenomena of terrorism of some form, more or less condensed, in
> each family, if more closely inspected.[4]

Robert Kennedy phrased it more succinctly: "Except for war,
there is nothing in American life, nothing, which trains a boy
better for life than football."

Except that football begins to look effete compared with one
of the fastest-growing sports in the United States, the "National
Survival Game." Sometimes also called splatball, it pits teams
of men clad in camouflage fatigues against each other in a series
of forty-five-minute mock battles. Each team tries to capture
the enemy's flag while ambushing and eliminating enemy soldiers with air guns that fire gelatin capsules filled with water-
based paint. The annual national tournament awards a prize
of fourteen thousand dollars and draws teams from all over
the United States, teams with names like the Muthers, the Grim

Reapers, and the Ace of Spades. Defenders of the sport claim it gets players out into the country each weekend, and promotes exercise and strategic thinking, "like chess for the physically active." Specialists in aggressive behavior, among them Leonard Berkowitz of the University of Wisconsin (Madison), deplore the sport, observing that it provokes a reduction in the inhibitions against violence, trivializes war, inures devotees to killing, and is "morally obscene." But forty thousand people now play the game each weekend in the United States, and it's almost as popular in Japan. It has spawned three magazines, plus various indoor versions for children, like "laser tag." Corporations are using the game in company retreats to "promote communication" and "build camaraderie" among employees lacking in teamwork. Lately, the sport is experiencing an arms race of its own: tanks, booby traps, paint-grenades, and paint-mines are becoming all the rage, and Tippman Pneumatics, a former manufacturer of machine guns, has introduced the SM-60, an automatic gun that fires six hundred paint-ball rounds per minute. (Purists sniff that all this gimmicky materiel detracts from the individual competitiveness and skill of the game— tracking, tactics, cunning.) Some women are involved, primarily wives and girlfriends of aficionados. But well over 85 percent of the players are men, most in their late twenties and early thirties; many are currently in the military, but the majority are average businessmen. These men speak of "falling in love with the game," "needing the game," "getting addicted to that adrenalin rush each weekend." One player (a team captain) explained his participation in this way: "Oh, it's fun and it's nonviolent. I couldn't do war for real. I'm a pacifist."[5]

Other such "pacifists" have been exercising their own freedom of expression on the roads of California lately. From mid-June to late August 1987, 119 incidents of highway violence in that state left four people dead and nineteen injured in what the governor called an "escalating violence that terrorized millions of California motorists." Analysts said the traffic was so bad, especially at freeway ramp entries, that motorists simply had taken to rolling down their windows and firing shots at one another.[6] California appears to be a stressful state, carrot juice and granola notwithstanding. In July of the same year, Joe Hunt, age twenty-seven and leader of the Billionaire Boys Club, was sentenced in the slaying of a former colleague Hunt thought had duped him in an investment deal. The Billionaire Boys Club members are all under age thirty-five, all graduates of the exclusive Harvard Preparatory School in the San Fernando Valley, all sons of wealthy and socially prominent families. Hunt himself is a handsome young man known for his politeness and charm.[7]

Ted Bundy and Angelo Buono, Jr., were also known for their charm—before, during, and after their convictions as mass murderers of women.

In a 1984 British television documentary entitled "No Apparent Motive," an FBI agent discussed the difficulty of ascertaining who is a serial sex murderer and who isn't:

> In the case of many of these individuals, they lead a kind of secret life, in the sense that they and they alone know what they may be doing and yet they live an apparently rather normal life when they're not doing the criminal activity. . . . a person [sic] who commits a series of twenty or thirty murders frequently is going to be a very nice guy, to talk to, to deal with, and they're not gonna be abnormal.[8]

And a psychiatrist chimed in:

> Most [serial sex murderers] are very normal and very friendly. . . . you maybe went into a pub to have a drink and you'd sit there and talk to him and he'd all of a sudden become one of your good friends, you can't look at him and tell that this is something strange about him, they're very normal.[9]

The many recent studies on psychopaths have determined that they show an unusual pattern of brain organization, exhibit glibness in language, are facile in social graces, seem incapable of feeling any emotion deeply, cannot make connections with other people, and cannot comprehend being thwarted in any of their own desires. They are rarely apprehended unless the criminal behavior practiced is acute: researchers estimate that less than 10 percent are ever charged with any crime. Researchers also estimate that more than 80 percent of all psychopaths are male.[10]

Back when I was less free than I am now because I didn't realize I was in here yet, back when I was concerned with being reasonable and proving things in a painstaking manner, information like that would confuse me. I would sit for hours with a document like the one about psychopaths and an article like the one in which Martha Crenshaw noted that "the outstanding characteristic of terrorists is their normality."[11] And I would think about it and resist it and think about it and resist it. You know how it is. One doesn't want to believe the worst. It seems so, well, simple-minded. It seems crazy. Then I would think, Who defined crazy? And I'd be off again. That sort of brooding makes you nervous. Because you suspect it may strike you sane.

Then I would read the conclusions of child psychiatrists studying children in war situations—things like "The body and mind handle terror in the same way, whether you were beaten by your father or by Pol Pot's soldiers"—and I would think about the escalating statistics on child abuse and the saying "If you can't beat 'em, join 'em," and wonder how the psychiatrists defined a war situation. This was unreasonable of me. After all, they were talking about children in Northern Ireland or Cambodia, "boys as young as 8 and 9 . . . being recruited and trained as soldiers in Central America, Africa, and the Middle East." They were talking about little boys who "had done a lot of killing when they were as young as 8 years old and continued to assassinate people until they were around 14." Such kids were "psychologically intact as long as they stayed with the Khmer Rouge. But when they finally came to a refugee camp filled with Pol Pot's victims, they fell apart."[12]

And I would think about it and resist it. It was my way of staying out there by denying I was in here, or rather denying that "out there" *was* "in here" and I'd never even known anyplace else. Oh, I studied lots of things back then. I made it my duty to learn as much as I could about this whole subject. It added to the confusion, which helped the denial. For instance, I knew that expressing emotion was acceptable for female people in every culture in the world, but was nowhere as acceptable for male people—unless the emotion was expressed violently. That was comforting, because it put the blame for violence on "society." Then I would remember what "society" was and who defined it and controlled it, and I'd get anxious again.

Sometimes, now, in here, I'm amazed at how I lived so long with all the confusion and anxiety that comes from being reasonable. In retrospect, *that* seems simple-minded to me. But one can't rush these realizations. The most one can do is not resist them, and that in itself is a full-time job.

Like the simplicity of this cell. I have nothing to collect or save here. I know all of the stones—how many of them there are, and the particular configuration, texture, and varying shades of slate of every single stone in this cell. I know the way light from the high small window leaks in stripes between bars of shadow across the wall and then across the floor, how it changes according to season. I can recognize the different footsteps of each one of my guards. Even when they assign new ones—you'll learn about that in time, how they rotate personnel, and at first it really throws you—it takes me only a matter of hours to recognize the new footsteps as well as the old. I can almost always anticipate their moods now: when they'll decide to punish me or reward me, how arbitrary those decisions are, when they'll come with the ritual prewritten statement for me to read before the videotape camera, when they'll try to lift my spirits by saying it looks like release is near, when they'll try to unhinge me by saying I'll rot in here until I die. Don't misinterpret me, I'd never be so naive as to say that they've done all they can to me and I'm beyond fearing whatever else they can invent, oh no. But I do see them more clearly all the time. It even has occurred to me that you don't exist, there in the neighboring cell, that they've hinted to me you're in there to trick me into writing this. But I could swear I've heard you moving around, pacing, soundlessly crying. I do not imagine you. And it's worth the risk of their tricking me and finding out what I really think, if this reaches you and makes you feel a little less alone. The night I thought I heard you singing softly to yourself in there for company, I knew. "That's another woman in there, singing to keep from going sane," I told myself. That's when I decided to write you this message.

But I'm not unvigilant. I can tell by the way the light now borders on the seventy-eighth stone up from the floor, which is also the twelfth stone out from the far wall, that they'll be coming soon for the daily lecture about the rightness of their cause, about humanism and brotherhood and how we're all just people, about how it's really human nature or the way of the world or the lay of the land or the alignment of the stars or karma, about how pain is all in the imagination and I needn't feel it and it's my own fault if I do and I'm the one who's keeping me here and how can I still be so unreasonable. So this goes back under the stone for now.

———

You probably wonder how I managed to get paper and writing materials, especially since there's no commissary here and no mail or packages are allowed in. For security's sake, as always. Some people in these circumstances have written microscopic words using their own blood as ink on fragments of toilet paper. Others have chiseled letter by agonized letter onto chunks of stone. I won't divulge my own method. There's no need for you to know—for your own protection. I will tell you, though, that I've done some things I'm not particularly proud of, in order to get hold of these materials. Still, it's worth it, at least so far. Although I confess there are days when I feel the way a deciduous tree must feel in autumn. Leaf after leaf flames, crisps—then releases and falls. Some cling to the last possible moment, despite buffeting by the harshest blasts of wind—and then let go of a sudden when the air is utterly still. Writing may be like that. In this strange stripping down of the self.

But for now, this message. Because you need to hear it, need to understand you're not so alone as you may fear. Forgive me, I've wandered from my point—easy enough when you have, as they remind you, no vantage point to begin with. My point that I don't have was about the problem I began to notice with these categories and being reasonable/proving things/keeping the classifications neat. For instance, another one was:

Category: Economics

In this one I piled items like the following:
  • In 1987 Rabbi Meir Kahane completed a lecture tour of the United States during which he raised over fifty thousand dollars (less than his usual annual yield) in support of his ultramilitant Kach party in Israel. Some of the profits were to be shared with the U.S. Jewish Defense League, to finance the legal defense of League members who had been indicted for a wave of bombings in New York City. Kahane lectures mostly in temples and synagogues. His supporters include such people as attorney Barry Slotnick, who has successfully defended alleged mobster John Gotti. Kahane himself maintained a close friendship with Joseph Colombo, Sr., the late *capo* of the Colombo crime "family."[13]
  • The IRA's funding primarily comes from two sources: donations from Irish Americans, and the IRA's commercial venture in Northern Ireland—taxicab companies. The taxi business became more lucrative once the IRA bombed the Belfast bus system.[14]
  • The Palestine Liberation Organization has tried to become self-sustaining and to rely less on foreign governments, which

can blow hot and cold. The PLO has built the Palestinian National Fund, which controls estimated assests of two billion dollars in liquid funds and investments in factories, farms, real estate, and import-export. The investments provide not only revenue but jobs for Palestinians, they establish the PLO as part of the economy in various localities, and they give PLO members an opportunity to gain experience as managers and "money men." Since renouncing terrorism and in 1975 proclaiming the new PLO policy of imposing death sentences or punishment at hard labor for members committing terrorist acts, the PLO has been hit by a severe economic slump. "Rejectionist" and violent groups such as the PFLP, however, are increasing their collective assets, now approaching three billion dollars.[15]

I would read this sort of stuff and get confused again. About the categories, that is. I would look back at these three examples and think: No, they should be in "Category: Terror," not "Category: Economics." But then I'd come across one like this:

• Kanrisha Yosei Gakko is Japan's most famous business-management school; mid-level managers and executives from such companies as Nissan and Honda are sent by their corporations at a tuition fee of two thousand dollars per head. They are ordered to attend. Here they learn to "rededicate themselves to their companies" in thirteen days of samurai-style training and self-improvement. If they pass, they will be promoted; if they fail, their futures as managers are over. The students call it "hell camp." The school is patterned after the pre–World War II Kamikaze academies. Each class has 250 members (out of which an average of twelve pass). A student starts out bedecked with fourteen "badges of shame" symbolizing weaknesses. As a student progresses, he may remove a badge. He must learn to shout all his statements, to run—not walk—from place to place, to repeat by heart the Ten Commandments of Aggressive Salesmanship. He is taught that accuracy in a debate is less important than being loud and fast, that assertiveness is everything. He must learn the "Sales Crow

Song," with such lyrics as: "What you make with the sweat of your brow, you must sell with the sweat of your brow. What you make with tears, you must sell with tears. Don't be discouraged, Sales Crow, encourage yourself, and fight like a warrior." In one of the tests students are bussed into town to shout-sing the song to commuters at the local train station: this demolishes inhibition and promotes endurance through humiliation. Each dawn there are calisthenics with a harsh towel to toughen the skin, as in ancient samurai ritual. There are twenty-five-mile endurance hikes with deliberately misleading maps, competitions to see who can get back first; some students return by stretcher. Some run away, some must go into the hospital because of physical or mental breakdown. Those who don't pass bring shame to their employer and their family. Some are fired outright and commit suicide. Those who pass rise swiftly in the Japanese corporate world. The training techniques are being adopted by some U.S. and Australian companies, and in November 1987 a U.S. "branch" of the school (Japanese-run but with two American instructors, a retired U.S. Army colonel and a former police training officer) began advertising a thirteen-day course for $2,400 in the *Wall Street Journal;* the course is highly subscribed and booked well in advance.[16]

You see the problem. Does that piece of information fit into the Terror category, or into Economics? I used to believe that if I could only make these things fit properly, people would stop thinking that I invent them—even though in this case the story ran on national television and in a national news magazine.

For that matter, is it Economics or Normalcy or Terror that the majority of jobs created in the United States since 1980 (jobs which permit the administration to boast that unemployment has dropped) pay wages below the poverty level? That of all the single mothers living in New York City, 62.8 percent live well below the poverty line? That the number of wage-earning poor increased faster during the 1980s than the number of welfare poor did?[17] That in November 1987 the Reagan administration announced plans to further reduce "surpluses" of cheese, rice, and milk, and to cut by 50 percent the 1988 government distribution of these commodities, upon which almost nineteen million Americans, mainly women and children, depend for survival? Ninety-eight percent of the households receiving these commodities have incomes of less than $15,000 per year and 44 percent have incomes of less than $5,000; 38 percent consist of people age sixty or older and 48 percent of the households have children under age eighteen. The administration—which, under the Food Security Act of 1985, began paying fourteen thousand dairy farmers to stop milk production by slaughtering cows, and which has been encouraging farmers to dump rice and grain—explained that "the objective of the law was to achieve a better balance between supply and demand, and it seems to be accomplishing that purpose."[18]

Now, back when I was "out there" believing I wasn't a captive or hostage or refugee, I would get frantic not knowing where to categorize information like that. Where do you fit the way a woman feels when her child won't stop crying because she has nothing to feed it even though she lives in one of the richest countries in the world? Terror? Economics? Normalcy? It was items like this—when they wouldn't fit, no matter how I resisted—that helped me know I was going uncertifiably sane.

It was reading statements such as:

Violence is not the exclusive preserve of the exploiters; the exploited can use it, and what's more should use it.

And:

There is a violence that enslaves, and a violence that liberates.

And thinking well yes okay allright it's awful but I can understand it at least it's consistent and certainly reasonable—and discovering that the first was a quote from Ché Guevara and the second from Benito Mussolini.

It was learning that, in response to street demonstrations and general strikes—part of the 1987–88 Intifada, the popular uprising protesting the treatment of Palestinians in the Occupied Territories—the Israeli government posted ten thousand additional troops on round-the-clock patrol in the West Bank and the Gaza Strip; that for three days at the end of March 1988, all 650,000 residents of the Strip were confined to their homes under an "iron fist" policy of "collective-punishment curfew." It was learning that there were over four hundred deaths and severe injuries in one week in Gaza alone, and that UNRWA had to take extraordinary measures, which included keeping some clinics in Gaza open twenty-four hours a day, organizing special feeding programs, and more than doubling its international staff. It was learning that, despite an official policy of "no beatings," soldiers of the Occupying Authority were beating women in labor, old women, nursing mothers, babies, and toddlers; that women were suffering miscarriages from tear gas; that women were being forced to clean the streets with their bare hands after demonstrations; that nonetheless, women were organizing in neighborhood committees to secure food under curfew, care for the wounded, and try to rescue and hide children about to be arrested. It was learning that each of the 400,000 adult Gazans was being forced to exchange her or his old green identity card for a pink one issued by the army; learning that the thousands of Palestinians standing in line to exchange the cards were being herded past Israeli soldiers carrying automatic rifles, toward rows of secretaries who punched the identity numbers into banks of IBM computers which immediately revealed such data as outstanding tax obligations and past arrest records; learning that each Palestinian must "clear up" such "problems" before being issued the new card—without which it is impossible to receive rations, register a marriage, obtain a driver's license or a birth or death certificate, accept a paycheck, do any banking, or pass through the numerous army checkpoints. It was learning that as of August 1988 almost nine thousand Palestinians were in makeshift prison camps awaiting trial, including two thousand Palestinians being held under administrative detention orders which allow the suspect to be jailed for ongoing renewable six-month periods without any judicial review; learning that the Israeli army had imposed tight restrictions on the domestic and the international press and had severed all international telephone connections with the Occupied Territories. It was learning that Israel's Prime Minister Yitzhak Shamir was repeating that such repressive tactics were necessary to end the violence, to keep the peace, to stop terrorism.[19] And it was remembering the words of "Rabbi Yzertinsky," a key figure in the Stern Gang who used clerical disguises during his terrorist career and who proudly recollected that "it was the question of an idea, an aim to be achieved . . . a political goal. There are many examples of what we did to be found in the Bible—Gideon and Samson, for example." Rabbi Yzertinsky was the code name of Yitzhak Shamir.[20]

It was not knowing how to classify war casualities, today 80 to 90 percent civilians, or the world arms trade, 75 percent of which is directed at developing countries. It was not knowing where to fit the 145 million children in the world's official labor force (not counting, as always, rural work, farm work, housework, care of younger siblings, water hauling and fuel gathering, and not counting bonded labor, prostitution, domestic servitude, and hidden-economy sweatshop labor). Economics? It was not knowing where to place fifty million refugees, with women and children the overwhelming majority. Normalcy? Or the tuberculosis, body lesions, malnutrition, and venereal disease rife among the world's eighty million street children, an estimated thirty million of whom are in Brazil alone.[21] Terror?

I was never able to make it *fit*, you see. It swelled. It brimmed and spilled over all the container edges just as my eyes did when I read it, as my brain did when I heard it, as my guts did

when I saw and smelled and touched it. Even now, even understanding where I am at last, I can't get over it. Even right now,
I can't put down these words anymore for a while, because I
can't see to write because these simple-minded emotional
unreasonable tears get in the way. Even in here. Even after all
this time. Even now.

———

Yesterday they told me they would never make peace with their
enemy. Today they told me negotiations were proceeding and
the talks were "constructive, frank, fruitful." They're always
so puzzled when I laugh at these reports. Sometimes they strike
out—not always at the face or the belly, sometimes with a blow
to the brain or the soul—in rage that I find them so funny. But
you know how it is. When you try to stifle laughter it just gets
worse. It gurgles and bubbles and rises until you're ready to
explode with it—like in church or in a judge's chambers or in
a business meeting or at any of those rituals they perform out
there, insisting they're not in here. The more you try to smother
laughter, the more it leaks out. I mean, you could choke from
trying not to laugh when you really have to. You can gulp back
tears if necessary. You can certainly swallow words you know
will get you into trouble if you speak them. You can grind your
teeth and not cry out in pain. But there's just no way to swallow laughter, real laughter, for any "reasonable" period of time.
So they tell me these things and I laugh. I laugh until my ribs
ache. Like when they tell me that technology will solve human
suffering and I laugh until my lungs are desperate for gasps of
air. It bewilders them. They punish me, well, yes. But then they
leave me in peace for a while. So here's a tip to put back the
pleasure in your traveling: their thinking you're mad is a reliable form of safety—freedom, almost. Like being able to write
you this message, for instance.

Anway, there I was back then, beginning to be skittishly cured
by degrees—of *their* sanity, I mean. There I was, observing
observations like this one: "The goal of terrorism is not to kill

or to destroy property but to break the spirit of the opposition."[22]

I would underline those last six words and think about it
and still resist it—though I was resisting it less and less all the
time, which made me want to resist it more. I would think
about how hard it was to perceive what was going on when
you had no legitimate vantage point for perception. I would
think this must be my failing. But I couldn't help noticing how
other women had a similar problem. Was it just a resistance
to knowing? A disbelief? A denial? The lack of a vantage
point?

I would think about what to "break the spirit of the opposition" meant. Oh, I don't mean the obvious ways, like the fire-
bombing of the only women's radio program in Italy, *Radio
Donna,* in 1979. Or the murder on average each week in the
favela slums of Rio de Janeiro of twenty-five women, whose
deaths never make the newspapers. Or the chaining of six young
girls between the ages of ten and twelve to their beds in a child
brothel on the resort island of Phuket, in Thailand, where their
charred skeletons were found after a fire in 1984. Or how the
propaganda of pornography promulgates the lie that fear is
arousing, that terror is orgasmic, that women enjoy being afraid
because being afraid is women's natural state because nice
friendly guys are on the loose in the pub and the prep school
and every time another woman dies the rest get jumpy which
is the point of the vantage because if women are jumpy all the
time it must mean that being afraid is their natural state which
means they enjoy it which means give them more of the same
because fear is arousing and terror is orgasmic.

No, I don't mean these obvious ways in which they try to
"break the spirit of the opposition." I mean the normal, everyday ways, the ways we call living. So I tried to make a category.
I really did try. But by then I was beginning to have an impossible time with classification.

Category: Men/Sex/Love/Crime/Marriage/
Battery/Reproduction/Rape/Slave Traffic/
Government/Economics/Technology/Terror/
Breaking the Spirit

There certainly was Normalcy here. There was marine lieutenant colonel James L. Jones instructing his troops not to talk
freely in bars: "Men, if you ever wanted to lie to women, this
is the time to do it."[23] Or the observation of a wife-beater on
probation, "Violence isn't learned. It's something in your own
mind that makes you overreact," and the response of another
man in his therapy group, "All of society, not just families within
it, is violent. If you're nonviolent, you're nonviolent because
everyone else is so violent. If you're violent, you're just fitting
in."[24]

    There certainly was Economics here. There was a statement
by Bai Waiba, a member of parliament in Papua New Guinea,
where a 1986 survey disclosed that 67 percent of rural women
and 56 percent of urban women are regularly beaten or "wife
bashed." In some parts of the island, the percentages run much
higher. The relative importance of different causes reverses, in
mirror-image fashion, according to class. The survey reported
that "women from 'elite' marriages cited sexual jealousy as the
main trigger, followed by money problems and alcohol, while
low-income women gave the same reasons but in reverse order."
(A class analysis is always so clarifying, don't you think? I used
to think so, back when I was being a Marxist and reasonable.)
When the government tried to institute anti-battery laws, most
members of parliament were "violently against the idea of parliament interfering with traditional family life." That's when
Waiba said, "I paid for my wife, so she should not overrule my
decisions because I am the head of the family." Well, that's
definitely Economics. But another member of parliament, William Wi, even as he agreed, said that the issue was irrelevant

and "we are wasting our time debating the issue, because wife-beating is an accepted custom."[25] Now where does *that* go? Under Economics, Tradition, Government, Marriage, Battery, Sex, Love, or Terror?

I wasn't the only one having these categorization problems. Many women were. One of them was Jane Caputi, who in her book *The Age of Sex Crime* argued that sensationalized murders by such men as Jack the Ripper, the Son of Sam, and the Hillside Strangler were sexually political crimes that functioned as a form of patriarchal terrorism.[26]

No matter where I focused, the content overflowed whatever purported to contain it. How could the local custom in Papua New Guinea have spread so as to be accountable for the battering in Leningrad of Natalia Malakhovskaya by her celebrated Soviet dissident husband?[27] Then I realized that Papua New Guineans must travel a lot, because the identical local custom prevailed in Ireland.

There, according to Paul Theroux in *The Kingdom by the Sea*, virtually all social duties had been assumed by women, leaving the men with few responsibilities except manliness, idleness, religion, and violence. He found Ulster "a collection of secret societies, to which only men were admitted. The men dressed up, made rules, beat drums, swore oaths, invented handshakes and passwords, and crept into the dark and killed people." Yet life rolled along as usual: ". . . everything happened at once—the festival concert and talent show and bicycle race and cooking exhibit, along with mass frisking, soldier patrols, bomb threats, and arrests. There was the traditional football game and a festival art exhibition; and on the opening day there was a grotesque killing."[28] Theroux found a "cult of death" in Ulster and Derry both: disproportionate sheafs of newspaper pages devoted to long flowery obituaries, anniversary-of-death commemorations, poems, songs, invocations to the dead. He found jovial men and fatigued women, but he was too horrified at the public violence around him to notice what was festering underneath. After all, he was surrounded by bombs and murders, by "people's hands being hacksawed off, or men having their kneecaps shot off as a punishment for disloyalty, or the tar-and-feathering of young girls for socializing with soldiers. . . . it was worse than frightening: it was unbearable. . . . there was quite a bit of rural crime in the border areas—cattle maiming . . . to take revenge on farmers, some of the republican country folk sneaked into pastures at night and knifed off cows' udders."[29]

But in 1979, Gena Corea had already written:

> During my ten weeks in Northern Ireland, I came to see terrorism against women—a terrorism used to keep them in their place—as the central political issue in Ulster. . . . domestic violence is more widespread, more frequent, and much less lamented [than street violence]. Most important, the two are connected. For many women, it does not matter who wins the various battles of domination going on over their heads, . . . men will still beat women.[30]

Women's Aid, an organization that provides refuge for battered wives, claimed family violence was epidemic, based on the local cultural concept that a wife and children are a man's property—a tradition reinforced by laws of Church and State. Audrey Middleton, a founder of Belfast Women's Aid, warned that "battery is not the issue. Degradation is. Degradation can come out in the way you're forced to cook, the way you're forced to dress, the way you're imprisoned in the house. It can come out in bed. To isolate battering is a cop-out—because other suffering women can sit back and say, 'Well, I'm not battered. Thank God for that.' "[31]

Corea observed the by-now-familiar eerie respect between men who were declared enemies, "the respect of one warrior for another. One UDA [Ulster Defense Association] bomber who was responsible for 177 explosions told me that in the prison hospital, UDA and IRA men even helped each other in escape attempts."[32] She noted that extensive figures were kept on terrorist attacks, the number of bombs exploded and soldiers shot, but the Belfast police and hospital officials kept no count of the battered women with whom they dealt—first, because the matter was not important enough to investigate, and second, because in sheer numbers the batterings reached plague proportions. But Audrey Middleton kept notes on the cases who came to her shelter: the woman who had spoken only in whispers for twenty years; the woman whose husband doused her naked body with gasoline and then danced around her, flicking matches; the woman whose man poured a kettle of boiling water over her vagina just before she went into child-birth labor.[33] Marlene McConnell, who worked at another refuge, in Limerick, in the Republic of Ireland, said that incest/child rape was also common: "A father will start on a daughter when she's nine, have incest on her until she's eleven or twelve, and then get on with the next sister. He will rape her for a few years before moving on to the next child."[34] It has not gone unnoticed by these women that while everyone deplores the public violence in the history of Ireland, no one spends much time on the private violence. These women quoted the Irish hero Patrick Pearse, who before his execution in 1916 said, "Bloodshed is a cleansing and a sanctifying thing, and the nation which regards it as the final horror has lost its manhood." And these women further observed that for the street violence to end, the domestic violence at its root must end, "the nation must lose its manhood."[35]

Well, I used to study such data until I had nightmares about it, even when wide awake. One does so want to be reasonable and respectful of local customs. But I would get terrible headaches trying to work out how come the Republic of Ireland and Northern Ireland both could be populated by settlers from Russia and Papua New Guinea. It seemed clear, however, that Irish-Russian-New Guinean migration must explain why over 52 percent of (official) reported child maltreatment in the United States targeted female children. Which was distinct from the fact that over 40 percent of teenage pregnancies in the United States were caused by rape committed by father, brother, or uncle—even though the girls got blamed for "promiscuity." What I couldn't decide was whether all this fitted under Reproduction or Crime, under Family or Terror, under Love or Slavery. I felt very stupid.

I seriously wondered, for example, whether Lisa McElhaney had ever been to Leningrad, or Ulster, or North Waghi. Then again, I couldn't even figure out what she really died of. Her seventeen-year-old body was found in a plastic bag in Columbus, Ohio, in April 1987. Her father was an alcoholic, her mother had tried to get an abortion when pregnant with Lisa, but couldn't afford it. Lisa was raped as a child, became pregnant and miscarried at age fifteen, was thrown out by her family, became addicted to drugs, and worked in pornography and prostitution to support her habit. Each time she ran afoul of the law and was incarcerated in a home for delinquents, social workers noted on her file that she displayed an eagerness for relationships and was "starved for affection." But the system was set up to rehabilitate, not to provide relationships or affection, so Lisa withdrew and "would sit for hours and hours, staring into space." When photographs of her performing sexual acts were discovered by the police, she was subpoenaed to testify in a child-pornography case against Larry Miller, the pornographer. Although Miller was a suspect in her murder, police believed the killer was a client of hers, Rob Roy Baker, a thirty-four-year-old truck driver who had been linked to similar attacks on other prostitutes. When police came to question him, Baker shot himself to death in a house filled with pictures of nude women cut from pornographic magazines.[36]

So I would ask myself, did Lisa die of assault? Which assault? The lack of affordable abortion for her mother? The beating from her john? Did she die of the disease called "family" or the disease called "rehabilitation," of poverty or drugs or pornography, of economics or sexual slavery or a broken body? Or a broken spirit? When she stared into space for hours was it because she knew she was in here but had no way of trying to reach anyone in the neighboring cell?

Perhaps she died of unknown causes.

You will understand well enough by now why I can't help

these irreverent bursts of hilarity when they come to me, telling me that when women dwell on these things we fall into "victimization thinking," assuring me that they care about human rights, that they esteem women, cherish children, and revere life. You will understand why, when they speak of respect for their law—which they differentiate from the law of their enemy, in a distinction I can't follow because of my lack of perspective—or they speak of the higher law of their gods, I keel over, holding my sides in stitches. When I still thought I was out there I counted hundreds of cases of forced sterilization of women of color. I remember other cases where judges ordered caesarean sections despite the refusal of the pregnant women because doctors claimed the fetuses were at risk, cases where women were brought to court for rejecting certain surgical procedures to prevent miscarriage, or for taking nonprescription drugs while pregnant, or even for taking a prescription drug that might discolor the teeth of the unborn.[37] I remember the "fetal protection" policies of companies like American Cyanamid—which demanded that five women submit to surgical sterilization so that they could work in a certain department, which was closed shortly thereafter.[38] I remember much furor over occupational hazards in the workplace in a world where a woman's workplace was everywhere and where being a woman was a lifetime occupational hazard in itself. I remember that illegal, botched abortion was known to be responsible for almost half of the estimated one million "maternal" deaths annually; that 99 percent of those deaths were in the Third World, where complications in pregnancy and abortion are the primary killers of all women in their twenties and thirties; that butchered abortions were the leading cause of death for all Brazilian women: for every seven who gave birth, another ten aborted, and one of the ten died—with a toll of 400,000 a year as of 1988.[39]

Oh, if only I knew there were some way this could reach you. I still hear you singing sometimes, little snatches of melody with no words, or muttering unintelligible words with no music. Perhaps I do imagine you, after all. Yet you exist. Perhaps it is a lie that I write this to help you feel less alone. Perhaps I write for myself—but with the identical purpose. Sometimes I knock softly on our shared wall. Sometimes I think I hear an answering knock from your side.

———

Were you ever to receive this, you might hate me. That's a possibility I've considered, I assure you. Nobody likes the bearer of bad tidings. Although the truth is that in this place it's hard to see how things could get more gruesome (but that thought could be a dangerous invitation). At least it's hard to see why any tidings of human communication from a source other than *them* wouldn't be a relief of sorts. But I admit being afraid of frightening you. Which would be funny in itself, considering our situation. Or of boring you. I guess wanting to prove myself or my arguments to you is probably the final temptation, the one that remains even though I've quite given up wanting to prove anything to them. The day I realized that, I knew I had been struck sane, I was beyond reason and reasons. In their terms, you understand, the terms from which they had forfeited all vantage points for observing or judging. They could no longer tell sex from death or love from loathing, money from flesh, crime from law, government from slavery. No wonder, in their sanity of necrophilia, they perceived two women embracing as perverse: it was too wholesome. And if one has become a necrophiliac, isn't it an act of love to make of the entire world a graveyard?

So I made one last attempt at a category. But I had been driven wild. I might as well have labeled it "Everything."

———

Category: The World

This was, as you might expect, rather a large classification. I haven't the time—even with all the time I have that they let me have which is all I have—to list what went into this category, and I certainly haven't the writing materials, not to mention not knowing when I may be able to get hold of more, if ever. But you will get the point, if not the vantage, from these hints.

• One million species, out of a total of five million (20 percent of all species), are at risk of extinction by the year 2000.[40]

• The rate of plant and animal extinction is likely to reach several hundred per day in the next ten to thirty years.[41]

• Since the Chernobyl nuclear disaster, there have been 250 other less-publicized nuclear "incidents" world wide, as chronicled by the International Atomic Energy Agency. But by the end of 1986, 21 new reactors had been added to the 373 already on line in twenty-six countries.[42]

• Acid rain is on the increase. Norway suffers under its drift from England, Canada under its drift from the United States. Already, fourteen thousand lakes in eastern Canada and thirteen salmon-bearing rivers in Nova Scotia are "acid dead." It is estimated that acid rain causes up to fifty thousand premature deaths annually in the United States and Canada alone.[43]

• Twenty-five billion tons of arable topsoil vanish from the world's cropland every year. Enough timberland to cover forty Californias will disappear by the end of the twentieth century.[44]

Well, it just went on and on in that fashion. You know all this, of course. You knew it back then, when you were out there not knowing you were already in here, didn't you? But—and I say this as no criticism of you because I did the same thing—didn't you ever notice how they dealt with it? With keeping us calm and convinced that we weren't in here, captives, refugees, hostages? Didn't you ever notice what they would do after disasters? They would set up more study panels, survey committees, investigatory commissions. They would ask questions like:

How can human beings assimilate this kind of experience?

How can people better accommodate themselves to stress?

What are the psychological effects of living under conditions of violence and repression?

Now, without meaning to sound flippant, I must tell you

that one day I discovered a vantage point. I realized that the psychological effects were what they termed sanity. I realized further that rather than assimilate and accommodate myself to that state of mind I would leave it.

I can't claim it was any bravery on my part. No, it was simply having no other place to go—like the woman who is being battered or the woman who is trying to flee Lebanon. No place to go but into our vantage point and out of their minds.

So I am here. But I *know* I am here. I do not imagine me. And that's an odd sort of power, bounded in a nutshell, counting myself a queen of infinite space. How peculiar—finding *oneself* is the opposition whose spirit is still unbroken! Because being here and knowing what I know, I have no choice but to invent some other way of existing. I can't do that all by myself, though. Which is where you come into the picture.

If I've imagined you, then that's already some other way of existing.

If I haven't imagined you, you might even understand that you need me as much as I need you.

I'm going to try to break out, you see, break free of this space. But I can't leave without you, knowing you're in there just beginning to glimpse fully where you are. It's not anything nobly sacrificial, I'm as selfish as the next one. I would go if I could, even without you—but I can't. I need you to invent another way of existing, together with me. Or, if you like, forget me. Do it yourself. But pass it on.

I know it's simple-minded, but I think I love you, you there singing wordlessly to yourself in the neighboring cell.

I have no way of knowing if these words will ever reach you. But I have to try.

Tap three times if you receive this.

CHAPTER 10

꧁꧂꧁꧂꧁꧂꧁꧂꧁

BEYOND TERROR:
THE POLITICS OF EROS

I am the First and the Last,
I am the Whore and the Holy One.
I am She whose wedding is great
yet I have never taken a husband.
I am the voice whose sound is manifold
and the silence whose manifestation is multiple.
I am She who cries out.
Why have you hated me in your counsels?
I am the one whom you have despised,
yet you reflect on me.
I am the one from whom you have hidden,
yet you appear to me.
Whenever you hide yourselves,
I myself will appear.
I am the knowledge of my inquiry.
I am the utterance of my name.

/ "Thunder, Perfect Mind," VI 13, 1–21, 32,
from the Nag Hammadi Gnostic texts

*L*ook closely at her.

She is the only qualified expert on her existence in the entire universe.

There are things she knows that she does not know she knows.

For this, she needs her lifetime in which to teach herself what it is she knows. But there are things she knows now that she dares not say. For this, she needs to break silence.

There is a silence that *will* not speak. When this silence explodes, it does so in violence from and for terror's sake. This is Achilles brooding in his tent. This is Oliver North citing the military slogan "Silence means consent" to back his claim that his White House superiors gave implicit support to his actions. This is active violence. This is the way of the Demon Lover.

There is a silence that *may* not speak. Violence *im*plodes this silence, from and for erasure's sake. This is the way she is violent—against herself, "for the sake of peace." Remaining in this silence (even if it is an enforced one) is reactive violence.

His violence provokes fear, which provokes silence. Her silence lends her the hope of surviving. The former pretends a false erasure (false because she does exist, because she does not imagine herself). The latter pretends a false safety (because silent or not, she and all around her are perishing from his violence).

Where is her self-interest in identifying with such psychosis?

Must she try a drastic perception shift, as if she had just landed from the Crab Nebula System? How else can she fully perceive the madness so as to totally de-identify with it? Where is the risk in doing this if she is dying anyway, being threatened, poisoned, inched toward extinction? Isn't it a greater risk to do nothing, or to do something imitative of his demonic Thanatos?

At last she begins to fear her own silence as much as or more than the violence he visits upon her if she speaks. Her silence is within her own power to break, even if his violence is not. Silence is the first thing within the power of the enslaved to shatter. From that shattering, everything else spills forth.

What would happen if she became *incapable* of "realizing what is impossible"?

She would be unafraid.

Terror is merely fear's by-product, fear's neon shriek for help. Fear longs to be dissolved, yet we manufacture it faster than any other emotion. A bleak brilliance, this ugliest and coldest of energies annunciates itself in the negative, by absences—the absence of trust, the absence of light, the absence of love. Fear requires consequent force: it would control what cannot be controlled. Failing that, it would destroy what cannot be controlled. Failing *that,* it would destroy itself rather than continue to feel itself. This is the love-death. This is Thanatos.

In the Demon Lover's world system of perception and practice, fear is central to power, and fear is defined as multiple while power is defined as singular. We speak often of having "fears," but rarely of having "powers." The religious directive "As God is to man, so man is to woman" is one example of a deliberate and accurate representation of the channel of power (singular) vested in the male, along the continuum from family through State to the manner in which we are required to perceive the universe: one power, one type of power, one mode of using it (power over)—and one vehicle for exercising it: male. Yet this construct, of fear as multiple and power as singular, is the reverse of all organic logic. Such logic implies rather that all fears—physical, emotional, mental, spiritual—really lead back to one, the sole source: fear of loss of consciousness / loss of self / obliteration (i.e., death). Whether the fear is of illness or of aging, of rejection or of loneliness, of war or of earthquake, of going mad or of selling out, the source is the same—fear of ceasing to exist, cessation of the knowledge that one is existing. And organic logic also implies that power, far from being a singular, quantifiable either / or object, is actually plural, a repertoire, a menu of possibilities: the power of an active volcano *and* that of an ailanthus shoot managing to grow through a concrete city pavement; the power of a bat's radar *and* that of the invention of writing; the power of an undertow *and* that of music; the power of a generator *and* that of the cyclone that causes a "power failure." Indeed, one could argue that the most pernicious use of power is the one that would convince us of its singularity.

Listen to her:

Death, whether faced in actual dying or in the inner awareness of one's own mortality, is perhaps the most antipolitical experience there is. It signifies that we shall disappear from the world of appearances and shall leave the company of our fellow-men [sic], which are the conditions of all politics. As far as human experience is concerned, death indicates an extreme loneliness and impotence. But faced collectively and in action, death changes its countenance; now nothing seems more likely to intensify our vitality than its proximity. Something we are usually hardly aware of, namely, that our own death is accompanied by the potential immortality of the group we belong to and, in the final analysis, of the species, moves into the center of our experience. It is as though life itself, the immortal life of the species, nourished, as it were, by the sempiternal dying of its individual members, is "surging upward," is actualized in the practice of violence.[1]

Those are the words of Hannah Arendt, the articulations of a first-rate mind straining itself to the limits of analytical thought *within* an (only partially challenged) androcentric context. One aches to cry out to that mind: *What if there is no such thing as an antipolitical experience?* What if one realizes that because everything is interactive, everything is in the deepest sense political? What if there exists an entire body of human consciousness that has already been made to disappear (by force) from the "world of appearances" and to leave (by force) the company of "fellow-men"? Is that constituency outside "the conditions of all politics" or outside the conditions of a politics delineated by those "fellow-men"? By "fellow-men" Arendt of course meant non-genderized humanity—but by the use of the masculine as the generic term for "human" she came closer to the real meaning than her own intuition may have suspected. One longs to ask her: Death (under patriarchy) may be experienced as loneliness when individuated yet as vitality when collectivized—but what if one stands *outside* that "collective"? Is death then less lonely, less impotent? Is death then *not* a means to vitality? What if one is made to stand outside by exclusion? What if one stands outside at last by choice? And what if the hitherto prevailing concept (that nature requires individual or collective death to nourish the immortality of the species and other life) has in this century undergone a major shift? Because now the fellow men can deliver a death equal to the *extinction* of the species—and of the entire biosphere we call earth.

Death is one thing; an end to birth is something else.

Those trapped inside the closed-system thinking of patriarchy, no matter how scintillant their intelligence, cannot perceive another "world of appearances," a different kind of company, an alternative collective action, or ways of living (and even dying) that would not be lonely, impotent, *or* vitalized by violent proximity to death. That task can be imagined and activated only by those who are attempting to appear in that other world, approach that different company, become a whole people, and engage in that alternative action, even now.

The sole source of fear for such a people is the loss (or theft) of *consciousness* while still alive, a death-in-life that *is* the "fate worse than death." Patriarchal power is employed toward that exact end; this requires the monopolizing of power, which in turn requires the monodefining of power as a static and singular object, the better to monopolize it. Fluid, multiple powers cannot be employed to such an end because they are not so controllable, because the more powers there exist, the more likely they are to be distributed via many vehicles and channels, and the more channels, the less likely it is that consciousness can be destroyed. Recognizing these qualities of power / powers is a political act.

Power (like women) does not exist only in the world of appearances and only in the company of our fellow men. It is diverse, multi-definable, and active.

For example, fame is a sort of power, but power is not necessarily a sort of fame. Wealth is a form of power, but power isn't necessarily a form of wealth. Youth (and age) are types of power, but power isn't a quality of age. Wisdom, truth, serenity, love are kinds of power—but power isn't necessarily inherent in any of them. Squeezing power into a monodefinition is imperative for the monopolizing of it. The more "powerful" you become (in the Demon Lover's politics of Thanatos), the more rigid and abstract are the laws you forge and follow; the more "powerless" you are (in his system), the more fluid and specific are your realities.

What if that were turned inside out?

The specific inevitably leads to an awareness of the unique, to a respect for differences. A respect for differences means one does not wish to make multiplicity uniform, to *control* (persons, resources, nations) for the sake of some old tradition or some new efficiency. A respect for differences implies a respect for a variety of integrities, for change, growth, process. A respect for differences approaches the universal through celebrating the specific, and a respect for the specific is an act of desire—as energy yearns toward matter, as the unspecifiable expresses itself through metaphor and the precision of form. A respect for the specific synthesizes differences into new wholes by recognizing and expressing their disparate longings. It implies a respect for the *movement* of life. It implies a totally different politics—of celebration, of creative collaboration. Mary Daly has termed this politics "biophilic": life-loving. Yes. I would also call it the politics of Eros, and not only because, as Arendt put it, "love-making is the most glorious manifestation of life." I would call it the politics of Eros because the energy of this desire, of erotic intelligence, is inherently the expression of respect, of fierce tenderness, of caring-in-totality, of humor, friendship, amity, and trust. By expressing this longing for integrity in loving, this rejection of fetishized body parts and compartmentalized relationships, this refusal to isolate physical sensuality from emotional affection, women have shown themselves, in masculinist terms, notoriously remiss. What happens, then, as women's expression of that longing becomes more clearly "politicized"?

Reclaiming the erotic in our own terms, redefining power(s) in our own terms, are inseparable acts for women. So far, we have barely begun on individual levels—achieving relatively "freer" sexuality, more visibility in the workplace, the emergence of the gender gap in electoral politics. Collectively our actions have been more reactive than active. Now the gravity of global crisis requires a strategic shift on our part. We face possibilities for creative tactics never before conceivable. One classic justification for (insurgent) terrorism is that such action is the only recourse for an oppressed *minority* to confront the oppressor. We need not be bound by these rules, since we are not bound by those numbers. As the human *majority*, and as people increasingly insisting on our own empowerment, women can utterly change the terms on which power is held or seized, on which the world is sustained or destroyed. This will require us to defuse the Demon Lover, refuse the *Liebestod* (in our own lives and for humanity), no longer lust after selflessness, no longer be satisfied by tokenism (of the Right or the Left), no longer define ourselves as non-men or "liberate" ourselves by imitating men, no longer settle for passion as violence or violence as normalcy. The powers of female sexuality, in all of their expressions *and* redefinitions (maternal, celibate, bisexual, lesbian, and heterosexual) have the potential of forming completely different relationships in the twenty-first century. Those relationships need not be only between individuals but, as metaphor and totality in practice, can be between groups, nations, and regions. Rhetoric won't get us there. "Making it" within his system won't get us there. Even blueprints for action won't get us there. But the energy of female erotic intelligence freed from the Demon Lover, combined with our numbers as a majority and our growing indigenous tactical sophistication, *can* get us there. This would mean an end to terrorism, its causes and effects and self-propagation, because it would mean an end to the sexuality of terrorism—which has given violence its power to destroy us all.

If for centuries women have been accused by the Right of being dangerously radical creatures and by the Left of being dangerously conservative ones, it is because the sub-patriarchal reality in which women live is a third politics altogether. That is the reality now starting to manifest in the "world of appearances."

We have never had a chance on the wheel of revolution: it revolves between the father and the son. We can neither turn it nor ride it, because we are not *on* it. We have, however, been trapped *inside* it. We have been the hub that has held it together for the sake of our own misused and abused altruism.

But we have seen that revolution is insufficient. *Transformation* is necessary to save ourselves, sentient life on the planet, the biosphere itself. Transformation requires that we recognize our own just anger as being so vast that mere violence could not possibly address it. Transformation requires more than mere seeing; it requires all forms of perception, including remembering, imagining, intuiting, hallucinating, dreaming, and empathizing. And transformation requires that we *act,* that we *step off the wheel, outside the prescribed boundaries altogether.* Transformation requires that we enter history on our own terms and audaciously place ourselves at the center of it.

Gerda Lerner declares:

> The shift in consciousness we must make occurs in two steps: we must, at least for a time, be woman-centered. We must, as far as possible, leave patriarchal thought behind.[2]

Lerner describes a "woman-centered" consciousness as assuming "that it is inconceivable for anything ever to have taken place in the world in which women were not involved, except if they were prevented from participation through coercion and repression." It means ignoring "all evidence of women's marginality. . . . Women cannot be put into the empty spaces of patriarchal thought and systems—in moving to the center, they transform the system." As for stepping outside of patriarchal thought:

> Being skeptical toward every known system of thought: being critical of all assumptions, ordering values and definitions . . . , devel-

oping intellectual courage, . . . the challenge to move from the desire for safety and approval to the most "unfeminine" quality of all—that of intellectual arrogance, the supreme hubris which asserts to itself the right to reorder the world.[3]

This audacity, which would literally center itself in the future of history, must begin *at* the center.

Look closely at her.

The Self

She asks, How long must we let them research what we already know, how long let them indulge in endlessly self-propagating *re*-search as the ultimate procrastination against action?

She decides to step outside the wheel.

Being herself, she does not do this precipitously or violently, but with small incremental motions, not always perceptible at first, even to herself.

She knows that women are acculturated to be responsible not only for children but for others, including men. She knows, too, that men are acculturated to be self-enclosed, so that if they hurt or kill others they need not feel it as keenly (also one of the characteristics, she recalls, of psychopaths). She sees that *for him to become responsible for himself, she must cease being so.*

She enters her own psychic and psychological space, what Daly has called the thirteenth hour, beyond patriarchy's midnight.[4]

Since she has ceased being responsible for him, she now has time to notice her own history of thralldom to Thanatos. She begins to see what, when, and why she was drawn to what he claimed was power. From this perspective, that history and that power seem worse than repellent, seem pathetic, puerile, literally beneath her—who was always so kept beneath them. As she positions herself in this center of her own perceptions, she

begins to experience this field as one vibrating with powers—
of intellectual rigor and emotional strength, of space to breathe
and think, to notice what she's feeling, to acknowledge an urge
to act not out of desperation but out of affirmation. She enjoys
this.

She touches, as if it were the permeable membrane into
another dimension, the grace of the comedic.

So addicted has she been to tragic beauty, that she is tempted
to lie about this. But her biophilic audacity gives her the strength
to tell the truth. She remembers that it was Camus—one of the
Demon Lover's almost-renegade sons—who said, "Freedom is
the right not to lie." She reminds herself that there are differences between men. She discovers that her truths constitute a
fragile new-found freedom—and that they are part of her powers.

She begins to like herself.

> Yonder they do not love your flesh. They despise it. . . . Love your
> hands! Love them. Raise them up and kiss them. Touch others
> with them, pat them together, stroke them on your face 'cause they
> don't love that either. *You* got to love it, *you!* . . . This is flesh I'm
> talking about here. Flesh that needs to be loved. . . . And all your
> inside parts. . . . The dark, dark liver—love it, love it, and the beat
> and beating heart, love that, too. More than eyes or feet. More
> than lungs that have yet to draw free air. More than your life-
> holding womb and your life-giving private parts, hear me now,
> love your heart. For this is the prize.[5]

Toni Morrison in her novel *Beloved* could be—and should be—
every woman calling to every woman.

So she begins to love herself, to love her own flesh, to love
her own genius. She begins to *deserve* herself.

This is political.

This is the discovery of ecstasy not as a "standing outside
of" the self but as a standing, for the first time, inside the self.

She begins to imagine what she deserves from others. She
begins to imagine what others deserve.

Now, from this ecstatic perspective inside herself, she looks around her.

The Female Community

She looks at the world. She thinks, I have no idea what to do to change all this; *but those in power don't know what they're doing, either.*

She hears, as if for the first time, Clausewitz saying, "War is the continuation of politics by other means," and Berit Ås replying, "A patriarchal state is one which is either rehabilitating from war, is presently at war, or is preparing for war."

She thinks, as if for the first time, Why do men marching to battle wear keys to a promised heaven while women fleeing from battle wear keys to a lost home?

She is afraid to think there is an inherent difference.

But she does wonder, as if for the first time, why there are no articles titled "Men *Can* Be Violent: A Hidden History of Male Capacity for Force," and no books titled *Why Women Resist Pacifism.*

She reads the words of well-meaning women who emphasize that women are just as responsible for violence as men, who deny and excuse and are reasonable: "Males are always going to have an 'excess' of androgen (it's an excess only if one sets up the female as a single human norm, which doesn't seem quite fair)."[6] She notices that men have been setting themselves up as the single human norm for millennia.

But she is still afraid to believe in a basic difference between them.

So she tiptoes her small, incremental steps, to try to change the world without looking too closely at what she fears.

Like Margarita Chant Papandreou, president of the Women's Union of Greece, she can say, "I *do* want to argue that women's values, whether they are biologically imbedded or culturally instilled, are clearly more anti-war, more anti-violence, more for the preservation of life than are male values."[7] But she is not quite comfortable settling for this. She suspects there's something more.

She supports strategies which themselves, though humble, are cumulative and important. She affirms a plurality of feminisms because she respects differences between women (though she is still reluctant to see the difference between women and men). She peers behind the stereotypes and reads behind the headlines.

She demands that all girls be taught self-defense in required courses at the primary-school level. She knows this demand is consistent with genuine anti-violence, because if there are no prey there can be no predator, and because such forms as judo and aikido wittily turn the attacker's own strength against himself. She tries to think of other ways of turning an aggressor's strength against the aggressor.

She remembers that there are places in the world where women still cannot vote, so she uses her ballot as a potentially radical lever. She doesn't wish to say that she will never vote for any man and always vote for women, because she knows there are women in the Demon Lover's party-caucus harems as well as in the harems of his cells and underground collectives. Yet she also knows that at this point in history no man can truly represent her, because no man can conceive what her experience is. But she is still afraid of being "anti-male." So she says instead that she will never vote for any man who has a military record. (She knows this will not mean that he has avoided being physically or emotionally violent in other ways, but it is at least a place to begin.) It occurs to her that if, instead of being a plus for a candidate, having a military record were to disqualify one from holding public office, that in itself would be quite a gain. It could also mean that after a single election, a majority of officeholders would be women.

She rather likes that one.

But she can also agree with Marilyn J. Waring, who has been in public office and reports from the inside, "I suppose it

might be said that a woman in government changes attitudes—
but ethics? There I am skeptical. If women are seen as an
important voter population, if the government has a small
majority, then policies might change, but expediently, not ethically."[8]
She listens carefully for all hints of audacity.

The Industrial Revolution gave a major turn to history. Out of it
emerged industrial capitalism and, as a reaction to it, Marxism in
its various forms. Together these have given rise to the great social
upheavals of our time. The two have followed different paths but
their ethos is basically materialistic. All that begins must end. And
the seeds of the ending are present from the very beginning. What
we have witnessed—the two world wars, the possible approach of
a third, so much more destructive and disastrous, and the struggle
for power are the end of the road for the existing order of compet-
ing systems. Out of this chaos a new order is struggling to be born.[9]

That was no marginal visionary speaking. That was the leader
of a nation of 700 million people. That was a highly pragmatic
politician—pragmatic as only a woman can be. That was the
late prime minister of India Indira Gandhi, also chair of the
Movement of Non-Aligned Countries, addressing the UN General Assembly in 1983.

She ponders Indira Gandhi, who stopped short of naming
the old order for what it is, of naming the new order for what
it can be. She ponders Cory Aquino, another pragmatic woman
politician. She learns that Aquino, in her capacity as president
of the Philippines, and Margarita Papandreou, in her (secondary, other) capacity as wife of the male prime minister of Greece,
have said publicly what no woman in either position has ever
said before—that the clicking, stamping, shouting, saluting,
flourishing of guns, and firing of cannons in an official State
welcome disgusts them. (She is not deterred by Margaret
Thatcher. She is in fact bored at having Margaret Thatcher
thrown at her; she knows men will pounce upon such an

example *because* it has been cloned in their own image and is so much an exception to the rule.)

She tries to work it out:

Even if women are "the same" and can be "as violent" as men, women seem to have some *override* that stops or slows the violence. Is it ambivalence? If, as human beasts together, men and women share a "killer instinct" (in which she no longer believes), then this override is a positive, mutant, evolutionary leap. To be affirmed. To be learned and imitated by *men*.

She tries to work it out in the specific:

If a woman who is being beaten fears striking back, it is because she knows, first, that he can come for her and kill her in retaliation, and, second, that if *she* kills in her own defense, then not he but his State will come for her. Women know that we cannot win by force—*that no one really can*—and therefore women seek to resolve problems by other means. Far from being the utopian and naive approach it is regarded as, this is an eminently *practical* approach.

She is stunned that women, these most rational of beings, who know what won't work from experience and who therefore do not resort to it, are as a result considered irrational.

This seems to her "unreasonable."

The momentum of her own intelligence is propelling her further outside the wheel of his thought, the circles of his hell.

But she is still afraid to leave him (so she thinks) behind.

She clings to his voice whenever it echoes a hint of audacious biophilia.

Some of the principal laws of science, like the second law of thermodynamics, arose out of industrial experience. This law (e.g., in any process involving a flow of energy there is always some loss) resulted from efforts to improvise the working of the steam engine so as to advance industry. It is this connection between physics and economics that also helps explain the colonizing thrust of science. C. V. Seshadri *finds the second law ethnocentric, and therefore outside science.* Because of its industrial origins, it has presented a definition of energy in a way calculated to favor the allocation of resources for the purpose of big industry, often depriving the rest of the population of them. . . . Seshadri points out [that] both nature and the non-Western world are losers in this new definition. . . . A civilization based on modern science provides itself with an arbitrary criterion and justification for taking over the processing of all resources. . . . This monopoly [of centralized knowledge] is based on the premise that all other forms of acquisition or accumulation of knowledge, all other epistemologies, are worthless, antiquated, magical, and must be eliminated . . . [so that] science-based technologies replace experience-based systems, even if, when all things are considered, the latter fulfill their purposes better.[10]

It comforts her that this was written by a man, Claude Alvares, commenting approvingly on the theories of another man, C. V. Seshadri. So they *can* reject Thanatos when they choose to! And to state flat-out that the second law of thermodynamics is ethnocentric and therefore outside of science! She is impressed. How she admires their ease and familiarity with an audacity she still finds awesome in herself. Then she stops and rethinks just who is leaving whom behind. She looks at the Third World being ripped in two between its own elites who buy into the Western scientific megamachine and the bulk of its people who are crushed by the disregard for their experience-based systems. She sees and hears what Alvares and Seshadri stop short of seeing, hearing, naming.

She sees where women stand in that picture.

She thinks: I resent being different from men when *men* are defining that difference.

She thinks: Both nature and the female world are losers in that definition.

She thinks: Ethnocentrism itself is androcentric, and *therefore* outside science.

She thinks: Do I resent being different from men when I and other women are defining the difference? Do I resent that difference if a singular power is not at work to enforce it, but our multiple powers are at work to explore it?

She builds her own epistemology.

She studies the accumulating research in the neurosciences about sex and gender differences: hormonal impact, chromosomal differentiation, brain lateralization. She is amused at the finding that the *corpus callosum,* which communicates information between the two hemispheres of the brain, is larger and bulkier in female brains than in male brains, implying a greater "ease and frequency of communication" between right and left brain in females than in males.[11] She is unsurprised at the growing number of studies linking formative testosterone (in utero), as well as that circulating post-puberty, with aggression and with "homicidal violence, whether spontaneous and outlawed or organized and sanctioned for military purposes."[12] She wonders about conceiving a society wise enough to compensate for biological difference, should it be proven. She worries about who holds the power (singular) to attribute worth to certain characteristics and worthlessness to others. She retains a healthy distrust of the we-can't-change propaganda inherent in the pseudo-science of sociobiology, but also remains skeptical of any either/or dogmatists, whether biological determinists or societal determinists. She knows that just as cultural behavior and societal structures affect the brain (the most obvious examples being malnutrition, protein denial, food taboos), so the brain in turn affects cultural behavior and society—and can alter both. She worries about who is doing the research, who is funding it, who will interpret it, who will apply it and to what purpose.

She studies the work of Finnish feminist theorist Hilkka Pietilä and Norwegian feminist theorist Berit Ås. Her experience-based knowledge resonates in agreement that women and men currently exist in two cultures; that women approach communication differently (with more body language, more linguistic agility and clarity, possibly due to interaction with the practical life of family and children); that women regard tools and technology differently (with more user orientation, more interest in a machine for what it can *do* than for what it *is* or symbolizes); that women organize differently (with more volunteerism, more consensus); and use time differently (with less linearity than men, being more accustomed to performing multiple tasks simultaneously). She studies the conclusions of Swedish feminist Rita Liljeström—that women's time is organic and keyed to the duration it takes to get something (or many things) done, as opposed to men's time, which is one-dimensional; that women's time is "unsold" time, "uncoordinated" time, and "indistinct" time, i.e., it adapts to the needs and context around it.[13] None of these feminist theorists can yet "prove" that these differences are biological, genetic, or socio-cultural. But all recognize that the difference exists—and do so from a consciousness which is female and is *doing the defining,* for the first time, *of that difference.*

One day it occurs to her to turn a standard phrase inside out, to say instead: "Men are really the same as women." Absurd. Or: "Men are really different from women." Obviously.

All at once, she understands that despite his denials, to him different always meant inferior.

All at once, she is less afraid.

She remembers Nina Simone's reply, on being asked to define freedom: *"No fear."*

She remembers Virginia Woolf's elegant response to male "pacifist" appeals for aid: "We can best help you to prevent war not by repeating your words and following your methods but by finding new words and creating new methods, . . . not by joining your society but by remaining outside your society."[14]

Outside the company of the fellow men.

She begins to conceive of herself as the next evolutionary leap. Then she smiles at herself—but in her new-found simultaneity of time and multiplicity of powers, she smiles in complete seriousness.

She takes another step. She is much less afraid now, because stepping farther outside his wheel of revolution is irrelevant if one is at the center of an entirely incomparable kind of ring. It will move with her, around her, surrounding and protecting her.

She can extend her realization of differences between women, and her realization of differences between men, to her own realization of difference between genders. It is effortless now, though it implies a profound responsibility.

From this position she finds she can see farther and more clearly than ever before.

The Metanational Community

Stepping out and *dropping* out are, she realizes, very different. "Dropping out" is not an authentic option, for a number of reasons. First, most women on the planet can't even consider it as any kind of option at all; second, not only is the personal political, but the political is also personal; and third, dropping out would be, well, lazy (and being a woman, she is anything but lazy). She suspects that there are still more reasons for finding this non-option distasteful, but she finds it tedious even to list them further. She wants to *do* something.

She watches, learns, and tries to adopt the unpredictable organic strategies of other women.

· In November 1987, hundreds of Greek Cypriot women bearing white banners scrambled across the line dividing their country. The Turkish sentry summoned fifty comrades as reinforcements. They arrived with bazookas. The women said, "We come in peace. We will leave now. But when you least expect us, we will return."[15]

She finds this laudably reasonable.

· In Kausani, in the Indian Himalayas, village mountain women have organized to preserve the environment and to make themselves self-sufficient; they see these two issues as one, since the average woman in this extremely poor region (where there is one gynecologist for 300,000 women) spends over four hours a day gathering firewood and fetching water. The women began mobilizing in 1974, when twenty-four of them started to embrace trees to protect them from commercial logging; this was the origin of the Chipko Movement (*chipko* means "to embrace"). The women have agitated against deforestation, mining, and the sale of liquor in the hills, which they say promotes battery. Their tactics have been called magical and mad, but they persist and succeed. One now-famous anecdote involves the government's effort to support the loggers by sending in troops to shoot anyone embracing the trees. The women clung to the trees, and the troops were too ashamed to fire. So the government and the loggers sent in elephants to trample the women who were draping themselves around the trees. The huge animals moved forward on command. The women left the trees and approached the elephants, singing a ritual song that Hindu women sing at the annual festival of the elephant god, when they bedeck temple elephants with garlands. But these were not temple elephants, they were army elephants. Still, the women approached, singing, and then they swarmed over the animals, stroking them, embracing the massive trunks and feet. Was this a tactic or a prayer? Did the women believe in an elephant god? Did they think they were performing a religious ritual and might evoke a miracle? Or did they hope pragmatically that their action would shame the elephant drivers as it had the soldiers? Or did they act in this manner simply because retreat was unthinkable and they saw no other option? No one knows, and the women will not say.

But the elephants stopped. The elephants knelt. The elephants would not budge. The troops and the loggers withdrew, acknowledging defeat before a group of women who were hugging trees. Bina Kala, coordinator of eighteen local women's forums in the district, explains, "When awakened, Hindu goddesses are known to be more powerful and awesome than their male counterparts. Women here have now become conscious of their *shakti* (energy). They will exercise it whenever necessary."[16]

In her growing epistemology, she finds Chipko an example of the politics of Eros.

Anna Marcondes Faria is one of forty women who are *fav-*

ela presidents, community-elected leaders in the slums of Brazil. One of these women heads the largest such community (over 200,000 people) in the country. These women are building their own movement in the *favelas*—755 of which are in Rio de Janeiro alone—outside all political parties. Anna Marcondes Faria says, "Of course women do all the work here. Of course nothing ever changes unless women change it."

She finds this a quite proper, woman-centered, intellectual arrogance.

• In 1987, the Women's Peace Movement in Northern Ireland, comprised of both Protestant and Catholic women, was reviving. It had crested in the mid-1970s with mass marches and the awarding of the Nobel Peace Prize to its two founders, Betty Williams and Mairead Corrigan, then fallen into disarray under threats, taunts, accusations, and assaults from the two warring factions. Yet it was resurrecting itself. In 1988, in reaction to the atrocities of ethnic civil war between the Tamils and the Sinhalese in Sri Lanka, a group of women from different ethnic, economic, social, and political backgrounds in that country formed Women for Peace. They initiated a massive pro-peace signature drive, organized a poster blitz and a public-education campaign, formed a "mothers' front" protesting the arrest and disappearance of children, established structures to aid refugees, and protested both government and insurgent military forces' harassment of women.

She respects such stubborn rejections of tragedy as acts of comedic grace.

• The Israeli group that began in 1982 as Women Against the Invasion of Lebanon now calls itself Women Against Occupation. It demonstrates regularly, carrying signs that read *We Won't Be Alibis For Murder*. The group makes all its decisions by consensus and does not exclude any women, including committedly Zionist women: "Actually, the only positions one has to agree with when joining are women's liberation (broadly defined), Israel out of Lebanon and the Occupied Territories, and self-determination for the Palestinians. We see this as the broadest possible political basis on which women can organize as feminists here, since we see the state of war between Israel and our Arab neighbors and the oppression of Palestinians' rights as the main issue blocking women's emancipation. . . . [in our demonstrations] we emphasize exposing the links between militarism and the subjugation of women."[17] The group's slogan adopts—and carries one step further in meaning—the military saying "Silence means consent."

She loves these women. She loves them as she loves herself. She echoes Virginia Woolf: ". . . as a woman, I have no country. As a woman I want no country. As a woman my country is the whole world."[18]

But, she frets to herself, what effect are these women really having? They have no *plan*, they don't fully know what they're *doing*. Then she thinks, What effect are these *men* really having? And they claim they *have* a plan, that they fully *know* what they're doing.

Oppression, she suddenly recognizes, always structures itself along the same monotonous pattern. Oppression is predictable.

What we are, she flashes, is unpredictable. Like freedom. And what we must dare become is *more* unpredictable.

She comprehends: So it is not merely the absence of war but the presence of peace, not merely the absence of tragedy but the presence of comedy, not merely the absence of hate but the presence of love, not merely the absence of ignorance but the presence of intelligence, not merely the absence of death but the presence of life. And it is not merely the absence of fear, but the presence of trust.

She comprehends that she is leaving no one behind, because it is not about the absence of men but about the presence of women.

Here, in her own centrality, she sees to her astonishment that he is awkwardly, slowly, being drawn to *it*, to *her* magnetism, methods, imaginings, desires. He stumbles, lurches, still brings others down with him when he falls. But a few of him begin to take, as she did, small, incremental steps—truly caring for a child, trying to study peace, moving to the place *her* job requires, not merely "helping her with the housework," voting for her, listening to her, trying to talk about this politics with other men, trying to make the connections. The irony is that for the first time in her collective memory she has done nothing for the sake of drawing him; it is a side effect; she is the issue, she and these women. This is a new humanity, in which she feels for the first time fully human. What he is drawn to is her energy, an energy that is squared (or circled?) in heightening intensity as she connects with other women. Seemingly leaderless, these groupings of women in actuality pass different kinds of leadership among themselves, varying their strengths as the situation requires. They speak myriad languages but they converse in female. They exchange glances that communicate intimate knowledge. They help one another to grieve, they teach one another to laugh, they excite one another to survive, they arouse one another to act. They recognize each other. They recognize that each other exists.

There are no models for this. He has mapped no terrain beyond the revolutions of his own racking wheel.

Yet this terrain is authentic. She is experiencing it in all her senses, hungrily, rapidly, as if she were giving birth to herself as a new life form, as if she were being welcomed onto the planet by the planet itself.

There are no models for this?

The Biospheric Community

Like a young doe in the forest, she lifts her head and listens:

• The wheeling of ten thousand starlings in formation over a wheat field—or the shimmer of a million minnows, threatened by a predator, summing themselves up instantly into a single array—may seem to be choreographed motions. They are not. "The fluidity of a seeming intelligence" that far transcends the

apparent ability of individual members appears to be responsible. Hitherto, scientists have assumed that the intricate order
of flocking and schooling had to have a high level of coordina-
tion and a hierarchy of leaders. Now they acknowledge that
this is not the case—although they have yet to figure out how
the movements are made. "No conventional answer," they state,
will necessarily emerge, but such theories as "biological radio,"
"magnetic field perturbation," "a sense of distant touch," and
"thought transference" are being proposed. What baffles the
scientists is that "no individual is a leader, or in another sense,
every individual is. . . . there's no conceptual model. . . . You
have emergent properties that have nothing to do with the
original rules."[19]

Although the scientists are able to observe the schooling
"tactics" of fish in laboratory tanks, they're stumped when it
comes to flocking: "Nobody has figured out how to get 10,000
starlings in a big cage and get them to do anything." The scientists seem unable to comprehend that the fluid-seeming motion
is neither determined by a "central mind, a flock mind"[20] nor
preplanned and formally led. ("But even jet pilots in formation
can't do it this way!") Any third way seems too formidable for
them to grasp.

· In 1952, scientists conducting an experiment in animal
behavior on the Japanese island of Koshima gave wild monkeys sweet potatoes coated in sand. One eighteen-month-old
female monkey, who came to be nicknamed Imo, discovered
that the potatoes tasted better if she washed them first in a
nearby stream. She taught her playmates this trick, and she
taught it to her mother as well. Soon her playmates had taught
their mothers. Between 1952 and 1958, all the young monkeys
learned to wash their potatoes—but the only adults who did so
were those willing to learn from their offspring. Approximately a hundred monkeys were washing their potatoes on
Koshima when, in the autumn of 1958, the new skill spontaneously "jumped" to colonies of monkeys on the mainland;
monkeys at Takasiyama, as well as on some other islands, began

to wash dirt and sand off *their* sweet potatoes. The scientists still don't understand how this "jump" could have happened, but some have posited that a leap in awareness, once shared by a sufficient number of intelligences, makes possible a leap in communication of that awareness via a "field of thought" similar to a field of energy. The experiment and subsequent theory have come to be known as "the one hundredth monkey phenomenon."[21]

· The catastrophic warming effect of the planet's atmosphere, caused by manufactured chemicals and environmental abuse, is evoking a reaction—an organic attempt at an antidote. The globe may be regulating its temperature through a "planetary thermostat," an intricate feedback loop involving atmospheric gases, the formation of clouds, and oceanic plankton. "The key actors are tiny plankton—algae floating in vast numbers near the ocean surface. . . . [they] emit a sulfurous gas, dimethylsulfide. When it reaches the atmosphere, it reacts with oxygen to form aerosols, particles in the air. The particles . . . serve as seeds for cloud droplets, which then reflect the sun's radiation back out to space."[22] Warmth may increase the plankton's growth, but the algae emissions in turn are creating a climate of increasing cloudiness, as moisture condenses around the particles. The result is a natural cooling affect.

The newest scientific hypothesis of how the universe works—chaos theory—has fallen upon a platitude with an air of great discovery: that an imperceptible and implicit order is at work beneath a seeming disorder. The new connoisseurs of chaos, or "chaologists," are researching patterns of behavior—whether in the arcs of roulette balls, the frequency of ice ages, or the turbulence of flowing water—and finding that the patterns are in fact the order within the chaos. The human heart itself beats not like a metronome, but in subtly chaotic rhythms. Furthermore, each movement within the field of "chaos" affects every other. As meteorologist Edward Lorenz of MIT put it, "if a butterfly flapped its wings in Brazil, it might produce a tornado in Texas. Unlikely as it seems, the tiny air currents that a butterfly creates travel across thousands of miles, jostling other breezes as they go and eventually changing the weather."[23]

She refuses to sentimentalize or anthropomorphize starlings, fish, plankton, or pattern-defying patterns, as she refuses to sentimentalize or ethnomorphize women of other cultures. But she can't help feeling a burst of affection for them all—for instance, for these millions of tiny algae that spontaneously, "magically," and in no-nonsense fashion set about their business of cooling the atmosphere. This she understands—each individual planktonic organism bubbling to the surface as its own center, its own leader, knowing exactly "what must be done" without Lenin and the central committee of a vanguard party to inflict directions; each minuscule entity somehow undaunted by the enormous task facing it, each comic little alga farting into space its existential biophilic gesture of plain practicality, its contribution to the shared task of earthkeeping.

She is exhilarated by the model that isn't a model, the cheerful disorderly order, the unchaotic chaos. She no longer has any patience for the myopia of phallocentric, ethnocentric, androcentric, or even gynocentric perceptions. She is female, she is human—and she is animal, too.

Men have called her catty, cowlike, a bitch. Men have named her pigeon, chick, vixen, shrew, tomato, peach, lemon. Men have spat out their contempt for her and for the natural world in the same pejorative slang, attacking two birds with the identical stone, mistaking the character of both targets.

So, she smiles to herself, have I been so domesticated that I no longer know the wildness in myself? Then I will hiss and growl my rage, I will snap and shriek and snarl it, aloud. I will be unripe for their plucking and I will be bitter on their puckered tongues. I will move together with all the women who have left "the company of our fellow-men," and with all the life forms who—like myself and those women—have always been invisible in the "world of appearances."

She perceives powers she can embrace in common with creatures wild as herself, the ultimately untamable. Yet she doesn't confuse herself with them or settle for thinking that "woman is nature"—because she respects the specific and can celebrate differences. But now she can glory in her own desire for living in a newly imagined space and a newly conceived manner, approachable by *her* tactics. And if those tactics are as multiple or serial or mystifying to him as her orgasm, why should she descend to the level a Marighella could understand? The Demon Lover is as beneath her as she is beyond him, in her warm-hearted passion for the small blue planet and all that lives upon it. Nor is there any pseudo-mysticism in her rapture: just as her anger is not so cheap as to be bought by violence, so is her grace not so cheap as to be sold by gurus. She longs after no past lives or future immortalities. This life and the living of it, in all its fragile, transient beauty, is what she requires, demands, and honors, as if she had just arrived in it, as if she were being welcomed into the universe by the universe itself.

The Community of Energy

• "Asymptotic freedom" is the term physicists use to describe the relation of one quark to another. "The closer quarks get to each other, the freer they 'feel' "— and act. A second aspect of this relation has been misnamed (through either/or misperception) "infrared slavery," because at a distance the quarks seem most under one another's influence and least able to separate themselves into autonomy.[24] This misnaming ignores the Balance of Miracle: the miracle that each can still feel and act freely in close proximity to the other, and the miracle that each can still "hear" and affect the other no matter how remote, which is not a slavery at all.

She hears—and she is affected.

• Solitons are coherent packets or pulses of energy that retain their shape over incredible distances. These peculiar indestructible waves are puzzling the theoretical physicists who are trying to explain high-temperature superconductivity. Ordinary waves tend to spread out and fade as they journey through a substance, but solitons are, physicists say, "mystifying" because they interact in a special way, colliding and passing through one another without ever losing their integrity. The physicists are quite confused: "It brings us into a new conceptual domain. . . . Usually you think of starting out with bare particles in a vacuum and putting them into a medium. The soliton is a wrinkle of the medium itself. It's self-focusing, and it just doesn't dissipate." The soliton flows in perfect "magical efficiency," the scientists say, through a crystalline arrangement of molecules, and is the closest thing in nature to perpetual motion: an electrical current in a loop of superconducting material will flow forever. "From the outside, it looks completely chaotic," complain the physicists, "but in fact it's completely organized." They just can't understand *how*. They do know that "when the influences on a wave are linear, as they are for light traveling through a vacuum, solitons cannot occur."[25] (Just as when the politics on a planet are linear, as they are for intelligence traveling through a vacuum of perception, transformation cannot occur.) Physicists confess that they seem unable to gain control over the mechanisms of superconductivity.

She finds herself dazzled by the discovery of her own indestructible shape. She knows how to flock with other women—and how to separate but remain connected, how to combine yet retain her integrity. The model for what she is and what she can do is everywhere around her, one energy, evincing itself in multiple forms, omnipresent, erotic: the model is herself and her selves. And she begins to laugh, freely, irrepressibly, uncontrollably. She still doesn't know "what must be done," but she is on her way to doing it, and she has no time to waste on those who insist they know when they don't.

Look closely at her.

She crosses a city street or walks down a dirt road—but she is carrying herself now. She is the homemaker who "never thought about politics" who suddenly organizes her whole town to fight against a toxic-waste dump going into their backyards;

she is the Kenyan farmer planting trees to create a Green Belt; she is the woman teaching her daughter to defend herself, the woman gently prying her son's hand from a rifle butt; she is the woman serene in the arms of another woman; she is the woman saying No to what is and Yes to what she knows can be.

She has manifested herself from an unexpected, faintly ridiculous direction, unreasonably, as the substitute for the hitherto final arbiter in international affairs—violence. *What* she is, she shares, like her powers, with an entire cosmos of wit, magic, and majesty, a natural universe evolving toward practical joy. *Who* she is, is beautifully herself: a woman awakening for the first time into the reality of her own desire, as if into a dawn greener with summer than any she has ever known, the air clear, the water pure, the earth fertile, the creatures and humans at peace with one another—and herself unafraid.

NOTES

❧❧❧❧❧❧❧❧❧

CHAPTER I
EVERYMAN'S POLITICS: THE DEMOCRATIZATION
OF VIOLENCE

1. C. Wright Mills, *The Power Elite* (New York and London: Oxford University Press, 1956), p. 171.
2. Hannah Arendt, *On Violence* (New York and London: Harcourt Brace Jovanovich, 1970), p. 5.
3. See *Sisterhood Is Global: The International Women's Movement Anthology,* ed. Robin Morgan (Garden City, N.Y.: Anchor Press/Doubleday, 1984).
4. Gary Sick, op-ed page, *New York Times,* April 27, 1986.
5. *Asiaweek,* Hong Kong, July 12, 1985, as excerpted in "Born in the U.S.," *World Press Review,* September 1985, pp. 39–40. See also Timothy K. Smith, "War Games in Alabama's Woods," *Wall Street Journal,* August 19, 1985.
6. "Measures to Prevent International Terrorism Which Endangers or Takes Innocent Human Lives or Jeopardizes Fundamental Freedoms and Study of the Underlying Causes of Those Forms of Terrorism and Acts of Violence Which Lie in Misery, Frustration, Grievance and Despair and Which Cause Some People to Sacrifice Human Lives, Including Their Own, in an Attempt to Effect Radical Changes" (Report of the Secretary General A/40/445), Sep-

tember 20, 1985; Resolution Adopted by the General Assembly (on the Report of the Sixth Committee A/40/1003), January 14, 1986; "Measures to Prevent International Terrorism ..." (Report of the Secretary General A/42/519), September 8, 1987; "Report of the Special Committee on Enhancing the Effectiveness of the Principle of Non-Use of Force in International Relations" (General Assembly 42nd Session, Supplement No. 41, A/42/41).

7. Quoted in John Lamperti, letter to the editor, *New York Times*, June 6, 1987. See also *Patterns of Global Terrorism*, U.S. Department of State Annual Survey, Washington, D.C.; and Richard Falk, "Thinking about Terrorism," *Nation*, June 28, 1986, p. 873.

8. "Lost in the Terrorist Theater" (Forum based on proceedings of the Jonathan Institute's Second Conference on International Terrorism, Washington, D.C., June 1984), *Harper's*, October 1984, p. 45.

9. Richard Clutterbuck, *Living with Terrorism* (London: Faber, 1975), pp. 27, 28, 57.

10. Anthony M. Burton, *Urban Terrorism: Theory, Practice and Response* (London: Leo Cooper, 1975), p. 5.

11. Ernst Halperin, *Terrorism in Latin America* (Beverly Hills, Calif.: Sage Publications, 1976), pp. 71–72.

12. Adolphe D. Jonas, M.D., "Paper for the Berlin Conference," *Terrorism: An International Journal*, Vol. 3, Nos. 3/4 (1980).

13. Yehezkel Dror, "Challenge to the Democratic Capacity to Govern," in *Terrorism, Legitimacy, and Power: The Consequences of Political Violence*, ed. Martha Crenshaw (Middletown, Conn.: Wesleyan University Press, 1983), p. 68.

14. Paul Wilkinson, *Political Terrorism* (London: Macmillan, 1974), p. 13.

15. Irving Louis Horowitz, "The Routinization of Terror," in *Terrorism, Legitimacy, and Power*, ed. Crenshaw, pp. 40–41.

16. Luigi Bonanate, "Some Unanticipated Consequences of Terrorism," *Journal of Peace Research*, Vol. 16, No. 3 (1979), pp. 197–210.

17. Edward Hyams, *Terrorists and Terrorism* (London: J. M. Dent & Sons, 1975), p. 13.

18. Conor Cruise O'Brien, "Terrorism under Democratic Conditions," in *Terrorism, Legitimacy, and Power*, ed. Crenshaw, p. 94.

19. Martha Crenshaw, "The Causes of Terrorism," *Comparative Politics*, July 1981, pp. 379–399.

20. Crenshaw, Introduction ("Reflections on the Effects of Terrorism") and Conclusions, in *Terrorism, Legitimacy, and Power*, ed. Crenshaw, pp. 1–37, 143–49.

21. Crenshaw, "The Causes of Terrorism," pp. 381–82.

22. Ibid., p. 382. See also P. N. Grabosky, "The Urban Context of Political Terrorism," in *The Politics of Terrorism*, ed. Michael Stohl (New York and Basel: Marcel Dekker, 1979).

23. Quoted in "As Violence Spreads, Is U.S. Next?" *U.S. News and World Report,* September 14, 1981, p. 34.
24. George Wald in *The New Yorker,* March 22, 1969, pp. 29–31.
25. Arendt, p. 83.
26. J. Bowyer Bell, *Transnational Terror* (Washington, D.C., and Stanford: American Enterprise Institute for Public Policy Research/Hoover Institution, 1975), p. 15.
27. See *Political Terrorism and Business,* ed. Yonah Alexander and Robert A. Kilmark (New York: Praeger, 1979).
28. Dror, "Challenge," p. 78n.
29. Steven R. Weisman, "In Sri Lanka, the Civilians Are Losing," *New York Times,* June 6, 1987.

CHAPTER 2
THE DEADLY HERO: THE OLDEST PROFESSION

1. See Nancy F. Cott, *The Grounding of Modern Feminism* (New Haven, Conn.: Yale University Press, 1987). See also Dorothy Brown, *Setting a Course: American Women in the 1920's* (Boston: G. K. Hall, 1987).
2. Georges Sorel, *Reflections on Violence,* trans. T. E. Hulme and J. Roth, with an introduction by Edward A. Shils (Glencoe, Ill.: The Free Press, 1950).
3. Jillian Becker, "The Most Important Question," *Terrorism: An International Journal,* Vol. 4 (1980), p. 319.
4. Edward Hyams, *Terrorists and Terrorism* (London: J. M. Dent & Sons, 1975).
5. Martha Crenshaw, "The Causes of Terrorism," *Comparative Politics,* July 1981, p. 382.
6. Quoted in Rae Corelli, "The Menacing Face of the New Terrorism," *Maclean's,* April 26, 1986, p. 24.
7. Joseph Campbell, *The Hero with a Thousand Faces,* Bollingen Series XVII (Princeton, N.J.: Princeton University Press, 1968), p. 16.
8. Ibid., pp. 38, 162.
9. James Frazer, *The Golden Bough,* abridged edition (New York: Collier Books, Macmillan, 1922), p. 71.
10. Campbell, *Hero with a Thousand Faces,* pp. 26–27.
11. Charles A. Russell and Bowman H. Miller, "Profile of a Terrorist" (revised version of their article in *Terrorism: An International Journal,* Vol. 1, No. 1 [1977]), in *Perspectives on Terrorism,* ed. Lawrence Zelic Freedman and Yonah Alexander (Wilmington, Del.: Scholarly Resources, Inc., 1983).
12. Ibid., p. 49.
13. Ibid.
14. Ibid., p. 47.
15. Ibid., p. 54.

16. Ibid., p. 55.
17. Ibid., p. 51.
18. Ibid.
19. Fatima Mernissi, *Beyond the Veil: Male–Female Dynamics in Modern Muslim Society* (Bloomington: Indiana University Press, Midland Books, 1987), pp. xviii–xxii.
20. Quoted in Daniel Goleman, "The Roots of Terrorism," *New York Times*, September 2, 1986, pp. C1, C8.
21. Ibid.
22. Campbell, *Hero with a Thousand Faces*, p. 40.
23. Female genital multilation in its various forms is erroneously thought by many to be an Islamic practice, but it predates Muhammad, who himself counseled reform and moderation of the procedures. In the fifth century B.C.E., Herodotus mentioned it as a practice of the Phoenicians, Hittites, Egyptians, and Ethiopians. Furthermore, in addition to being performed by some Islamic peoples, clitoridectomy and/or infibulation is practiced by some Coptic Christians, members of various indigenous tribal religions, some Catholics and Protestants, and some Falasha (members of an ancient Jewish sect living in Ethiopia). In addition, such procedures are not unknown in the so-called developed world: clitoridectomy was practiced in nineteenth-century London (as a cure for the "epilepsy" it was thought would result from female orgasm), and as late as the 1940s in the United States (as a cure for female masturbation and "deviance"); during the 1970s in the United States an Ohio gynecologist offered an operation involving vaginal reconstruction "to make the clitoris more accessible to direct penile stimulation." In addition, the psychic clitoridectomy legitimized by Freud (who wrote that "the elimination of clitoral sexuality is a necessary precondition for the development of femininity") has caused inestimable female suffering in the West. As of 1988, estimates differ on the number of women alive today enduring various forms of physical genital mutilation: the figures range from 65 million to 75 million. Clitoridectomy is usually performed by midwives, and the age of the female child varies— between nine and forty days after the child's birth (Ethiopia), between four and six years (Egypt), and near puberty (the Sudan). The severe health consequences include primary fatalities due to shock, hemorrhage, or septicemia, and such later complications as incontinence, calcification deposits in the vaginal walls, recto-vaginal fistulas, vulval abscesses, recurrent urinary retention and infection, keloid formation, infertility, and an array of grave obstetric, sexual, and psychological complications. Overt justifications include such contradictory explanations as custom, religion, family honor, cleanliness, initiation, insurance of virginity at marriage, and prevention of female promiscuity. Yet such courageous women as Nawal El Saadawi, Marie Angélique Savané, Edna Adan Ismail, Marie Bassili Assad, Esther Ogunmodede, Fawzia Assad, and many others in the regions directly concerned have for years been

doing studies on the effects of this custom and have been pressuring governments and international agencies to oppose the practice. Some governments have taken a stand (the Sudan outlawed infibulation in 1946, Egypt passed legislation against clitoridectomy in the 1970s, and in 1982 President Daniel arap Moi of Kenya publicly denounced the practice and Kenyan medical authorities forbade it). Some nongovernmental organizations (including the Association of African Women in Research and Development, the Voltaic Women's Federation, the Somali Women's Democratic Organization, the International Commission for the Abolition of Sexual Mutilations, and the coalition of African, Arab, and Western women who formed the Women's Action Group on Female Excision and Infibulation), and some United Nations agencies—notably UNICEF (the United Nations Children's Fund) and WHO (the World Health Organization)—have organized conferences and seminars to develop creative education and/or legislative strategies that would effectively combat the practice of female genital mutilation. Clitoridectomy is the practice of excising the clitoris. "Sunna circumcision" is the removal of the prepuce and/or tip of the clitoris; full clitoridectomy consists of the removal of the entire organ (both prepuce and glans) plus adjacent parts of the *labia minora*. Clitoridectomy is practiced in more than twenty-six countries from the Horn of Africa and the Red Sea across to the Atlantic coast of the African continent, and from Egypt in the north to Mozambique in the south, also including Botswana and Lesotho. According to the Senegalese writer Awa Thiam, the practice of clitoridectomy can also be found in the two Yemens, Saudi Arabia, Iraq, Jordan, Syria, and southern Algeria. Some researchers cite evidence of the practice in such diverse areas as Indonesia, Malaysia, Australia, Brazil, El Salvador, Pakistan, and among the Skoptsy (members of a Christian sect in the Soviet Union). Infibulation (from the Latin *fibula*, or "clasp") is the removal of the entire clitoris, the *labia majora*, and the *labia minora*—and the joining of the scraped sides of the vulva across the vagina, where they are secured with thorns or sewn with thread or catgut; a small opening is maintained by inserting a sliver of wood (commonly a matchstick) into the wound during the healing process, to permit passage of urine and menstrual blood. An infibulated woman must be cut open to permit intercourse and cut further to permit childbirth; often, she is closed up again after delivery, and so may be subjected to such procedures repeatedly during her reproductive life. The practice of infibulation still exists (sometimes despite legal proscription) in certain areas of the Sudan, Somalia, Ethiopia, Nigeria, Upper Volta, Ivory Coast, Kenya, and Mali. The Sudanese name for infibulation credits its origin to Egypt ("Pharaonic circumcision"); the Egyptians call the same operation "Sudanese circumcision." (See *Sisterhood Is Global: The International Women's Movement Anthology,* ed. Robin Morgan [Garden City, N.Y.: Anchor Press/Doubleday, 1984].)

24. Campbell, *Hero with a Thousand Faces*, pp. 116, 120–21.

25. Ibid., p. 147.
26. Ibid.
27. Ibid., p. 353.
28. Frazer, *Golden Bough*, pp. 309, 337.
29. Martha Crenshaw, Introduction to *Terrorism, Legitimacy, and Power: The Consequences of Political Violence*, ed. Crenshaw (Middletown, Conn.: Wesleyan University Press, 1983), p. 8.
30. Crenshaw, Conclusions, in *Terrorism, Legitimacy, and Power*, ed. Crenshaw, pp. 148–49.
31. Hannah Arendt, *On Violence* (New York and London: Harcourt Brace Jovanovich, 1970), pp. 48–49.
32. Crenshaw, "The Causes of Terrorism," p. 394.
33. Frantz Fanon, *The Wretched of the Earth* (New York: Grove Press, 1968), p. 85.
34. Crenshaw, "The Causes of Terrorism," p. 395.
35. Ibid., p. 395.
36. Alessandra Stanley, "Faith in a True Believer," *Time*, February 16, 1987, p. 23.
37. This passage from *Catechism of a Revolutionist* is from the translation by M. Confino, in *Daughter of a Revolutionary* (London: Alcove Press, 1974), as reprinted in *The Terrorism Reader*, ed. Walter Laqueur (Philadelphia: Temple University Press, 1978), pp. 68–72.
38. Carlos Marighella, *Handbook of an Urban Guerrilla* (London: n.d.).
39. Christopher Dobson and Ronald Payne, *The Weapons of Terror: International Terrorism at Work* (London: Macmillan, 1979), p. 21.
40. Quoted in Ché Guevara, forematter to *Reminiscences of the Cuban Revolutionary War* (New York: Monthly Review Press, 1968).
41. "The Cadre, Backbone of the Revolution," in *Venceremos! The Speeches and Writings of Ché Guevara*, ed. John Gerassi (New York: Macmillan, 1968), p. 206.
42. *Quotations from Chairman Mao Tse-Tung* (Peking: Foreign Languages Press, 1967), pp. 92–94.
43. Luigi Bonanate, "Some Unanticipated Consequences of Terrorism," *Journal of Peace Research*, Vol. 16, No. 3 (1979), p. 207.
44. Conor Cruise O'Brien, "Thinking about Terrorism," *Atlantic Monthly*, June 1986, p. 63.
45. Becker, "The Most Important Question," p. 321.
46. See *Sisterhood Is Global*, ed. Morgan.
47. Ibid.
48. Robert Graves, *The White Goddess* (New York: Vintage Books, 1958), p. viii.
49. "The Epic of Creation," Tablet IV, adapted from the translation by L. W.

King, *Babylonian Religion and Mythology* (London and New York: Kegan Paul, Trench, Trubner and Co., 1899).

50. Jeanne N. Knutson, "The Terrorists' Dilemmas," *Terrorism: An International Journal*, Vol. 4 (1980), p. 217.

51. Lawrence Zelic Freedman, "Why Does Terrorism Terrorize?" *Terrorism: An International Journal*, Vol. 6, No. 3 (1983), p. 400.

CHAPTER 3
THE LOVE-DEATH: RELIGION, PHILOSOPHY, AND AESTHETICS

1. Moshe Amon, "Religion and Terrorism—A Romantic Model of Secular Gnosticism," in *The Rationalization of Terrorism*, ed. David C. Rapoport and Yonah Alexander (Frederick, Md.: University Publications of America, 1982), p. 82.

2. Mikhail Bakunin, *Selected Writings*, ed. Arthur Lehning (London: Jonathan Cape, 1973), pp. 112–14.

3. David C. Rapoport, "Terror and the Messiah: An Ancient Experience and Some Modern Parallels," in *The Morality of Terrorism: Religious and Secular Justifications*, ed. Rapoport and Yonah Alexander (New York: Pergamon Press, 1982), p. 14.

4. Apisai Tora quoted in *The Listener*, New Zealand, June 6, 1987, p. 17.

5. Bernadette Devlin, *The Price of My Soul* (New York: Alfred A. Knopf, 1969), p. 53.

6. Quoted in Peter Ross Range et al., "Islam: Seeking the Future in the Past," *U.S. News and World Report*, July 6, 1987, p. 33.

7. Melinda Beck, "The Suicide Bombers," *Newsweek*, November 14, 1983, p. 71.

8. Robert D. McFadden, "Death in Mecca," *New York Times*, August 3, 1987; and John Kifner, "Moslems Assail Mecca Clash," *New York Times*, August 5, 1987.

9. Amir Tahéri, "Islamic Terrorism: A Growing Peril," *World Press Review*, May 1987, pp. 17–19.

10. Howard W. French, "Three JDL Members Seized in Bombings," *New York Times*, May 9, 1987.

11. "Holy Terror," *Time*, March 19, 1984, p. 31.

12. See Ida B. Wells's great autobiography, *Crusade for Justice*, ed. Alfred M. Duster (Chicago: University of Chicago Press, 1970). See also Gerda Lerner, *Black Women in White America: A Documentary History* (New York: Vintage Books, 1972).

13. "Target of New Laws," Associated Press story, *New York Times*, June 30, 1987, p. A24.
14. Mark Starr et al., "Violence on the Right," *Newsweek*, March 4, 1985, pp. 23–26.
15. Ibid., p. 26.
16. Watt, Robertson, and Reagan quoted in Martin Gardner, "Giving God a Hand," *New York Review of Books*, August 13, 1987, pp. 17–23.
17. L. J. Davis, "Ballad of an American Terrorist," *Harper's*, July 1986, pp. 53–62.
18. Ibid., p. 58.
19. See Andrea Dworkin, *Right-Wing Women* (New York: Putnam/Perigee, 1983).
20. See the following by Robin Morgan: *Lady of the Beasts* (New York: Random House, 1976), *Going Too Far: The Personal Chronicle of a Feminist* (New York: Random House/Vintage Books, 1977), and *The Anatomy of Freedom* (Garden City, N.Y.: Anchor Press/Doubleday, 1982). See also Margaret A. Murray, *The Witch Cult in Western Europe* (London: Oxford at the Clarendon Press, 1962); Margaret A. Murray, *The God of the Witches* (London: Oxford University Press, 1970); and *Witch Hunting and Witch Trials*, ed. C. L'Estrange (London: Kegan Paul, Trench, Trubner and Co., 1929).
21. *New York Post*, August 18, 1976, and *Time*, September 6, 1976.
22. Statistical Preface to "German Democratic Republic," in *Sisterhood Is Global: The International Women's Movement Anthology*, ed. Robin Morgan (Garden City, N.Y.: Anchor Press/Doubleday, 1984), pp. 240–41. See also Gloria Steinem, "If Hitler Were Alive, Whose Side Would He Be On?—The Nazi Connection," in Steinem, *Outrageous Acts and Everyday Rebellions* (New York: Holt, Rinehart and Winston, 1983), pp. 305–26.
23. Kenneth Kaunda, *The Riddle of Violence* (New York and San Francisco: Harper and Row, 1980).
24. Paul Lewis, "Nicaraguan at U.N.," *New York Times*, October 9, 1987, p. A10.
25. Wilhelm Reich, *The Mass Psychology of Fascism* (New York: Orgone Institute Press, 1946), p. 197.
26. See John R. Pottenger, "Liberation Theology: Its Methodological Foundation for Violence," in *The Morality of Terrorism*, ed. Rapoport and Alexander, pp. 99–126.
27. Mario Praz, *The Romantic Agony* (London and New York: Oxford University Press, 1970), p. 157.
28. Vytautas Kavolis, "Models of Rebellion," in *The Morality of Terrorism*, ed. Rapoport and Alexander, pp. 53–56.
29. Martha Crenshaw, "The Causes of Terrorism," *Comparative Politics*, July 1981, p. 395.
30. Friedrich Nietzsche, *The Twilight of the Idols*, trans. R. J. Hollingdale (Middlesex, England: Penguin Books, 1968), p. 92.

31. Deborah Cameron and Elizabeth Frazer, *The Lust to Kill: A Feminist Investigation of Sexual Murder* (Cambridge, England: Polity Press in association with Basil Blackwell, 1987), p. 58.

32. Albert Camus, "The Absurd Man," in *The Myth of Sisyphus and Other Essays,* trans. Justin O'Brien (New York: Alfred A. Knopf, 1955), p. 73.

33. Albert Camus, "The Rebel," in *The Rebel: An Essay on Man in Revolt,* trans. Anthony Bower (New York: Vintage Books, 1956), p. 21. See also Camus, *Resistance, Rebellion, and Death* (New York: Alfred A. Knopf, 1961).

34. Camus, *The Rebel,* pp. 275–76.

35. Praz, *Romantic Agony,* p. 238.

36. Ibid., pp. 79–80.

37. Ibid., p. 80.

38. Jean Bethke Elshtain, *Women and War* (New York: Basic Books, 1987), p. 212.

39. Paul Fussell, "The Muse at War," *Boston Globe,* October 2, 1984, p. 14.

40. Gertrude Stein, *Wars I Have Seen* (New York: Random House, 1945).

41. Kate Millett, *Sexual Politics* (Garden City, N.Y.: Doubleday, 1970).

42. Joseph Conrad, *The Secret Agent* (1907; reprint, Middlesex, England: Penguin English Library, 1963), p. 67.

43. *Der Spiegel* interview, quoted in "Lost in the Terrorist Theater" (Forum based on proceedings of the Jonathan Institute's Second Conference on International Terrorism, Washington, D.C., June 1984), *Harper's,* October 1984, p. 51.

44. André Malraux, *Man's Fate,* trans. Haakon M. Chevalier (New York: Vintage Books, 1961), pp. 304, 177–78, 182.

45. Free translation from Julio Cortazar, *Libro de Manuel* (Buenos Aires: Editorial Sudamericana, 1973).

46. Andrea Dworkin, *Pornography: Men Possessing Women* (New York: Putnam/Perigee, 1981), pp. 13–14.

47. Paul Wilkinson, *Political Terrorism* (London: Macmillan, 1974).

48. Jillian Becker, "The Most Important Question," *Terrorism: An International Journal,* Vol. 4 (1980), p. 318.

49. Cameron and Frazer, *The Lust to Kill,* p. 60.

50. Conrad, *The Secret Agent,* p. 94.

51. Dworkin, *Pornography,* p. 13.

CHAPTER 4

OFFICIAL TERRORISM: THE STATE OF MAN

1. Paul Lewis, "World Hunger Found Still Growing," *New York Times,* June 28, 1987.

2. Ibid.

3. Herbert Marcuse, *Eros and Civilization* (Boston: Beacon Press, 1955), p. 85.

4. Quoted in Robert Conquest, "Lenin's Guffaw," *New Republic*, September 15/22, 1986, p. 19.

5. Richard Bernstein, "Barbie No Different in Exile, Aide Says," *New York Times*, May 15, 1987, p. A3.

6. Quoted in *Boletin de las Madres de Plaza de Mayo*, Vol. 1, No. 6 (May 1985). See also Nora Amalia Femenía, "Argentina's Mothers of Plaza de Mayo," *Feminist Studies 13*, No. 1 (Spring 1987); and Marjorie Agosin, "Refusing Terror: Women and the Disappeared," *Sojourner*, May 1987, pp. 10–11.

7. Gerda Lerner, *The Creation of Patriarchy* (New York: Oxford University Press, 1986), p. 213.

8. Risto Fried, "Quotations on Terrorism," *Terrorism: An International Journal*, Vol. 3, Nos. 3/4 (1980), p. 223.

9. Michel Foucault, *Power/Knowledge: Selected Interviews and Other Writings, 1972–1977*, ed. Michael Gordon (New York: Pantheon Books, 1981), p. 187–88.

10. Alice Miller, *For Your Own Good: Hidden Cruelty in Child-Rearing and the Roots of Violence*, trans. Hildegarde and Hunter Hannum (New York: Farrar, Straus, and Giroux, 1983), pp. 142–97.

11. Martha Crenshaw, Conclusions in *Terrorism, Legitimacy, and Power: The Consequences of Political Violence*, ed. Crenshaw (Middletown, Conn., Wesleyan University Press, 1983), pp. 148–49.

12. Michael Stohl, "International Dimensions of State Terrorism," in *The State as Terrorist: The Dynamics of Governmental Violence and Repression*, ed. Stohl and George A. Lopez (Westport, Conn.: Greenwood Press, 1984), pp. 43–44.

13. Gerald Holton, "Reflections on Modern Terrorism," *Terrorism: An International Journal*, Vol. 1, Nos. 3/4 (1978), pp. 269, 271–72.

14. Clyde Haberman, "In Hiroshima, Wiesel Finds New Horror," *New York Times*, May 23, 1987.

15. John G. Stoessinger, *Henry Kissinger: The Anguish of Power* (New York: Norton, 1976), p. 73.

16. See *The State as Terrorist*, ed. Stohl and Lopez; Walter Shapiro et al., "Assassination: Is It a Real Option?" *Newsweek*, April 28, 1986, p. 21; David M. Alpern, "The Man Who Wasn't There—Bill Casey's Off-the-Books CIA," *Newsweek*, October 5, 1987, pp. 44–45; and "The Congo, 1960: State Terrorism and Foreign Policy," *Harper's*, October 1984, p. 52.

17. Philip Agee, *Inside the Company: CIA Diary* (New York: Bantam Books, 1975).

18. Bob Woodward, *VEIL: The Secret Wars of the CIA 1981–1987* (New York: Simon and Schuster, 1987).

19. Franceschini quoted in Juan Arias, *El Pais* (Madrid, n.d.), as excerpted in translation in *World Press Review*, June 1988, p. 25.

20. Richard Falk, "Thinking about Terrorism," *Nation*, June 28, 1986, p. 886.

21. Conrad V. Hassel, "Terror: The Crime of the Privileged," *Terrorism: An International Journal*, Vol. 1, No. 1 (1977), p. 12.

22. Brian Jenkins, "Research Note: Rand's Research on Terrorism," *Terrorism: An International Journal*, Vol. 1, No. 1 (1977), p. 87.

23. Richard J. Barnet, *Roots of War: The Men and Institutions behind U.S. Foreign Policy* (New York: Penguin, 1971), pp. 109–10, 119.

24. *Women's Foreign Policy Council Directory*, Mim Kelber, editorial director (New York: Women's Foreign Policy Council, 1987).

25. George A. Lopez, "A Scheme for the Analysis of Government as Terrorist," in *The State as Terrorist*, ed. Stohl and Lopez, p. 69.

26. Quoted in Barnet, *Roots of War*, p. 115.

27. Quoted in "On Semantic Somersaults," *New York Times*, July 21, 1987.

28. Helen Caldicott, *Missile Envy: The Arms Race and Nuclear War* (Toronto: Bantam Books, 1986).

29. Carol Cohn, "Sex and Death in the Rational World of Defense Intellectuals," *Signs: Journal of Women and Culture in Society*, Vol. 12, No. 4 (1987), pp. 687–718.

30. Edgar Ulsamer, "Missiles and Targets," *Air Force Magazine*, July 1987, pp. 68–74.

31. *Action for Children*, Vol. 1, No. 3 (1986), p. 7.

32. Klaus Theweleit, *Male Fantasies: Volume One—Women, Floods, Bodies, History*, trans. Stephen Conway in collaboration with Erica Carter and Chris Turner (Minneapolis: University of Minnesota Press, 1987).

33. Hans Josef Horchem, "'European Terrorism: A German Perspective," *Terrorism: An International Journal*, Vol. 6, No. 1 (1982), p. 27.

34. Marilyn J. Waring, *If Women Counted: A New Feminist Economics* (New York and San Francisco: Harper and Row, 1989).

35. "Regional Report: Europe," *World Press Review*, June 1987, p. 36.

36. Marilyn J. Waring, *If Women Counted*.

37. F. Gentry Harris, "Hypothetical Facets or Ingredients of Terrorism," *Terrorism: An International Journal*, Vol. 3, Nos. 3/4 (1980), pp. 240–41.

38. Antal Deutsch, "On the Economics of Terrorism," *Terrorism: An International Journal*, Vol. 5, No. 4 (1982), p. 363.

39. Sam Siebert et al., "Israel Tries Vanunu," *Newsweek*, September 7, 1987, p. 41.

40. Quoted in Brian Jenkins "International Cooperation in Locating and Recovering Stolen Nuclear Materials," *Terrorism: An International Journal*, Vol. 6, No. 4 (1983), p. 566.

41. Quoted in John H. Cushman, Jr., "Rising Nuclear Trade Stirs Fear of Terrorism," *New York Times*, November 5, 1987, p. A5. See also, on the hazards of airborne plutonium, "Plane Foolishness," *Greenpeace*, Vol. 12, No. 3 (July–September, 1987), p. 4.

42. Thomas J. Knudson, "Russians Tour U.S. Chemical Arms Stockpile," *New York Times,* November 20, 1987.

43. Quoted in Rae Corelli, "The Menacing Face of the New Terrorism," *Maclean's,* April 28, 1986, p. 25.

44. Vanessa Griffen, "The Pacific Islands: All It Requires Is Ourselves," in *Sisterhood Is Global: The International Women's Movement Anthology,* ed. Robin Morgan (Garden City, N.Y.: Anchor Press/Doubleday, 1984), pp. 517–24. See also Statistical Preface to "The Pacific Islands," in *Sisterhood Is Global,* ed. Morgan, pp. 515–16.

45. T. R. Milton, "Nuclear Virginity," *Air Force Magazine,* May 1985, p. 44.

46. Regan and Ridgway quoted in "Arms and the Woman," *New York Times,* June 29, 1987.

47. Marian C. Diamond, letter to the editor, *New York Times,* June 23, 1987.

48. Berit Ås, "More Power to Women!" in *Sisterhood Is Global,* ed. Morgan, p. 514.

49. Wallace Stevens, "Connoisseur of Chaos," in *Collected Poems* (New York: Alfred A. Knopf, 1982), p. 215.

CHAPTER 5

WARGASM: THE REVOLUTIONARY HIGH

1. Quoted in A. James Gregor, "Fascism's Philosophy of Violence and the Concept of Terror," in *The Morality of Terrorism: Religious and Secular Justifications,* ed. David C. Rapoport and Yonah Alexander (New York: Pergamon Press, 1982), p. 154.

2. "Terrorista per forza," *L'espresso,* October 8, 1978 (trans. from *Libération*), quoted in Luigi Bonanate, "Some Unanticipated Consequences of Terrorism," *Journal of Peace Research,* Vol. 16, No. 3 (1979), p. 207n.

3. Albert Camus, "The Rebel," in *The Rebel: An Essay on Man in Revolt,* trans. Anthony Bower (New York: Vintage Books, 1956), p. 17.

4. Camus, "State Terrorism and Irrational Terror," in *The Rebel,* p. 177. See also Camus, "Individual Terrorism," in *The Rebel,* pp. 149–76.

5. Paulo Freire, *Pedagogy of the Oppressed* (New York: Seabury Press, 1968), pp. 21–36, 127.

6. Frantz Fanon, *The Wretched of the Earth* (New York: Grove Press, 1968), pp. 254–70.

7. Ibid., pp. 275–92.

8. Ibid., pp. 314–16.

9. Jean-Paul Sartre, Preface to Fanon, *The Wretched of the Earth,* pp. 17, 21.

10. Harry R. Targ, "Social Structure and Revolutionary Terrorism," in *The Pol-*

itics of Terrorism, ed. Michael Stohl, (New York and Basel: Marcel Dekker, 1979), p. 137.

11. Michele Wallace, *Black Macho and the Myth of the Superwoman* (New York: Dial Press, 1979), p. 15.

12. Ibid., p. 35.

13. *Der Spiegel of Hamburg*, May 11, 1985, excerpted in "The Eco-Terrorists," *World Press Review*, May 1985, p. 58.

14. David Gelman, with Rich Thomas, "Banality and Terror," *Newsweek*, January 6, 1986, p. 60.

15. John Kifner, "Mecca Pilgrims Say Iranians Concealed Weapons," *New York Times*, August 8, 1987.

16. Michael Selzer, *Terrorist Chic: An Exploration of Violence in the Seventies* (New York: Hawthorn Books, 1979), p. xv.

17. Abraham Kaplan, "The Psychodynamics of Terrorism," *Terrorism: An International Journal*, Vol. 1, Nos. 3/4 (1978), pp. 245–46.

18. Abu Nidal in an interview in *Der Spiegel*, quoted in Rod Nordland et al., "The 'Evil Spirit,' " *Newsweek*, January 13, 1986, pp. 23–24.

19. Interview with Debray in the *Hindustan Times*, New Delhi, excerpted in "Political Transition," *World Press Review*, September 1987, p. 58.

20. Patricia G. Steinhoff, "Portrait of a Terrorist: An Interview with Kozo Okamoto," *Asian Survey*, Vol. 16 (September 1976), p. 843.

21. George Black, "A Terrorist Odyssey: Delle Chiaie—From Bologna to Bolivia," *Nation*, April 25, 1987, pp. 538–41.

22. Steinhoff, "Portrait of a Terrorist," p. 845. See also Claire Sterling, *The Terror Network* (New York: Holt, Rinehart and Winston, 1981). The second source is confirmed in this case by the first, but in general Sterling's book is a less than reliable, sensationalistic treatment of the entire subject.

23. Samuel G. Freedman, "Abortion Bombings Suspect: A Portrait of Piety and Rage," *New York Times*, May 7, 1987, pp. B1–B4. See also *New York Times*, August 5 and September 3, 1987.

24. Fox Butterfield, "North: From 'National Hero' to Reluctant Witness," *New York Times*, July 7, 1987, p. A3.

25. Donald Moore, quoted in George Hackett, with Richard Sandza, "With Ollie North in the 'Eye of the Hurricane,' " *Newsweek*, July 13, 1987, p. 17.

26. Ibid., pp. 16–18.

27. Conrad V. Hassel, "Terror: The Crime of the Privileged," *Terrorism: An International Journal*, Vol. 1, No. 1 (1977), p. 5.

28. Eugene V. Walter, *Terror and Resistance*, (New York: Oxford University Press, 1972).

29. William F. May, "Terrorism as Strategy and Ecstasy," *Journal of Social Research*, Vol 41 (Summer 1974), pp. 285–87.

30. Ibid., pp. 290, 294–95, 296–98.

31. H. H. A. Cooper, "Woman as Terrorist," in *The Criminology of Deviant Women,* ed. Freda Adler and Rita Simon (Boston: Houghton Mifflin, 1979).
32. Details of the Murphy story are from Tom Morganthau, with Rod Nordland, "Losing Control," *Newsweek,* April 28, 1986, p. 33; and Russell Watson et al., "Brothers in Arms," *Newsweek,* May 5, 1986, pp. 31–32.

CHAPTER 6

TOKEN TERRORIST: THE DEMON LOVER'S WOMAN

1. See Robin Morgan, "From Riches to Rags: A Conversation with Patricia Hearst," *Ms.,* March 1979. See also Kathleen Barry's superb in-depth feminist analysis of the Hearst case, "Patricia Hearst: Did I Ever Have a Chance?" chapter 7 in Barry, *Female Sexual Slavery* (New York: New York University Press, 1979).
2. Quoted in Morgan, "From Riches to Rags," p. 60.
3. Elvia Alvarado, *Don't Be Afraid, Gringo: A Honduran Woman Speaks from the Heart,* trans. Medea Benjamin (San Francisco: The Institute for Food and Development Policy, 1987), p. 133.
4. J. K. Zawodny, "Internal Organizational Problems and the Sources of Tensions of Terrorist Movements as Catalysts of Violence," *Terrorism: An International Journal,* Vol. 1, Nos. 3/4 (1978), pp. 280–81.
5. Ibid., p. 281.
6. Vera Broido, *Apostles into Terrorists: Women and the Revolutionary Movement in the Russia of Alexander II* (New York: Viking Press, 1977), p. vi.
7. Daniel E. Georges-Abeyie, "Women as Terrorists," *Terrorism: An International Journal,* Vol. 1, No. 1 (1977), pp. 77–81.
8. Ibid., p. 77.
9. See Susan Stern, *With the Weathermen: The Personal Journal of a Revolutionary Woman* (Garden City, N.Y.: Doubleday, 1975); and Jane Alpert, *Growing Up Underground* (New York: William Morrow, 1981).
10. Georges-Abeyie, "Women as Terrorists," pp. 82–84.
11. Quoted in Vincent Bugliosi, with Curt Gentry, *Helter Skelter* (New York: Norton, 1974), p. 85.
12. William H. Blanchard, "V. I. Lenin: The Stoic," in Blanchard, *Revolutionary Morality* (Oxford, England, and Santa Barbara, Calif.: ABC-Clio Information Services, 1984), p. 223.
13. Quoted in Adam B. Ulam, *In the Name of the People* (New York: Viking Press, 1977), pp. 146–47. See also Broido, *Apostles into Terrorists;* and Jay Bergman, "Vera Zasulich, the Shooting of Tropov and the Growth of Political Terrorism in Russia, 1878–1881," *Terrorism: An International Journal,* Vol. 4 (1980), p. 37.

14. V. I. Zasulich, *Sbornik statei* (St. Petersburg, 1907), quoted in Bergman, "Vera Zasulich," p. 45.

15. See Elzbieta Ettinger, *Rosa Luxemburg: A Life* (Boston: Beacon Press, 1987); and Peter Nettl, *Rosa Luxemburg* (London: Oxford University Press, 1969).

16. Emma Goldman, *Living My Life*, 2 vols. (New York: Alfred A. Knopf, 1931).

17. Statistical Preface to "China," in *Sisterhood Is Global: The International Women's Movement Anthology*, ed. Robin Morgan (Garden City, N.Y.: Anchor Press/Doubleday, 1984), p. 149.

18. Ts'ai Ch'ang, eyewitness recollection, quoted in Joan M. Maloney, "Women in the Chinese Communist Revolution," in *Women, War, and Revolution*, ed. Carol R. Berkin and Clara M. Lovett (New York: Holmes and Meier, 1980), p. 169.

19. Statistical Preface to "China," in *Sisterhood Is Global*, ed. Morgan, pp. 148, 150. See also "Ding Ling: To Write What Others Would Not Dare," *Connexions*, Spring 1982; and *Ting Ling—Purged Feminist* (Tokyo, Femintern Press, n.d.).

20. Jacob W. F. Sundberg, "Lawful and Unlawful Seizure of Aircraft," *Terrorism: An International Journal*, Vol. 1, Nos. 3/4 (1978), pp. 428–29.

21. Colin Smith, *Carlos: Portrait of a Terrorist* (London: Deutsch, 1976), p. 149.

22. Craig Canine et al., "What Becomes a Legend Most," *Newsweek*, April 2, 1978, p. 49; and Elaine Sciolino, "Nicaragua's U.N. Voice," *New York Times Magazine* cover story, September 28, 1986.

23. Leonard Weinberg and William Lee Eubank, "Italian Women Terrorists," *Terrorism: An International Journal*, Vol. 9, No. 3 (1987), pp. 255, 259.

24. Vittorfranco S. Pisano, "A Survey of Terrorism of the Left in Italy, 1970–78," *Terrorism: An International Journal*, Vol. 2, Nos. 3/4 (1979), p. 180.

25. John Castellucci, *The Big Dance: The Untold Story of Kathy Boudin and the Terrorist Family That Committed the Brink's Robbery* (New York: Dodd, Mead, 1986), p. 126. See also Ellen Frankfort, *Kathy Boudin and the Dance of Death* (New York: Stein and Day, 1983).

26. Shirley Christian, "Santiago Journal: The Exile Returns, Embodying the Agony of '73," *New York Times*, July 2, 1987.

27. Testimony of Pia Lasker, *Judgment Proceedings*, pp. 188, 93, 46, 94, quoted in Jacob W. F. Sundberg, "Operation Leo: Description and Analysis of a European Terrorist Operation," *Terrorism: An International Journal*, Vol. 5, No. 3 (1981), pp. 210–11.

28. *Judgment Proceedings*, p. 122, quoted in Sundberg, "Operation Leo," p. 221.

29. Sundberg, "Operation Leo," pp. 200–202.

30. Ibid. See also Jillian Becker, *Hitler's Children* (London: Grenada Publishing, 1977); Becker, "Another Final Battle on the Stage of History," *Terrorism: An International Journal*, Vol. 5, Nos. 1/2 (1981); and Christopher Dobson and Ronald Payne, *The Weapons of Terror: International Terrorism at Work* (London: Macmillan, 1979).

31. *Der Baader-Meinhof Report*, Aus Akten des Bundeskriminalamtes, der "Sonderkommission Bonn" und des Bundesamts für Verfassungsschutz (v. Hase und Koehler Verlag Mainz, 1972), p. 97, quoted in translation in Raymond R. Corrado, "Ethnic and Student Terrorism in Western Europe," in *The Politics of Terrorism*, ed. Michael Stohl (New York and Basel: Marcel Dekker, 1979), p. 241.

32. Quoted in Anthony M. Burton, *Urban Terrorism: Theory, Practice and Response* (London: Leo Cooper, 1975), p. 33.

33. "Guru's City in Desert Sits Nearly Empty," *New York Times*, August 9, 1987.

34. Quoted in Smith, *Carlos*, p. 111.

35. Smith, *Carlos*, pp. 113–14.

36. Leila Khaled, *My People Shall Live: The Autobiography of a Revolutionary* (New York: Bantam Books, 1975).

37. Smith, *Carlos*, p. 83.

38. Quoted in Elvira Ganter, "Conversation with Leila Khaled," *Courage Aktuelle Frauenzeitung*, West Berlin, No. 8 (August 1981).

39. Andrea Dworkin, "Amsterdam," unpublished essay written in 1972, quoted by the author's permission.

40. The Three Marias, *New Portuguese Letters* (New York: Bantam Books, 1975), p. 87.

41. Association of Salvadoran Women, "We Cannot Wait . . . ," in *Sisterhood Is Global*, ed. Morgan, p. 213.

42. Marie Angélique Savané, "Elegance amid the Phallocracy," in *Sisterhood Is Global*, ed. Morgan, p. 598.

43. Fatima Mernissi, "The Merchant's Daughter and the Son of the Sultan," in *Sisterhood Is Global*, ed. Morgan, pp. 447–53.

44. Lidia Falcón, "Women Are the Conscience of Our Country," in *Sisterhood Is Global*, ed. Morgan, pp. 626–31.

45. Ama Ata Aidoo, "To Be a Woman," in *Sisterhood Is Global*, ed. Morgan, p. 264.

46. Robin Morgan, "On Women as a Colonized People" (originally published in *Circle One* [Colorado Springs: Colorado Women's Health Network, 1974], collected in Morgan, *Going Too Far: The Personal Chronicle of a Feminist* (New York: Random House/Vintage Books, 1977).

CHAPTER 7

LONGING FOR CATASTROPHE: A PERSONAL JOURNEY

1. See Robin Morgan, *Going Too Far: The Personal Chronicle of a Feminist* (New York: Random House/Vintage Books, 1977).

2. Norman Hill, ed., *The Violent Women* (New York: Popular Library, 1971).

3. See Morgan, Preface to "Three Articles on WITCH," in *Going Too Far*, pp. 71–75.

4. Susan Stern, *With the Weathermen: The Personal Journal of a Revolutionary Woman* (Garden City, N.Y.: Doubleday, 1975).

5. Robin Morgan, "The Fall of a Sparrow," in Morgan, *Depth Perception: New Poems and a Masque* (Garden City, N.Y.: Doubleday, 1982), p. 97.

6. William A. Reuben and Carlos Norman, "The Women of Lexington Prison," *Nation*, June 27, 1987, pp. 881–84. See also B. Drummond Ayres, "Prisoner Charges Poor Conditions Are U.S. 'Psychiatric Experiment,' " *New York Times*, June 8, 1988.

7. Thomas Burdick, "Radical Departure: Bernardine Dohrn," *Savvy*, August 1986, pp. 50–53.

8. Quoted in "As Violence Spreads, Is U.S. Next?" *U.S. News and World Report*, September 14, 1981, p. 34.

CHAPTER 8

"WHAT DO MEN KNOW ABOUT LIFE?": THE MIDDLE EAST

1. Communiqué dated May 5, 1986, from the Chargé d'Affaires of the Permanent Mission of Israel to the United Nations, to the Secretary General (ECOSOC E 1986/78).

2. "Survey of Population and Labour Force in the Agricultural Sector, First Quarter, 1967" (Amman: Government of Jordan, 1968), pp. 7–8, quoted in Suha Hindiyeh, "Social Change and Agriculture in the West Bank, 1950–1967: Aspects of Sharecropping and Commercialization," unpublished doctoral thesis, University of Kent, Canterbury, England, 1985, p. 155.

3. *Can It Happen Again: A Report on Mass Poisoning in the Palestinian Territories under Israeli Occupation* (London: Jerusalem Center for Development Studies, 1985). See also *New York Times*, March 28, 1983; and the UN General Assembly and Security Council "Communiqué of 30 March, 1983, from the Chairman of the Committee on the Exercise of the Inalienable Rights of the Palestinian People" to the Secretary General (A/38/128).

Note: The United Nations Relief and Works Agency for Palestine Refugees in the Near East publishes information in Arabic, English, French, German, Italian, Norwegian, Spanish, and Swedish. It regularly publishes a quarterly newsletter, *Palestine Refugees Today;* a quarterly briefing paper, *UNRWA Report;* and a fortnightly bulletin, *UNRWA News;* these, and the Agency's occasional publications, are available free. A catalogue of all publications, plus posters, maps, and wallsheets, films, tapes, and slide sets, is obtainable from UNRWA Public Information Division, P.O. Box 700, Vienna International

Centre, A-1400 Vienna, Austria, or from UNRWA Liaison Office, Room DC 2–550, United Nations, New York, N.Y. 10017.

CHAPTER 9

THE NORMALIZATION OF TERROR: A NOTE PASSED BETWEEN HOSTAGES

1. Andy Lightbody, *The Terrorism Survival Guide* (New York: Dell Publishing Co., 1987), pp. 2, 5, 7, 8, 10, 14–15, 21.
2. Quoted in David Gelman, with Rich Thomas, "Banality and Terror," *Newsweek*, January 6, 1986, p. 60.
3. Quoted in Thomas L. Friedman, "My Neighbor, My Enemy: A Report from Israel," *New York Times Magazine*, July 5, 1987, p. 31.
4. Martti Siirala, "Some Theses on Terrorism," *Terrorism: An International Journal*, Vol. 3, Nos. 3/4 (1980), pp. 311–12.
5. Lindsey Gruson, " 'Most Dangerous Game' Is Gaining as a Sport," *New York Times*, August 24, 1987.
6. "Measure Is Sought on Road Violence in California," *New York Times*, August 23, 1987.
7. "Leader of Club for Those Seeking More Wealth Gets Life Term for Killing," *New York Times*, July 7, 1987.
8. Quoted in Deborah Cameron and Elizabeth Frazer, *The Lust to Kill: A Feminist Investigation of Sexual Murder* (Cambridge, England: Polity Press in association with Basil Blackwell, 1987), p. 157.
9. Ibid.
10. Daniel Goleman, "Brain Defect Tied to Utter Amorality of the Psychopath," *New York Times*, July 7, 1987, Science Times section.
11. Martha Crenshaw, "The Causes of Terrorism," *Comparative Politics*, July 1981, p. 390.
12. Quoted in Daniel Goleman, "Terror's Children: Mending Mental Wounds," *New York Times*, February 23, 1987, pp. C1, C12.
13. Robert I. Friedman, "How Kahane Shakes the U.S. Money Tree," *Washington Post*, November 23, 1987, National Weekly edition, p. 24.
14. James Adams, *The Financing of Terror* (London: New English Library, 1987).
15. Ibid.
16. "How To Succed in Business" (aired July 19, 1987, on *60 Minutes*), transcript in *CBS News*, Vol. 19, No. 44, pp. 6–8. See also Edwin M. Reingold, "Welcome to 'Hell Camp,' " *Time*, March 7, 1988, Economy and Business Section, p. 55.
17. Theresa Funiciello, "New York's 'Work-Not-Welfare' Program," *Dissent*, Fall 1987, pp. 557–60.

18. Robert Pear, "Handouts of Cheese, Milk, and Rice Face 50% Cuts Next Year," *New York Times*, November 17, 1987, pp. A1, A24.

19. Data on the Occupied Territories 1987–88 assembled from the following sources: personal communications from Gaza residents; UNRWA quarterly *Report*; UNRWA, *Palestine Refugees Today*; emergency communiqués of the Palestine Human Rights Campaign; reports in the *Jerusalem Post, Al Fajr* of Jerusalem, the *Washington Post*, the *International Herald Tribune*, and the *New York Times*; see especially Joel Brinkley, "Latest Israeli Weapon: Bureaucracy," *New York Times*, May 11, 1988.

20. Nicholas Bethell, *The Palestine Triangle* (New York: Putnam, 1979).

21. *Action for Children*, Vol. 1, No. 3 (1986), p. 3.

22. Roland Gaucher, *The Terrorists*, trans. Paula Spurlin (London: Secker and Warburg, 1968), p. 298.

23. Quoted in "Overheard," *Newsweek*, September 7, 1987, p. 13.

24. Both quoted in Douglas Martin, "Family Violence: Seeking Answers by Sharing Pain," *New York Times*, November 7, 1987.

25. All quoted in the British publication *Independent*, as excerpted in *World Development Forum*, Vol. 5, No. 20 (November 1987).

26. Jane Caputi, *The Age of Sex Crime* (Bowling Green, Ohio: Bowling Green University Popular Press, 1987).

27. Robin Morgan, "First Feminist Exiles from the U.S.S.R.," *Ms.*, cover story, November 1980.

28. Paul Theroux, *The Kingdom by the Sea* (Boston: Houghton Mifflin, 1983), pp. 228, 230.

29. Ibid., pp. 232–33, 237.

30. Gena Corea, "Northern Ireland: The Violence Isn't All in the Streets," *Ms.*, July 1979, p. 94.

31. Quoted in ibid.

32. Corea, "Northern Ireland," p. 97.

33. Ibid., p. 98.

34. Quoted in Ibid., pp. 98–99.

35. Quoted in Ibid., p. 99.

36. Dirk Johnson, "Lisa: A Street Girl's Short, Bitter Life," *New York Times*, May 28, 1987, p. A14.

37. Janet Gallagher, J.D., "Fetus as Patient," Abstract prepared in 1987 for the forthcoming Forum on Reproductive Laws for the 1990s.

38. Joan E. Bertin, J.D., "Reproductive Health Hazards in the Workplace: Proposals for Legislative, Educational, and Public Policy Initiatives," Abstract prepared in 1987 for the forthcoming Forum on Reproductive Laws for the 1990s.

39. Jodi Jacobson of the Worldwatch Institute, quoted in J. Cook, "Abortion Update," *International Dateline*, bulletin of the Center for Population Communications, April 1988, pp. 1–2.

40. "On the Brink of Extinction," Worldwatch paper, quoted in *World Development Forum,* Vol. 5, No. 20 (November 1987), p. 3.
41. Ibid.
42. "Eco-Notes," *Greenpeace,* Vol. 12, No. 3 (July–September 1987), p. 5.
43. Ibid.
44. Ibid.

CHAPTER 10
BEYOND TERRORISM: THE POLITICS OF EROS

1. Hannah Arendt, *On Violence* (New York and London: Harcourt Brace Jovanovich, 1970), pp. 67–68.
2. Gerda Lerner, *The Creation of Patriarchy* (New York: Oxford University Press, 1986), p. 228.
3. Ibid.
4. Mary Daly, with Jane Caputi, *Webster's First New Intergalactic Wickedary of the English Language* (Boston: Beacon Press, 1987), p. 172. See also the following by Daly: *Beyond God the Father* (Boston: Beacon Press, 1973); *Gyn/Ecology* (Boston: Beacon Press, 1978); and *Pure Lust* (Boston: Beacon Press, 1984).
5. Toni Morrison, *Beloved* (New York: Alfred A. Knopf, 1987), pp. 88–89.
6. Jean Bethke Elshtain, *Women and War* (New York: Basic Books, 1987), p. 247.
7. Margarita Chant Papandreou, Welcoming Address to the November 1986 Meeting of Women for a Meaningful Summit, Athens, Greece.
8. Marilyn J. Waring, *Women, Politics, and Power* (Wellington, New Zealand, London, and Boston: Allen and Unwin in association with Port Nicholson Press, 1985), pp. 12–13.
9. Thirty-eighth Session of the United Nations General Assembly, Address by Prime Minister of India Indira Gandhi in her capacity as Chair of the Movement of Non-Aligned Countries, September 28, 1983.
10. Claude Alvares, "Science, Imperialism, and Colonialism," excerpted in *Work in Progress* (UNU: United Nations University) Vol. 10, No. 3 (October 1987), p. 11.
11. C. de LaCoste-Utamsing and R. Holloway, "Sexual Dimorphism in the Human Corpus Callosum," *Science,* Vol. 216 (1982), pp. 431–32, and J. Durden-Smith and D. DeSimone, *Sex and the Brain* (New York: Arbor House, 1983), both cited in Alice S. Rossi, "Gender and Parenthood" (1983 presidential address to the American Sociological Association), *American Sociological Review,* Vol. 49 (February 1984), p. 14.
12. Norwegian government study on aggression, by Dr. Dan Olweus, and studies

by G. Raisman and P. M. Field, as summarized in Dr. Melvin Konner, "The Aggressors," *New York Times Magazine,* August 14, 1988, pp. 33–34.

13. For essays in English by Pietilä, Ås, and Liljeström, see *Sisterhood Is Global: The International Women's Movement Anthology,* ed. Robin Morgan (Garden City, N.Y.: Anchor Press/Doubleday, 1984).

14. Virginia Woolf, *Three Guineas* (New York: Harcourt, Brace and Company, 1938), p. 219.

15. Alan Cowell, "Greek Cypriot Women Cross Turks' Line," *New York Times,* November 23, 1987, p. A3.

16. Rajiu Tiwari, "Uphill Struggles of Himalayan Housewives," *Popline*/World Population News Service, Vol. 9, No. 6 (June 1987), pp. 7–8.

17. Spokeswoman quoted in "Women Against the Occupation," *Connexions,* Winter 1984.

18. Woolf, *Three Guineas,* p. 166.

19. James Gleick, "New Appreciation of the Complexity in a Flock of Birds," *New York Times,* November 24, 1987, pp. C1, C17.

20. Ibid., p. C17.

21. Lyall Watson, *Lifetide* (New York: Bantam Books, 1980), pp. 147–48.

22. James Gleick, "Hints of More Cloudiness Spur Global Study," *New York Times,* June 30, 1987, pp. C1, C6.

23. Quoted in James Gleick, *Chaos: Making a New Science* (New York: Viking Penguin, 1987).

24. A. Zee, *Fearful Symmetry: The Search for Beauty in Modern Physics* (New York: Macmillan, 1986), pp. 205–6.

25. James Gleick, "Indestructible Wave May Hold Key to Superconductors," *New York Times,* December 15, 1987, pp. C1, C4.

ADDITIONAL SOURCES CONSULTED

꧁꧁꧁꧁꧁꧁꧁꧁꧁꧁

For authors whose works are quoted, or to whose work direct reference is made, see Index.

Alexander, Yonah, and Alan O'Day. *Terrorism in Ireland.* New York: St. Martin's Press, 1984.

Arendt, Hannah. *The Human Condition.* Chicago: University of Chicago Press, 1958.

———. *The Origins of Totalitarianism.* New York: Harcourt, Brace and World, 1968.

———. *On Revolution.* New York: Penguin Books, 1977.

Böll, Heinrich. *The Safety Net.* New York: Alfred A. Knopf, 1982.

Cambridge Women's Peace Collective. *My Country Is the Whole World: An Anthology of Women's Work on Peace and War.* Boston: Pandora Press, 1984.

Campbell, D'Ann. *Women at War with America.* Cambridge, Mass.: Harvard University Press, 1985.

Deming, Barbara. *We Cannot Live without Our Lives.* New York: Grossman, 1974.

Dobson, Christopher, and Ronald Payne. *The Carlos Complex.* New York: Hodder and Stoughton, 1977.

Faure, Christine. *Terre, terreur, liberté.* Paris: F. Maspero, 1979.

Foucault, Michel. *Madness and Civilization: A History of Insanity in the Age of Reason.* New York: Vintage, 1973.

———, and Ludwig Binswanger. *Dream and Existence: Studies in Existential Psychology and Psychiatry.* Ed. Keith Hoeller. Seattle: Review of Existential Psychology and Psychiatry, 1986.

Goldberg, Rochelle Lois. *"The Russian Women's Movement, 1859–1917."* Ph.D. dissertation, University of Rochester (New York), 1976.

Gouldon, Joseph C., with Alexander W. Raffio. *The Death Merchant: The Rise and Fall of Edwin P. Wilson.* New York: Simon and Schuster, 1984.

Hills, Denis Cecil. *Rebel People.* London and Boston: Allen and Unwin, 1978.

Lewy, Guenter. *Religion and Revolution.* New York: Oxford University Press, 1974.

Livingston, Marius H., with Lee Bruce Kress and Marie G. Wanek. *International Terrorism in the Contemporary World.* Westport, Conn.: Greenwood Press, 1978.

Lorde, Audre. "Uses of the Erotic: The Erotic as Power." In *Take Back the Night: Women on Pornography.* Ed. Laura Lederer. New York: William Morrow, 1980.

Mackey, Janet, ed. *Terrorism and Political Self-Determination.* Chicago: World without War Council, 1980.

MacKinnon, Catherine A. *Feminism Unmodified: Discussions on Life and Law.* Cambridge, Mass.: Harvard University Press, 1987.

Mallin, Jay, comp. and ed. *Terror and Urban Guerrillas: A Study of Tactics and Documents.* Coral Gables, Fla.: University of Miami Press, 1971.

Mazumdar, Satyendra Narayan. *In Search of a Revolutionary Ideology and Programme: A Study in the Transition from National Revolutionary Terrorism to Communism.* New Delhi: People's Publishing House, 1979.

McKnight, Gerald. *The Mind of the Terrorist.* London: Joseph, 1974.

Melchiori, Barbara Arnett. *Terrorism in the Late Victorian Novel.* London and Dover, N.H.: Croom Helm, 1985.

Mickolus, Edward F. *Transnational Terrorism: A Chronology of Events, 1968–1979.* Westport, Conn.: Greenwood Press, 1980.

Norton, Augustus R., and Martin H. Greenberg. *International Terrorism: An Annotated Bibliography and Research Guide.* Boulder, Colo.: Westview, 1980.

Negri, Antonio. *Dominio e sabotaggio.* Milan: Feltrinelli, 1978.

Rivers, Gayle. *The Specialist: Revelations of a Counterterrorist.* New York: Stein and Day, 1985.

Rossiter, Margaret L. *Women in the Resistance.* New York: Praeger, 1986.

Rowbotham, Sheila. *Women, Resistance and Revolution.* New York: Pantheon Books, 1972.

Rupp, Leila J. *Mobilizing Women for War.* Princeton, N.J.: Princeton University Press, 1978.

Rush, Florence. *The Best Kept Secret: Sexual Abuse of Children.* Englewood Cliffs, N.J.: Prentice-Hall, 1980.

Russell, Diana E. H., and Nicole Van de Ven, eds. *The Proceedings of the International Tribunal on Crimes Against Women*. Palo Alto, Calif.: Frog in the Well Press, 1984.

Schmid, Alex Peter. *Violence As Communication: Insurgent Terrorism and the Western News Media*. Beverly Hills, Calif.: Sage Publications, 1982.

Sjöö, Monica, and Barbara Mor. *The Great Cosmic Mother: Rediscovering the Religion of the Earth*. New York and San Francisco: Harper and Row, 1987.

Stiehm, Judith, *Women in Men's Wars*. New York: Pergamon Press, 1983.

Terrorism: An International Journal (New York). Published quarterly since 1977.

Trible, Phyllis. *Texts of Terror: Literary-Feminist Readings of Biblical Narratives*. Philadelphia: Fortress Press, 1984.

Wilson, Carolyn F. *Violence Against Women: An Annotated Bibliography*. Boston: G. K. Hall, 1981.

Women's Education Resources. *Violence Against Women, Causes and Prevention: A Literature Search and Annotated Bibliography*. Project directors Carolyn F. Wilson and Kathryn F. Clarenbach. Rockville, Md.: National Clearinghouse on Domestic Violence, 1980.

INDEX

Afterword

The following three letters were originally sent as e-mails. I wrote the first the day after the September 11, 2001, attacks, as a way of replying swiftly to more messages of concern than I could respond to individually. Friends and colleagues then apparently forwarded that first letter on to their own lists and list-servers. Rather than diminish the flood of e-mails, this increased it, and now messages arrived from utter strangers, urgently requesting more eyewitness reports and continued political analysis "outside" what they were gleaning from mass media. Sometimes writers feel as if we're sending out proverbial messages in a bottle, so it was both privilege and comfort, in a time of anguish, to be able to exercise one's art and craft in a way that addressed real hunger for real information. Besides, as the days passed and the scope of the disaster began to reveal itself, the immediacy of the first letter seemed quite naive. So I wrote the second, "Ghosts and Echoes," a week later. Astonishingly, it took on a life of its own: it apparently was reprinted as the editorial of a major English-language Hong Kong newspaper, published in two leading South African dailies, translated into Portuguese and read on Brazilian television, posted on hundreds of Web sites. The response has continued to grow with the third letter. As this edition of *The*

Demon Lover is being rushed to press, there have so far been three Letters from Ground Zero, all printed below. There may or may not be more to come. The reaction to them has deepened my respect for the power of the Internet and intensified my gratitude for the power of the word.—R.M.

Letters from Ground Zero

I. *The Day After* (Wednesday, 12 September 2001)

Dear Friends,

Forgive the mass e-mailing of this letter, but in this situation it seems more important to get some personal, basic lower-Manhattan news/impressions to you all than take the time to reply one-on-one to each of your many moving messages. I've received e-mails and phone calls from women in 18 different countries over the last 24 hours—from South Africa to Jordan, Malaysia to Brazil, Nepal to Canada, Australia to the Caribbean, the Philippines to Peru, all across Europe and the USA—and from West Bank and the Gaza Strip. I also know that many of you tried to telephone all day yesterday but couldn't get through—although e-mail seems to be working even when the land-phone lines are clogged; cell-phones have been working only erratically.

First, thank you from my heart for all your thoughts, concerns, invitations to come stay with you, expressions of sadness, solidarity, and political anxiety. So many of you have astonishingly cited *The Demon Lover* as an expression/analysis of what has just happened that even in the midst of grief you have renewed my belief that art, an attempted clarity of thought, and a stubborn politics of transformation do make a contribution, make a difference. But so far, as we know all too hideously, not enough.

I am well and safe, as are those dearest to me. (I've also been in touch with friends who were in transit around the U.S., who are safe, though some are stranded in hotels and airports.) Here in Greenwich Village we are, as many of you have worried, in lower Manhattan, but north—about a mile and a half—of the catastrophic area. We have electric power, water, the basics. Friends who live(d) much closer to it staggered here yesterday morning, covered with ash, shaking with fear, and spent the day and last night here. It is bizarre that my little city garden is untouched by all this: late summer roses blossoming, finches singing, vegetables ready to harvest. But you can hear fighter jets overhead now and then. From my street corner, looking south down Seventh Avenue, there used to be a clear view of the Twin Towers; I went out yesterday morning and saw the first tower burning—and was standing there watching in near disbelief while the second plane hit the second tower; later, I watched the south tower implode and collapse. It seemed totally surreal—as if Hollywood had produced yet another special-effects blockbuster. This morning early I went for a walk, looked down Seventh Avenue South, and saw nothing but massive billows of smoke. No towers anymore.

The city is holding together superbly; New Yorkers rise to such an occasion like the British did during the blitz. I live only a block and a half from St. Vincent's Hospital—which is the closest triage center to the disaster—so all day yesterday and last night the ambulances have been wailing; that and the planes overhead remind me of sounds I heard in Beirut at the height of the war there. All streets and avenues below 14th Street have been cleared of traffic, but evacuation has been enforced only for those below Canal Street (I live below 14th but above Canal.) You can walk right down the middle of major lower Manhattan avenues with only emergency vehicles whizzing by occasionally. People are volunteering all over the city, very touchingly; those of us near St. Vincent's Hospital have brought homemade food and coffee and cold drinks to the workers and the people milling about hoping for news of lost relatives. There's a doctors' conference in town, by fortunate coincidence—so a great many M.D.s have responded to hospitals' calls for help; apparently even more have shown up than the emergency rooms can use; same with nurses. Last night I wanted to give blood but there were by formal count over 1,000 people lined up ahead of me, with an estimated seven-hour wait, so I decided to try again in a day or two. The infrastructure of the city is holding extraordinarily well: subways and buses are already running again (though not south, near the site itself). There was a brief run on the banks and grocery stores but that seems to have passed. No food shortages have been felt yet, but since many bridges and tunnels and other approaches to Manhattan are closed or limited except for emergency vehicles, that may change. Still, people are calm, helping one another, not panicking—though they're clearly in a state of shock. I personally know three people who apparently have lost friends or family who worked in or near the Twin Towers. It's the stories about people hunkered down at the back of the hijacked planes, whispering into their cell phones "I love you" one last time, that bring tears. It's the children who will lose/have lost parents who especially crack one's heart.

The hospitals are now announcing that they are gravely concerned—they had expected thousands of emergency cases but are treating only hundreds—which means more fatalities than injuries. Emergency morgues are being set up in 10 locations around Manhattan. The number of already known dead approaches 1,000—mostly firefighters, emergency personnel, and police. Apparently 800 may have died in the Pentagon attack, and the passenger manifests of the four planes adds another almost 300. It appears that there will be massive fatalities, topping Pearl Harbor's 2,500.

The site itself has rubble as deep as 100 feet high, with breakaway fires still burning, some underground, making rescue of those trapped even more difficult, especially since the Twin Towers' foundation went down 70 feet below ground and there are reports of people still trapped there, calling out on cellphones. It sears the brain just to think about it.

Good news: a few more firefighters have just been pulled from the rubble . . .

This morning the National Guard arrived—and on my dawn walk I could just as well have been moving through a military state: police, state troopers, and emergency personnel on every corner below 14th Street, with trucks filled with Guardsmen, rifles bayoneted and at ready, beginning to roll through the streets. We have to be calm but also need to be truly vigilant, since in such a time of crisis, the danger of a turn to the extreme right is genuinely real. The press continues to roll, though no newspapers could be delivered below 14th Street.

Where I am, we've been fortunate, in that the winds have been prevailing to blow the dense smoke southeast out to sea—so although we could see the smoke plumes, there has been no stench or fallout of concrete or contaminants in my immediate vicinity. But just now the wind changed, and a smell like charred rubber or burning electrical wire pervades Greenwich Village.

Media coverage has been nonstop, and relatively cautious to avoid rumors (especially in the wake of misreporting last year's election results). As of this morning, the first "day after," the expected patriotic blabber and religious jargon had started, along with pundits and politicians already issuing media clichés about "beginning the healing process" and seeking "closure." Maddeningly, there have been frequently repeated airings of film clips of some Palestinian men in West Bank celebrating the attack with laughter, dancing, and v-signs—but unfortunately there has *not* been as frequently repeated press coverage of Palestinian leaders, Arab leaders, and leaders of the Arab-American community deploring it; equal time has *not* been given; only once in 24 hours have I heard major media announce the official statement of the Muslim community in the U.S. that heatedly denounced the attack. But there *has* been heartening comment—from journalists and from the mayor of NYC—warning against bigoted responses to this tragedy. As those of you with whom I've managed to speak know, in fact, that has been one of my great worries, because a few years ago, in the 48 hours after the Oklahoma City bombing (before it was discovered that the perpetrator was a white, Christian, right-wing male), three Arab Americans were lynched in the Midwest and South of the U.S. Already, mosques are being defaced and Internet chatrooms spewing hate against "all Arabs." We (feminists, progressives, etc.) are doing everything we can to avoid this kind of escalating nightmare—and a network of safe houses is already being set up to shelter and help innocent Arab or Muslim civilians who might be persecuted in the wake of this attack. This morning I was touched to learn that the Pagan and Wiccan community is doing the same thing, in the name of religious freedom from persecution they know all too well.

Politically—well, it's too early to say, of course. But some things might be hypothesized. It may be heartening that this disaster could deter Bush's Star Wars anti-missile fantasy—since, as so many of us have said for so long, *this* kind of attack, not missiles, is the real 21st-century threat (and it was amazingly low-tech: box cutters, pepper spray, commercial flights, four or five men per plane willing to die for a cause: simple). Furthermore (despite the expectable "let's all stand together behind our president" rhetoric) general press analysis plus public reaction seems so far fairly critical of Bush's handling, noting: (1) Bush's previous policy of withdrawal from/abandoning Mideast peace-process talks, (2) Bush's administration having ignored warnings three weeks ago of an imminent "unprecedented" attack against the U.S., and (3) Bush being seemingly so far incapable of evoking confidence or projecting an aura of basic competence. In talking with colleagues in feminist leadership, a number of us have noted that for years we've tried everything to get the U.S. to put pressure on the Taliban, given their unprecedented human-rights violations against women and girls in today's Afghanistan—and each time we've been impeded by the powerful boys of Big Oil, who care only for their beloved pipelines. It took this, finally, to get their attention.

As I write this, news breaks that the FBI has picked up possible "suspects" in Florida and in Boston . . . but that kind of story you will hear or read as it evolves, in your own press, or if you can access CNN, where you are.

So I will sign off for now. I trust with all my heart that you will each do all you possibly can in your own countries, cities, and situations to educate people as to *why* this kind of tragedy happens—that it is *not* just "madmen" or "monsters" or "subhuman maniacs" who commit dramatic violence, but that such acts occur in a daily climate of patriarchal violence so epidemic as to be invisible in its normality—and that such tactics as this attack come from a complex set of circumstances, including despair over not being heard any other way; desperation over long-term, even generational, suffering; calcification of sympathy for "the other"; callousing of sensibilities, blatant economic and political injustice, tribal/ethnic hatreds and fears, religious fundamentalisms, and *especially* the eroticization and elevation of violence as the expression of "manhood." Violence *is* psychosis—but it's a psychosis that contemporary incumbent leaders of most nations share with their insurgent opponents.

Even as we mourn, somehow, we need to continue audaciously daring to envision and re-vision a different way, a way out of this savage age, to a time when our species will look back and gasp, recoiling at its own former barbarism. Even as we weep, we must somehow reorganize to reaffirm our capacity to change the world, each other, and ourselves—to insist, even in the teeth of despair, on a politics that is both possible and necessary: a politics not of Thanatos and death, but of Eros and joy.

I send each of you my gratitude and my deep affection.

Robin Morgan
New York City

* * *

II. *Ghosts and Echoes* (Tuesday, 18 September 2001)

Dear Friends,
Your response to the e-mail I sent on Day 2 of this calamity has been overwhelming. In addition to friends and colleagues, absolute strangers—in Serbia, Korea, Fiji, Zambia, all across North America—have replied, as have women's networks in places ranging from Senegal and Japan to Chile, Hong Kong, Saudi Arabia, even Iran. You've offered moving emotional support and asked for continued updates. I cannot send regular reports/alerts as I did during the elections last November or the cabinet confirmation battles last year. But here's another try.

I'll focus on New York—my firsthand experience—but this doesn't mean any less anguish for the victims of the Washington or Pennsylvania calamities. Today was Day 8. Incredibly, a week has passed. Abnormal normalcy has settled in. Our usually contentious mayor (previously bad news for New Yorkers of color and for artists) has risen to this moment with efficiency, compassion, real leadership. The city is alive and dynamic. Below 14th Street, traffic is flowing again, mail is being delivered, newspapers are back. But very early this morning I walked east, then south almost to the tip of Manhattan Island. The 16-acre site itself is closed off, of course, as is a perimeter surrounding it controlled by the National Guard, used as a command post and staging area for rescue workers. Still, one is able to approach nearer to the area than was possible last weekend, since the law-court district and parts of the financial district are now open and (shakily) working. The closer one gets the more one sees—and smells—what no TV report, and very few print reports, have communicated. I find myself giving way to tears, again and again, even as I write this.

If the first sights of last Tuesday seemed bizarrely like a George Lucas special-effects movie, now the directorial eye has changed: it's the grim lens of Agnes Varda, juxtaposed with images so surreal they could have been framed by Bunuel or Kurosawa.

This was a bright, cloudless, early autumnal day. But as one draws near the site, the area looms up out of a dense haze: one enters an atmosphere of dust, concrete powder, and plumes of smoke from fires still raging deep beneath the rubble (an estimated two million cubic yards of debris). Along lower Second Avenue, 10 refrigerator tractor-trailer trucks are parked, waiting; if you stand there a while, a New York City medical examiner van arrives—with a sagging body bag. Thick white ash, shards of broken glass, pebbles, and chunks of concrete cover street after street of parked cars for blocks outside the perimeter. Handprints on car windows and doors—handprints sliding downward—have been left like frantic graffiti. Sometimes there are messages finger-written in the ash: "U R Alive." You can look into closed shops, many with cracked or broken windows, and peer into another dimension: a wall-clock stopped at 9:10, restaurant tables meticulously set but now covered with two inches of ash, grocery shelves stacked with cans and produce bins piled high with apples and melons—all now powdered chalk-white. A moonscape of plenty. People walk unsteadily along these streets, wearing nose-masks against the still particle-full air, the stench of burning wire and plastic, of erupted sewage; the smell of death, of decomposing flesh.

Probably your TV coverage shows the chain-link fences aflutter with yellow ribbons, the makeshift shrines of candles, flowers, scribbled notes of mourning or of praise for the rescue workers that have sprung up everywhere—especially in front of firehouses, police stations, hospitals. What TV doesn't show you is that near Ground Zero the streets for blocks around are still, a week later, adrift in bits of paper—singed, torn, sodden pages: stock reports, trading print-outs, shreds of appointment calendars, half of a To-Do list. What TV doesn't show you are scores of tiny charred corpses now swept into the gutters. Sparrows. Finches. They can fly higher than the larger-bodied pigeons, so they would have exploded outward, caught midair in a rush of flame, wings on fire as they fell. Who could have imagined it: the birds were burning.

From a distance, you can see the lattices of one of the Towers, its skeletal bones the sole remains, eerily beautiful in asymmetry, as if a new work of abstract art had been erected in a public space. Elsewhere, you see the transformation of institutions: The New School and New York University are missing persons' centers. A movie house is now a rest shelter, a Burger King a first-aid center, a Brooks Brothers clothing store a body parts morgue, a record shop a haven for stranded animals. Libraries are counseling centers. Ice rinks are morgues. A bank is now a supply depot: in the first four days, it distributed 11,000 respirators and 25,000 pairs of protective gloves and suits. Nearby, a mobile medical unit housed in a McDonald's has administered 70,000 tetanus shots. The brain tries to process the numbers: "only" 50,000 tons of debris had been cleared by yesterday, out of 1.2 million tons. The medical examiner's office has readied up to 20,000 DNA tests for unidentifiable cadaver parts. At all times, night and day, a minimum of 1,000 people live and work on the site.

Such numbers daze the mind. It's the details—fragile, individual—that melt numbness into grief. An anklet with "Joyleen" engraved on it—found on an ankle. Just that: an ankle. A pair of hands—one brown, one white—clasped together. Just that. No wrists. A burly welder who drove from Ohio to help, saying softly, "We're working in a cemetery. I'm standing in—not on, *in*—a graveyard." Each lamppost, storefront, scaffolding, mailbox is plastered with homemade photocopied posters, a racial/ethnic rainbow of faces and names: death the great leveler, not only of the financial CEOs—their images usually formal, male, white, older, with suit-and-tie—but the mailroom workers, receptionists, waiters. You pass enough of the MISSING posters, and the faces, names, descriptions become familiar. The Albanian window-cleaner guy with the bushy eyebrows. The teenage Mexican dishwasher who had an American flag tattoo. The janitor's assistant who'd emigrated from Ethiopia. The Italian-American grandfather who was a doughnut-cart tender. The 23-year-old Chinese American junior pastry chef at the Windows on the World restaurant who'd gone in early that day so she could prep a business breakfast for 500. The firefighter who'd posed jauntily wearing his green shamrock necktie. The dapper African American midlevel manager with a small gold ring in his ear who handled "minority affairs" for one of the companies. The middle-aged blond secretary laughing up at the camera from her wheelchair. The maintenance worker with a Polish name, holding his newborn baby. Most of the faces are smiling. Most of the shots are family photos. Many are recent wedding pictures. . . .

I have little national patriotism, but I do have a passion for New York—partly for our gritty, secular energy of endurance, and because the world does come here: 80 countries had offices in the Twin Towers; 62 countries lost citizens in the catastrophe; an estimated 300 of our British cousins died, either in the planes or the buildings. My personal comfort is found not in ceremonies or prayer services, but in watching the plain, truly heroic (a word much misused) work of ordinary New Yorkers we take for granted every day, who have risen to this moment unpretentiously, too busy even to notice they're expressing the splendor of the human

spirit: firefighters, medical aides, nurses, ER doctors, police officers, sanitation workers, construction workers, ambulance drivers, crane operators, rescue worker "tunnel rats". . . .

Meanwhile, across the U.S., the rhetoric of retaliation is in
full-throated roar. Flag sales are up. Gun sales are up. Some radio
stations have banned playing John Lennon's song, "Imagine."
Despite appeals from all officials, mosques are being attacked,
firebombed; Arab Americans are hiding their children indoors;
two murders in Arizona have already been categorized as hate
crimes—one victim a Lebanese-American man and one a Sikh
man who died merely for wearing a turban. (Need I say that there
were not nationwide attacks against white Christian males after
Timothy McVeigh was apprehended for the Oklahoma City
bombing?)

Last Thursday, right-wing televangelists Jerry Falwell and Pat
Robertson (our homegrown American Taliban leaders) appeared
on Robertson's TV show *The 700 Club,* where Falwell blamed
"the pagans, and the abortionists, and the feminists and the gays
and lesbians . . . the American Civil Liberties Union, People for
the American Way" and groups "who have tried to secularize
America" for the attacks. Robertson replied, "I totally concur."
After even the Bush White House—deeply indebted to the
Christian right—called the remarks "inappropriate," Falwell
apologized (though he did not take back his sentiments);
Robertson hasn't even apologized. (The program is carried by the
Fox Family Channel, recently purchased by the Walt Disney
Company—in case any of you would like to register a protest.)

The sirens have lessened now. But the drums have started.
Funeral drums. War drums. A state of emergency, with an initial
call-up of 50,000 reservists to active duty. The Justice
Department is seeking increased authority for wider surveillance,
broader detention powers, wiretapping of persons (not, as previously, just phone numbers), and stringent press restrictions on
military reporting.

And the petitions have begun. For justice but not vengeance.
For a reasoned response but against escalating retaliatory violence. For vigilance about civil liberties. For the rights of innocent

Muslim Americans. For "bombing" Afghanistan with food and medical parcels, *not* firepower. For reviving the Middle East peace talks. There will be the expected peace marches, vigils, rallies. . . . One member of the House of Representatives—Barbara Lee, Democrat of California, an African American woman—lodged the sole vote in both houses of Congress against giving Bush broadened powers for a war response, saying she didn't believe that a massive military campaign would stop terrorism. (She could use letters of support: e-mail her, if you wish, at: barbara.lee@mail.house.gov.)

Those of us who have access to the media have been trying to get a different voice out. But ours are complex messages with long-term solutions—and this is a moment when people yearn for simplicity and short-term, facile answers.

Still, I urge each of you to write letters to the editors of newspapers, call in to talk radio shows, and, for those of you who have media access—as activists, community leaders, elected or appointed officials, academic experts, whatever—to do as many interviews and TV programs as you can. Use the tool of the Internet. Talk about the root causes of terrorism, about the need to diminish this daily climate of patriarchal violence surrounding us in its state-sanctioned normalcy; the need to recognize people's despair over ever being heard short of committing such dramatic, murderous acts; the need to address a desperation that becomes chronic after generations of suffering; the need to arouse that most subversive of emotions, empathy, for "the other"; the need to eliminate hideous economic and political injustices, to reject *all* tribal/ethnic hatreds and fears, to repudiate religious fundamentalisms of *every* kind. Especially talk about the need to understand that we *must expose the mystique of violence*, separate it from how we conceive of excitement, eroticism, and "manhood"; the need to comprehend that violence thrives along a spectrum, as do its effects—from the battered child and raped woman who live in fear to an entire populace living in fear.

Meanwhile, we cry and cry and cry. I don't even know who my tears are for anymore, because I keep seeing ghosts, I keep hearing echoes. . . .

The world's sympathy moves me deeply. Yet I hear echoes dying into silence: the world averting its attention from Rwanda's screams . . .

Ground Zero is a huge mass grave. And I think: Bosnia. Uganda.

More than 6,300 people are currently missing and presumed dead (not counting the Washington and Pennsylvania deaths). Even the TV anchors choke up: civilians, they say, my god, *civilians*. And I see ghosts. Hiroshima. Nagasaki. Dresden. Vietnam.

I watch the mask-covered mouths and noses on the street turn into the faces of Tokyo citizens who wear such masks every day against toxic pollution. I watch the scared eyes become the fearful eyes of women forced to wear the *hijab* or *chodor* or *burka* against their will . . .

I stare at the MISSING posters' photos and think of the Mothers of the Disappeared, circling the plazas in Argentina. And I see the ghosts of other faces. In photographs on the walls of Holocaust museums. In newspaper clippings from Haiti. In chronicles from Cambodia. . . .

I worry for people who've lost their homes near the site, though I see how superbly social-service agencies are trying to meet their immediate and longer-term needs. But I see ghosts: the perpetually homeless who sleep on city streets, whose needs are never addressed. . . .

I watch normally unflappable New Yorkers flinch at loud noises, parents panic when their kids are late from school. And I see my Israeli feminist friends like Yvonne, who've lived with this dread every day for decades and still (even yesterday) stubbornly continue to issue petitions insisting on peace. . . .

I watch sophisticates sob openly in the street, people who've lost workplaces, who don't know where their next paycheck will come from, who fear a contaminated water or food supply, who are afraid for their sons in the military, who are unnerved by security checkpoints, who are wounded, who are in mourning, who feel terrified, humiliated, outraged. And I think of my friends like Zuhira in the refugee camps of Gaza or West Bank,

Palestinian women who have lived in precisely that same emotional condition—for four generations.

Last weekend, many Manhattanites left town to visit concerned families, try to get away for a break. As they streamed out of the city, I saw the ghosts of other travelers: hundreds of thousands of Afghan refugees streaming toward their country's borders in what is to them habitual terror, trying to escape a drought-sucked country so war-devastated there's nothing left to bomb, a country with 50,000 disabled orphans and two million widows whose sole livelihood is begging; where the life expectancy of men is 42 and women 40; where women hunch in secret whispering lessons to girl children forbidden to go to school, women who risk death by beheading—for teaching a child to read.

The ghosts reach out their hands. *Now you know,* they weep, gesturing at the carefree, insulated, indifferent, golden innocence that was my country's safety, arrogance, and pride. *Why should it take such horror to make you see?* the echoes sigh, *Oh please do you finally see?*

This is calamity.

And opportunity.

The United States—what so many of you call America—could choose now to begin to understand the world. And join it.

Or not.

For now my window still displays no flag, my lapel sports no red-white-and-blue ribbon. Instead, I weep for a city and a world. Instead, I cling to a different loyalty, affirming my un-flag, my un-anthem, my un-prayer—the defiant un-pledge of a madwoman who also had mere words as her only tools in a time of ignorance and carnage, Virginia Woolf: "As a woman I have no country. As a woman I want no country. As a woman my country is the whole world."

If this is treason, may I be worthy of it.

In mourning—and in absurd, tenacious hope,

Robin Morgan
New York City

*   *   *

III. *Redefining Normal* (Tuesday, 25 September 2001)

Dear Friends,

Two weeks ago today, the attack on the Twin Towers ruptured reality as we thought we knew it. Images from that day are indelibly etched on our individual and collective memory. Here in Manhattan, we live with daily reminders that re-shock the brain and re-spasm the heart. Omnipresent MISSING posters, now rain-blurred and wind-torn, flap half-affixed to store windows and lampposts. Melted parking meters slump like Salvador Dali sculptural sentinels near the site, what some call "the hot zone" because it still smolders with buried fires. Everywhere you go, you can't help but overhear snatches of conversations, from passers-by, people on the bus, diners at the next table, shoppers at the checkout line—all, always, talking about It: where they were when it happened, what they're feeling. We share a new, quite un-urban, interest in any changing direction of the wind. Newspapers' obituary sections thicken with additional pages, as more bodies are found or identified and the formal death toll rises. Bereft families visit the site—what some call the killing ground—to mourn and to see for themselves where the pulverized fragments of someone they loved are forever buried in the dust; when the families pass through, the site workers pause, remove headgear, stand silently. Memorial services have begun to replace funerals, for the still unidentified or the still missing dead. Almost 1,500 relatives of the missing have forced themselves to face the inevitability of loss and applied for death certificates, so they can access accelerated benefits for needy families. Day and night, workers still swarm over the debris pile—but they are professionals now, not volunteers, because the current levels of excavation require engineering and demolition expertise. They estimate it will take at least nine months to clear Ground Zero, which is now the largest demolition/construction site in the world. The days grow cooler, the nights crisper. October nears. By now, usually, stores already display Halloween costumes—skeletons, death masks. Instead, you can spot only a few orange and black streamers, a pumpkin or two. We live in a state of uncertainty, ricocheting between trying to function and then becoming undone by renewed mourning.

But we're New Yorkers, so in a way we might be better equipped to handle such a condition than other people, partly because we're right *in* it, without the buffering effect folks in other parts of the country and world are valiantly trying to bridge, and partly because our notoriously edgy street-smarts might just help us deal with the residue of fear.

Still, the sadness keeps washing back over you, in waves. Yesterday I allowed myself the brief indulgence of mourning another, little-noticed, and, in the scale of things, relatively minor yet crucial casualty: language. I care about words—their power, their potential for communicating truths, clarity, comfort, comprehension. So this administration's more-than-usually-insensitive tin ear plus Bush's frequent gaffes—culminating in his lamentable reference to a "crusade"—fill me with frustration. The new department's name, "Homeland Security," rings a reminder of South Africa's former apartheid euphemisms for race-restricted areas as "homelands." Any reference to the perpetrators of the WTC attack as "cowardly" degrades the lucidity of language: you can list a hell of a lot of negative adjectives about the attackers (fanatical, ruthless, simplistic, megalomaniacal, homicidal), but being obsessively committed to dying as "martyrs" for what they believed was *not*, literally, "cowardly." (In fact, this kind of manly bravery is precisely the problem.) Then there's the U.S. military response initially being named "Infinite Justice" (one of the Muslim attributes of Allah) and now being renamed "Enduring Freedom" (which sounds as if it describes Attorney General Ashcroft's feeling resigned at having to put up with democracy). If we each simply took care to say what we mean and mean what we say, that in itself would be a vital political act toward comprehension.

Last night I found myself thinking that we've all been witness to—in fact participants in—an archetype, complete with the enormous powers and resonances therein. Not only because this has been and is a huge collective event in which the entire city, country, and most of the world has been and is involved. Not only because the immediate aftermath brought forth waves of an altruism so far apparently evocable mostly by calamity. Not only because that altruism expressed the longing in all of us for a sense of authentic community, as opposed to the Disneyland versions marketed to us every day. And not only because the magnitude of sheer high drama these past weeks, in relentless real time, put us in touch with the entire range of raw emotions and the accompanying feeling of being intensely alive (sometimes with attendant guilt); not only because such real-life drama put into sobering perspective the previous popularity of "reality TV" shows with their cheap, safe, fake, vicariously experienced "survivor thrills." All this, yes. But last night I realized we've been inhabiting an archetype for another reason, too. I've been fond of Tarot cards for years, not for any so-called prophetic faculties but because I'm a sucker for a good metaphor, and these ancient visual images are psychologically insightful and archetypally profound. Last night I finally realized why the flaming shapes of the buildings had seemed eerily familiar. Card XVI of the major trumps, The Tower, depicts a golden-crowned turret ablaze and crumbling, with human figures flailing, falling headfirst from its heights. Various interpretations refer to the card as representing unforeseen catastrophe, immense loss, and the leveling of arrogance—but also significant change, the breakdown of old beliefs.

And change there is, albeit subtle. Thirty years ago, the U.S. charged unilaterally into any wars it chose (whether or not they were misnamed "interventions," "engagements," or "police actions"). Today, even a conservative administration of a now-sole superpower has to *try* for at least the appearance—and preferably the reality—of a coalition (no matter how corruptive or cynical); it must try, too, for the UN's seal of approval. Such an incremental shift is hideously small, horribly slow, tragically late, appallingly inadequate. Still, for those of us who care passionately about social change to ignore or dismiss that shift would be foolish; it would be to collaborate in the erasure of our own lifelong efforts, and to invite deeper despair.

Pundits, politicians, and religious leaders are addressing the legacies of September 11—rising fear and continuing grief—with various rhetorics, some even well meaning. But many people are clinging to fear, as if to let down their vigilance is to become even more vulnerable than, terrified, they already are. And people may cling to grief because letting grief go can seem the ultimate disloyalty. "Crueler than the loss of love, the surrendering/of loss. Worse than the disease,/the affliction of its healing," I wrote once in a poem. Still, energy *will* rack us mercilessly into life again, whether we give it permission or not. The question is, what quality of life?

Experts urge us to "return to normal": that sleepwalking, unquestioning, luxury of dailiness that fixates on getting to the bank before it closes or remembering to pick up stuff at the cleaners. Yet maybe this is a chance for us—individually, collectively, nationally—*not* to return to "normal" but to *redefine* normal, broadening its meanings in every conceivable way, from the personal to the political (still one and the same).

And if we find ourselves wrenched back and forth between choking with rage and thirsting for peace, what if we actually *claimed* that—claimed our frail, imperfect, human ambivalence as the virtue it is? A lack of ambivalence can't tolerate complexity, hesitation, or contradiction. A lack of ambivalence never flinches from judgment. A lack of ambivalence is considered the hallmark of leadership—on aircraft carriers where right now they are revving up missiles and bombers, and in mountain caves where right now they are setting up antiaircraft guns. A lack of ambivalence has been made to seem honorable, manly, heroic. *The men who organized and carried out the September 11 attacks suffered from a total lack of ambivalence.*

If we could acknowledge and affirm ambivalence we could make another small gesture toward seeing ourselves—all of ourselves—as *ourself*, the single species we are. And we might begin to stop killing ourself.

Understanding *who* we are might be a beginning. All over this country, well-intentioned, confused Americans are now waking up and asking why so many people around the globe hate and fear us. It's good that at least the question is finally being asked—and we shouldn't scoff in contempt at the questioners, because the education system and the media have failed to educate the U.S. public, and decades of isolationist policies have furthered that ignorance. Here's one tool—possibly familiar to some of you, yet still useful—to help us see who we are and perhaps answer a few questions:

If the world were a village and its population were comprised of 100 people (based on existing ratios), this is who and how they'd be: 53 would be female, 58 would be under age 25, 70 would be people of color, 70 would be non-Christian; 58 would be Asians/Pacific, 21 would be Africans, 21 would be Europeans (of which 14 would be Americans, south and north). Of the 100, 80 would live in poverty-level housing, 70 (50 of whom would be female) would be illiterate, 50 would be starving or malnourished; 6 would own 59 percent of all the wealth and all 6 would be from the U.S.; one would own a computer and one would have a college education, both from the U.S.

In our shock over civilian casualties, we should also know that "civilian casualties" globally translates to mean women and children, since men are (voluntarily or forcibly) in armed conflict. Amnesty International has noted that women's fatality in war— 5 percent of all victims in World War I, rising to 50 percent in World War II—*soared to nearly 80 percent* in the 1990s. Women and children also make up almost 90 percent of all refugee and displaced populations.

So. There is fear. Understanding doesn't necessarily lessen the fear. It may even sharpen it. What to do about *that*, then?

On an ordinary day, you and I wake and move through the hours in a state of deliberately unacknowledged risk. It's a strange sanity of denial, as if the continual consciousness that we're actually hurtling through the dark matter of outer space, riding a delicate blue marble, would be too intolerable a burden to bear in mind. Each day, we act out a series of small, multiple trusts. We trust that with a turn of the wrist on the cold-water faucet, hot water won't scald us. We trust that the motorist bearing down on the crosswalk will observe the same traffic-light change as the pedestrian stepping off the curb. We trust the key that fit the lock this morning will still fit the lock tonight. We trust that when we bare our teeth at strangers, they will understand it as a smile.

These and many more are, if you think about them, acts of remarkable risk-taking. That our expectations are largely met is, if you dwell on it, miraculous in a mundane sort of way. If we recognized these commonplace risks and humdrum miracles as such, we might live each day more intensely without the jolt of cataclysm to prompt us. We might also realize that we're better prepared to deal with fear than we think we are. It takes an ability to balance conflicting possibilities at the same time, like acknowledging threat and proceeding anyway. It takes a capacity for irony, resilience—and ambivalence.

I think of women I've met and work with still, in the vertical-slum favelas of South America, the rice paddies of Asia, the townships of South Africa; I think of their familiarity with acute suffering and chronic fear, and the simple yet sophisticated skills they've developed for transcending it. I think of women in the refugee camps of the Middle East where, like banners of survival, laundry is always hanging to dry—miles of it strung above and between shelters, like banners insisting on cleanliness amidst filth—and where, camp after camp, amazingly, there are stubborn attempts at gardens. In a two- or three-foot square of rocky sand beside a cramped one-room shelter housing 14 people: a garden. The women grow subsistence food in these tiny spaces: some squash or zucchini, a tomato plant, a grapevine. And always at least that one flower—a crimson hibiscus, a bougainvillea. I think of Aziza in Beach Camp in the Gaza Strip, showing me what she managed to grow in this ridiculous space and inhospitable soil where 41,000 people are compressed into a single camp. She has no tools, and water is a precious commodity. Why then devote space and water to flowers? "Because," Aziza grins at the translator and pokes me as if I'm teasing her, "*you* know why." She laughs, "The soul—it needs to be fed, too."

Today, my little city garden is still dripping with the autumn rain that fell all last night into the dawn. I could hear it through my open windows: few sounds so plain in loveliness as softly falling water. But this morning, the wind had changed again, and the stench was back. This morning, I went to vote in the primary election: a lackluster set of choices, but the act of choosing was the point. People died for the right of suffrage; women fought for a century to win me mine. Women in Kuwait are still denied that right; women and men alike are denied it in Saudi Arabia—and in Afghanistan. Then, after drafting and signing petitions and going to meetings and returning phone calls and answering e-mails, I returned to these words—ambivalently—as if performing an act of irony as well as an act of trust. As if calling for long-term solutions at a moment of short-term reactions made sense. As if words on a page or as electronic impulses or as sounds from a human throat could make a difference.

Now, as this country circles war, I'll go into the garden, where I've been for perhaps only ten minutes during the past two weeks. And I'll probably cry again. And, ambivalently, I'll perform another act of irony and trust, toward another long-term solution. I'll plant some bulbs—"poet's narcissus," they call them. Because the soul needs to be fed. I'll bury them while mourning: small, gnarled, pocked, dead-looking nuggets in the moist soil. I'll do this in the hope of another spring. I'll do this in the hope that months from now—cold months of short gray days and long dark nights—slender-stemmed, double-petaled, creamy flowers iridescent as pearl might poke through and rise, brazening their fragrant glory in a transcendence of suffering. Improbable. Miraculous.

In our great shared sorrow, but in defiance of despair,

Robin Morgan
New York City